COMPREHENSIVE GUIDE TO CLINICAL RESEARCH REGULATIONS

THEORY AND PRACTICE

DR. C. RONALD DARWIN, DR. PRAFUL J KUMAR,
DR. A. R. VIJAYAKUMAR

Copyright © Dr. C. Ronald Darwin, Dr. Praful J Kumar, Dr. A. R. Vijayakumar
All Rights Reserved.

This book has been self-published with all reasonable efforts taken to make the material error-free by the author. No part of this book shall be used, reproduced in any manner whatsoever without written permission from the author, except in the case of brief quotations embodied in critical articles and reviews.

The Author of this book is solely responsible and liable for its content including but not limited to the views, representations, descriptions, statements, information, opinions and references ["Content"]. The Content of this book shall not constitute or be construed or deemed to reflect the opinion or expression of the Publisher or Editor. Neither the Publisher nor Editor endorse or approve the Content of this book or guarantee the reliability, accuracy or completeness of the Content published herein and do not make any representations or warranties of any kind, express or implied, including but not limited to the implied warranties of merchantability, fitness for a particular purpose. The Publisher and Editor shall not be liable whatsoever for any errors, omissions, whether such errors or omissions result from negligence, accident, or any other cause or claims for loss or damages of any kind, including without limitation, indirect or consequential loss or damage arising out of use, inability to use, or about the reliability, accuracy or sufficiency of the information contained in this book.

Made with ♥ on the Notion Press Platform
www.notionpress.com

Contents

Preface   v

COMPREHENSIVE GUIDE TO CLINICAL RESEARCH REGULATIONS: THEORY AND PRACTICE   vii

ABOUT THE AUTHORS   ix

1. Introduction To Clinical Research And Drug Development   1
2. Phases Of Clinical Trials   18
3. Phase 0 Studies   29
4. Phase I Studies   40
5. Phase II Studies   53
6. Phase III Trials   65
7. Phase IV And Post-Marketing Studies   79
8. Clinical Investigation And Evaluation Of Medical Devices   94
9. Historical Perspectives On Ethics In Clinical Research   108
10. The Belmont Report And Declaration Of Helsinki   122
11. The Origin Of ICH-GCP Guidelines   134
12. Ethics Of Randomized Clinical Trials   147
13. The Role Of Placebo In Clinical Trials   164
14. Ethical Considerations For Special Populations   180
15. Institutional Review Boards (IRB) And Independent Ethics Committees (IEC)   196
16. Data Safety Monitoring Boards (DSMB)   210
17. Informed Consent Process And Documentation   226
18. Clinical Research Regulations In India – Schedule Y   241
19. USA Clinical Research Regulations (FDA)   254
20. Clinical Research Regulations In The European Union (EMA)   268
21. Good Clinical Practice (GCP) Guidelines – ICH E6   282
22. Indian Good Clinical Practice Guidelines   295
23. ICMR Ethical Guidelines For Biomedical Research   309

Contents

24. Regulatory Guidance On Efficacy And Safety (ICH Guidelines)	322
25. Post-Market Surveillance And Safety Reporting	336
Glossary of Key Terms and Definitions	349
Bibliography	359
Chapter wise Contents	363

Preface

The field of **clinical research** plays a pivotal role in the advancement of medical science, bringing hope to millions of patients through the discovery and development of innovative therapies. The increasing complexity of clinical trials and the rigorous regulations governing them demand a thorough understanding of both **theoretical knowledge** and **practical applications**. This book, *Comprehensive Guide to Clinical Research Regulations: Theory and Practice*, is designed to bridge that gap, offering a well-rounded resource for students, professionals, and researchers engaged in clinical studies.

In this book, we aim to provide an **exhaustive guide** that addresses the essential elements of clinical research, from **ethical considerations** and **regulatory requirements** to the **phases of clinical trials** and post-marketing surveillance. We have taken special care to simplify complex topics, using a structured approach that ensures clarity while maintaining the depth of content required for academic and professional excellence. With **25 comprehensive chapters** and numerous **illustrations**, this book covers everything needed to navigate the regulatory landscape in clinical research effectively.

The regulatory frameworks of key organizations such as the **FDA, EMA,** and **CDSCO** are thoroughly explored, ensuring that readers have a global understanding of clinical research protocols. In addition, **case studies** are incorporated to provide real-world examples, illustrating the challenges and intricacies of clinical trials. Each chapter is designed to offer practical insights, helping readers apply theoretical concepts in real-life clinical settings.

This work is the culmination of contributions from esteemed experts in the field of **clinical research** and **pharmacology**. We would like to extend our gratitude to all who have contributed their expertise and knowledge. The authors, **Dr. C. Ronald Darwin, Dr. Praful J Kumar,** and **Dr. A. R. Vijayakumar,** and the editor, **Dr. A. Muralidhar Rao,** have shared their years of experience and insights, making this guide both authoritative and practical.

We hope this book serves as an invaluable resource to the next generation of clinical researchers, educators, and healthcare professionals. Our goal is to make this guide a cornerstone in the study and application of clinical research, helping to shape the future of healthcare through the ethical and effective conduct of clinical trials.

Dr. C. Ronald Darwin
Dr. Praful J Kumar
Dr. A. R. Vijayakumar
Editor: Dr. A. Muralidhar Rao

Comprehensive Guide To Clinical Research Regulations: Theory And Practice

AUTHORS

Dr. C. Ronald Darwin, M.Pharm., PhD.
Professor & Head, Pharmacology
School of Pharmaceutical Sciences
Vels Institute of Science Technology & Advanced Studies
Chennai - 600117, India

Dr. Praful J Kumar, MBBS, M.D.
PG Resident,
Dept of General Medicine,
Stanley Medical College,
Chennai - 600001, India

Dr. A. R. Vijayakumar, M.Pharm., PhD., FASc.
Professor & HoD, Department of Pharmacology
Faculty of Pharmacy,
Sree Balaji Medical College and Hospital
Bharat Institute of Higher Education and Research (BIHER),
Chromepet, Chennai, Tamil Nadu - 600044, India

Editor
Dr. A. Muralidhar Rao, M.Pharm., PhD., FISCA., FICPHS., FICCP
Principal,
St. Mary's College of Pharmacy,
Secunderabad, Telangana, India

Published by Notion Press
Notion Press, Inc.
800, West El Camino Real #180,
California, USA 94040
Email ID: publish@notionpress.com

About The Authors

Dr. Ronald Darwin C

Dr. Ronald Darwin C is a distinguished Professor and Head of the Department of Pharmacology at the School of Pharmaceutical Sciences, VISTAS. Dr. Darwin holds a Ph.D. in Pharmacology from The Tamil Nadu Dr. MGR Medical University, Guindy, Chennai, where he also completed his M.Pharm and B.Pharm degrees.

With a teaching and research career spanning over a decade, Dr. Darwin has made significant contributions to the fields of neuropharmacology and pharmacology education. His expertise in animal study design and neuropharmacology research has been widely recognized and has led to the publication of 32 high-impact research articles, the highest of which boasts an impact factor of 15.8. Additionally, his inventive prowess is demonstrated by his 9 patents and substantial contributions to textbook and chapter writing, including seven textbooks and several book chapters published by renowned publishers such as Springer Nature.

Dr. Darwin has been an integral part of the academic and professional growth of countless students, having guided three Ph.D. scholars to completion and currently mentoring eight. He has also overseen 42 MD Siddha research works and supervised numerous M.Pharm projects.

ABOUT THE AUTHORS

A life member of several prestigious pharmacy and pharmacology associations, Dr. Darwin has been recognized with multiple awards from national and international bodies for his contributions to science and education. His commitment to advancing pharmaceutical sciences is unwavering, as evidenced by his active participation in various capacities within the scientific community.

Dr. Darwin's approach to education and research is characterized by a profound dedication to excellence and innovation, making him a respected leader in his field.

ABOUT THE AUTHORS

Dr. Praful J Kumar

Dr. Praful J Kumar's illustrious career began as Team Leader at Tamilnadu's Govt's pioneering Emergency Care Centre. Leveraging his exceptional clinical expertise and acumen, he successfully treated critically ill, trauma, medical, and surgical emergencies, saving countless lives. Notably, several of his challenging and intersting cases have been published in esteemed magazines and journals.

Committed to serving the underserved, Dr. Praful joined a Rural Primary Health Care Centre as Medical Officer. He conducted numerous medical camps, blood donation drives, school health initiatives, vaccination programs, and community outreach activities. His tireless efforts upgraded his PHC's facilities and services to National standards, earning the National Quality Assurance Standards award from Tamilnadu's Honourable Health Minister.

During the COVID-19 pandemic, Dr. Praful played a crucial role in district's covid control efforts. His stringent measures, community awareness campaigns, patient treatment, and vaccination initiatives achieved 100% coverage, earning recognition from the District Collector on the occasion of Republic Day.

Currently, Dr. Praful is pursuing his postgraduate studies at Chennai's prestigious Govt. Stanley Medical College. His passions include teaching and mentoring fellow medical professionalls, clinical innovation, sharing expertise through knowledge dissemination

ABOUT THE AUTHORS

Dedicated to healthcare excellence, Dr. Praful's contributions have significantly impacted countless lives, communities, and the medical fraternity.

ABOUT THE AUTHORS

Dr. A. R. Vijayakumar

Dr. A. R. Vijayakumar, M.Pharm., Ph.D., FASc., serves as Professor and Head of the Department of Pharmacology at Faculty of Pharmacy, Sree Balaji Medical College and Hospital, Bharath Institute of Higher Education and Research (BIHER), Chromepet, Chennai, Tamil Nadu, India.

Dr. Vijayakumar embarked on his illustrious educational journey at The Tamil Nadu Dr. M. G. R. Medical University, Chennai, where he completed his Bachelor's degree in Pharmacy in 2003 and his Master's Degree in Pharmacology in 2005. He earned his Ph.D. in Medical Sciences from 2008 to 2013 at Dr. RPC, All India Institute of Medical Sciences (AIIMS), New Delhi. His profound commitment to pharmacology has been recognized with several accolades, including the prestigious Dr. Dev Raj Bajaj Research Award for the best paper on the development of newer techniques and instrumentation in pharmacology at APPICON – 2016, AIIMS, Patna, Bihar.

A Fellow of the Academy of Sciences for Animal Welfare (FASc), Dr. Vijayakumar was honoured for his significant contributions to animal welfare in science. Throughout his career, he has secured multiple travel grants to participate in national conferences, reflecting his active engagement in the academic community.

With over 34 publications in esteemed PubMed, Scopus, and Web of Science indexed journals, and around 9 book chapters, Dr. Vijayakumar

ABOUT THE AUTHORS

is a respected reviewer for numerous national and international scientific journals. His scholarly work not only advances the field of pharmacology but also serves as a beacon for upcoming researchers in the medical sciences.

CHAPTER ONE

Introduction to Clinical Research and Drug Development

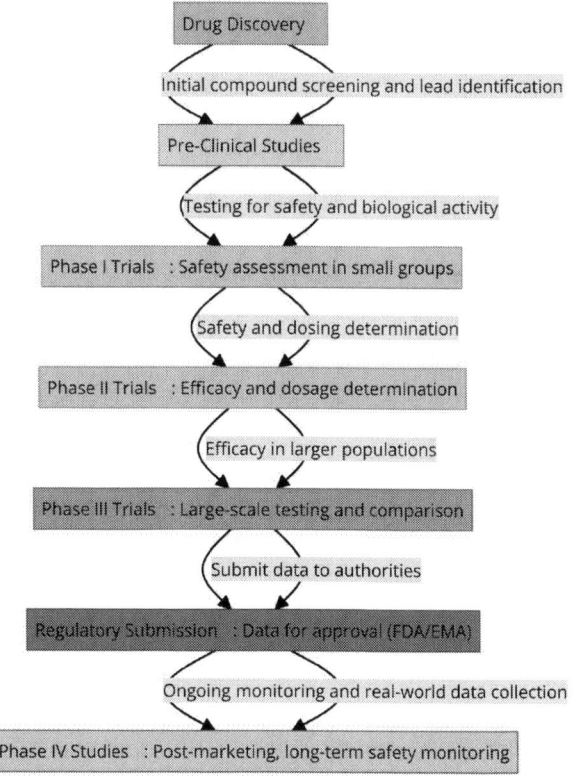

1.1 History of Clinical Research and Drug Development

1.1.1 Early Drug Discovery Methods
The journey of drug discovery began long before modern scientific methods emerged. In ancient times, drug discovery relied heavily on natural resources, including plants, minerals, and animal products. Civilizations like the Egyptians, Chinese, and Indians used herbs and natural compounds in their traditional medicine systems. The Ayurvedic system of medicine, which originated in India more than 3000 years ago, is one of the earliest recorded examples of structured medicinal practices, using various herbs and compounds to treat ailments. However, the scientific basis behind these treatments was not well understood. The early drug discovery process was more of a trial-and-error method, where healers would observe the effects of substances on the body and make deductions about their medicinal value. Without standardized clinical trials or knowledge of drug metabolism, the efficacy and safety of these early medicines were often questionable. Even though many drugs like quinine from cinchona bark for malaria, or opium from poppy plants for pain relief, were discovered during this period, the absence of structured research limited their full potential. It wasn't until the 19th and 20th centuries, with the advent of chemical synthesis and a growing understanding of biology, that systematic drug discovery began to emerge.

1.1.2 Milestones in Clinical Research
The field of clinical research has witnessed numerous milestones that have revolutionized medical science. One of the earliest milestones was the scurvy trial conducted by James Lind in 1747, which is often regarded as one of the first controlled clinical trials. Lind's trial, which demonstrated that citrus fruits could cure scurvy, introduced the idea of testing hypotheses in human subjects under controlled conditions. Fast forward to the mid-20th century, the Randomized Controlled Trial (RCT) emerged as a gold standard for clinical research. The introduction of RCTs allowed for the comparison of treatments with control groups, reducing biases and increasing the reliability of results. This was a critical shift in clinical research methodology, providing the basis for modern drug testing. Another major milestone was the adoption of Good Clinical Practice (GCP) guidelines in the 1990s, which standardized clinical trial procedures globally. The establishment of regulatory bodies such as the U.S. Food and

Drug Administration (FDA) in 1906 and the European Medicines Agency (EMA) in 1995 were significant as well, as they introduced stricter regulations for drug testing and approval, ensuring the safety and efficacy of new drugs before they reached the market.

1.1.3 Evolution of Drug Development Regulations

Drug development regulations have evolved over the last century in response to various public health disasters. One of the earliest regulatory changes came after the 1937 Elixir Sulfanilamide tragedy in the United States, where more than 100 people died due to the toxic solvent used in the drug formulation. This incident led to the Federal Food, Drug, and Cosmetic Act of 1938, which required companies to prove the safety of their drugs before marketing them. Over the years, similar regulations were introduced globally, often in response to drug-related tragedies. The thalidomide disaster of the 1960s, where thousands of babies were born with birth defects after their mothers took thalidomide during pregnancy, prompted stricter drug testing requirements and the introduction of regulatory oversight for clinical trials. The 1962 Kefauver-Harris Amendment to the U.S. Federal Food, Drug, and Cosmetic Act was a direct result, mandating drug manufacturers to prove not just the safety, but also the efficacy of their products through controlled trials. The development of ICH-GCP guidelines in the 1990s further standardized clinical trial processes, ensuring ethical conduct, participant protection, and high-quality data across global trials. Today, regulatory bodies like the FDA, EMA, and CDSCO in India work collaboratively under harmonized guidelines, ensuring that new drugs are thoroughly tested for safety and efficacy before they reach patients.

1.2 Ethical Considerations in Clinical Research

1.2.1 Importance of Ethics in Clinical Research

Ethics play a crucial role in clinical research, particularly when human subjects are involved. The main objective of ethics in clinical research is to protect the rights, safety, and well-being of participants while ensuring that the study produces valid scientific data. Ethical considerations guide the design, conduct, and reporting of clinical research, balancing the pursuit of scientific knowledge with the need to safeguard human dignity. Key ethical principles such as respect for persons, beneficence, and justice, as outlined in the Belmont Report, are foundational to modern clinical research. The role of Institutional Review Boards (IRBs) and Ethics Committees (ECs) in overseeing research is critical, as they ensure that the study protocols comply with ethical guidelines. These bodies review research proposals to assess whether risks are minimized and that informed consent is obtained from participants. They also monitor ongoing trials to ensure that participants are not exposed to undue risks. Without such ethical oversight, clinical trials could potentially exploit vulnerable populations, leading to harm or injustice. The Declaration of Helsinki, adopted in 1964 by the World Medical Association, further strengthens the ethical framework of clinical research by providing guidelines on obtaining informed consent and maintaining transparency with research subjects.

1.2.2 Impact of Unethical Research (Examples: Tuskegee, Thalidomide)

The importance of ethics in clinical research is often highlighted by examples of unethical studies that have caused widespread harm. One such example is the Tuskegee Syphilis Study (1932-1972), where 600 African-American men with syphilis were misled and denied treatment in order to study the natural progression of the disease. The participants were not informed of their diagnosis, nor were they given access to penicillin when it became the standard treatment for syphilis in the 1940s. This study caused a public outcry when it was revealed, leading to new regulations that protected human subjects in research. Another infamous example is the Thalidomide tragedy, where a drug prescribed to pregnant women for morning sickness in the late 1950s led to over 10,000 cases of severe birth defects worldwide. Thalidomide had not been adequately tested for safety in pregnant women, highlighting the need for stringent regulatory oversight in clinical trials. These incidents were pivotal in shaping modern ethical guidelines and regulations, emphasizing the need for informed consent, transparency, and rigorous testing of drugs before they are approved for widespread use.

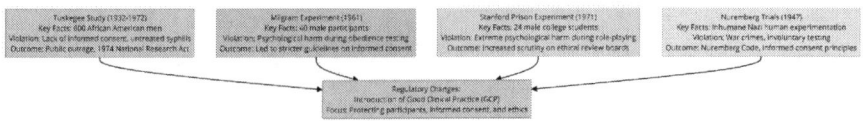

Major Ethical Violations in Clinical Research History

1.2.3 Development of International Ethical Guidelines

In response to historical ethical violations, international guidelines were developed to protect human subjects in clinical research. The Nuremberg Code, formulated after World War II, was one of the earliest documents to emphasize the voluntary consent of participants in medical research. This was followed by the Declaration of Helsinki in 1964, which provided ethical principles for medical research involving human subjects. The Declaration of Helsinki is widely regarded as the cornerstone of clinical research ethics, outlining key principles such as the importance of obtaining informed consent and conducting research that benefits society. Over time, these guidelines have evolved to address new challenges in research, such as genetic studies and research involving vulnerable populations. The ICH-GCP guidelines, developed in the 1990s, further formalized ethical requirements in clinical trials by establishing standards for designing, conducting, and reporting research. These guidelines are now adopted worldwide, ensuring that ethical standards are upheld in clinical trials regardless of where they are conducted. Today, clinical research is governed by a complex framework of international and national ethical guidelines, designed to protect participants and ensure that scientific research is conducted with integrity.

1.3 Different Types of Clinical Studies

1.3.1 Observational Studies

Observational studies play a vital role in understanding the epidemiology of diseases and assessing the real-world effectiveness of treatments. Unlike interventional studies, observational studies do not involve any manipulation or intervention by the researchers. Instead, they observe and record data on subjects as they go about their normal lives. Observational studies can be prospective, where data is collected in real time, or retrospective, where existing data is analyzed. A classic example of an observational study is the Framingham Heart Study, which began in 1948 and has provided valuable insights into the risk factors for cardiovascular diseases. Observational studies are typically less expensive and less time-consuming than randomized controlled trials (RCTs), making them an essential tool in public health research. However, because they do not involve randomization, they are more prone to bias, and establishing causality is more challenging. Despite these limitations, observational studies have contributed significantly to medical knowledge, particularly in understanding the long-term effects of exposures such as smoking, diet, and environmental factors.

1.3.2 Interventional Studies

Interventional studies are designed to test the effectiveness of a treatment, intervention, or drug by assigning participants to different groups, typically an experimental group and a control group. The most well-known type of interventional study is the randomized controlled trial (RCT), which is considered the gold standard in clinical research. In an RCT, participants are randomly assigned to receive either the treatment being tested or a placebo/control. This randomization helps eliminate bias and ensures that the groups are comparable at the start of the study. Blinding, where participants and/or researchers do not know which group a participant is in, is often used to prevent bias in outcome assessments. Interventional studies provide strong evidence of a treatment's efficacy because they control for variables and use rigorous statistical analysis. For example, the RCTs conducted for COVID-19 vaccines, such as the Pfizer-BioNTech and Moderna trials, were crucial in demonstrating the vaccines' safety and efficacy. These trials followed thousands of participants over several months to monitor the incidence of infection and adverse effects, providing the robust data needed for regulatory approval.

1.3.3 Comparative Studies (Case-Control, Cohort, Randomized Controlled Trials)

Comparative studies, including case-control studies, cohort studies, and randomized controlled trials, are fundamental to clinical research as they allow researchers to compare different groups of individuals to determine the effects of exposures or interventions. Case-control studies are retrospective, comparing individuals with a specific condition (cases) to those without the condition (controls). These studies are particularly useful in studying rare diseases, where it would be impractical to follow a large group over time. Cohort studies, on the other hand, are prospective and follow a group of individuals over time to observe the development of outcomes based on their exposures. A well-known example is the Nurses' Health Study, which has been tracking the health of over 100,000 nurses since 1976 to study the impact of diet and lifestyle on chronic diseases. While case-control and cohort studies provide valuable insights, they are more prone to biases compared to RCTs. RCTs remain the gold standard for comparing treatments, as randomization helps to eliminate selection bias and confounding factors. By assigning participants to either the experimental or control group, RCTs provide the highest level of evidence in determining the efficacy and safety of new interventions.

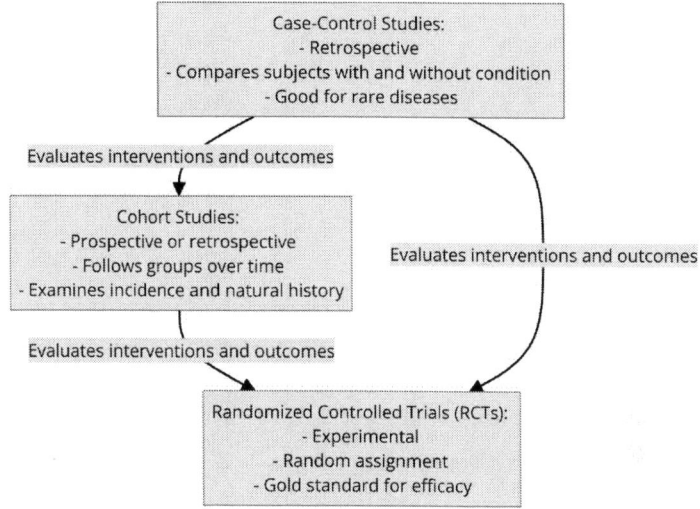

Comparison of Study Designs: Case-Control, Cohort, and RCTs

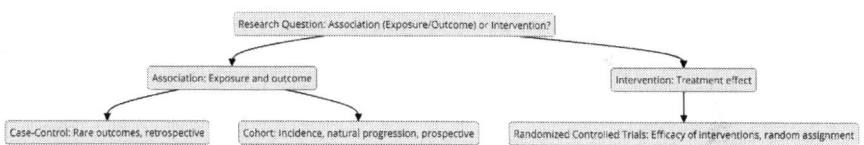

Study Design Selection Flowchart

1.4 Drug Development Process Overview

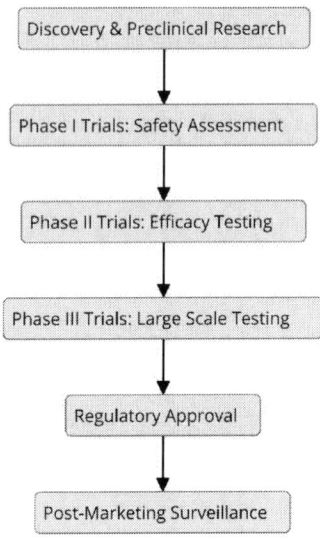

Fig 1: Drug Development Process

1.4.1 Pre-Clinical Trials

Pre-clinical trials are the first step in the drug development process, conducted before a drug is tested in humans. These trials involve laboratory testing on cells and animals to determine the safety and efficacy of a drug. In vitro studies, which involve testing in a controlled laboratory environment outside of a living organism, help scientists understand how the drug interacts with biological targets. In vivo studies, conducted on animals, are used to evaluate the drug's pharmacokinetics (how the drug is absorbed, distributed, metabolized, and excreted) and pharmacodynamics (how the drug affects the body). Pre-clinical testing is essential for identifying potential toxic effects before progressing to human trials. Regulatory agencies such as the FDA and EMA require extensive pre-clinical data before approving a drug for human testing. This stage is crucial as it helps to minimize risks in later phases of drug development, where human participants are involved. For example, the average cost of pre-clinical testing can range from $10 million to $30 million, depending on the complexity of the drug and the number of animal studies required.

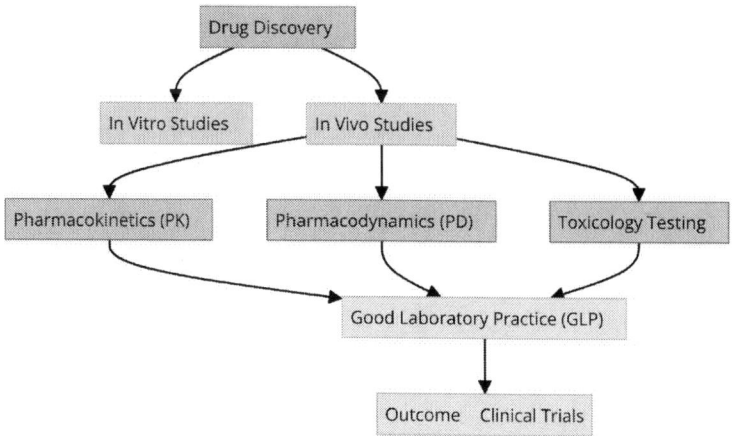

Pre-Clinical Trials: From Discovery to Clinical Trials

1.4.2 Clinical Trials

Clinical trials are the backbone of the drug development process, involving human participants to assess the safety, efficacy, and dosage of new treatments. Clinical trials are conducted in phases, each with specific objectives. Phase I trials are the first stage of human testing, focusing on safety and dosage in a small group of healthy volunteers or patients (typically 20-100 participants). Phase II trials expand the study to a larger group (100-300 participants) to assess efficacy and further evaluate safety. Phase III trials are large-scale studies involving several thousand participants across multiple locations to confirm efficacy, monitor side effects, and compare the new treatment to standard therapies. These trials are critical for regulatory approval, as they provide the data needed to prove that the drug is safe and effective for its intended use. Following regulatory approval, Phase IV trials, also known as post-marketing studies, continue to monitor the drug's long-term safety and effectiveness in the general population.

1.4.3 Drug Approval and Marketing

Once clinical trials have demonstrated the safety and efficacy of a drug, the next step is obtaining regulatory approval. In the United States, drug developers submit a New Drug Application (NDA) to the FDA, which includes all pre-clinical and clinical trial data, as well as information on the drug's manufacturing and labeling. In Europe, a Marketing Authorization Application (MAA) is submitted to the EMA. The approval process involves a thorough review by regulatory authorities to ensure that the benefits of the drug outweigh the risks. On average, the NDA/MAA review process can take 6 to 12 months, depending on the drug's complexity and the quality of the data provided. Once approved, the drug can be marketed to the public, but post-marketing surveillance (Phase IV trials) is required to monitor long-term safety and rare side effects that may not have been detected in earlier trials.

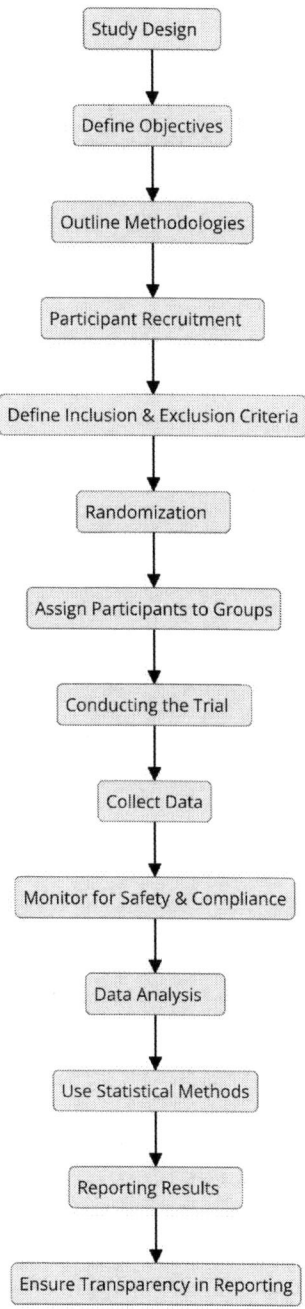

Fig: 2 Clinical Trial Process

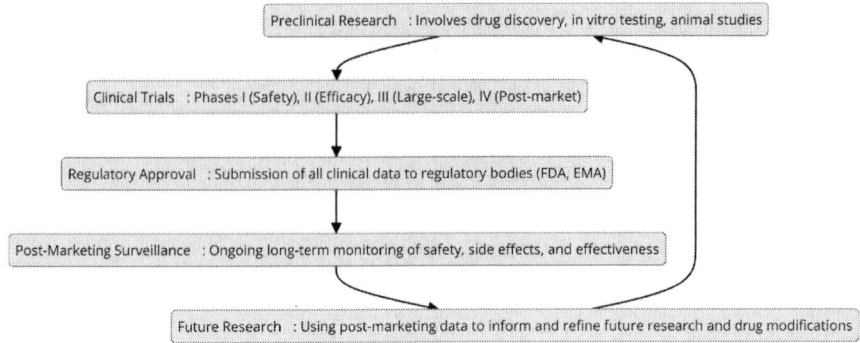

Fig: 3 Clinical Research Cycle

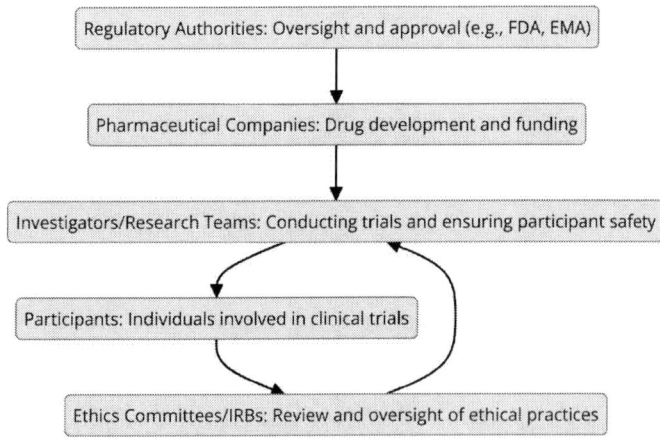

Roles of Key Stakeholders in Clinical Research Illustration

1.5 Challenges in Clinical Drug Development

1.5.1 Time and Cost Factors

Drug development is a highly time-consuming and expensive process. On average, it takes 10-15 years and costs approximately $2.6 billion to bring a new drug from discovery to market. The high cost is largely due to the long and complex process of conducting clinical trials, where each phase becomes progressively more expensive. For example, Phase III trials, which involve thousands of participants across multiple sites, can cost upwards of $100 million. In addition to the direct costs of running trials, delays in recruitment, data analysis, and regulatory approvals can significantly increase the overall cost. The financial risk is further compounded by the fact that only a small percentage of drugs that enter clinical trials ultimately receive regulatory approval. It is estimated that only 10% of drugs that enter Phase I trials make it to market, meaning that the majority of the investment is lost.

1.5.2 Regulatory Hurdles

Navigating the regulatory landscape is one of the most significant challenges in drug development. Regulatory requirements vary from country to country, and obtaining approval in multiple regions can be a lengthy and costly process. For example, the time to obtain regulatory approval for clinical trials in the United States can range from several months to over a year, depending on the complexity of the drug and the FDA's review workload. Similarly, in Europe, the EMA's review process can take up to a year. In addition to the time required for regulatory approvals, drug developers must also comply with various local regulations regarding patient consent, data protection, and safety reporting. These regulatory hurdles are further complicated in multinational trials, where different countries may have conflicting requirements. To address these challenges, efforts have been made to harmonize regulations through initiatives such as the International Council for Harmonisation (ICH), which seeks to streamline the drug approval process across major markets.

1.5.3 Patient Recruitment and Retention

One of the most critical challenges in clinical trials is recruiting and retaining enough participants to complete the study. Patient recruitment can be particularly difficult in trials for rare diseases, where the pool of eligible participants is limited. On average, 30% of clinical trials fail to recruit enough participants, leading to delays or even the termination of the trial. Even when patients are successfully recruited, retaining them throughout the duration of the study can be challenging. Long-term studies, in particular, have high dropout rates, which can skew results and reduce the statistical power of the study. To address these challenges, trial sponsors use a variety of strategies, including digital recruitment platforms, patient advocacy groups, and financial incentives for participants. However, recruitment and retention remain significant obstacles to the success of many clinical trials.

1.6 Globalization of Clinical Trials

1.6.1 Multinational Trials

As the pharmaceutical industry becomes more globalized, multinational clinical trials have become increasingly common. These trials involve multiple countries and regions, allowing drug developers to collect data from diverse populations and accelerate the recruitment process. One of the largest multinational trials in recent years was the SOLIDARITY trial, coordinated by the World Health Organization (WHO), which tested multiple treatments for COVID-19 across more than 30 countries. Multinational trials offer several advantages, including faster recruitment, broader demographic representation, and the ability to meet regulatory requirements in multiple regions simultaneously. However, conducting trials across different countries also presents challenges, such as coordinating between multiple regulatory agencies, ensuring consistent trial protocols, and addressing cultural and linguistic differences among participants.

Phase I : Safety and tolerability Participants: 20-100 Duration: Months	Phase II : Efficacy and dosage Participants: 100-300 Duration: Months-Years	Phase III : Confirmatory trials Participants: 1,000-3,000 Duration: Years	Phase IV : Post-marketing studies Participants: Thousands Duration: Ongoing

Comparative chart for the drug development phases

1.6.2 Regulatory Harmonization

The globalization of clinical trials has highlighted the need for regulatory harmonization, as drug developers must navigate different regulatory frameworks in each country where the trial is conducted. The International Council for Harmonisation (ICH) has played a key role in harmonizing clinical trial regulations across major markets, including the United States, Europe, and Japan. ICH guidelines, such as Good Clinical Practice (GCP), provide a common framework for conducting clinical trials, ensuring that the data generated is accepted by regulatory authorities in multiple regions. Regulatory harmonization has reduced the time and cost of conducting multinational trials by eliminating the need for duplicate studies in different countries. For example, ICH guidelines have streamlined the process of submitting clinical trial data to multiple regulatory agencies, allowing drug developers to submit a single dossier for review by the FDA, EMA, and other agencies.

1.6.3 Impact of Globalization on Trial Design and Outcomes

The globalization of clinical trials has also influenced trial design and outcomes. Multinational trials are often designed to include diverse populations, allowing researchers to assess the efficacy and safety of treatments across different ethnic and demographic groups. For example, trials for cardiovascular drugs often include participants from different racial backgrounds, as certain populations may respond differently to treatment due to genetic variations. Globalization has also led to the development of adaptive trial designs, which allow researchers to modify the trial protocol based on interim data. Adaptive designs have become increasingly popular in multinational trials, as they allow for greater flexibility and can reduce the time needed to reach a conclusion. However, conducting trials across multiple regions can also introduce variability in outcomes due to differences in healthcare systems, patient adherence, and cultural factors. To address these challenges, trial sponsors must carefully standardize protocols and ensure that data is collected consistently across all sites.

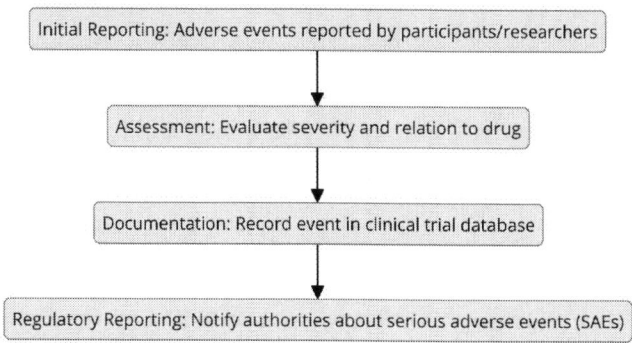

Process of adverse event monitoring in clinical trials

Review Questions

1. What are the key milestones in the history of clinical research and drug development?

2. How have drug discovery methods evolved over the years?
3. Discuss the impact of historical unethical research events, such as the Tuskegee Syphilis Study, on the development of modern drug regulations.
4. Why was the Thalidomide disaster significant in the evolution of drug development regulations?
5. Why are ethical guidelines essential in clinical research, and what are their primary objectives?
6. Explain the role of the Nuremberg Code and the Declaration of Helsinki in shaping modern clinical research ethics.
7. How do international ethical guidelines prevent the recurrence of unethical research practices?
8. Give examples of unethical research practices from history and how they changed modern clinical research standards.
9. What are the primary differences between observational studies and interventional studies?
10. Describe the characteristics of case-control studies, cohort studies, and randomized controlled trials.
11. How do comparative studies help in the development of clinical treatments?
12. Discuss the advantages and limitations of randomized controlled trials in clinical research.
13. Outline the stages of the drug development process, from discovery to marketing.
14. What is the role of pre-clinical trials in drug development?
15. How do clinical trials progress through the different phases (I, II, III, IV), and what is the primary objective of each phase?
16. Discuss the regulatory approval process for a new drug after clinical trials are completed.
17. What are some of the common challenges faced by pharmaceutical companies during clinical drug development?
18. How do time and cost factors impact the drug development process?
19. What regulatory hurdles must be overcome during the drug development process?
20. Explain the difficulties in recruiting and retaining patients for clinical trials.
21. How has the globalization of clinical trials changed the landscape of drug development?

22. Discuss the benefits and challenges of conducting multinational clinical trials.
23. What role does regulatory harmonization play in global clinical trials?
24. How does globalization impact trial design, participant diversity, and trial outcomes?

CHAPTER TWO

Phases of Clinical Trials

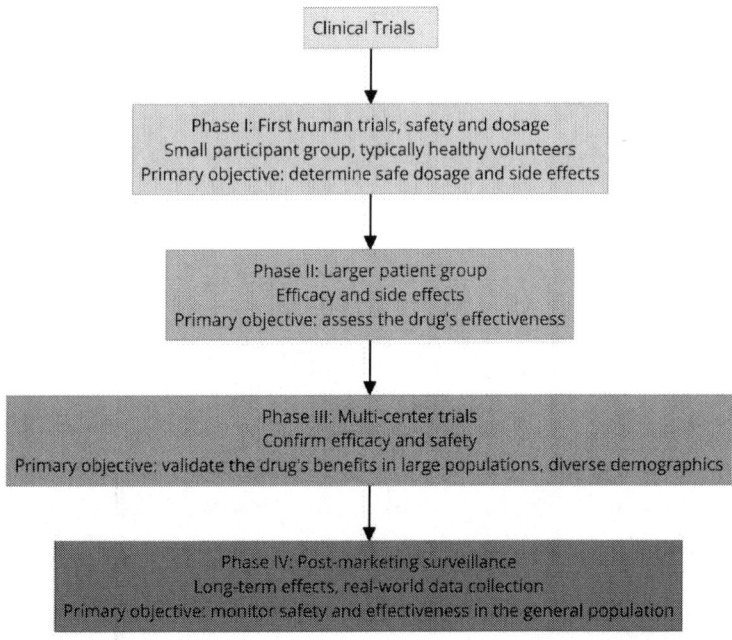

The Four Phases of Clinical Trials: A Detailed Overview

2.1 Overview of Clinical Trial Phases

2.1.1 Introduction to Clinical Trial Phases

Clinical trials are a series of meticulously designed studies conducted to evaluate the safety and efficacy of a drug or medical treatment before it reaches the general population. These trials are divided into distinct phases, each serving a unique purpose in the overall development of a drug. The progression from one phase to the next is determined by the results obtained at each stage. The primary goal of the clinical trial process is to ensure that the benefits of a new treatment outweigh any risks or side effects, making it both safe and effective for human use. While pre-clinical research, conducted in the laboratory and on animals, forms the foundation of drug development, clinical trials begin once the potential of a drug is established. This phase-by-phase approach allows researchers to systematically gather data, address uncertainties, and minimize risks associated with the drug before making it widely available. The clinical trial process ensures that no stage is skipped, and all potential risks are identified and addressed at the appropriate time.

2.1.2 Differences Between Trial Phases

The four main phases of clinical trials—Phase 0, I, II, III, and IV—differ in terms of objectives, scale, and participants. Phase 0 trials are exploratory, involving very small groups and ultra-low doses of the drug to collect preliminary data on pharmacokinetics and pharmacodynamics. In contrast, Phase I trials involve a larger group of healthy volunteers and are designed to assess safety, determine dosage ranges, and study the drug's metabolism and excretion. Phase II trials, which enroll several hundred participants with the targeted disease, focus on assessing the drug's efficacy and further evaluating safety. The primary aim here is to gather enough evidence to justify larger trials. Phase III trials are pivotal in nature, involving thousands of participants across multiple centers or even countries. These trials confirm the drug's efficacy on a large scale and provide comprehensive safety data for regulatory submission. Finally, Phase IV trials, conducted post-approval, monitor the drug's performance in real-world settings to identify any rare or long-term adverse effects that may not have been apparent during earlier phases.

2.1.3 Importance of Sequential Progression Through Phases

Sequential progression through each phase of clinical trials is crucial to ensuring the safe development of a drug. Moving through these phases in order allows researchers to build upon data collected at each stage, refining their understanding of how the drug works, what doses are appropriate, and what safety concerns need to be addressed. Starting with small, controlled groups in Phase 0 and I minimizes the risk to human participants while gathering initial insights into the drug's behavior in the body. As trials advance to Phase II, where efficacy is tested on patients with the target condition, researchers can fine-tune dosage levels and study the potential benefits in real-world applications. By the time Phase III trials are conducted, the drug's efficacy and safety have been largely established, allowing for broader testing and paving the way for regulatory approval. Skipping phases or prematurely advancing could lead to incomplete data, resulting in unforeseen safety issues or failure to meet efficacy standards, which could have serious consequences for patients and developers alike.

2.2 Phase 0 Clinical Trials

2.2.1 Role of Phase 0 Trials in Drug Development

Phase 0 clinical trials, also referred to as "micro-dosing studies," play a relatively new but essential role in modern drug development. These trials allow researchers to gather early data on how a drug interacts with the human body without exposing participants to the full therapeutic dose. The primary objective of Phase 0 trials is to assess pharmacokinetics (how the drug is absorbed, distributed, metabolized, and excreted) and pharmacodynamics (the drug's biological effects). These trials are typically conducted with a very small number of participants, often fewer than 15, and involve minimal doses that are far below those that would produce therapeutic effects. By obtaining this early data, drug developers can make informed decisions about whether to proceed with further clinical testing, potentially saving time and resources. Phase 0 trials are especially useful for ruling out compounds that have poor bioavailability or show rapid clearance from the body, which would make them unsuitable for further development. Although Phase 0 trials do not replace Phase I trials, they serve as an efficient initial screening tool.

2.2.2 Micro-Dosing Studies

In micro-dosing studies, participants receive a fraction of the full therapeutic dose—typically less than 1%—to minimize the risk of adverse effects while allowing researchers to study the drug's pharmacokinetics. These doses are too low to produce any significant pharmacological effects, but they provide valuable information on how the drug is absorbed, distributed, and eliminated by the body. Micro-dosing studies use advanced analytical techniques, such as accelerator mass spectrometry (AMS), to detect and measure the drug's concentration in biological samples. This approach is particularly useful for studying drugs with complex structures or those that require precise dosing for efficacy. Micro-dosing studies are also valuable for early decision-making in drug development, as they can reveal whether a drug is likely to succeed in later phases. If a drug shows poor pharmacokinetics in a micro-dosing study, developers may choose to modify its structure or abandon the project before investing in larger, more expensive trials.

2.2.3 Exploratory IND (Investigational New Drug) Applications

To conduct Phase 0 trials, researchers must submit an Exploratory Investigational New Drug (IND) application to regulatory authorities. This application is a streamlined version of the traditional IND, focused on providing enough safety data to justify limited human exposure. The exploratory IND includes results from pre-clinical testing, such as in vitro and animal studies, that demonstrate the drug's potential safety for humans. While Phase 0 trials do not require the extensive data needed for later-phase trials, the exploratory IND must still show that the risk to participants is minimal. Once approved, the exploratory IND allows researchers to proceed with micro-dosing studies and gather the necessary pharmacokinetic data. Exploratory IND applications help accelerate the drug development process by providing a faster, more efficient path to human testing, especially for compounds that show early promise but require further refinement before moving to larger trials.

2.3 Phase I Clinical Trials

2.3.1 Key Objectives: Safety and Dosing

Phase I clinical trials are the first step in testing a drug on humans and are primarily focused on assessing safety and determining the appropriate dosage range. These trials are usually conducted with a small group of healthy volunteers, ranging from 20 to 100 individuals, although patients with the target condition may be included in certain cases, particularly in oncology trials. The main objectives of Phase I trials are to identify potential side effects, establish the maximum tolerated dose (MTD), and study the drug's pharmacokinetics and pharmacodynamics. By starting with low doses and gradually increasing them, researchers can assess how the drug behaves in the human body and identify any adverse reactions. Phase I trials are critical for laying the groundwork for subsequent phases, as they provide the first insights into the drug's safety profile and help determine the appropriate dosage for future trials. The information gathered in Phase I trials also informs the design of Phase II and III trials, ensuring that the drug is tested in a way that maximizes its potential benefits while minimizing risks.

2.3.2 Single Ascending Dose (SAD) Studies

Single Ascending Dose (SAD) studies are a common feature of Phase I trials and involve administering a single dose of the drug to different groups of participants, with each group receiving a progressively higher dose. The goal of SAD studies is to evaluate the drug's pharmacokinetics, including how it is absorbed, distributed, metabolized, and excreted, as well as to monitor for any immediate side effects. By increasing the dose in a stepwise fashion, researchers can determine the maximum tolerated dose (MTD) and identify the dose at which adverse effects begin to occur. SAD studies provide critical information on the drug's safety and help establish the starting dose for future trials. These studies are particularly important for new molecular entities, where the effects of the drug on humans are largely unknown. The data from SAD studies are used to guide dosing decisions in later phases of development, ensuring that participants receive the safest and most effective dose possible.

2.3.3 Multiple Ascending Dose (MAD) Studies

Multiple Ascending Dose (MAD) studies are conducted alongside SAD studies to evaluate the effects of repeated dosing over a period of time. In MAD studies, participants receive the drug at increasing doses over several days or weeks, allowing researchers to assess how the body responds to sustained exposure. MAD studies are particularly important for drugs that are intended to be taken chronically, as they provide insights into the drug's accumulation in the body and its potential long-term effects. The results of MAD studies help researchers determine the appropriate dosing regimen for Phase II trials and provide valuable data on the drug's safety and pharmacokinetics. For example, MAD studies were instrumental in the development of many chronic disease treatments, where understanding the effects of repeated dosing is critical for ensuring long-term safety. The data gathered in MAD studies also help identify potential drug-drug interactions, which are important for drugs that are likely to be used in combination with other therapies.

2.4 Phase II Clinical Trials

2.4.1 Proof of Concept Studies

Phase II clinical trials, often referred to as "proof of concept" studies, are the first trials to evaluate the drug's efficacy in patients with the target condition. These trials typically involve a few hundred participants and are designed to provide preliminary data on whether the drug works as expected. Phase II trials are divided into two sub-phases: Phase IIa, which focuses on dose-finding, and Phase IIb, which evaluates the drug's efficacy at the optimal dose. The primary goal of Phase II trials is to determine whether the drug provides a therapeutic benefit that justifies further testing in larger trials. In addition to assessing efficacy, Phase II trials continue to monitor the drug's safety profile, identifying any side effects that may not have been observed in Phase I trials. The success of a drug in Phase II is critical for determining whether it will proceed to the larger and more expensive Phase III trials. If a drug shows promise in Phase II, researchers can move forward with confidence, knowing that the drug has a reasonable chance of success in later stages of development.

2.4.2 Dose-Ranging Studies

Dose-ranging studies are a key aspect of Phase II trials, designed to identify the optimal dose that provides the greatest therapeutic benefit with the fewest side effects. These studies test multiple doses of the drug in different groups of participants, allowing researchers to evaluate the relationship between dose and efficacy. Dose-ranging studies help refine the dosing regimen for Phase III trials, ensuring that participants receive the most effective and safest dose. For example, dose-ranging studies were essential in the development of many cancer therapies, where finding the right balance between efficacy and toxicity is critical. These studies also play a crucial role in developing treatments for chronic diseases like asthma and rheumatoid arthritis, where long-term dosing must be carefully managed.

2.4.3 Safety and Efficacy Balance

One of the main challenges in Phase II trials is achieving the right balance between safety and efficacy. While Phase I trials focus primarily on safety, Phase II trials must demonstrate that the drug is not only safe but also effective. This requires a careful evaluation of the drug's therapeutic benefits relative to its risks. In some cases, a drug may show promising efficacy but have significant side effects, requiring further refinement before it can proceed to Phase III. Conversely, a drug that is safe but lacks sufficient efficacy may need to be modified or abandoned. The safety and efficacy balance is especially important in fields like oncology, where drugs with high toxicity may still be used if they provide significant survival benefits. Data from Phase II trials help inform decisions about whether to proceed with larger-scale testing and guide the design of Phase III trials.

2.5 Phase III Clinical Trials

2.5.1 Pivotal Trials for Regulatory Approval

Phase III clinical trials are the most crucial in the drug development process. These trials are conducted on a large scale, typically involving thousands of participants, and are designed to provide definitive evidence of the drug's efficacy and safety. Unlike the earlier phases, Phase III trials aim to confirm the findings from Phase II by testing the drug on a larger and more diverse population. These trials are often referred to as pivotal trials because they are essential for gaining regulatory approval. The data generated from Phase III trials is submitted to regulatory agencies like the U.S. FDA or European Medicines Agency (EMA) to demonstrate that the drug is both safe and effective for widespread use. Phase III trials also help identify less common side effects that might not have been detected in smaller studies. The success of a drug in Phase III trials is critical, as it determines whether the drug will be approved for the market. For example, the COVID-19 vaccines were subjected to large Phase III trials, involving tens of thousands of participants, to assess their effectiveness in preventing infection across various age groups and demographics.

2.5.2 Multi-Center and Multinational Trials

Phase III trials often involve multiple centers, and in many cases, are conducted in several countries. These multi-center and multinational trials allow for a broader representation of participants, ensuring that the drug's effects are tested in diverse populations. By involving different regions and countries, researchers can evaluate how factors like genetics, environmental conditions, and healthcare practices influence the drug's performance. This is particularly important for diseases that affect people globally, such as diabetes or cardiovascular diseases, where treatment responses might vary across different populations. Additionally, conducting trials across multiple centers accelerates patient recruitment, which is crucial for large-scale studies. A major advantage of multinational trials is that they allow pharmaceutical companies to gather data that meets the regulatory requirements of different countries simultaneously, thus speeding up the process of obtaining approvals in multiple markets.

2.5.3 Registration Studies and Global Trials

Phase III trials are often known as registration studies because their primary goal is to provide the data needed for regulatory submission. Upon successful completion of these trials, the drug sponsor can submit a New Drug Application (NDA) to regulatory authorities such as the FDA, or a Marketing Authorization Application (MAA) to the EMA. These applications include detailed data from the Phase III trials, along with information on the drug's manufacturing process, labeling, and proposed dosage. Global trials, which involve participants from different countries, have become increasingly common as pharmaceutical companies seek to market their products internationally. By conducting global trials, companies can submit a single dossier to multiple regulatory agencies, reducing the time and cost of obtaining approvals in various markets. However, global trials also present challenges, such as the need to comply with different regulatory requirements and address logistical issues like language barriers and cultural differences in patient populations.

2.6 Phase IV Clinical Trials (Post-Marketing)

2.6.1 Post-Marketing Surveillance

Once a drug is approved and made available to the public, it enters Phase IV, also known as post-marketing surveillance. While the earlier phases focus on proving a drug's safety and efficacy in controlled settings, Phase IV trials monitor the drug's performance in the real world. These trials are critical for identifying rare or long-term side effects that may not have been observed during earlier clinical trials. Since Phase IV trials involve a much larger and more diverse population than the controlled settings of Phase III, they provide valuable insights into how the drug performs in everyday medical practice. For example, some drugs may interact with other medications in ways that were not apparent during pre-market testing, or certain side effects may only appear after prolonged use. Regulatory authorities require ongoing safety monitoring through Phase IV trials to ensure that the drug remains safe for long-term use. An example of post-marketing surveillance can be seen in the withdrawal of drugs like Vioxx, which was initially approved but later found to increase the risk of heart attacks after being widely used.

2.6.2 Pharmacovigilance

Pharmacovigilance is an integral part of Phase IV trials. It involves the continuous monitoring of adverse effects and safety data related to approved drugs. Regulatory agencies have established pharmacovigilance systems, such as the FDA's MedWatch and the European Medicines Agency's EudraVigilance, where healthcare professionals and patients can report any adverse events or side effects. The goal of pharmacovigilance is to detect, assess, and prevent adverse reactions to medications, ensuring that the benefits of the drug continue to outweigh the risks. Through this process, regulatory agencies can take action if new safety concerns arise, such as updating drug labels with additional warnings, restricting use in certain populations, or even withdrawing the drug from the market if necessary. Pharmacovigilance is a proactive approach to drug safety, ensuring that patients remain protected even after a drug has been approved and marketed.

2.6.3 Real-World Evidence and Long-Term Safety Data

Phase IV trials also provide important real-world evidence (RWE) and long-term safety data, which are essential for understanding how the drug performs outside of the controlled conditions of clinical trials. Real-world evidence is collected from sources such as electronic health records, patient registries, and observational studies, offering insights into how the drug works in different patient populations, including those with co-morbidities or those taking other medications. This data is invaluable for healthcare providers, as it helps them make informed decisions about prescribing the drug to their patients. Long-term safety data is particularly important for drugs that are intended for chronic use, as side effects may not become apparent until the drug has been taken over a prolonged period. For example, statins, which are widely prescribed to lower cholesterol, have been the subject of numerous Phase IV studies to monitor their long-term safety and efficacy in reducing the risk of cardiovascular events. By continuing to collect and analyze real-world data, pharmaceutical companies and regulatory agencies can ensure that the benefits of the drug remain consistent with its initial approval.

Review Questions

1. What is the main purpose of each phase in clinical trials, and how do they differ from one another?
2. Why is it important for clinical trials to progress sequentially through the different phases?
3. What are the objectives of Phase 0 clinical trials, and how do they fit into the drug development process?
4. Explain the concept of micro-dosing in Phase 0 trials and its importance in early-stage drug testing.
5. What is the role of Exploratory Investigational New Drug (IND) applications in Phase 0 studies?
6. What are the key objectives of Phase I clinical trials?
7. How does the Single Ascending Dose (SAD) study design work in Phase I trials, and what is its purpose?
8. What is the purpose of Multiple Ascending Dose (MAD) studies, and how do they differ from SAD studies?
9. Why is safety monitoring a crucial component of Phase I clinical trials?
10. What is the significance of dose escalation in Phase I studies, and how is the Maximum Tolerated Dose (MTD) determined?
11. Explain the role of pharmacokinetics (PK) and pharmacodynamics (PD) in Phase I trials.
12. What are "proof of concept" studies in Phase II trials, and why are they important for drug development?
13. How do dose-ranging studies in Phase II trials help determine the optimal therapeutic dose?
14. What challenges are commonly faced during patient recruitment and selection in Phase II clinical trials?
15. How are adverse events monitored and reported in Phase II studies?
16. Why are multi-center and multinational trials commonly used in Phase III clinical trials?
17. What role do Phase III trials play in the regulatory approval process for new drugs?
18. What is the importance of primary and secondary endpoints in Phase III trials, and how are they defined?
19. Explain the role of Phase IV clinical trials in post-marketing surveillance.

20. How does pharmacovigilance contribute to the safety monitoring of approved drugs in Phase IV studies?
21. What are Periodic Safety Update Reports (PSURs), and why are they essential in post-marketing studies?
22. How does real-world evidence gathered in Phase IV trials impact drug safety and efficacy?
23. What is the role of Risk Management Plans (RMPs) in post-marketing studies?
24. Discuss the challenges and benefits of using real-world data in post-marketing surveillance.
25. How do regulatory authorities, such as the FDA and EMA, monitor post-marketing drug safety?

CHAPTER THREE

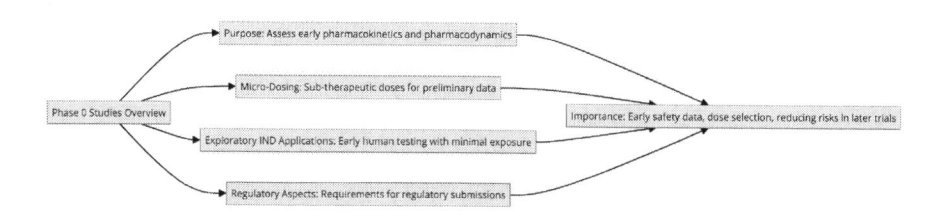

Phase 0 Studies

- Purpose: Assess early pharmacokinetics and pharmacodynamics
- Micro-Dosing: Sub-therapeutic doses for preliminary data
- Phase 0 Studies Overview
- Exploratory IND Applications: Early human testing with minimal exposure
- Importance: Early safety data, dose selection, reducing risks in later trials
- Regulatory Aspects: Requirements for regulatory submissions

Key Components of Phase 0 Clinical Trials

3.1 Definition and Purpose of Phase 0 Studies

3.1.1 Role of Phase 0 in Early Drug Development

Phase 0 studies serve as an early exploration in the drug development process, providing valuable insights without committing extensive resources to full-scale trials. Unlike traditional clinical trials, Phase 0 trials involve very limited human exposure to the investigational drug, usually in the form of micro-doses. These trials are designed to gather early data on the drug's pharmacokinetics (PK) and pharmacodynamics (PD), which refer to how the drug is absorbed, distributed, metabolized, and excreted in the human body. By testing the drug in small, carefully controlled doses, researchers can determine whether it behaves as expected, based on preclinical studies conducted in animals or in vitro systems. This phase helps identify any early signs of poor bioavailability, rapid metabolism, or other pharmacokinetic properties that could hinder the drug's success in later stages. Additionally, Phase 0 trials are critical for minimizing the risk associated with later-phase trials. By identifying problems early, developers can make informed decisions about whether to modify the drug's formulation, dosage, or route of administration before proceeding to Phase I. Phase 0 trials, while relatively new in the landscape of drug development, are becoming increasingly important as pharmaceutical companies seek to streamline the development process and reduce costs by eliminating ineffective drugs early.

3.1.2 Differences from Phase I Trials

While both Phase 0 and Phase I trials involve testing new drugs in humans, they differ significantly in terms of their goals, scope, and participant exposure. Phase I trials are traditionally the first stage of clinical testing in humans, focusing primarily on determining the safety, tolerability, and maximum tolerated dose (MTD) of a drug. These trials involve a gradual increase in dose, starting from a low dose and increasing until adverse effects or toxicity are observed. In contrast, Phase 0 trials are designed to test much smaller, non-therapeutic doses—usually less than 1% of the anticipated therapeutic dose. The primary aim of Phase 0 is to gather preliminary data on pharmacokinetics and pharmacodynamics, not to assess the drug's safety or efficacy at therapeutic levels. This distinction is critical because Phase 0 trials involve far fewer participants, typically fewer than 15, compared to the larger sample sizes used in Phase I. Additionally, while Phase I trials often include patients with the target disease, Phase 0 trials are usually conducted in healthy volunteers to minimize risks. The information obtained from Phase 0 trials helps developers decide whether to proceed with Phase I, making it a key decision point in the drug development process.

3.1.3 Regulatory Requirements for Phase 0 Studies

Conducting Phase 0 trials requires approval from regulatory authorities, just like any other phase of clinical research. In the United States, drug developers must submit an exploratory Investigational New Drug (IND) application to the Food and Drug Administration (FDA), which reviews the preclinical data and proposed trial design to ensure participant safety. The exploratory IND differs from a full IND application in that it is designed to support limited human exposure, focusing on pharmacokinetic and pharmacodynamic data rather than safety and efficacy. To obtain approval, drug developers must provide detailed information on the drug's chemistry, manufacturing, and control processes, as well as preclinical data from animal studies that demonstrate its safety at the proposed micro-doses. The FDA reviews this information to ensure that the risk to human participants is minimal. Once approved, the Phase 0 trial can proceed under strict monitoring and reporting requirements. In Europe, the European Medicines Agency (EMA) follows similar guidelines, requiring sponsors to submit an application under the Clinical Trial Directive, which includes a review of the drug's preclinical data and the proposed micro-dosing study design. The goal of regulatory oversight in Phase 0 trials is to ensure that the trials are scientifically sound, ethically conducted, and that participant safety is a top priority.

3.2 Micro-Dosing in Phase 0 Trials

3.2.1 Concept of Micro-Dosing

The concept of micro-dosing is central to Phase 0 trials, where extremely small doses of a drug are administered to participants to gather early pharmacokinetic data without exposing them to the potential risks of higher therapeutic doses. A micro-dose is typically defined as less than 1% of the dose required to produce a therapeutic effect, and it is chosen based on preclinical data that suggest it will not cause any significant pharmacological activity. The purpose of micro-dosing is not to test the efficacy of the drug, but to determine how the drug behaves in the human body—specifically, how it is absorbed, distributed, metabolized, and eliminated. By administering these small doses, researchers can assess whether the drug has suitable pharmacokinetic properties to justify further development. For example, if a drug is poorly absorbed or rapidly eliminated, it may require modification before moving to higher-dose studies. Micro-dosing allows developers to make these assessments early in the process, potentially saving time and resources. Furthermore, because the doses are so low, the risk to participants is minimal, making micro-dosing a safe and efficient method for obtaining valuable early data.

3.2.2 Ethical and Safety Considerations

Despite the minimal risk associated with micro-dosing, ethical and safety considerations remain paramount in Phase 0 trials. Participants must be fully informed about the purpose of the trial and the fact that the doses they receive are unlikely to have any therapeutic benefit. Informed consent is a critical ethical requirement, and participants must understand that Phase 0 trials are designed to gather pharmacokinetic data rather than to treat a disease. Furthermore, although the doses are low, the drug's safety must be thoroughly assessed in preclinical studies to ensure that even at micro-dose levels, there are no unforeseen toxicities. Regulatory agencies closely monitor Phase 0 trials to ensure that all ethical guidelines are followed and that participants are protected from harm. Additionally, because Phase 0 trials involve healthy volunteers or, in some cases, patients with no other treatment options, the ethical justification for exposing participants to a new, unproven drug must be clear. The risks and benefits must be carefully weighed, and the trial must be designed to minimize any potential harm while maximizing the scientific value of the data collected.

3.2.3 Applications of Micro-Dosing in Drug Discovery

Micro-dosing has several applications in drug discovery, particularly in the early stages of development. One of the most significant advantages of micro-dosing is that it allows researchers to gather early pharmacokinetic data without committing to the time and cost of full-scale clinical trials. This can be especially useful for compounds that have complex pharmacokinetics or uncertain bioavailability. For example, if a drug shows rapid clearance from the body in a micro-dosing study, developers may decide to modify the formulation or dosage before moving forward with higher-dose studies. Additionally, micro-dosing can be used to test different drug formulations or delivery methods, helping researchers determine the best way to administer the drug for optimal absorption and distribution. Another important application of micro-dosing is in personalized medicine, where researchers can use micro-doses to study how individual genetic or metabolic differences affect drug metabolism. By testing micro-doses in a small group of participants, researchers can gather valuable data on inter-individual variability, which can inform dosing strategies in later trials. Overall, micro-dosing is a cost-effective and efficient way to gather critical early data, helping to streamline the drug development process and increase the likelihood of success in later phases.

3.3 Exploratory IND Applications

3.3.1 Requirements for an Exploratory IND

To conduct a Phase 0 trial, drug developers must submit an exploratory Investigational New Drug (IND) application to regulatory authorities like the FDA. The exploratory IND is a streamlined version of the traditional IND, designed to support early-phase research with limited human exposure. The key components of an exploratory IND include data from preclinical studies that demonstrate the drug's safety at micro-dose levels, as well as information on the drug's chemistry, manufacturing, and control processes. Preclinical studies must include in vitro and animal testing that provides insights into the drug's potential toxicity, pharmacokinetics, and pharmacodynamics. The exploratory IND also requires a detailed study protocol that outlines the trial design, including participant selection criteria, dosing strategies, and methods for data collection and analysis. Unlike traditional INDs, which are designed to support full-scale clinical trials, exploratory INDs focus on gathering early data to inform decisions about whether to proceed with further development. The regulatory review process for an exploratory IND is typically faster than for a full IND, allowing developers to begin Phase 0 trials more quickly and efficiently.

3.3.2 Key Regulatory Approvals Needed

Before a Phase 0 trial can begin, regulatory approval is required from agencies such as the FDA, EMA, or CDSCO. The exploratory IND application must be submitted to the appropriate regulatory agency, which reviews the preclinical data and proposed trial design to ensure that the risks to participants are minimized. The approval process involves a thorough review of the drug's pharmacology and toxicology, as well as the proposed dosing regimen and participant safety monitoring. Regulatory agencies may also require additional data or modifications to the trial design before granting approval. Once approved, the trial is subject to ongoing oversight by the regulatory agency, which monitors for any adverse events or safety concerns. In the event of serious safety issues, the regulatory agency has the authority to suspend or terminate the trial. This rigorous regulatory process ensures that Phase 0 trials are conducted ethically and that participant safety is prioritized at all times.

3.3.3 Advantages of Exploratory IND Applications

One of the key advantages of exploratory IND applications is that they allow drug developers to gather early human data without committing to the time and cost of full-scale clinical trials. This can be particularly useful for drug candidates that are still in the early stages of development, where the pharmacokinetics and pharmacodynamics are not yet fully understood. Exploratory INDs provide a more flexible regulatory pathway, allowing developers to test their drug in humans early and make informed decisions about whether to proceed with further trials. Another advantage is that exploratory INDs require less extensive preclinical data than traditional INDs, which can reduce the time and cost of preparing the application. By providing a faster and more efficient route to human testing, exploratory

INDs help accelerate the drug development process, increasing the likelihood of success in later-phase trials.

3.4 Study Design in Phase 0 Trials

3.4.1 Participant Selection

Participant selection in Phase 0 trials is one of the most critical aspects of the study design. Since these trials involve administering micro-doses of a drug, the risk to participants is generally lower than in later-phase trials, but the criteria for selecting participants remain stringent to ensure safety and reliability of data. Typically, healthy volunteers are chosen for Phase 0 trials to avoid any underlying medical conditions that could interfere with the study's outcomes. In some cases, patients with no other treatment options may be included, particularly when the drug being tested is intended for a life-threatening condition. The inclusion and exclusion criteria for participants are designed to minimize risk and ensure that the data collected is relevant to the drug's future development. For example, participants with impaired liver or kidney function might be excluded from Phase 0 trials, as these organs play a key role in drug metabolism and excretion. Before the trial begins, each participant undergoes thorough medical screening, including blood tests and physical exams, to ensure they are suitable for participation. The small sample size, usually fewer than 15 participants, allows for close monitoring and detailed analysis of the drug's effects.

3.4.2 Drug Administration and Dosing Strategies

In Phase 0 trials, the dosing strategy is carefully designed to minimize risks while providing valuable data on how the drug behaves in the human body. The drug is administered at extremely low doses—less than 1% of the anticipated therapeutic dose—based on preclinical data from animal studies. These micro-doses are unlikely to produce any therapeutic effects or significant side effects, but they provide critical information on the drug's absorption, distribution, metabolism, and excretion (ADME). The drug may be administered orally, intravenously, or through other routes, depending on the intended method of delivery in later phases of development. Researchers may also use different dosing strategies, such as single-dose or multiple-dose regimens, to study how the drug behaves under various conditions. For example, a single-dose regimen might be used to gather initial pharmacokinetic data, while a multiple-dose regimen could help researchers understand how the drug accumulates in the body over time. By carefully controlling the dose and monitoring participants closely, researchers can gather early data on the drug's safety and pharmacokinetics, which will inform dosing strategies for later-phase trials.

3.4.3 Data Collection and Analysis

The primary focus of data collection in Phase 0 trials is to gather detailed information on the drug's pharmacokinetics and pharmacodynamics. Blood samples are taken at regular intervals to measure the concentration of the drug and its metabolites in the bloodstream. This allows researchers to create a pharmacokinetic profile, which describes how the drug is absorbed, distributed, metabolized, and eliminated from the body. Other biological samples, such as urine, saliva, or tissue biopsies, may also be collected to provide additional insights into the drug's behavior. The data collected from these samples are analyzed using advanced techniques like mass spectrometry or liquid chromatography, which can detect even trace amounts of the drug in biological samples. The results of this analysis help researchers understand how the drug behaves in humans and determine whether it is suitable for further development. In addition to pharmacokinetic data, researchers may also collect pharmacodynamic data, which describes the drug's biological effects on the body, even at micro-dose levels. Although the doses used in Phase 0 trials are too low to produce therapeutic effects, subtle biological responses can provide valuable insights into the drug's potential efficacy.

3.5 Limitations of Phase 0 Trials

3.5.1 Limited Sample Size and Power

One of the most significant limitations of Phase 0 trials is their small sample size, which limits the statistical power of the study. With fewer than 15 participants typically involved, the data collected may not be representative of the broader population. This small sample size makes it difficult to draw definitive conclusions about the drug's safety, efficacy, or pharmacokinetics. While Phase 0 trials are valuable for gathering early data, they are not designed to detect rare side effects or long-term safety concerns, which can only be identified in larger, more comprehensive trials. The limited sample size also restricts the ability to explore variations in drug metabolism or response among different demographic groups, such as differences based on age, gender, or ethnicity. As a result, the findings from Phase 0 trials must be interpreted with caution, and further testing in larger populations is essential to confirm the drug's safety and efficacy.

3.5.2 Restrictions in Data Applicability

Another key limitation of Phase 0 trials is that the data collected may not be fully applicable to later stages of development. Because Phase 0 trials use micro-doses that are far below the therapeutic levels required for treating a disease, the pharmacokinetic and pharmacodynamic data obtained may not accurately reflect how the drug will behave at higher, clinically relevant doses. For example, a drug that shows promising absorption and distribution at micro-dose levels may exhibit different behavior at therapeutic doses due to factors such as saturation of transport mechanisms or non-linear pharmacokinetics. Additionally, Phase 0 trials do not provide data on the drug's efficacy in treating the target condition, as the doses used are too low to produce a therapeutic effect. This means that while Phase 0 trials can provide valuable early insights, they cannot replace the need for full-scale clinical trials, which are necessary to assess the drug's safety, efficacy, and therapeutic potential.

3.5.3 Ethical Challenges

Phase 0 trials also present unique ethical challenges, particularly because they involve exposing healthy volunteers or patients to a drug that is in the very early stages of development. Since Phase 0 trials are designed to gather pharmacokinetic data rather than to treat a disease, participants do not receive any direct therapeutic benefit from the trial. This raises ethical questions about the justification for exposing participants to potential risks, even though those risks are minimal due to the low doses used. Informed consent is critical in Phase 0 trials, as participants must be fully aware that the trial is designed to gather early data and that the drug may not progress to later stages of development. Researchers must ensure that participants understand the purpose of the trial, the risks involved, and the potential outcomes. Regulatory agencies play a key role in ensuring that Phase 0 trials are conducted ethically and that the rights and safety of participants are protected. By closely monitoring the trial design and participant consent process, regulatory agencies help mitigate the ethical challenges associated with Phase 0 trials.

3.6 Regulatory Aspects of Phase 0 Trials

3.6.1 Regulatory Agencies and Phase 0 Trials

Regulatory agencies such as the U.S. Food and Drug Administration (FDA),

European Medicines Agency (EMA), and India's Central Drugs Standard Control Organization (CDSCO) are responsible for overseeing the conduct of Phase 0 trials. These agencies play a vital role in ensuring that Phase 0 trials adhere to strict safety and ethical guidelines. Before a Phase 0 trial can be initiated, the drug sponsor must submit an exploratory Investigational New Drug (IND) application to the relevant regulatory agency. This application includes data from preclinical studies, such as animal testing, that demonstrate the drug's safety at micro-dose levels, as well as the proposed trial design and dosing strategy. Regulatory agencies review this information to ensure that the risks to human participants are minimized and that the trial is scientifically sound. Once the trial is approved, the regulatory agency continues to monitor its progress, requiring regular safety reports and adverse event notifications. The oversight provided by regulatory agencies ensures that Phase 0 trials are conducted with the highest ethical standards and that participants are protected throughout the study.

3.6.2 Reporting Requirements

Reporting requirements for Phase 0 trials are stringent, reflecting the need for transparency and participant safety. Drug sponsors are required to submit regular reports to the regulatory agency, detailing the progress of the trial and any adverse events or safety concerns that arise. These reports include data on the drug's pharmacokinetics and pharmacodynamics, as well as any side effects observed in participants. In the event of a serious adverse event, the trial may be temporarily suspended or terminated, depending on the severity of the issue and the findings of the safety review. Regulatory agencies require that all adverse events, even minor ones, be documented and reported to ensure that any potential safety concerns are addressed early. These reporting requirements are essential for maintaining the integrity of the trial and ensuring that participants are not exposed to unnecessary risks.

3.6.3 Comparison of Phase 0 Regulations in Different Regions

While the basic principles of Phase 0 trials are consistent across different regions, there are some variations in the regulatory requirements for these trials. In the United States, the FDA has specific guidelines for exploratory IND applications, which streamline the approval process for early-phase trials. The European Medicines Agency (EMA) follows a similar approach, with its guidelines emphasizing participant safety and data quality. In India, the CDSCO oversees Phase 0 trials, with regulations that align closely with international standards. However, there may be differences in the specific requirements for preclinical data, participant selection, and reporting in different regions. For example, some regulatory agencies may require additional safety data before approving a Phase 0 trial, depending on the drug's chemical structure or therapeutic area. Drug sponsors conducting multinational Phase 0 trials must ensure that they comply with the regulations of each region in which the trial is conducted. By understanding and adhering to these regional differences, drug developers can ensure that their trials meet all necessary regulatory requirements and progress smoothly.

Review Questions

1. What is the purpose of Phase 0 studies in drug development?
2. How do Phase 0 studies differ from Phase I trials?
3. Explain the concept of micro-dosing in Phase 0 studies.
4. What are the ethical and safety considerations involved in Phase 0 trials?
5. How do exploratory IND applications play a role in Phase 0 studies?
6. Describe the study design and participant selection in Phase 0 trials.
7. What are the limitations of Phase 0 trials in terms of sample size and data applicability?
8. How do regulatory agencies view Phase 0 trials?

CHAPTER FOUR

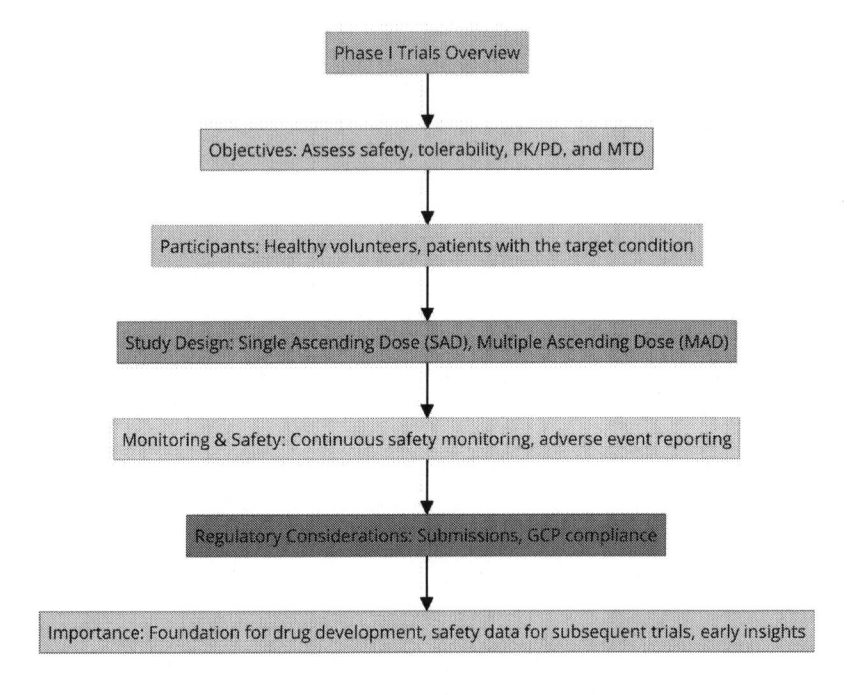

Phase I Studies

```
Phase I Trials Overview
        ↓
Objectives: Assess safety, tolerability, PK/PD, and MTD
        ↓
Participants: Healthy volunteers, patients with the target condition
        ↓
Study Design: Single Ascending Dose (SAD), Multiple Ascending Dose (MAD)
        ↓
Monitoring & Safety: Continuous safety monitoring, adverse event reporting
        ↓
Regulatory Considerations: Submissions, GCP compliance
        ↓
Importance: Foundation for drug development, safety data for subsequent trials, early insights
```

Phase I Trials: Objectives, Design, and Importance

4.1 Objectives of Phase I Trials

4.1.1 Safety Assessment

The primary objective of Phase I clinical trials is to assess the safety of a new drug or treatment in human participants. This phase is the first time the drug is administered to humans, usually involving a small group of healthy volunteers or, in some cases, patients with the target disease. Safety assessment is critical because it helps identify potential adverse effects and the overall tolerability of the drug at various doses. In Phase I, researchers closely monitor participants for any side effects, ranging from mild reactions like headaches or nausea to more serious events such as organ toxicity or allergic reactions. These trials provide crucial information on the drug's safety profile, ensuring that the risks associated with the treatment are well understood before progressing to later phases. The safety assessment is ongoing throughout the trial, with participants undergoing regular medical exams, blood tests, and monitoring to detect any adverse effects. The data collected helps determine whether the drug is safe enough to continue to Phase II trials, where efficacy will be evaluated alongside safety.

4.1.2 Determination of Appropriate Dosing

Another key objective of Phase I trials is to determine the appropriate dosing for the drug. This includes identifying the minimum effective dose, the optimal therapeutic dose, and the maximum tolerated dose (MTD). Dosing is carefully adjusted during the trial, starting at a low level and gradually increasing until either the desired pharmacological effect is achieved or adverse effects occur. This process is known as dose escalation, and it helps researchers identify the dose range that is both safe and effective for future trials. Determining the correct dose is critical because it directly affects the drug's efficacy and safety in later phases. Too low a dose may result in inefficacy, while too high a dose can lead to toxicity. Through careful monitoring of how participants respond to different doses, researchers can pinpoint the optimal dose for the drug, which will guide dosing regimens in Phase II and Phase III trials. This process ensures that participants in later trials receive the best possible therapeutic benefit with minimal risk of adverse effects.

4.1.3 Pharmacokinetic and Pharmacodynamic Evaluation

Phase I trials also focus on evaluating the pharmacokinetics (PK) and pharmacodynamics (PD) of the drug. Pharmacokinetics refers to how the drug is absorbed, distributed, metabolized, and excreted in the body, while pharmacodynamics refers to the drug's biological effects and its mechanism of action. Understanding these aspects is crucial for determining how the drug interacts with the body and how it produces its intended effects. For example, PK data helps researchers understand how long the drug stays in the bloodstream, how it is metabolized by the liver, and how it is eliminated through the kidneys or other routes. PD data, on the other hand, provides insights into the drug's biological activity, such as its impact on specific cellular targets or biochemical pathways. By studying these parameters, researchers can ensure that the drug reaches the intended site of action in the body and produces the desired therapeutic effects. The PK and PD data collected in Phase I trials are essential for designing subsequent trials and ensuring that the drug's safety and efficacy are thoroughly evaluated.

4.2 Types of Phase I Trials

4.2.1 Single Ascending Dose (SAD) Studies

Single Ascending Dose (SAD) studies are a common design used in Phase I trials to evaluate the safety and pharmacokinetics of a new drug. In these studies, small groups of participants receive a single dose of the drug at increasing levels, with each group receiving a higher dose than the previous one. The goal of SAD studies is to determine how the body processes the drug at different doses and to identify the maximum dose that can be safely administered without causing significant adverse effects. By starting with low doses and gradually increasing them, researchers can minimize the risk of harm to participants while gathering valuable data on how the drug behaves in the human body. SAD studies are particularly useful for identifying dose-dependent side effects, such as nausea, dizziness, or changes in blood pressure, which may only occur at higher doses. The data collected from these studies provide a foundation for determining the optimal dose range for future trials, ensuring that the drug can be safely and effectively administered to larger populations.

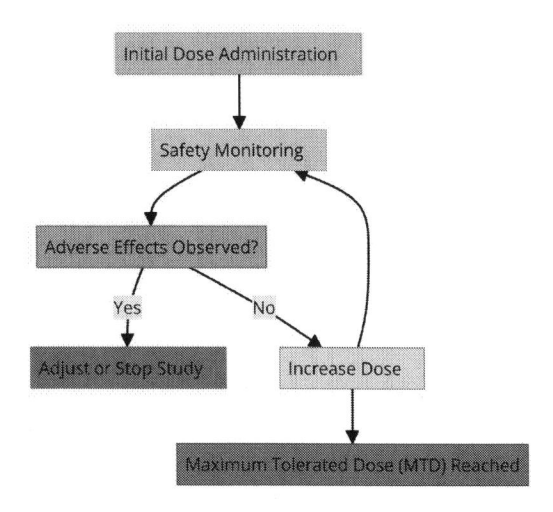

```
Initial Dose Administration
        ↓
   Safety Monitoring ←──────┐
        ↓                   │
 Adverse Effects Observed?  │
    ↙ Yes      No ↘         │
Adjust or Stop Study    Increase Dose
                           ↓
              Maximum Tolerated Dose (MTD) Reached
```

Single Ascending Dose (SAD) Study Process

4.2.2 Multiple Ascending Dose (MAD) Studies

Multiple Ascending Dose (MAD) studies build on the findings from SAD studies by administering the drug to participants over multiple doses, rather than a single dose. These studies are designed to evaluate the drug's safety and pharmacokinetics during repeated administration, allowing researchers to assess how the body responds to the drug over time. MAD studies are particularly important for drugs that are intended to be taken chronically or over extended periods, as they provide insights into how the drug accumulates in the body and whether repeated dosing leads to increased side effects. In these studies, participants receive the drug at increasing doses over a series of days or weeks, with each group receiving a higher dose than the previous group. Researchers monitor the participants for any signs of toxicity or adverse reactions, while also collecting data on how the drug is metabolized and eliminated. MAD studies are essential for understanding the long-term safety and tolerability of a drug, ensuring that it can be safely administered at therapeutic doses in future trials.

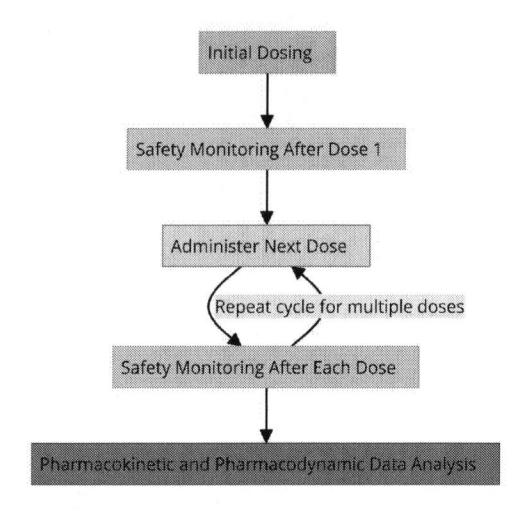

COMPREHENSIVE GUIDE TO CLINICAL RESEARCH REGULATIONS

Diagram illustrating the Multiple Ascending Dose (MAD) Study Process

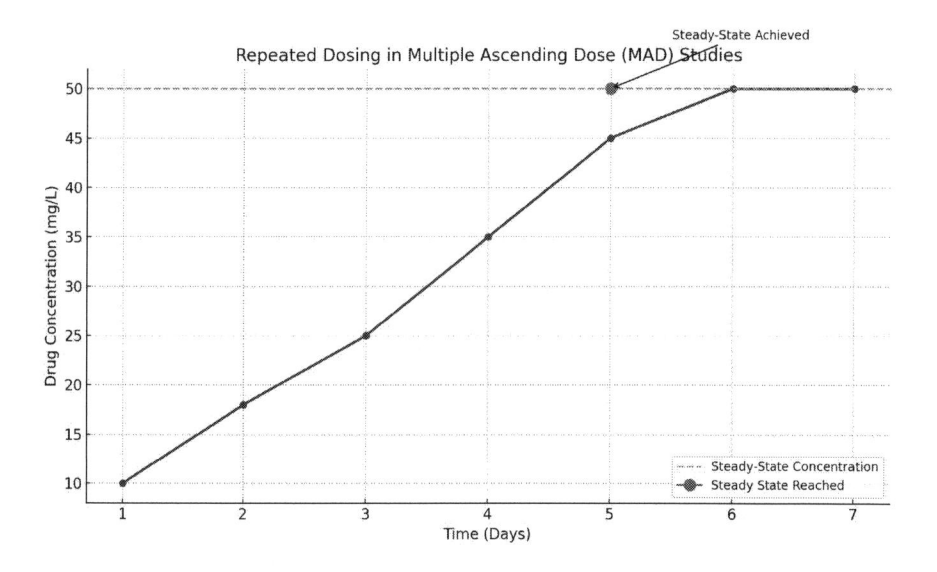

Graph illustrating Repeated Dosing in Multiple Ascending Dose (MAD) Studies. It shows how drug concentration builds up over time with each dose until the steady-state concentration is reached, which is marked by a horizontal line and an annotation.

4.2.3 Special Studies (Food Effect, Drug-Drug Interaction)

In addition to SAD and MAD studies, Phase I trials often include special studies designed to evaluate specific factors that may affect the drug's safety and efficacy. Food effect studies, for example, are conducted to determine how the presence of food in the stomach impacts the drug's absorption and bioavailability. These studies involve administering the drug to participants under both fasting and fed conditions to assess whether food increases or decreases the drug's absorption. Drug-drug interaction studies are another important type of special study, designed to evaluate how the drug interacts with other medications that participants may be taking. These studies are critical for identifying potential interactions that could alter the drug's effectiveness or increase the risk of adverse effects. For example, if the drug inhibits the metabolism of another medication, it could lead to higher levels of the other drug in the body, increasing the risk of toxicity. By conducting these special studies in Phase I, researchers can identify potential issues early in the development process and take steps to mitigate any risks before the drug is tested in larger populations.

4.3 Dose Escalation and Safety Monitoring

4.3.1 Dose Escalation Methods

Dose escalation is a key component of Phase I trials, where the drug is administered to participants at increasing doses to determine the maximum tolerated dose (MTD). The most common method of dose escalation is the traditional 3+3 design, in which groups of three participants are treated at each dose level. If no serious adverse effects are observed, the next group of participants receives a higher dose. If one or more participants experience significant side effects, the dose is either reduced or maintained, and additional participants may be added to further assess safety. This method allows researchers to gradually increase the dose while minimizing the risk of serious harm to participants. Other dose escalation methods, such as the continual reassessment method (CRM) or Bayesian adaptive designs, are used in more complex trials to allow for more flexible dose adjustments based on real-time safety data. These methods help ensure that the dose escalation process is as safe and efficient as possible, allowing researchers to identify the MTD while minimizing the number of participants exposed to potentially harmful doses.

Dose Escalation in Phase I Trials

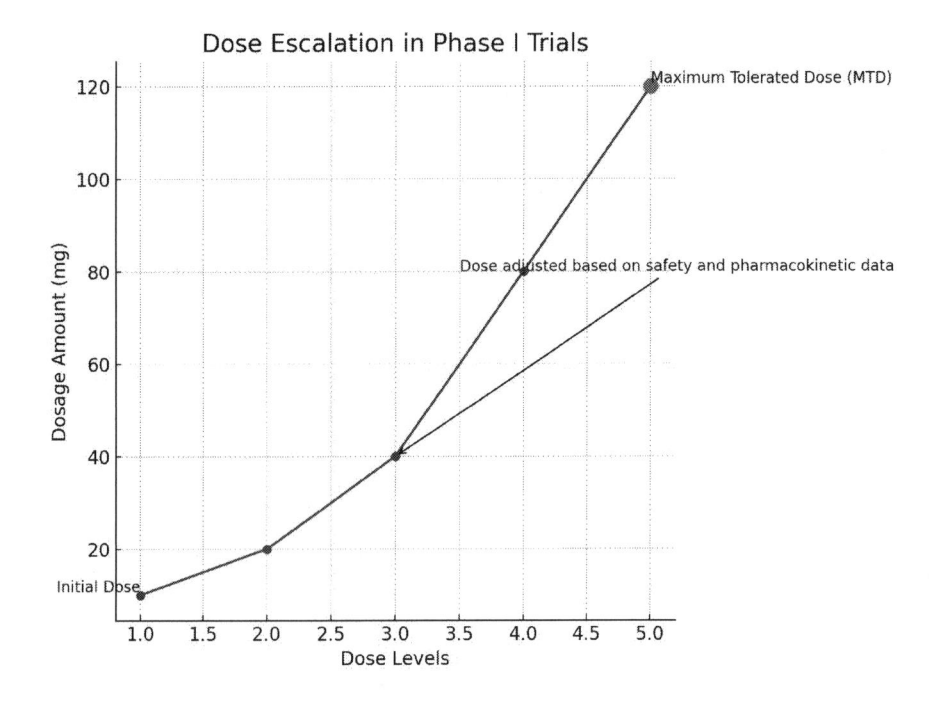

Dose Escalation in Phase I Trials graph, showing the gradual increase in dosage levels. The graph highlights the Initial Dose and the Maximum Tolerated Dose (MTD), along with annotations explaining how doses are adjusted based on safety and pharmacokinetic data.

4.3.2 Maximally Tolerated Dose (MTD) Determination

Determining the maximum tolerated dose (MTD) is one of the primary goals of dose escalation in Phase I trials. The MTD is defined as the highest dose of the drug that can be administered without causing unacceptable side effects. This dose is critical for guiding the design of future trials, as it provides the upper limit for dosing in later phases. The MTD is typically determined by gradually increasing the dose in small increments until participants begin to experience significant adverse effects, such as severe nausea, liver toxicity, or changes in heart function. Once the MTD is identified, researchers can use this information to establish a safe and effective dose range for Phase II and III trials. It is important to note that the MTD may vary depending on the population being studied, as factors such as age, gender, and underlying health conditions can affect how participants respond to the drug. As a result, the MTD determined in Phase I trials may need to be adjusted for specific patient populations in later trials.

4.3.3 Continuous Safety Monitoring Protocols

Safety monitoring is a continuous process throughout Phase I trials, with strict protocols in place to ensure that participants are protected from harm. Participants undergo regular medical examinations, blood tests, and other diagnostic procedures to monitor for any signs of toxicity or adverse reactions. In addition to routine monitoring, researchers may also implement real-time safety monitoring protocols, where data on adverse events is reviewed continuously as it is collected. This allows for rapid identification of any safety concerns, enabling researchers to adjust the dosing regimen or suspend the trial if necessary. Safety monitoring also includes the use of stopping rules, which are predefined criteria that dictate when the trial should be paused or stopped altogether. For example, if a certain number of participants experience severe side effects, the trial may be temporarily halted to assess the cause and determine whether it is safe to continue. Continuous safety monitoring ensures that participants are protected throughout the trial and that any risks are promptly addressed.

4.4 Pharmacokinetics and Pharmacodynamics in Phase I

4.4.1 PK/PD Endpoints

Pharmacokinetics (PK) and pharmacodynamics (PD) are key endpoints in Phase I trials, as they provide critical information about how the drug interacts with the body. PK endpoints include measurements of how the drug is absorbed, distributed, metabolized, and excreted, while PD endpoints focus on the drug's biological effects and its mechanism of action. These endpoints help researchers understand the drug's behavior in the human body and provide insights into its potential efficacy and safety. PK data is typically collected through blood samples, which are analyzed to determine the concentration of the drug and its metabolites at various time points after administration. PD data, on the other hand, may be gathered through a variety of methods, including biomarker analysis or clinical assessments of the drug's effects on specific biological targets. By studying both PK and PD endpoints, researchers can develop a comprehensive understanding of the drug's pharmacological profile and use this information to guide dosing decisions in future trials.

4.4.2 Role of Bioavailability and Bioequivalence

Bioavailability and bioequivalence are critical concepts in Phase I trials, particularly when evaluating different formulations of a drug. Bioavailability refers to the proportion of the drug that reaches the bloodstream after administration, while bioequivalence refers to the comparison of bioavailability between two different formulations or delivery methods. Understanding these concepts is important for ensuring that the drug is delivered effectively to the target site in the body. For example, a drug that has poor bioavailability may need to be reformulated or administered through a different route (e.g., intravenously rather than orally) to ensure that it reaches therapeutic levels in the bloodstream. Phase I trials often include bioavailability studies to compare different formulations and determine which one provides the best absorption and distribution. These studies are essential for optimizing the drug's delivery and ensuring that it can be administered safely and effectively in later phases.

4.4.3 Interpretation of PK/PD Data

The interpretation of pharmacokinetic and pharmacodynamic data is a complex but essential part of Phase I trials. Researchers must analyze the data collected from blood samples and other assessments to develop a detailed understanding of how the drug behaves in the body. This includes determining key PK parameters such as the drug's half-life, clearance rate, and volume of distribution, as well as PD parameters such as the drug's potency and efficacy at different doses. By interpreting this data, researchers can identify trends and patterns that help guide dosing decisions in future trials. For example, if the PK data shows that the drug is eliminated from the body rapidly, researchers may need to increase the dose or administer the drug more frequently to maintain therapeutic levels. Conversely, if the drug accumulates in the body over time, the dose may need to be reduced to prevent toxicity. The interpretation of PK and PD data is critical for ensuring that the drug is administered at the optimal dose and frequency in subsequent trials.

4.5 Ethical Considerations in Phase I Studies

4.5.1 Participant Safety and Informed Consent

Participant safety is the foremost concern in Phase I trials, as this is the first stage of testing new drugs in humans. Since the risks and side effects of the drug are not fully known at this stage, ensuring the safety of participants through rigorous monitoring and ethical guidelines is essential. All participants must give informed consent before enrolling in the trial, which means they must be fully aware of the potential risks, the trial's objectives, and the fact that the drug is in an early stage of development. The informed consent process is not just a one-time event; it involves ongoing communication between the researchers and participants throughout the trial. Participants are given detailed information about the study, including the procedures involved, possible side effects, and their right to withdraw from the trial at any time without penalty. Researchers are responsible for ensuring that participants understand the risks involved, and they must be available to answer any questions or address concerns. The informed consent process is critical for protecting participants' rights and ensuring that they are not exposed to undue risks.

4.5.2 Ethical Approval Processes

Before a Phase I trial can begin, it must receive ethical approval from an Institutional Review Board (IRB) or an Independent Ethics Committee (IEC). These bodies are responsible for reviewing the study protocol to ensure that the trial is designed ethically and that the rights and safety of participants are protected. The ethical approval process involves a thorough review of the study design, including the dosing regimen, participant selection criteria, and safety monitoring procedures. The IRB or IEC evaluates whether the potential benefits of the study outweigh the risks to participants and whether appropriate safeguards are in place to protect vulnerable populations. For example, if the study involves patients with a terminal illness who may have no other treatment options, the ethical committee will consider the potential risks and benefits of the new drug in light of the participants' condition. Ethical approval is a critical step in the clinical trial process, ensuring that the trial is conducted according to the highest ethical standards and that participants are treated with respect and fairness.

4.5.3 Protecting Vulnerable Populations

Protecting vulnerable populations is an important ethical consideration in Phase I trials. Vulnerable populations include groups such as children, the elderly, pregnant women, and individuals with cognitive impairments, who may be at greater risk of harm or exploitation in clinical trials. Special care must be taken when including these groups in Phase I trials, as they may have different physiological responses to the drug or may be unable to fully understand the risks involved. For example, children metabolize drugs differently than adults, so extra caution is needed when determining dosing levels. In cases where vulnerable populations are included in the trial, additional safeguards must be put in place to ensure their safety. This may include obtaining consent from legal guardians, providing extra monitoring, or limiting the dose escalation in these groups. Researchers must also ensure that the trial is designed in a way that does not exploit vulnerable populations, such as by offering undue financial incentives or coercion. Protecting these groups is essential for maintaining the ethical integrity of the trial and ensuring that all participants are treated fairly.

4.6 Regulatory Guidelines for Phase I Studies

4.6.1 Key Regulations Governing Phase I Trials

Phase I trials are governed by strict regulatory guidelines designed to ensure the safety of participants and the integrity of the data collected. In the United States, these trials are regulated by the Food and Drug Administration (FDA), while in Europe, the European Medicines Agency (EMA) oversees clinical trials. In India, the Central Drugs Standard Control Organization (CDSCO) is responsible for regulating Phase I trials. These regulatory bodies set forth guidelines that outline the requirements for conducting Phase I trials, including the need for preclinical data, safety monitoring protocols, and ethical approval. One of the key regulations governing Phase I trials is the requirement for an Investigational New Drug (IND) application, which must be submitted to the relevant regulatory agency before the trial can begin. The IND application includes detailed information on the drug's chemistry, manufacturing process, and preclinical testing, as well as the proposed trial design and dosing regimen. The regulatory agency reviews this information to ensure that the trial is scientifically sound and that the risks to participants are minimized. These regulations are essential for maintaining the safety and ethical conduct of Phase I trials.

4.6.2 Regulatory Submission and Approval Process

The submission and approval process for Phase I trials involves several key steps, beginning with the preparation of an IND application. This application must include data from preclinical studies that demonstrate the drug's safety in animals, as well as a detailed description of the proposed trial design, including the number of participants, dosing regimen, and safety monitoring protocols. The IND application is submitted to the regulatory agency, which reviews the data to determine whether the trial can proceed. The review process typically takes several months, during which the agency may request additional information or modifications to the trial design. Once the regulatory agency is satisfied that the trial is safe to proceed, it grants approval for the trial to begin. Throughout the trial, the drug sponsor must submit regular safety reports to the regulatory agency, detailing any adverse events or safety concerns that arise. This ongoing communication ensures that the regulatory agency remains informed of the trial's progress and can take action if necessary to protect participants.

4.6.3 International Regulatory Harmonization for Phase I Trials

As clinical trials increasingly involve multiple countries, international regulatory harmonization has become an important aspect of Phase I trials. Harmonization refers to the process of aligning regulatory standards across different regions to facilitate the conduct of multinational trials. The International Council for Harmonisation (ICH) plays a key role in this process by developing guidelines that are adopted by regulatory agencies in the United States, Europe, Japan, and other countries. These guidelines provide a common framework for conducting clinical trials, ensuring that data collected in one region is accepted by regulatory agencies in other regions. For example, ICH guidelines on Good Clinical Practice (GCP) set out the ethical and scientific standards for designing, conducting, and reporting clinical trials. By following these guidelines, drug sponsors can conduct Phase I trials in multiple countries without having to navigate conflicting regulatory requirements. Harmonization also helps to speed up the drug development process, as it reduces the need for duplicate studies in different regions and allows drug sponsors to submit a single dossier for approval in multiple markets. This approach benefits both drug developers and patients by ensuring that new treatments can be tested and approved more efficiently on a global scale.

Review Questions

1. What are the primary objectives of Phase I clinical trials?
2. How is safety assessed during Phase I trials?
3. What is the difference between Single Ascending Dose (SAD) and Multiple Ascending Dose (MAD) studies?
4. Why is dose escalation important in Phase I trials?
5. Explain the role of pharmacokinetics (PK) and pharmacodynamics (PD) in Phase I studies.
6. How are participants monitored for safety during Phase I trials?
7. What are the ethical considerations in Phase I trials, particularly regarding vulnerable populations?
8. How do regulatory guidelines affect the design and execution of Phase I trials?

CHAPTER FIVE

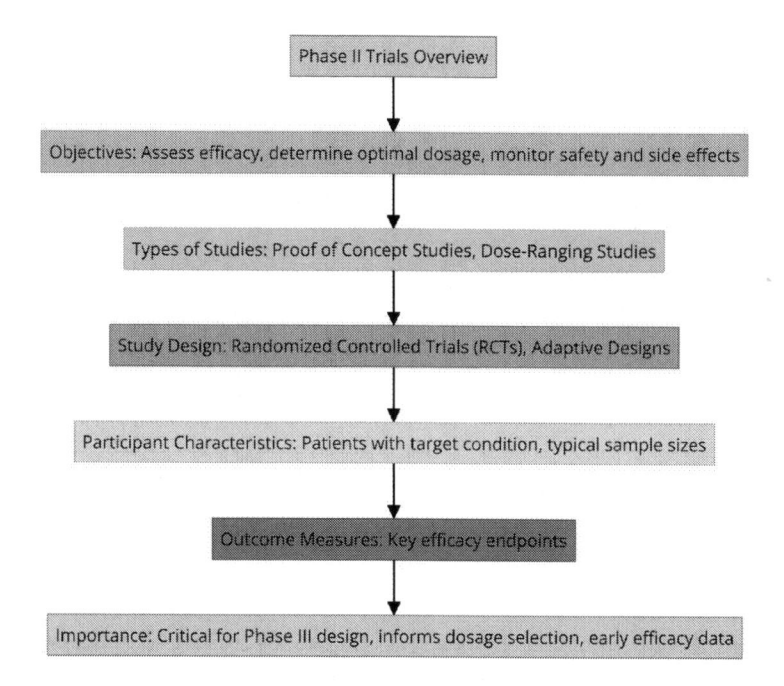

Phase II Studies

```
Phase II Trials Overview
          ↓
Objectives: Assess efficacy, determine optimal dosage, monitor safety and side effects
          ↓
Types of Studies: Proof of Concept Studies, Dose-Ranging Studies
          ↓
Study Design: Randomized Controlled Trials (RCTs), Adaptive Designs
          ↓
Participant Characteristics: Patients with target condition, typical sample sizes
          ↓
Outcome Measures: Key efficacy endpoints
          ↓
Importance: Critical for Phase III design, informs dosage selection, early efficacy data
```

Overview of Phase II Trials

5.1 Proof of Concept and Dose-Ranging Studies

5.1.1 Establishing Initial Efficacy

Phase II trials are often referred to as "proof of concept" studies because they provide the first indication of whether a drug works as intended in patients. The primary goal of these studies is to establish the initial efficacy of the drug in treating the target condition. While Phase I trials focus on safety and pharmacokinetics, Phase II trials introduce the concept of efficacy by evaluating how well the drug performs in patients who have the disease or condition being studied. Researchers aim to gather evidence that the drug produces a meaningful clinical effect, such as reducing symptoms or improving disease outcomes, compared to a placebo or standard treatment. For example, in a Phase II trial for a new hypertension medication, the efficacy could be measured by the drug's ability to lower blood pressure in patients over a specific period. Establishing initial efficacy is critical because it provides the foundation for moving the drug forward into larger, more definitive trials in Phase III. If the drug does not show sufficient efficacy in Phase II, it may not proceed to the next stage of development.

5.1.2 Dose-Response Relationship Studies

Another important aspect of Phase II trials is studying the dose-response relationship, which refers to how the drug's effect changes with different doses. The goal is to identify the dose that provides the optimal balance between efficacy and safety. Dose-response studies involve administering the drug at varying doses to different groups of patients and measuring the effects on clinical outcomes. By analyzing how the drug's efficacy increases or decreases with each dose, researchers can determine the minimum effective dose (the lowest dose that produces a meaningful clinical effect) and the maximum tolerated dose (the highest dose that can be administered without causing unacceptable side effects). These studies are crucial for identifying the dose that should be used in Phase III trials, where the drug will be tested on a larger scale. For example, in a Phase II trial for a cancer treatment, the dose-response relationship might be evaluated by measuring tumor shrinkage or progression-free survival at different dose levels. Understanding this relationship helps ensure that patients receive the most effective and safest dose in future trials.

5.1.3 Balancing Safety and Efficacy

Balancing safety and efficacy is one of the key challenges in Phase II trials. While the primary focus is on establishing the drug's efficacy, safety remains a critical consideration. Researchers must carefully monitor patients for any adverse effects that occur at the doses being tested, ensuring that the benefits of the drug outweigh the risks. This balance is particularly important in conditions where the drug may have significant side effects, such as in oncology or autoimmune diseases. For example, a cancer drug that shows strong efficacy in shrinking tumors may also cause severe side effects like nausea, fatigue, or immune suppression. In such cases, researchers must weigh the potential benefits of tumor reduction against the risk of harm to the patient's overall health. Achieving the right balance between safety and efficacy is crucial for the success of the drug in later-phase trials and ultimately for its approval by regulatory agencies.

5.2 Study Design in Phase II Trials

5.2.1 Randomized Controlled Trials (RCTs)

Randomized controlled trials (RCTs) are the gold standard in Phase II trial design because they provide the most reliable data on the efficacy and safety of a new drug. In an RCT, participants are randomly assigned to one of two or more groups: a treatment group that receives the investigational drug and a control group that receives a placebo or standard treatment. This randomization ensures that any differences in outcomes between the groups are due to the drug itself, rather than other factors. RCTs help eliminate bias and provide robust evidence on whether the drug works as intended. For example, in a Phase II RCT for an asthma treatment, one group of patients might receive the new drug while another group receives a placebo. By comparing the outcomes between the two groups, researchers can determine whether the drug significantly improves lung function or reduces asthma symptoms. The randomization process ensures that the results are scientifically valid and can be used to support the drug's progression to Phase III trials.

5.2.2 Double-Blind, Placebo-Controlled Designs

Double-blind, placebo-controlled designs are a common feature of Phase II trials, ensuring that neither the participants nor the researchers know which treatment the participants are receiving. This blinding is critical for reducing bias in the trial, as it prevents participants from changing their behavior based on their knowledge of the treatment they are receiving and stops researchers from interpreting data in a biased way. The use of a placebo control provides a baseline for comparison, helping researchers determine whether the investigational drug produces a greater effect than no treatment at all. For example, in a Phase II trial for a new antidepressant, participants would be randomly assigned to receive either the drug or a placebo, and neither they nor the researchers would know which treatment they were receiving. By comparing the improvement in depression symptoms between the two groups, researchers can determine whether the drug has a true therapeutic effect. Double-blind, placebo-controlled designs are crucial for ensuring the validity of the trial results.

5.2.3 Adaptive Trial Designs

Adaptive trial designs are becoming increasingly popular in Phase II trials because they allow for greater flexibility and efficiency. In an adaptive trial, the study design can be modified based on interim data, allowing researchers to make real-time adjustments to the trial without compromising its scientific integrity. For example, if early data suggests that one dose is particularly effective, the trial can be adapted to focus on that dose, or if a certain subgroup of patients is responding better to the treatment, the trial can be adjusted to include more patients from that subgroup. Adaptive designs can also allow for early termination of the trial if it becomes clear that the drug is not effective or if safety concerns arise.

This approach helps streamline the drug development process by allowing researchers to make informed decisions based on emerging data, potentially accelerating the progression to later-phase trials. Adaptive designs are particularly useful in conditions where patient populations are small, or where the drug's effects are expected to vary significantly between different groups of patients.

5.3 Patient Recruitment and Selection in Phase II Trials

5.3.1 Inclusion and Exclusion Criteria

Defining clear inclusion and exclusion criteria is a critical step in patient recruitment for Phase II trials. These criteria determine who is eligible to participate in the trial and ensure that the study population is appropriate for answering the research questions. Inclusion criteria specify the characteristics that participants must have to be included in the trial, such as age, gender, disease stage, or specific biomarker levels. Exclusion criteria, on the other hand, outline factors that would prevent someone from participating, such as certain medical conditions, use of conflicting medications, or a history of allergic reactions to similar treatments. Establishing these criteria helps create a homogeneous study population, reducing variability and increasing the likelihood that any differences in outcomes can be attributed to the drug. For example, in a Phase II trial for a diabetes medication, inclusion criteria might require participants to have a specific range of blood sugar levels, while exclusion criteria might eliminate individuals with a history of kidney disease. By carefully selecting participants, researchers can ensure that the trial produces meaningful and reliable results.

5.3.2 Recruitment Challenges and Strategies

Recruiting patients for Phase II trials can be challenging, particularly in rare diseases or conditions where the patient population is limited. Even in more common conditions, finding enough eligible participants who meet the strict inclusion and exclusion criteria can be difficult. Recruitment challenges may also arise from patients' concerns about potential risks or side effects, as Phase II trials involve investigational drugs that have not yet been fully tested for efficacy. To overcome these challenges, researchers often use a variety of recruitment strategies, including outreach through patient advocacy groups, online platforms, and referrals from healthcare providers. Offering financial incentives or covering travel expenses can also help attract participants, although these must be carefully balanced to avoid coercion. Clear communication about the potential benefits and risks of participation is essential for building trust with patients and encouraging them to join the trial. Recruitment is a critical component of trial success, and without adequate patient enrollment, the study may be delayed or fail to produce reliable results.

5.3.3 Ethical Considerations in Patient Selection

Ethical considerations play a significant role in patient selection for Phase II trials. Researchers must ensure that participants are selected fairly and that vulnerable populations are not exploited. For example, patients with limited treatment options, such as those with terminal illnesses, may be particularly eager to participate in a trial, even if the risks are high. In such cases, researchers must carefully weigh the potential benefits against the risks and ensure that patients fully understand what participation entails. Informed consent is a critical part of the ethical process, as participants must be made aware of the potential risks, benefits, and uncertainties associated with the trial. Ethical considerations also extend to ensuring diversity in the study population, so that the trial results are applicable to a broad range of patients. This includes making efforts to recruit participants from different age groups, genders, and ethnic backgrounds, ensuring that the drug is tested in a representative sample of the population.

5.4 Safety Monitoring in Phase II Studies

5.4.1 Monitoring Adverse Events

Safety monitoring is one of the most critical components of Phase II trials, where the drug's efficacy is tested in a larger group of patients who have the target condition. While Phase I trials primarily assess safety in a small, controlled group, Phase II trials expand this safety assessment by monitoring for adverse events in a more diverse patient population. Adverse events (AEs) are any undesirable effects that occur after the drug is administered, ranging from mild symptoms like headaches or fatigue to more severe effects such as organ damage or allergic reactions. In Phase II trials, participants are closely monitored for any signs of AEs, which are systematically recorded and classified based on their severity and likelihood of being related to the drug. This data is critical for understanding the safety profile of the drug and determining whether the benefits outweigh the risks. For example, a Phase II trial for a new asthma medication would monitor participants for both common AEs, such as throat irritation, and more serious events, such as difficulty breathing or changes in lung function. Identifying and managing AEs early in the drug development process helps ensure patient safety and informs dosing adjustments for future trials.

5.4.2 Safety Data Collection and Reporting

The collection and reporting of safety data are central to ensuring that Phase II trials adhere to regulatory standards and ethical guidelines. All adverse events must be systematically documented and reported to the regulatory authorities, such as the FDA or EMA, and to the study's Data Safety Monitoring Board (DSMB). The safety data collected in Phase II trials is critical for assessing the overall risk-benefit profile of the drug, which will inform decisions about whether the drug can move forward to Phase III. Safety data is typically collected through various means, including patient self-reports, clinical assessments, laboratory tests, and imaging studies. For example, in a Phase II trial for a cardiovascular drug, researchers might collect blood pressure measurements, electrocardiogram results, and blood tests to monitor for any potential adverse effects on the heart or blood vessels. This data is analyzed to determine the frequency, severity, and duration of adverse events, as well as to identify any potential trends or patterns that could indicate a safety concern. Regular safety reports are submitted to the regulatory authorities, ensuring that any significant risks are promptly identified and addressed.

5.4.3 Role of Data Safety Monitoring Boards (DSMBs)

Data Safety Monitoring Boards (DSMBs) play a crucial role in overseeing the safety of participants in Phase II trials. A DSMB is an independent committee of experts, typically composed of physicians, statisticians, and bioethicists, who are responsible for monitoring the trial's progress and reviewing safety data. The DSMB regularly reviews the accumulating data from the trial to ensure that participants are not being exposed to unnecessary risks. If the DSMB identifies any safety concerns, such as a higher-than-expected rate of adverse events, they have the authority to recommend modifications to the trial protocol, such as adjusting the dose or halting the trial altogether. The DSMB also ensures that the trial is conducted ethically and that participants' rights are protected. For example, in a Phase II trial for a cancer drug, the DSMB might closely monitor the incidence of severe side effects, such as liver toxicity or immune-related adverse events, to determine whether the trial should continue. The involvement of a DSMB is essential for maintaining the integrity of the trial and ensuring that participant safety is the top priority.

5.5 Interim Analyses and Adaptive Trials

5.5.1 Importance of Interim Analyses

Interim analyses are an essential tool in Phase II trials, providing an opportunity to evaluate the progress of the trial before it is completed. These analyses are conducted at predefined points during the trial, allowing researchers to assess key outcomes, such as efficacy and safety, based on the data collected up to that point. Interim analyses can provide early insights into whether the drug is working as expected and whether any adjustments to the trial design are needed. For example, if the interim analysis shows that the drug is producing significant benefits without causing serious side effects, the trial may continue as planned or even be expedited. Conversely, if the interim analysis reveals safety concerns or a lack of efficacy, the trial may be modified or halted early. Interim analyses are particularly valuable in Phase II trials, where the goal is to gather preliminary data on the drug's efficacy and safety. By conducting these analyses, researchers can make informed decisions about whether to continue, modify, or stop the trial, potentially saving time and resources in the drug development process.

5.5.2 Adaptive Trial Methodologies

Adaptive trial designs are an innovative approach in clinical research that allows for greater flexibility in how the trial is conducted. In an adaptive trial, the study design can be modified based on interim data without compromising the integrity of the trial. This flexibility can include changes to the dosing regimen, sample size, or even the inclusion of additional patient subgroups. Adaptive trials are particularly useful in Phase II studies, where researchers are still exploring the optimal dose and patient population for the drug. For example, if an interim analysis shows that one dose is particularly effective, the trial can be adapted to focus on that dose, while discontinuing less effective doses. Adaptive trials also allow for the possibility of stopping the trial early if it becomes clear that the drug is not effective or if safety concerns arise. This approach helps streamline the drug development process by allowing researchers to make real-time decisions based on emerging data, potentially accelerating the progression to Phase III trials.

5.5.3 Regulatory Considerations for Adaptive Trials

While adaptive trial designs offer significant advantages in terms of flexibility and efficiency, they also present unique regulatory challenges. Regulatory agencies, such as the FDA and EMA, require that adaptive trials are carefully planned and that any potential modifications to the trial design are predefined in the trial protocol. This ensures that the integrity of the trial is maintained and that any changes are based on sound scientific principles. For example, the trial protocol must specify the criteria for making changes, such as how interim data will be analyzed and under what conditions the trial will be modified. Regulatory agencies also require that adaptive trials include robust statistical methods to account for the potential biases introduced by making changes to the trial design. Additionally, adaptive trials must undergo the same level of scrutiny as traditional trials, with regular safety and efficacy updates submitted to the regulatory authorities. By adhering to these regulatory requirements, researchers can ensure that their adaptive trials are conducted in a scientifically rigorous and ethically sound manner.

5.6 Regulatory Pathways for Phase II Trials

5.6.1 Key Regulatory Submissions for Phase II

Before a Phase II trial can begin, drug developers must submit a detailed application to the relevant regulatory authorities, such as the FDA, EMA, or CDSCO. This application includes data from Phase I trials, which demonstrate that the drug is safe to proceed to the next phase of testing, as well as a comprehensive study protocol for the Phase II trial. The regulatory submission must provide detailed information on the trial design, including the number of participants, dosing regimen, safety monitoring procedures, and endpoints for measuring efficacy. The application also includes preclinical data, manufacturing information, and a summary of the drug's pharmacokinetics and pharmacodynamics. The regulatory agency reviews this information to ensure that the trial is scientifically sound and that the risks to participants are minimized. In some cases, the regulatory authorities may request additional data or modifications to the trial design before granting approval. Once the Phase II trial is approved, the sponsor must submit regular safety reports and updates to the regulatory agency throughout the duration of the trial.

5.6.2 Differences in Regulatory Pathways by Region

While the basic principles of drug development are similar across regions, there are differences in the regulatory pathways for Phase II trials depending on the country or region where the trial is conducted. For example, in the United States, Phase II trials are regulated by the FDA under the Investigational New Drug (IND) program, while in Europe, the EMA oversees clinical trials through the Clinical Trials Directive or the newer Clinical Trials Regulation. In India, the Central Drugs Standard Control

Organization (CDSCO) is responsible for approving and overseeing clinical trials. Each regulatory agency has its own set of guidelines and requirements for conducting Phase II trials, and drug developers must ensure that they comply with the specific regulations of the region in which the trial is being conducted. For example, some regions may have stricter requirements for safety monitoring or more extensive reporting obligations. Understanding these regional differences is critical for conducting multinational trials and ensuring that the trial data is accepted by regulatory agencies in different countries.

5.6.3 Fast-Track, Breakthrough, and Orphan Drug Designations

In certain cases, drugs that address unmet medical needs or treat rare diseases may qualify for special regulatory designations that expedite the development and approval process. In the United States, the FDA offers several programs designed to accelerate the development of promising drugs, including fast-track designation, breakthrough therapy designation, and orphan drug designation. Fast-track designation is granted to drugs that treat serious conditions and fill an unmet medical need, allowing for more frequent interactions with the FDA and the possibility of rolling submissions. Breakthrough therapy designation is granted to drugs that show substantial improvement over existing treatments in early clinical trials, providing expedited development and review. Orphan drug designation is granted to drugs that treat rare diseases, offering incentives such as tax credits, market exclusivity, and reduced regulatory fees. These designations can be applied to drugs in Phase II trials, allowing for a more efficient path to approval if the drug shows promise. Similar programs exist in other regions, such as the EMA's Priority Medicines (PRIME) scheme and the CDSCO's accelerated approval pathway.

Review Questions

1. What are the main objectives of Phase II trials?
2. What is the role of proof of concept studies in Phase II trials?
3. How do dose-ranging studies help determine the optimal therapeutic dose?
4. What are the key challenges in recruiting participants for Phase II studies?
5. How are safety and efficacy balanced in Phase II trials?
6. What is the role of Data Safety Monitoring Boards (DSMBs) in Phase II trials?
7. How are interim analyses used in Phase II trials to inform trial decisions?
8. What are the regulatory pathways for advancing a drug from Phase II to Phase III trials?

CHAPTER SIX

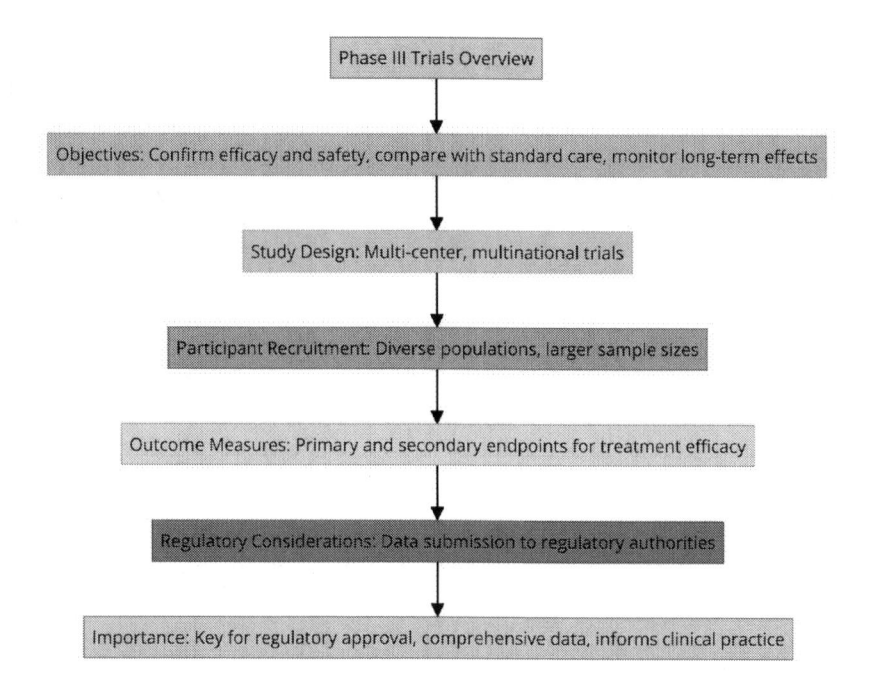

Phase III Trials

```
Phase III Trials Overview
    ↓
Objectives: Confirm efficacy and safety, compare with standard care, monitor long-term effects
    ↓
Study Design: Multi-center, multinational trials
    ↓
Participant Recruitment: Diverse populations, larger sample sizes
    ↓
Outcome Measures: Primary and secondary endpoints for treatment efficacy
    ↓
Regulatory Considerations: Data submission to regulatory authorities
    ↓
Importance: Key for regulatory approval, comprehensive data, informs clinical practice
```

Overview of Phase III Trials

6.1 Objectives of Phase III Trials

6.1.1 Confirming Safety and Efficacy in Large Populations

Phase III trials are the critical stage in drug development where the safety and efficacy of the investigational drug are confirmed in large, diverse patient populations. Unlike Phase II, which typically involves smaller patient groups to test for efficacy and safety, Phase III trials expand the sample size significantly, often enrolling thousands of participants across multiple sites. This increase in population size allows researchers to identify rare side effects and confirm that the drug's therapeutic effects are consistent across a wider range of individuals. For example, in a Phase III trial for a new hypertension medication, researchers would recruit patients from different regions, with varying ages, ethnicities, and comorbidities, to ensure that the drug works effectively and safely in the general population. Phase III trials also provide a final opportunity to assess any potential long-term risks associated with the drug, such as cardiovascular or hepatic side effects that might not have appeared in earlier phases.

The larger scale of Phase III trials also allows for a more comprehensive analysis of the drug's efficacy across different subgroups of patients. This is particularly important in conditions that affect diverse populations differently, such as diabetes or heart disease, where factors like genetics, lifestyle, and environmental conditions may influence the drug's effectiveness. By enrolling a large and diverse patient population, researchers can ensure that the drug will be effective and safe for a broad range of individuals once it reaches the market. The data collected in Phase III trials are essential for informing regulatory decisions about whether the drug should be approved for widespread use.

6.1.2 Establishing Clinical Endpoints

A key objective of Phase III trials is to establish definitive clinical endpoints that will be used to evaluate the drug's success. Clinical endpoints are specific, measurable outcomes that indicate whether the drug is having the desired effect. These endpoints can include objective measures, such as blood pressure reduction or tumor shrinkage, as well as subjective measures, such as improvements in pain or quality of life. In a Phase III trial for a new oncology drug, for example, the primary endpoint might be overall survival, while secondary endpoints could include progression-free survival or tumor response rate. Establishing clear clinical endpoints is critical for determining whether the drug provides a meaningful benefit to patients.

In addition to primary and secondary endpoints, Phase III trials often include exploratory endpoints, which are used to gather additional data that may not be directly related to the primary outcomes but could provide useful information for future studies. For instance, in a trial for a new rheumatoid arthritis drug, exploratory endpoints might include biomarkers of inflammation or patient-reported outcomes related to joint stiffness and mobility. By carefully selecting and defining clinical endpoints, researchers ensure that the trial will provide robust data on the drug's efficacy and safety, which is necessary for regulatory approval.

6.1.3 Registration Studies for Drug Approval

Phase III trials are often referred to as registration studies because they are designed to provide the comprehensive data needed for regulatory approval. The results from these trials form the basis of the drug's submission to regulatory agencies, such as the FDA, EMA, or CDSCO, and are used to determine whether the drug is safe and effective enough to be marketed to the public. For example, after completing a successful Phase III trial for a new cholesterol-lowering medication, the drug sponsor would submit the trial data as part of a New Drug Application (NDA) to the FDA, seeking approval to sell the drug in the United States. Similarly, in Europe, the data would be submitted as part of a Marketing Authorization Application (MAA) to the EMA.

Registration studies must meet strict regulatory requirements to ensure that the data is of high quality and that the trial was conducted ethically and according to Good Clinical Practice (GCP) guidelines. These trials are often the most expensive and time-consuming part of drug development, as they involve large patient populations, long follow-up periods, and rigorous safety monitoring. However, they are essential for ensuring that the drug is safe and effective for widespread use. Once the data from Phase III trials are submitted to regulatory agencies, it undergoes a thorough review process, during which regulators assess the trial's design, conduct, and results to determine whether the drug should be approved.

6.2 Study Design in Phase III Trials

6.2.1 Multi-Center and Multinational Trials

Phase III trials often involve multi-center and multinational designs, which are necessary to recruit the large number of participants needed to demonstrate the drug's safety and efficacy across diverse populations. Multi-center trials are conducted at several different locations, often in different cities or countries, to ensure that the trial results are representative of the broader patient population. This is particularly important for diseases that affect people differently depending on geographic, genetic, or environmental factors. For example, a Phase III trial for a new type 2 diabetes medication might be conducted at multiple sites across the United States, Europe, and Asia to ensure that the drug works effectively in patients of different ethnic backgrounds and with varying lifestyles.

Multinational trials also help to speed up the drug development process by allowing researchers to collect data from a large number of patients in a relatively short period of time. For instance, a Phase III trial for a new cancer therapy might enroll thousands of patients at dozens of sites worldwide, allowing the trial to reach its enrollment targets and produce results more quickly than if it were conducted in a single country. These trials also help drug developers meet regulatory requirements in multiple regions, as the data collected from multinational trials can be used to support drug approval applications in several countries. However, conducting multi-center and multinational trials also presents challenges, such as coordinating between different regulatory authorities, ensuring consistent trial conduct across sites, and managing logistical issues related to patient recruitment, data collection, and monitoring.

6.2.2 Comparative Effectiveness Studies

Comparative effectiveness studies are a common feature of Phase III trials, where the investigational drug is compared to an existing treatment or standard of care to demonstrate its superiority or non-inferiority. These trials are critical for determining whether the new drug offers a meaningful improvement over current therapies, which is often required for regulatory approval and for market differentiation. In a Phase III trial for a new antihypertensive drug, for example, the investigational drug might be compared to the most commonly prescribed blood pressure medication. Researchers would measure outcomes such as the reduction in systolic and diastolic blood pressure, the incidence of side effects, and patient adherence to determine whether the new drug provides better or equivalent results.

Comparative effectiveness studies are designed with rigorous statistical methods to ensure that any differences in outcomes between the two treatments are statistically significant and not due to chance. This often involves using large sample sizes and stratified randomization to ensure that the treatment groups are well-balanced in terms of key demographic and clinical characteristics. For example, in a Phase III trial comparing two diabetes treatments, researchers might stratify patients by age, gender, baseline HbA1c levels, and comorbidities to ensure that the comparison is fair and that any observed differences in efficacy are due to the treatments themselves, rather than differences in the patient populations. Comparative effectiveness studies are essential for providing the evidence needed to position the new drug in the market and to support its use as a first-line or second-line treatment option.

6.2.3 Statistical Power and Sample Size Determination

The determination of statistical power and sample size is a critical component of Phase III trial design, as it ensures that the trial has enough participants to detect a meaningful difference between the investigational drug and the control or comparator treatment. Statistical power refers to the probability that the trial will detect a true effect if one exists, and it is influenced by factors such as the effect size (the magnitude of the difference between treatments), the sample size, and the variability in the outcome measures. In Phase III trials, researchers typically aim for a statistical power of at least 80%, meaning that there is an 80% chance of detecting a true treatment effect.

Determining the appropriate sample size involves balancing the need for sufficient statistical power with the practical considerations of patient recruitment, trial duration, and costs. For example, in a Phase III trial for a new heart failure drug, researchers would calculate the sample size needed to detect a statistically significant difference in the primary endpoint, such as all-cause mortality or hospitalization rates, based on the expected effect size and variability in the patient population. If the sample size is too small, the trial may fail to detect a meaningful difference, even if the drug is effective, leading to inconclusive results. On the other hand, if the sample size is too large, the trial may be unnecessarily expensive and time-consuming. By carefully calculating the sample size and ensuring that the trial is adequately powered, researchers can increase the likelihood of obtaining reliable and clinically meaningful results.

6.3 Multi-Ethnicity and Global Clinical Trials

6.3.1 Designing Trials for Diverse Populations

In the modern landscape of drug development, it is increasingly important for Phase III trials to be designed with multi-ethnicity in mind. Different populations may respond to drugs in varied ways due to genetic, environmental, or cultural factors, making it essential to ensure that clinical trials include participants from diverse ethnic backgrounds. For example, in a Phase III trial for a new antihypertensive drug, researchers must consider that African-American patients might have a different response to the drug compared to Caucasian or Asian patients due to genetic variations affecting drug metabolism or receptor sensitivity. To account for these differences, Phase III trials should be stratified by ethnicity to ensure that the drug's efficacy and safety are tested across a broad range of populations. This not only improves the generalizability of the trial results but also ensures that the drug is safe and effective for all groups once it is approved and marketed.

Designing trials for diverse populations also involves addressing potential socioeconomic and cultural barriers that may affect patient recruitment and retention. In some regions, access to healthcare or transportation may be limited, making it challenging for participants to attend study visits or follow the treatment regimen. Researchers must carefully consider these factors when selecting trial sites and designing study protocols to ensure that participants from different ethnic and socioeconomic backgrounds can be included. By designing inclusive trials, drug developers can ensure that their products are truly effective and safe for the global population, increasing the chances of regulatory approval in multiple regions.

6.3.2 Regulatory and Ethical Challenges in Multinational Trials

Conducting multinational clinical trials presents a host of regulatory and ethical challenges that must be addressed to ensure the integrity and success of the trial. Different countries have varying regulatory requirements for clinical trials, and navigating these differences can be complex. For example, while the FDA may have specific guidelines for adverse event reporting or patient informed consent, the EMA may have different requirements for these same processes. Drug developers must work closely with regulatory authorities in each country to ensure that the trial meets all local regulatory requirements, which may involve submitting separate applications to multiple agencies or conducting parallel reviews. Coordinating between multiple regulatory bodies can be time-consuming and costly, but it is essential for ensuring that the trial data will be accepted for drug approval in each region.

Ethical considerations also play a crucial role in multinational trials, particularly when trials are conducted in low- and middle-income countries. Researchers must ensure that the rights and welfare of participants are protected, regardless of the location of the trial. This includes ensuring that participants have given fully informed consent, that they understand the risks and benefits of participation, and that they are not being exploited for the benefit of wealthier nations. For example, in a Phase III trial for a new tuberculosis treatment conducted in both high-income and low-income countries, researchers must ensure that participants in all regions have equal access to the investigational drug and that the trial is conducted according to ethical standards, such as those outlined in the Declaration of Helsinki. Addressing these regulatory and ethical challenges is essential for ensuring the success and credibility of multinational trials, which are increasingly necessary for global drug development.

6.3.3 Harmonization of Regulatory Requirements

Harmonization of regulatory requirements across countries is an important goal for multinational trials, as it helps streamline the drug development process and reduces the burden on drug developers. Organizations such as the International Council for Harmonisation (ICH) have been instrumental in creating common guidelines for clinical trials, which are accepted by regulatory agencies in the United States, Europe, Japan, and other regions. These guidelines provide a framework for conducting trials that meet high ethical and scientific standards, regardless of where the trial is conducted. For example, the ICH's Good Clinical Practice (GCP) guidelines outline best practices for trial design, patient safety, and data management, ensuring that trials are conducted consistently across different countries.

Harmonization of regulatory requirements also facilitates the approval process, as data collected from multinational trials can be used to support drug approval applications in multiple regions. For instance, a Phase III trial conducted in both the US and Europe can use a single set of data to submit applications to both the FDA and EMA, rather than having to conduct separate trials for each region. This not only reduces the cost and complexity of drug development but also helps bring new treatments to patients more quickly. However, while significant progress has been made toward regulatory harmonization, challenges remain, particularly in emerging markets where local regulatory standards may differ from those in the US or Europe. Drug developers must continue to work closely with regulatory authorities to ensure that trials are conducted according to local regulations while adhering to global best practices.

6.4 Safety and Efficacy Monitoring in Phase III

6.4.1 Long-Term Safety Monitoring

In Phase III trials, long-term safety monitoring is critical because the drug is being tested in a much larger and more diverse patient population than in earlier phases. This provides an opportunity to identify rare but serious adverse events (SAEs) that may not have been detected in Phase I or II. Long-term monitoring is especially important for drugs intended for chronic use, as side effects may emerge only after months or years of treatment. For example, in a Phase III trial for a new cholesterol-lowering drug, researchers would monitor participants for long-term adverse effects such as liver toxicity, muscle damage, or cardiovascular issues that could arise from prolonged use. Safety monitoring protocols often include regular laboratory tests, imaging studies, and patient-reported outcomes to track any emerging safety concerns throughout the duration of the trial.

Long-term safety monitoring also involves the establishment of predefined safety endpoints, such as the incidence of specific adverse events or changes in key laboratory values. If these endpoints are exceeded, the trial may be paused, modified, or even terminated to protect participants. For example, in a trial for an immunosuppressive drug, if a certain percentage of participants develop severe infections, the trial may be stopped to reassess the dosing or safety protocols. This continuous safety monitoring ensures that any risks to participants are identified early and that appropriate actions are taken to mitigate these risks, protecting both the participants and the integrity of the trial.

6.4.2 Collection of Efficacy Data

The collection of efficacy data is one of the primary objectives of Phase III trials, as this data will be used to determine whether the investigational drug is effective enough to warrant approval. Efficacy data is typically collected through a combination of objective clinical measures, such as laboratory tests or imaging studies, and subjective measures, such as patient-reported outcomes. For instance, in a Phase III trial for a new asthma medication, researchers would collect data on lung function (e.g., FEV1 measurements), the frequency of asthma exacerbations, and patients' reported improvements in symptoms like shortness of breath or wheezing. This comprehensive approach ensures that the efficacy of the drug is thoroughly evaluated from multiple angles, providing robust evidence to support its potential therapeutic benefits.

Efficacy data is usually collected at regular intervals throughout the trial, with final efficacy assessments conducted at the end of the study. In addition to primary efficacy endpoints, Phase III trials often include secondary or exploratory endpoints to provide additional insights into the drug's effects. For example, in a Phase III trial for a new diabetes medication, the primary endpoint might be the reduction in HbA1c levels, while secondary endpoints could include weight loss, changes in lipid profiles, and improvements in quality of life. Collecting a wide range of efficacy data helps ensure that the drug's benefits are well-documented and that its therapeutic potential is fully understood before seeking regulatory approval.

6.4.3 Reporting Serious Adverse Events (SAEs)
Reporting serious adverse events (SAEs) is a crucial aspect of safety monitoring in Phase III trials, as these events can have significant implications for the drug's development. SAEs are defined as any untoward medical occurrence that results in death, is life-threatening, requires hospitalization, or results in persistent or significant disability. For example, in a Phase III trial for a new anticoagulant drug, SAEs might include severe bleeding events, strokes, or myocardial infarctions. When an SAE occurs, it must be reported immediately to the trial's Data Safety Monitoring Board (DSMB) and to regulatory authorities, such as the FDA or EMA, depending on the location of the trial. This ensures that the safety of participants is continuously monitored and that any potential risks are identified and addressed in real time.

The reporting process for SAEs involves a detailed assessment of the event, including whether it is related to the investigational drug or to other factors, such as the patient's underlying health condition or concomitant medications. If a pattern of SAEs emerges, the trial may be paused or modified to address the safety concerns. In some cases, the trial may be terminated if the risks outweigh the potential benefits of the drug. For example, if a Phase III trial for a new cancer treatment results in a high number of severe infections or organ failures, the trial may be stopped to prevent further harm to participants. Reporting SAEs is an essential component of the trial's ethical and regulatory responsibilities, ensuring that the risks to participants are minimized and that the trial can be modified or halted if necessary to protect their safety.

6.5 Endpoints and Outcomes in Phase III Trials

6.5.1 Primary and Secondary Endpoints
Endpoints in clinical trials serve as the critical measures that determine the success of the investigational drug. In Phase III trials, **primary endpoints**

are the most important outcomes that the trial is designed to assess, often directly related to the drug's therapeutic purpose. For instance, in a Phase III trial for a new cardiovascular drug, the primary endpoint might be the reduction in all-cause mortality or the number of major cardiovascular events, such as heart attacks or strokes. These endpoints are carefully selected based on their clinical relevance and their ability to demonstrate whether the drug provides a tangible benefit to patients. Regulatory agencies, such as the FDA or EMA, often require that primary endpoints be predefined and statistically powered to detect significant differences between the treatment and control groups.

In addition to primary endpoints, **secondary endpoints** are also established to provide additional insights into the drug's effects. While not the main focus of the trial, secondary endpoints help evaluate other important aspects of the drug's performance, such as improvements in quality of life, symptom relief, or reductions in secondary complications. For example, in a Phase III trial for a diabetes medication, while the primary endpoint might be a reduction in HbA1c levels, secondary endpoints could include changes in weight, improvements in cholesterol levels, or patient-reported outcomes like reduced fatigue or better overall health. Secondary endpoints add depth to the understanding of the drug's efficacy and safety, helping to guide clinical decision-making and the eventual use of the drug in practice. Together, the primary and secondary endpoints create a comprehensive picture of how the drug performs across multiple dimensions of patient health.

6.5.2 Surrogate Endpoints vs. Clinical Outcomes

In some Phase III trials, researchers use **surrogate endpoints**, which are indirect measures that predict the drug's effect on real clinical outcomes but are easier and faster to measure. Surrogate endpoints are often used when the clinical outcomes of interest, such as overall survival, would take too long to assess within the trial's timeframe. For example, in a Phase III trial for a cancer drug, tumor shrinkage (a surrogate endpoint) might be measured as an indicator of the drug's effectiveness, rather than waiting years to determine overall survival rates. While surrogate endpoints provide useful early indicators of a drug's potential efficacy, they must be validated to ensure that they accurately reflect meaningful clinical outcomes.

However, there is sometimes a trade-off between the use of surrogate endpoints and the collection of more meaningful **clinical outcomes**, such as reductions in morbidity or mortality. Clinical outcomes, while often more time-consuming and expensive to assess, provide the most definitive evidence of a drug's real-world benefits. For example, in trials for cardiovascular drugs, clinical outcomes such as the occurrence of heart attacks, strokes, or death are the gold standards for evaluating the drug's impact. Although surrogate endpoints can speed up the approval process and provide early evidence of efficacy, regulatory agencies require strong validation of these endpoints to ensure they correlate with real clinical benefits. Balancing surrogate endpoints with clinical outcomes is crucial for maintaining the scientific rigor and reliability of Phase III trials.

6.5.3 Statistical Analysis of Endpoints

Statistical analysis plays a crucial role in interpreting the results of Phase III trials, ensuring that the findings related to primary and secondary endpoints are valid and reliable. Researchers use a range of statistical methods to analyze the data collected during the trial and to determine whether the observed differences between treatment groups are statistically significant. **P-values** and **confidence intervals** are commonly used to assess whether the drug's effects on the primary endpoint are likely due to chance. For example, in a Phase III trial testing a new heart failure medication, a p-value less than 0.05 might indicate that the reduction in hospitalization rates observed in the treatment group is statistically significant, meaning it is unlikely to have occurred by chance.

In addition to assessing statistical significance, researchers also evaluate the **clinical significance** of the results, which considers whether the observed effects are meaningful and impactful for patients. For instance, a statistically significant reduction in blood pressure may be important, but the clinical significance depends on whether the reduction translates into fewer cardiovascular events or improved long-term outcomes. Researchers also use statistical methods to account for **confounding variables** and to perform **subgroup analyses**, which explore how different patient populations (e.g., by age, gender, or ethnicity) respond to the treatment. This in-depth analysis helps ensure that the trial results are robust, generalizable, and applicable to a wide range of patients, guiding both regulatory decisions and clinical practice.

6.6 Regulatory Approval Process Following Phase III

6.6.1 Submission of Data to Regulatory Agencies

After the successful completion of Phase III trials, the next critical step in drug development is the submission of the trial data to regulatory agencies for approval. This involves preparing a comprehensive dossier that includes all the data from preclinical studies, Phase I, II, and III trials, as well as information on the drug's manufacturing process and safety profile. The goal is to provide regulators with enough evidence to assess whether the drug is safe, effective, and of high quality. In the United States, this submission takes the form of a **New Drug Application (NDA)** or a **Biologics License Application (BLA)**, depending on whether the product is a chemical drug or a biologic. In Europe, the equivalent submission is the **Marketing Authorization Application (MAA)**, submitted to the European Medicines Agency (EMA).

The submission process is highly detailed and involves the presentation of thousands of pages of documentation, including clinical trial reports, statistical analyses, and summaries of the drug's risks and benefits. For example, in an NDA submission for a new cholesterol-lowering medication, the application would include a detailed description of the Phase III trial design, patient demographics, the efficacy results (e.g., reduction in LDL cholesterol), and the safety data (e.g., incidence of muscle pain or liver damage). Regulatory agencies then review the submission in detail, often requesting additional information or clarifications from the sponsor. This process can take several months to years, depending on the complexity of the drug and the trial results.

6.6.2 Common Technical Document (CTD) Format

The **Common Technical Document (CTD)** format is the standardized structure used for regulatory submissions in many regions, including the US, EU, Japan, and other ICH countries. The CTD format streamlines the submission process by providing a consistent template for presenting data, making it easier for regulators to review applications from different regions. The CTD is divided into five modules: Module 1 contains region-specific administrative information; Module 2 provides summaries of the drug's quality, nonclinical, and clinical data; Module 3 focuses on the drug's chemistry, manufacturing, and controls (CMC); Module 4 includes the nonclinical study reports (e.g., animal toxicity studies); and Module 5 contains the clinical study reports from Phase I, II, and III trials.

For example, in a Phase III trial for a new biologic drug targeting rheumatoid arthritis, the CTD submission would include detailed clinical data in Module 5, such as the trial's endpoints, statistical analyses, and safety monitoring results. This standardization of the submission process allows drug developers to submit the same CTD to regulatory agencies in multiple regions, facilitating simultaneous reviews by different authorities and potentially speeding up the drug's approval. The use of the CTD also reduces duplication of effort and ensures that all necessary information is presented clearly and consistently, improving the likelihood of a successful regulatory review.

6.6.3 Pathways to Approval: NDA, BLA, MAA

Once the data from Phase III trials are submitted, the next step is for regulatory agencies to review the application and decide whether to approve the drug for marketing. In the United States, there are two main pathways for drug approval: the **New Drug Application (NDA)** for chemical drugs and the **Biologics License Application (BLA)** for biologics, such as vaccines or monoclonal antibodies. Similarly, in Europe, drug developers submit a **Marketing Authorization Application (MAA)** to the EMA. Each pathway involves a rigorous review process, during which the regulatory agency assesses the drug's safety, efficacy, and quality based on the data provided in the CTD.

The review process typically includes input from various experts, including clinicians, statisticians, and toxicologists, who evaluate whether the benefits of the drug outweigh the risks for the intended patient population. For example, in an NDA review for a new antidepressant, the FDA would assess the results of the Phase III trials, looking at whether the drug significantly improves depressive symptoms compared to a placebo and whether the safety profile is acceptable, particularly regarding risks such as increased suicidal ideation or weight gain. If the regulatory agency is satisfied that the drug meets the necessary standards, it grants marketing approval, allowing the sponsor to begin selling the drug. However, if the agency identifies any concerns, such as inadequate safety data or manufacturing issues, it may request additional studies or modifications before granting approval. In some cases, the agency may grant **conditional approval**, allowing the drug to be marketed while additional data are collected, particularly for drugs that address unmet medical needs.

Review Questions

1. What is the primary objective of Phase III clinical trials?
2. Why are multi-center and multinational trials commonly used in Phase III studies?
3. How is safety monitoring conducted during Phase III trials?
4. What is the difference between primary and secondary endpoints in Phase III trials?
5. Explain the statistical considerations involved in determining sample size for Phase III trials.
6. How do Phase III trials contribute to the regulatory approval process for new drugs?
7. What are the ethical challenges in conducting Phase III trials across diverse populations?
8. How do Phase III trials ensure the collection of long-term safety and efficacy data?

CHAPTER SEVEN

Phase IV and Post-Marketing Studies

7.1 Introduction to Post-Marketing Studies

7.1.1 Purpose of Phase IV Trials

Phase IV trials, also known as post-marketing studies, serve an essential purpose by monitoring the safety and effectiveness of a drug after it has received regulatory approval and is available for use by the general population. These trials are designed to evaluate long-term effects, rare side effects, and the drug's performance in a much larger and more diverse patient population than was possible during the earlier phases of development. For instance, while Phase III trials typically involve several thousand participants, once a drug reaches the market, it may be used by millions of people, some of whom may have pre-existing conditions, be taking other medications, or fall into demographic categories underrepresented in earlier trials. The purpose of Phase IV trials is to gather data on how the drug performs in these real-world settings, ensuring its ongoing safety and efficacy. In some cases, these trials also explore new indications or combinations of the drug with other therapies.

Another key aspect of Phase IV trials is that they help identify any previously unrecognized adverse effects. Some side effects or drug interactions may be too rare to be detected during the earlier phases of clinical trials but may become apparent once the drug is widely used. For example, a drug might cause an adverse reaction in only 1 out of 10,000 patients, a rate that might not be observed in Phase III but could become evident during post-marketing surveillance. Phase IV trials, therefore, play a critical role in protecting public health by ensuring that any risks associated with the drug are identified and addressed as soon as possible.

7.1.2 Differences from Earlier Phases

Phase IV trials differ from earlier phases of drug development in several important ways. First, unlike Phase I, II, and III trials, which are conducted in controlled environments with carefully selected participants, Phase IV trials are conducted in real-world settings, where patients may have a range of comorbidities, be on multiple medications, and not follow strict protocols. This makes the data from Phase IV trials more reflective of how the drug will actually be used in daily clinical practice. Second, while earlier phases focus primarily on establishing the safety and efficacy of the drug, Phase IV trials expand their focus to include long-term safety monitoring, the identification of rare adverse effects, and assessments of the drug's overall benefit-risk profile in larger populations.

Another key difference is that Phase IV trials often assess additional indications for the drug, exploring whether it may be effective in treating conditions other than those for which it was initially approved. For example, a drug approved for hypertension may undergo Phase IV trials to investigate its potential benefits in patients with chronic kidney disease. This process allows drug manufacturers to expand the market for their products while providing physicians with more data on how to use the drug in a broader range of patients. Additionally, Phase IV trials are usually required by regulatory authorities as a condition of market approval, ensuring that the drug continues to meet safety standards after it is released to the public.

7.1.3 Regulatory Requirements for Post-Approval Trials

Regulatory agencies, such as the FDA, EMA, and CDSCO, often require the completion of Phase IV trials as a condition of the drug's market approval. These trials are essential for ensuring that the benefits of the drug continue to outweigh the risks once it is widely available. For example, the FDA may mandate a post-approval commitment from the manufacturer to conduct additional studies focused on long-term safety, particularly if there were any safety signals during earlier trials that warranted further investigation. Failure to comply with these requirements can lead to regulatory actions, including the suspension or withdrawal of the drug from the market.

Post-approval trials are also essential for meeting regulatory requirements related to **pharmacovigilance**, which refers to the ongoing monitoring of a drug's safety profile once it has been approved. Regulatory authorities often require companies to establish detailed plans for post-marketing surveillance and safety reporting as part of the approval process. These plans, known as **Risk Management Plans (RMPs)**, outline the measures that the company will take to monitor and mitigate any potential risks associated with the drug. RMPs are critical for ensuring that regulatory agencies can continue to evaluate the safety and efficacy of the drug throughout its lifecycle.

7.2 Post-Marketing Surveillance

7.2.1 Role of Pharmacovigilance

Pharmacovigilance is a key component of post-marketing surveillance, designed to detect, assess, understand, and prevent adverse effects or any other drug-related problems once the drug has been released to the public. The role of pharmacovigilance is to ensure that any safety issues that arise after the drug is marketed are identified and addressed in a timely manner. This is especially important because clinical trials, even large Phase III trials, cannot account for all potential risks, particularly those that occur in rare populations or under specific conditions. For instance, a drug that is found to be safe and effective in clinical trials might cause severe allergic reactions in a small subset of the population once it is widely used. Pharmacovigilance systems are designed to catch these rare events, allowing regulatory authorities and drug manufacturers to take action, such as updating labeling information, issuing safety warnings, or in extreme cases, withdrawing the drug from the market.

The scope of pharmacovigilance also includes monitoring drug interactions, especially as new drugs enter the market and are used in combination with existing therapies. For example, a drug might be safe when used alone but could cause harmful effects when taken with another medication that was not tested during earlier trials. Pharmacovigilance systems rely on the collection of data from a variety of sources, including healthcare providers, patients, and pharmaceutical companies. This data is then analyzed to identify any emerging safety concerns that need to be addressed.

7.2.2 Reporting Adverse Drug Reactions (ADRs)

One of the primary mechanisms for pharmacovigilance is the reporting of **adverse drug reactions (ADRs)**. ADRs are unwanted or harmful effects that occur as a result of taking a medication. These reactions can range from mild, such as headaches or nausea, to severe, such as liver damage or life-threatening allergic reactions. Healthcare providers, patients, and pharmaceutical companies are all encouraged to report ADRs to national pharmacovigilance centers or regulatory agencies, such as the FDA or EMA. The timely reporting of ADRs is essential for identifying potential safety issues before they become widespread.

Once an ADR is reported, it is typically categorized based on its severity and the likelihood that it is related to the drug. Regulatory authorities analyze this data to determine whether any action needs to be taken, such as updating the drug's safety labeling, issuing warnings to healthcare providers, or conducting further studies to investigate the issue. For example, if a significant number of ADR reports indicate that a new anticoagulant is causing severe bleeding in patients, the regulatory agency might require the manufacturer to add a black box warning to the drug's label or conduct additional Phase IV studies to better understand the risks. In extreme cases, the drug may be withdrawn from the market if the risks are found to outweigh the benefits.

7.2.3 Spontaneous Reporting Systems (e.g., FDA MedWatch)

Spontaneous reporting systems, such as the FDA's **MedWatch** program, play a crucial role in pharmacovigilance by providing healthcare professionals and patients with a platform to report ADRs and other safety concerns. These systems allow for the collection of real-time safety data from individuals who are using the drug in the real world, outside of the controlled environment of clinical trials. The MedWatch system, for example, allows anyone to report a potential safety issue with a drug, medical device, or dietary supplement. Once a report is submitted, the FDA reviews the information to determine whether further investigation or action is needed. This process helps ensure that any emerging safety issues are identified quickly and that appropriate measures are taken to protect public health.

Spontaneous reporting systems are vital because they provide a broad and decentralized method for monitoring drug safety. Unlike clinical trials, which involve a relatively small and controlled group of participants, spontaneous reporting systems collect data from millions of people who are using the drug in a wide variety of settings and conditions. This increases the likelihood of detecting rare or unexpected side effects that might not have been apparent during earlier phases of development. However, one limitation of spontaneous reporting systems is that they rely on voluntary reporting, which can lead to underreporting of ADRs. To address this, regulatory agencies encourage healthcare providers and patients to report any suspected adverse events, even if they are unsure whether the drug is the cause.

7.3 Pharmacovigilance Systems

7.3.1 National and International Systems

Pharmacovigilance systems operate both at the national and international levels, with the goal of monitoring the safety of medicinal products once they have been marketed. National pharmacovigilance systems are established by regulatory authorities in individual countries, such as the FDA in the United States, the EMA in Europe, and the CDSCO in India. These systems are responsible for collecting and analyzing data on adverse drug reactions (ADRs) and other drug-related issues from healthcare providers, pharmaceutical companies, and patients. For example, in India, the Pharmacovigilance Programme of India (PvPI) is overseen by the CDSCO and aims to ensure that all medicines in the country meet safety standards by continuously monitoring adverse effects.

At the international level, organizations like the World Health Organization (WHO) play a central role in coordinating pharmacovigilance efforts through programs such as the WHO Programme for International Drug Monitoring. This program involves collaboration with over 100 member countries, all of which contribute data to the WHO's global database, VigiBase. By pooling data from multiple countries, international pharmacovigilance systems can detect safety signals that might not be evident within individual nations due to smaller sample sizes or regional differences in drug use. For example, if a rare but serious adverse reaction to a new drug is reported in several countries, international collaboration through WHO can facilitate faster recognition of the issue, allowing regulatory authorities worldwide to take action.

7.3.2 Role of the Qualified Person for Pharmacovigilance (QPPV)

The Qualified Person for Pharmacovigilance (QPPV) plays a critical role in the oversight and implementation of pharmacovigilance activities, particularly in the European Union. Every pharmaceutical company that markets drugs in the EU is required to appoint a QPPV who is responsible for ensuring that the company complies with all pharmacovigilance regulations. The QPPV's responsibilities include monitoring the safety of the company's products, managing the collection and reporting of adverse drug reactions, and liaising with regulatory authorities regarding any safety concerns. For example, if a company receives reports of unexpected side effects associated with one of its drugs, the QPPV is responsible for investigating these reports, ensuring that they are communicated to regulatory bodies, and taking appropriate action to mitigate the risks.

The QPPV also oversees the preparation and submission of **Periodic Safety Update Reports (PSURs)** and other safety documentation required by regulators. This individual must have a deep understanding of pharmacovigilance regulations and clinical safety assessments, as well as the authority to make decisions regarding the safety of the company's products. For instance, if serious safety concerns arise during post-marketing surveillance, the QPPV may recommend that the drug be temporarily withdrawn from the market while further investigations are conducted. The QPPV's role is essential in ensuring that pharmacovigilance activities are conducted effectively and that patient safety remains the top priority.

7.3.3 Regulatory Requirements for Pharmacovigilance

Regulatory authorities around the world have established strict requirements for pharmacovigilance to ensure that drug safety is continuously monitored after a product has been approved. These requirements vary by region but generally include obligations for pharmaceutical companies to report adverse drug reactions, submit regular safety updates, and implement risk management plans (RMPs) to mitigate known risks. For example, in the European Union, the EMA requires companies to submit PSURs at regular intervals, detailing any new safety information that has emerged since the last report. Similarly, in the United States, the FDA requires companies to submit post-marketing safety reports, including serious adverse event reports and periodic safety updates, as part of their ongoing regulatory obligations.

In addition to these reporting requirements, pharmaceutical companies must also maintain comprehensive pharmacovigilance systems that are capable of detecting, assessing, and responding to safety signals in real-time. This includes having systems in place for collecting data from healthcare providers, patients, and other stakeholders, as well as conducting regular audits to ensure that pharmacovigilance activities are being carried out in compliance with regulatory standards. Failure to meet pharmacovigilance requirements can result in significant penalties, including fines, product recalls, or the suspension of marketing authorizations. For example, if a company is found to have failed to report serious adverse events associated with one of its products, it may face regulatory action, including the possibility of having the drug removed from the market.

7.4 Real-World Evidence and Long-Term Safety Monitoring

7.4.1 Real-World Data Collection
Real-world data collection is an increasingly important aspect of Phase IV trials and post-marketing surveillance, as it provides insights into how drugs perform in routine clinical practice outside the controlled environment of clinical trials. **Real-world evidence (RWE)** is gathered from sources such as electronic health records (EHRs), patient registries, insurance claims, and patient-reported outcomes. This data helps researchers and regulatory authorities assess how a drug works in a broader, more diverse population, including individuals with comorbidities, those on concomitant medications, and populations that may have been underrepresented in earlier trials. For example, real-world data collected from patients using a new diabetes medication might reveal that the drug is less effective in elderly patients or that it leads to higher rates of hypoglycemia when combined with certain other treatments.

The use of real-world data allows for the identification of rare side effects, drug-drug interactions, and other safety concerns that may not have been evident during the earlier phases of clinical trials. It also provides insights into the drug's long-term effectiveness and its impact on patient quality of life. For example, in a Phase IV trial for a new rheumatoid arthritis drug, real-world data might show that while the drug reduces symptoms in the short term, its long-term use leads to an increased risk of infections or cardiovascular events. Real-world data is invaluable for healthcare providers and regulatory authorities, as it provides a more comprehensive picture of a drug's safety and effectiveness over time.

7.4.2 Importance of Long-Term Safety Data
Long-term safety data is crucial for understanding the full risk profile of a drug, particularly for chronic conditions where patients may be on treatment for many years. While Phase I through III trials provide important information on the short-term safety of a drug, it is often only during Phase IV and post-marketing surveillance that long-term risks become apparent. For instance, drugs used to treat conditions such as hypertension, diabetes, or osteoporosis may need to be taken for decades, and it is essential to monitor for potential long-term adverse effects such as

organ toxicity, cancer, or cardiovascular events. For example, in long-term safety monitoring of a popular cholesterol-lowering medication, researchers might find that after several years of use, there is an increased risk of liver damage or muscle disorders.

This long-term data also helps guide clinical practice, as healthcare providers use it to make informed decisions about whether the benefits of continuing a particular therapy outweigh the risks for their patients. For example, in a post-marketing study for a new antidepressant, long-term safety data might reveal that patients are at higher risk for weight gain or metabolic syndrome, prompting providers to monitor patients more closely for these conditions. Additionally, long-term safety data is often required by regulatory authorities to maintain a drug's market approval and to ensure that it remains safe for widespread use.

7.4.3 Risk Management Plans (RMPs)

Risk management plans (RMPs) are an essential component of long-term safety monitoring and pharmacovigilance. These plans are required by regulatory authorities, such as the FDA, EMA, and CDSCO, and outline the steps that pharmaceutical companies will take to monitor and mitigate risks associated with their products once they are on the market. RMPs typically include a detailed description of the known risks associated with the drug, as well as plans for post-marketing surveillance, the collection of additional safety data, and strategies for minimizing risks. For example, an RMP for a new immunosuppressive drug might include measures to monitor for serious infections and cancers, both of which are known risks associated with long-term immunosuppression.

In addition to addressing known risks, RMPs also outline strategies for identifying and responding to new safety concerns that may emerge during post-marketing surveillance. This could include the establishment of patient registries to track long-term outcomes, the implementation of risk minimization measures such as restricted prescribing or additional patient monitoring, and the development of educational materials for healthcare providers and patients to ensure the safe use of the drug. RMPs are living documents that are continuously updated as new safety data becomes available, ensuring that regulatory authorities and pharmaceutical companies can respond quickly to any emerging risks.

7.5 Periodic Safety Update Reports (PSURs)

7.5.1 Structure and Content of PSURs

Periodic Safety Update Reports (PSURs) are crucial documents that pharmaceutical companies must submit to regulatory authorities after a drug has been approved for marketing. These reports are designed to provide a comprehensive overview of the safety profile of the drug, including any new information that has emerged since the drug was first marketed. The structure of a PSUR typically includes several key sections, such as a summary of new safety data, an analysis of adverse drug reactions (ADRs) reported since the last update, and an evaluation of the drug's overall benefit-risk balance. For example, if a pharmaceutical company is marketing a new antipsychotic medication, the PSUR would include details on any serious side effects, such as weight gain or diabetes, that have been reported since the drug's launch.

The content of a PSUR must be thorough and well-organized to ensure that regulatory authorities have all the information they need to assess the ongoing safety of the drug. This includes not only data from post-marketing surveillance but also any new data from clinical trials, observational studies, or literature reviews. For instance, if new research has been published linking the drug to an increased risk of cardiovascular events, this information would be included in the PSUR, along with an analysis of its relevance to the current patient population. The PSUR also provides an opportunity for the company to propose any changes to the product labeling or risk management plan based on the new safety data.

In addition to safety data, PSURs must also include an assessment of the drug's overall benefit-risk profile. This involves comparing the drug's therapeutic benefits to its potential risks, particularly in light of any new safety information. For example, if a new side effect is identified, the PSUR would analyze whether the benefits of the drug still outweigh the risks for the majority of patients. This analysis is critical for regulatory authorities, as it helps them decide whether any regulatory actions, such as changes to the product's labeling or additional warnings, are necessary to ensure patient safety.

7.5.2 Frequency of Reporting

The frequency with which pharmaceutical companies are required to submit PSURs varies depending on the regulatory authority and the specific risk profile of the drug. In general, PSURs are required more frequently during the first few years after a drug's approval, when its safety profile is still being fully established. For example, the European Medicines Agency

(EMA) typically requires companies to submit PSURs every six months for the first two years after a drug is marketed, then annually for the next two years, and biennially thereafter. This regular reporting schedule allows regulatory authorities to monitor the drug's safety in real-time and take action if any safety concerns arise during the early post-marketing period.

In some cases, the frequency of PSUR submission can be adjusted based on the drug's safety profile and the results of previous PSURs. For example, if a drug has been on the market for several years without any significant safety issues, regulatory authorities may decide to reduce the frequency of PSUR submissions to every two or three years. Conversely, if a new safety concern emerges, such as a high number of serious adverse events, the regulatory authority may require more frequent PSUR submissions to closely monitor the situation. This flexibility in the reporting schedule ensures that regulatory authorities can respond quickly to any new safety data while also reducing the burden on companies when the drug has demonstrated a stable safety profile over time.

In countries like India, the CDSCO also mandates the submission of PSURs at regular intervals as part of its pharmacovigilance requirements. The objective is the same—to ensure that the safety and efficacy of a drug are continuously evaluated, and any risks are mitigated promptly. By maintaining a structured and regulated frequency of PSUR submissions, regulatory authorities can ensure that the post-marketing safety of a drug is carefully tracked and that any potential risks to public health are addressed as soon as possible.

7.5.3 Regulatory Requirements for PSUR Submission

The submission of PSURs is a mandatory regulatory requirement in most regions, and pharmaceutical companies must comply with these requirements to maintain the marketing authorization for their products. Regulatory agencies, such as the FDA, EMA, and CDSCO, have strict guidelines on the content, structure, and timing of PSUR submissions, and failure to comply can result in significant penalties. For instance, if a company fails to submit a PSUR within the required timeframe or provides incomplete safety data, it may face fines, legal action, or even the suspension of the drug's marketing authorization. These strict requirements ensure that pharmaceutical companies take their post-marketing surveillance obligations seriously and that patient safety remains a top priority.

In addition to submitting PSURs to regulatory authorities, companies are also required to implement any recommendations or actions that arise from the review of these reports. For example, if a regulatory authority identifies a new safety concern based on the data in a PSUR, it may require the company to update the drug's labeling with new warnings or precautions. In some cases, regulatory authorities may even require the company to conduct additional Phase IV trials or observational studies to gather more data on the safety concern. For instance, if a PSUR for an anti-inflammatory drug reveals an increased risk of gastrointestinal bleeding, the EMA might require the company to conduct further studies to determine the severity and prevalence of this side effect in the general population.

Compliance with PSUR submission requirements is also monitored through regular audits and inspections by regulatory authorities. These audits ensure that companies have the necessary systems in place to collect, analyze, and report safety data in accordance with regulatory standards. For example, during an audit, the FDA may review the company's pharmacovigilance procedures to ensure that all adverse events are being properly recorded and reported in the PSURs. By enforcing strict regulatory requirements for PSUR submission, regulatory authorities help ensure that pharmaceutical companies maintain a high standard of drug safety and that any potential risks to patients are promptly identified and addressed.

7.6 Case Studies in Post-Marketing Studies

7.6.1 Examples of Successful Phase IV Trials

Several notable Phase IV trials have provided valuable insights into the long-term safety and efficacy of drugs after they have been marketed. One such example is the **Women's Health Initiative (WHI)** study, a large-scale Phase IV trial that evaluated the risks and benefits of hormone replacement therapy (HRT) in postmenopausal women. While HRT had been widely prescribed to manage menopausal symptoms, the WHI study revealed that long-term use of HRT was associated with an increased risk of breast cancer, stroke, and heart disease. As a result of these findings, healthcare providers significantly reduced the use of HRT, and regulatory agencies updated the labeling to include stronger warnings about the risks. This Phase IV trial demonstrated the importance of post-marketing studies in identifying risks that may not be apparent during earlier phases of clinical development.

Another example of a successful Phase IV trial is the **ALLHAT (Antihypertensive and Lipid-Lowering Treatment to Prevent Heart Attack Trial)**, which evaluated the long-term efficacy and safety of different classes of antihypertensive drugs. The study compared the effectiveness of newer drugs, such as calcium channel blockers and ACE inhibitors, with older, more established medications like diuretics. The results showed that diuretics were just as effective, if not more so, than the newer drugs in preventing heart attacks and strokes, and they had fewer side effects. These findings had a significant impact on clinical practice, leading many physicians to reconsider the use of diuretics as a first-line treatment for hypertension.

These examples highlight the value of Phase IV trials in providing real-world data on the long-term use of drugs, particularly in large and diverse populations. While earlier phases of clinical trials focus on proving a drug's efficacy and safety in controlled settings, Phase IV trials allow researchers to observe how the drug performs in everyday clinical practice. This real-world data is critical for understanding the broader impact of the drug, particularly in populations that may not have been fully represented in earlier trials, such as elderly patients, individuals with multiple comorbidities, or those on complex treatment regimens.

7.6.2 Regulatory Responses to Post-Marketing Issues

Post-marketing studies play a crucial role in identifying safety concerns that may not have been evident during the earlier phases of drug development, and regulatory agencies must respond quickly to these issues to protect public health. One well-known example is the case of **rofecoxib (Vioxx)**, a popular painkiller that was withdrawn from the market after post-marketing studies revealed a significant increase in the risk of heart attacks and strokes among users. Initially, Vioxx was approved based on data from Phase III trials that showed its effectiveness in relieving pain with fewer gastrointestinal side effects than traditional NSAIDs. However, as more patients began using the drug, Phase IV studies and post-marketing surveillance revealed that the cardiovascular risks outweighed the benefits for many patients, leading to its withdrawal in 2004. This case underscores the importance of robust post-marketing surveillance systems and the need for swift regulatory action when safety concerns arise.

Another example is the regulatory response to **fluoroquinolone antibiotics**, which have been widely used to treat bacterial infections. While these drugs were initially considered safe based on data from earlier clinical trials, post-marketing studies revealed that long-term use was associated with severe side effects, including tendon rupture, peripheral neuropathy, and central nervous system effects. In response to these findings, the FDA issued a series of safety alerts and updated the labeling to include warnings about these risks. The agency also recommended that fluoroquinolones should only be used when no other treatment options are available. These regulatory actions were critical in reducing the use of fluoroquinolones for conditions where the risks outweighed the benefits.

Regulatory responses to post-marketing issues are essential for ensuring that drugs remain safe for public use throughout their lifecycle. When safety concerns arise, regulatory agencies have a range of tools at their disposal, including updating labeling, issuing safety alerts, restricting the drug's use, or, in extreme cases, withdrawing the drug from the market. These actions help protect patients and ensure that the risks associated with the drug are minimized while still allowing access to effective treatments for those who need them.

7.6.3 Lessons Learned from Post-Marketing Surveillance

The lessons learned from post-marketing surveillance underscore the importance of ongoing safety monitoring throughout the entire lifecycle of a drug. One key lesson is that even well-conducted clinical trials cannot capture all potential risks, particularly those that are rare, long-term, or specific to certain populations. For example, the cardiovascular risks associated with Vioxx were not detected during the initial trials, which involved relatively small, homogenous patient populations, but became apparent only after millions of patients began using the drug. This highlights the need for robust post-marketing surveillance systems that can identify and address safety concerns in real time.

Another important lesson is the value of international collaboration in pharmacovigilance. Safety data collected from different countries and regions can provide a more comprehensive understanding of a drug's risks and benefits, particularly when rare adverse events are involved. For instance, in the case of the fluoroquinolones, reports of tendon rupture and neuropathy emerged from multiple countries, prompting regulatory agencies around the world to take coordinated action. This global approach to pharmacovigilance ensures that safety issues are addressed promptly and that patients are protected regardless of where they live.

Finally, post-marketing surveillance has shown that effective communication between regulatory agencies, healthcare providers, and the public is essential for ensuring drug safety. When safety concerns arise, it is important that regulatory agencies provide clear, timely, and accurate information to both healthcare professionals and patients. This allows providers to make informed decisions about whether to continue prescribing the drug and enables patients to understand the risks and benefits of their treatment. Clear communication is also critical for maintaining public trust in the regulatory process, particularly when difficult decisions, such as drug withdrawals, need to be made.

Review Questions

1. What is the purpose of Phase IV trials in post-marketing surveillance?
2. How do Phase IV trials differ from earlier phases of clinical trials?
3. What role does pharmacovigilance play in post-marketing studies?
4. How are adverse drug reactions (ADRs) reported during post-marketing studies?
5. What are Periodic Safety Update Reports (PSURs), and why are they important?
6. Explain the significance of real-world evidence in post-marketing surveillance.
7. What are Risk Management Plans (RMPs), and how are they implemented?
8. Discuss the role of regulatory authorities in monitoring post-marketing drug safety.

CHAPTER EIGHT

Clinical Investigation and Evaluation of Medical Devices

8.1 Introduction to Medical Device Clinical Investigations

8.1.1 Definition of Medical Devices and IVDs

Medical devices encompass a wide range of products used for diagnosis, treatment, or prevention of diseases or conditions, ranging from simple tools like bandages to complex technologies such as pacemakers and diagnostic imaging machines. The regulatory definition of a medical device often differs from that of pharmaceuticals in that devices typically work through mechanical, physical, or structural means, rather than chemical interactions. **In-Vitro Diagnostics (IVDs)**, a subclass of medical devices, are specifically used to perform tests on samples such as blood or tissue taken from the human body. Examples include blood glucose meters, pregnancy tests, and laboratory reagents. The distinction between devices and drugs lies in their mode of action—whereas drugs achieve their effects via chemical actions, medical devices generally function through physical means, making their development and evaluation pathways distinct.

IVDs play a critical role in modern medicine, providing essential diagnostic information that informs clinical decision-making. For example, a blood test to measure cholesterol levels using an IVD can help assess a patient's risk for cardiovascular diseases, guiding therapeutic decisions. The performance of IVDs must be rigorously tested to ensure they provide accurate and reliable results. This is why clinical investigations, including performance evaluation studies, are essential for both medical devices and IVDs before they can be approved for use. In clinical investigations, the devices are tested in real-world settings to confirm that they perform as expected and that they do not pose unacceptable risks to patients.

8.1.2 Differences Between Drug and Device Clinical Trials

While both drugs and medical devices undergo clinical investigations, the processes for evaluating them differ significantly due to the distinct ways they interact with the body. **Drug trials** often focus on evaluating the pharmacokinetics (how the drug is absorbed, distributed, metabolized, and excreted) and pharmacodynamics (the drug's effects on the body), while **medical device trials** focus more on mechanical performance, safety, and the device's interaction with human physiology. For example, a clinical trial for a cardiac stent would focus on how well the stent holds open arteries and prevents blockages, rather than on chemical effects. Additionally, because many medical devices are used in combination with surgical procedures (such as implants), device trials often include surgical outcomes as part of their evaluation metrics.

Medical device trials also tend to involve a more iterative process compared to drug trials. Devices may undergo several rounds of modification and testing before final approval, whereas drug trials usually follow a more linear path from preclinical testing through Phase I, II, and III trials. Furthermore, device investigations must account for usability, especially for products like diagnostic tools or wearables that patients or healthcare providers handle directly. This means that clinical investigations for devices often include user feedback and design adjustments based on real-world testing. Ultimately, while the goal of both drug and device trials is to ensure the product's safety and efficacy, the differences in how they achieve these outcomes are significant.

8.1.3 Importance of Clinical Investigations for Devices

The primary purpose of clinical investigations for medical devices is to ensure that they are both safe and effective when used by healthcare professionals or patients in real-world conditions. Unlike pharmaceuticals, where the primary focus is often on how the body processes a drug, medical device investigations must address a wide range of factors, including mechanical reliability, durability, and interaction with the human body. For instance, a clinical investigation of a knee replacement device would assess not only the implant's ability to function within the joint but also its longevity, how it wears down over time, and whether it causes complications like inflammation or infection. These evaluations are critical because devices, once implanted, are difficult to remove or replace compared to adjusting drug dosages.

Clinical investigations for medical devices also play a crucial role in the approval process for both new and significantly modified devices. Regulatory agencies like the FDA and EMA require robust clinical evidence to demonstrate that a device performs as intended and poses no undue risk to patients. In some cases, real-world testing may reveal unforeseen issues, such as device malfunctions or adverse reactions, which would not be apparent from preclinical laboratory tests or animal studies. Clinical investigations thus provide the final, critical step in ensuring that medical devices meet the stringent safety standards required for regulatory approval.

8.2 Regulatory Pathways for Medical Devices

8.2.1 Regulatory Approval for Medical Devices

The regulatory pathways for medical device approval differ from those for drugs and vary significantly depending on the region. In the United States, medical devices are classified by the FDA into three categories—Class I, II, and III—based on the level of risk they pose to patients. **Class I devices** (e.g., surgical gloves) are considered low-risk and typically do not require extensive clinical data for approval. **Class II devices** (e.g., infusion pumps) are moderate-risk and may require clinical evidence demonstrating safety and efficacy, while **Class III devices** (e.g., pacemakers) are high-risk and require rigorous clinical investigations. In the European Union, the European Medicines Agency (EMA) also classifies devices based on risk and requires that all devices meet the standards outlined in the Medical Device Regulation (MDR) before they can be sold in the EU market.

In India, the Central Drugs Standard Control Organization (CDSCO) regulates medical devices through a classification system similar to that used by the FDA. Devices are categorized based on their intended use and the risk they pose to patients, with higher-risk devices requiring more extensive clinical data for approval. For example, an implantable device like a coronary stent would undergo a rigorous evaluation to ensure that it meets safety and performance standards before receiving marketing authorization. In all regions, the goal of the regulatory process is to ensure that medical devices are safe, effective, and manufactured to high-quality standards, reducing the risk of harm to patients.

8.2.2 Investigational Device Exemption (IDE) Process

In the United States, the **Investigational Device Exemption (IDE)** process allows manufacturers to use their medical devices in clinical trials before they have been approved for marketing. An IDE is necessary for conducting clinical investigations on **Class III devices**, which pose the highest risk to patients and are subject to the strictest regulatory scrutiny. The IDE application must include detailed information about the device, including its design, intended use, and preclinical testing results. It must also outline the proposed clinical study protocol, detailing how the device will be tested in humans, what safety precautions will be taken, and how the data will be collected and analyzed.

The IDE process is designed to ensure that the risks associated with testing investigational devices in humans are minimized and that the study is conducted ethically and scientifically. For example, a manufacturer developing a new type of cardiac implant might apply for an IDE to conduct a clinical trial involving patients with severe heart disease. The trial would evaluate the device's ability to improve heart function while monitoring for potential risks, such as device failure or adverse reactions. Once the clinical investigation is complete and the data supports the device's safety and effectiveness, the manufacturer can submit a **Premarket Approval (PMA)** application to the FDA for full marketing authorization.

8.2.3 Overview of the FDA, EMA, and CDSCO Requirements

The regulatory requirements for medical device approval vary slightly between the **FDA (United States)**, **EMA (Europe)**, and **CDSCO (India)**, but all agencies follow a risk-based approach to device regulation. In the United States, the FDA's Center for Devices and Radiological Health (CDRH) is responsible for reviewing medical devices, with the level of regulatory oversight increasing based on the risk classification of the device. For high-risk devices, clinical evidence from well-controlled trials is typically required to demonstrate safety and effectiveness. In Europe, the EMA enforces the Medical Device Regulation (MDR), which requires devices to meet stringent safety and performance standards before they can be marketed. Devices must be evaluated by a **Notified Body**, which reviews the clinical data and ensures that the device complies with regulatory requirements.

In India, the CDSCO oversees the approval of medical devices through a process that includes both pre-market evaluation and post-market surveillance. Devices classified as moderate to high risk must undergo clinical trials in India, and manufacturers must submit clinical data that demonstrates the device's safety and performance in the Indian population.

The CDSCO also requires that manufacturers maintain ongoing post-market surveillance to monitor the long-term safety of devices once they are in use. While the specific requirements may differ slightly between regions, the overarching goal of all regulatory bodies is to ensure that medical devices are safe, effective, and of high quality.

8.3 Clinical Evaluation Methods for Medical Devices

8.3.1 Pre-Clinical and Clinical Evaluation

Before a medical device reaches the stage of clinical trials, it must undergo **pre-clinical evaluations** to ensure that it is safe and functional. These evaluations typically include laboratory-based tests, mechanical performance assessments, and sometimes animal studies to confirm the device's safety before it is tested in humans. For instance, an implantable orthopedic device such as a hip replacement would be subjected to mechanical stress tests to ensure that it can withstand daily activities without failing. Pre-clinical evaluations also include biocompatibility tests to ensure that materials used in the device do not cause adverse reactions when in contact with human tissues. Only after passing these pre-clinical evaluations can the device move on to clinical trials.

Once the device enters the clinical evaluation phase, **clinical trials** are conducted to gather data on its safety, performance, and efficacy when used in real-world conditions. For example, a clinical trial for a new glucose monitoring device would assess not only how accurately it measures blood sugar levels but also how easy it is for patients to use. This phase may involve randomized controlled trials, observational studies, or post-market surveillance, depending on the risk level of the device and regulatory requirements. The clinical evaluation helps to identify any potential risks that might not have been apparent during pre-clinical testing and confirms that the device provides the intended benefit to patients.

The clinical evaluation process must also comply with ethical standards, such as ensuring informed consent from participants and minimizing risks to patient safety. Regulatory agencies such as the FDA, EMA, and CDSCO require that all medical devices undergo a thorough clinical evaluation before they are approved for marketing. This process ensures that devices not only meet performance expectations but also do not pose unacceptable risks to patients. The data generated from clinical evaluations provide the evidence needed for regulatory authorities to make informed decisions about whether a device should be approved for use.

8.3.2 Safety and Performance Endpoints

The **safety and performance endpoints** of a medical device trial are the key outcomes that the trial is designed to measure. These endpoints are carefully selected to demonstrate that the device is both safe and effective for its intended use. For example, in a clinical trial for a new coronary stent, the primary performance endpoint might be the reduction in the incidence of heart attacks in patients with coronary artery disease, while the safety endpoint could involve monitoring for complications such as stent thrombosis or restenosis. Secondary endpoints might include patient-reported outcomes, such as improvements in chest pain or quality of life after the stent is implanted. These endpoints must be predefined in the trial protocol and are crucial for determining whether the device meets its intended clinical objectives.

In addition to performance endpoints, safety endpoints are a critical part of the evaluation. Safety endpoints often focus on potential risks associated with the device, such as device malfunction, infection, or other adverse events that could harm the patient. For instance, a clinical trial for an insulin pump might include safety endpoints related to device failures that could result in inaccurate insulin delivery, leading to hypoglycemia or hyperglycemia in patients. Monitoring safety endpoints throughout the trial helps ensure that any risks associated with the device are identified early and addressed before the device is approved for widespread use.

The selection of appropriate safety and performance endpoints is vital for ensuring that the clinical trial generates meaningful data. These endpoints provide the foundation for regulatory approval decisions, and the data collected must demonstrate that the device provides a clear clinical benefit while minimizing risks. If a device fails to meet its safety or performance endpoints, it may require further modifications and testing before it can be approved for use in patients.

8.3.3 Ethical Considerations in Medical Device Evaluation

The ethical considerations in the evaluation of medical devices are critical to ensuring that the rights, safety, and well-being of participants are protected throughout the clinical trial process. Just as with drug trials, medical device trials must adhere to ethical standards such as obtaining **informed consent** from participants, ensuring that they fully understand the risks and benefits of participating in the trial. For example, in a clinical trial for a new cochlear implant, participants would need to be informed of potential risks, such as surgical complications or device malfunction, and the trial's potential benefits. Informed consent ensures that participants voluntarily agree to participate with a full understanding of what the trial entails.

Additionally, **ethical review boards** or **Institutional Review Boards (IRBs)** are responsible for overseeing medical device trials to ensure that they meet ethical guidelines. These boards evaluate the trial protocol to confirm that it minimizes risks to participants, that the selection of participants is fair, and that vulnerable populations (such as children or individuals with disabilities) are protected from exploitation. For instance, a trial involving a pediatric ventilator device would require careful ethical review to ensure that the risks to children are minimized and that the trial is justified by the potential benefits. The role of the IRB is to ensure that ethical standards are maintained throughout the study, from participant recruitment to data collection and reporting.

Ethical considerations also extend to the **post-trial responsibilities** of device manufacturers, including the obligation to provide continued access to the device for participants if the trial demonstrates its efficacy. For example, if a clinical trial for a life-saving medical device shows that it significantly improves patient outcomes, the manufacturer may have an ethical responsibility to provide the device to participants after the trial ends, even before it receives full regulatory approval. Overall, ethical considerations are central to the clinical evaluation of medical devices, ensuring that patient safety is prioritized and that trials are conducted in a manner that respects the rights of all participants.

8.4 In-Vitro Diagnostics (IVD) Clinical Studies

8.4.1 Specific Requirements for IVD Clinical Trials

Clinical trials for **In-Vitro Diagnostics (IVDs)** have distinct requirements compared to those for other medical devices, due to the nature of their use in diagnosing diseases based on biological samples. IVDs are not typically used directly on or in the human body but are instead used in laboratories to analyze patient samples, such as blood or tissue. The primary focus of IVD clinical trials is to ensure the **accuracy, reliability, and reproducibility** of the diagnostic test. For example, a clinical trial for a new COVID-19 diagnostic test would need to demonstrate that the test accurately detects the virus in patient samples and that it produces consistent results across different laboratory settings.

One of the key challenges in IVD trials is selecting an appropriate patient population, as the test needs to be validated in both diseased and healthy individuals to confirm its specificity and sensitivity. **Specificity** refers to the test's ability to correctly identify individuals without the disease (i.e., avoiding false positives), while **sensitivity** refers to its ability to correctly identify those with the disease (i.e., avoiding false negatives). Regulatory agencies require IVD manufacturers to provide robust data showing that their tests meet these standards, particularly for high-stakes diagnostics like cancer screening tools or infectious disease tests. The clinical trial must be designed to evaluate the test in a variety of settings, using a diverse patient population, to ensure that it works as intended in real-world conditions.

In addition to performance metrics, IVD trials must also assess the **clinical utility** of the test, meaning whether the test provides information that improves patient care. For example, a genetic test for hereditary cancer risk may be accurate, but its clinical utility would depend on whether the information it provides leads to better preventive measures or treatments for patients. Therefore, IVD clinical trials not only focus on technical accuracy but also on the test's practical benefits in guiding healthcare decisions.

8.4.2 Study Design for IVDs

The study design for IVD clinical trials is tailored to assess both the technical performance of the diagnostic device and its impact on patient care. One of the most important aspects of IVD study design is ensuring that the trial includes a representative patient population that reflects the intended use of the test. For instance, in a trial for an IVD that screens for early-stage breast cancer, the study must include both healthy individuals and those with varying stages of breast cancer to assess the test's performance across a wide spectrum of cases. This helps ensure that the test is both sensitive to detecting disease and specific enough to avoid false positives in healthy individuals.

Another key consideration in the study design is the **reference standard** used to compare the IVD's results. The reference standard is typically the best available method for diagnosing the condition, such as a gold-standard laboratory test or a well-established clinical diagnostic procedure. For example, in a trial for a new IVD to detect diabetes, the reference standard might be the oral glucose tolerance test (OGTT), which is currently considered the most reliable method for diagnosing diabetes. The IVD's performance is then compared to the reference standard to determine how well it performs in identifying patients with and without the disease.

The study design must also account for variability in testing conditions, such as differences in laboratory environments or sample handling procedures. For instance, if an IVD is intended for use in remote or resource-limited settings, the clinical trial should include sites that reflect these conditions to ensure that the test performs consistently across different environments. By incorporating these elements into the study design, IVD trials can generate comprehensive data that demonstrates the test's reliability, accuracy, and usefulness in real-world clinical practice.

8.4.3 Regulatory Requirements for IVDs

The regulatory requirements for IVDs vary depending on the region, but most regulatory agencies follow a risk-based approach similar to that used for other medical devices. In the United States, the **FDA** classifies IVDs into three categories based on their risk level: Class I (low risk), Class II (moderate risk), and Class III (high risk). **Class III IVDs**, such as genetic tests for inherited diseases, require the most rigorous clinical evaluation, including data from well-designed clinical trials that demonstrate their safety, accuracy, and clinical utility. In the European Union, IVDs are regulated under the **In-Vitro Diagnostic Medical Device Regulation (IVDR)**, which requires manufacturers to demonstrate that their tests meet strict safety and performance standards before they can be marketed.

One of the unique regulatory challenges for IVDs is ensuring that they are **validated** for their intended use, meaning that the test must be shown to be effective in diagnosing the specific condition it is designed to detect. For example, a diagnostic test for HIV must be validated to ensure that it reliably detects HIV antibodies in patient samples, and it must be evaluated across different patient populations, including those with different stages of the disease or other comorbidities. Regulatory agencies require comprehensive data on the test's sensitivity, specificity, and clinical utility before granting marketing authorization.

Additionally, IVD manufacturers must implement post-market surveillance programs to monitor the ongoing performance of their tests once they are in widespread use. This includes collecting data on any **adverse events** associated with the test, such as inaccurate results that lead to incorrect diagnoses or unnecessary treatments. Regulatory agencies may require manufacturers to submit **Periodic Safety Update Reports (PSURs)** to ensure that the test continues to meet safety and performance standards over time. By adhering to these regulatory requirements, IVD manufacturers can ensure that their products provide reliable diagnostic information that improves patient care.

8.5 Key Concepts of Medical Device Clinical Evaluation

8.5.1 Clinical Performance vs. Safety Evaluation

In medical device clinical evaluations, both clinical performance and safety are key aspects that need to be rigorously assessed. **Clinical performance** refers to how effectively the device performs its intended function in real-world clinical settings, while **safety evaluation** focuses on identifying and mitigating any potential risks the device may pose to patients. For example, a clinical performance evaluation for a prosthetic heart valve would measure how well the valve helps maintain normal blood flow and heart function, while the safety evaluation would monitor for any adverse events, such as infections or blood clot formation. Balancing these two components is essential to ensure that the device offers meaningful clinical benefits without compromising patient safety.

The performance versus safety balance is critical because even devices that perform well in achieving their intended purpose could pose risks if they lead to harmful side effects or complications. For instance, a highly effective drug delivery device that introduces medication directly into the bloodstream might show excellent clinical performance, but if it causes frequent infections at the insertion site, its overall safety would be compromised. Regulators require manufacturers to demonstrate that the device provides sufficient clinical benefit to outweigh any potential risks. This is done through carefully designed clinical trials that assess both the performance of the device under various conditions and the safety outcomes over short- and long-term use.

8.5.2 Data Collection and Interpretation

The collection and interpretation of data in medical device trials are essential for providing evidence that the device is both safe and effective for its intended use. Data collection must be systematic and comprehensive, capturing a wide range of variables, such as the device's performance under different conditions, patient demographics, and any adverse events that occur during the trial. For instance, in a trial evaluating a new diagnostic device for detecting early-stage cancer, data on the device's sensitivity (the ability to correctly identify patients with cancer) and specificity (the ability to correctly identify those without cancer) would be collected. Such data would then be analyzed to determine whether the device meets regulatory standards for accuracy and reliability.

Interpretation of this data is a critical step in determining whether the device should be approved for market use. Statistical analyses are typically employed to assess whether the device's performance is statistically significant compared to existing alternatives or control groups. For example, data showing a statistically significant reduction in diagnostic errors compared to a standard diagnostic tool would strengthen the case for regulatory approval. Moreover, manufacturers must demonstrate that the data is robust and applicable to a wide range of real-world clinical scenarios. This means ensuring that the trial includes diverse patient populations and adequately reflects the intended use of the device in everyday medical practice.

8.6 Global Harmonization of Medical Device Regulations

8.6.1 Overview of the Global Harmonization Task Force (GHTF)

The **Global Harmonization Task Force (GHTF)** was established to streamline and harmonize medical device regulations across different countries, reducing the complexity and cost of bringing medical devices to the global market. The GHTF brought together regulators and industry representatives from regions such as the United States, Europe, Japan, Canada, and Australia to develop a common framework for the regulation of medical devices. One of the key outcomes of the GHTF's work was the development of guidelines for the classification of devices, clinical evaluation, and post-market surveillance. For example, the GHTF's classification system categorizes devices based on their risk, similar to the systems used by the FDA and EMA, ensuring that high-risk devices undergo more rigorous evaluation.

The GHTF's efforts have led to more consistent regulatory requirements across major markets, which has significantly benefited both manufacturers and regulatory bodies. For manufacturers, harmonization reduces the need to comply with multiple, often conflicting, regulatory systems, allowing them to bring products to the market more efficiently. For regulatory authorities, harmonized standards make it easier to assess the safety and performance of medical devices, especially those intended for global distribution. The work of the GHTF has since been continued by the

International Medical Device Regulators Forum (IMDRF), which builds on the GHTF's foundation and continues to promote regulatory convergence and cooperation among global regulatory bodies.

8.6.2 ISO 14155 Guidelines for Medical Device Trials

ISO 14155 is an internationally recognized standard that provides guidelines for the conduct of clinical investigations of medical devices for human subjects. These guidelines are essential for ensuring that medical device trials are conducted ethically and scientifically, with a focus on protecting the rights and safety of participants. The ISO 14155 standard covers all aspects of the clinical investigation process, including study design, protocol development, risk management, and data collection. For example, ISO 14155 requires that clinical trials include a clear risk-benefit assessment to ensure that the potential benefits of the device outweigh any risks posed to participants.

One of the key strengths of ISO 14155 is its emphasis on **Good Clinical Practice (GCP)**, which ensures that trials are conducted with the highest ethical standards. This includes obtaining informed consent from participants, maintaining confidentiality, and ensuring that the trial is scientifically sound. The guidelines also outline the responsibilities of the sponsor, investigator, and ethics committee, ensuring that each party plays a role in protecting the welfare of participants. By adhering to ISO 14155, manufacturers can ensure that their clinical trials meet the regulatory requirements of multiple regions, facilitating global approval of the device. The standard is widely accepted by regulatory authorities around the world, including the FDA, EMA, and CDSCO, making it an essential tool for manufacturers seeking to market their devices internationally.

8.6.3 Harmonization Efforts Across the EU, USA, and India

Harmonization of medical device regulations across the **European Union (EU)**, **United States (USA)**, and **India** has been an ongoing effort to create a more streamlined and efficient regulatory environment. In the EU, the **Medical Device Regulation (MDR)** provides a comprehensive framework for the regulation of devices, requiring rigorous clinical evaluation and post-market surveillance. Similarly, in the USA, the **FDA's Center for Devices and Radiological Health (CDRH)** regulates medical devices through a risk-based approach, classifying devices into three categories based on their potential risks. Both regions aim to ensure that devices are safe, effective, and of high quality, with a strong emphasis on clinical data to support regulatory approval.

In India, the **Central Drugs Standard Control Organization (CDSCO)** has been working to align its medical device regulations with international standards, including those set by the GHTF and ISO 14155. India's regulatory framework for medical devices now includes risk-based classification, clinical evaluation, and post-market surveillance, similar to the systems used in the EU and USA. This harmonization has made it easier for manufacturers to market their devices in multiple regions without the need to navigate vastly different regulatory systems. For example, a device approved under the MDR in the EU can now undergo a more streamlined approval process in India, thanks to the alignment of regulatory standards. These efforts toward harmonization not only benefit manufacturers by reducing regulatory burdens but also enhance patient safety by ensuring that devices meet consistent, high standards across all regions.

Review Questions

1. What are the key differences between drug and medical device clinical trials?
2. How do regulatory pathways for medical devices differ from those for drugs?
3. What are the key concepts involved in clinical evaluation of medical devices?
4. How do in-vitro diagnostics (IVD) differ from medical devices in clinical trials?
5. What ethical considerations are specific to medical device trials?
6. How does the Global Harmonization Task Force (GHTF) influence medical device regulations?
7. What are ISO 14155 guidelines, and how do they apply to medical device trials?
8. Discuss the challenges faced in the clinical investigation of medical devices.

CHAPTER NINE

Historical Perspectives on Ethics in Clinical Research

9.1 The Nuremberg Code

9.1.1 Background and Development of the Nuremberg Code

The **Nuremberg Code** was developed in the aftermath of the **Nuremberg Trials**, which took place after World War II to bring Nazi war criminals to justice, particularly those involved in unethical medical experiments on concentration camp prisoners. These experiments, often conducted without consent and under horrific conditions, highlighted the need for ethical guidelines to protect human subjects in medical research. The trials led to the creation of the Nuremberg Code in 1947, a set of 10 principles designed to ensure the protection of individuals participating in clinical research. The Code emphasized the need for **voluntary consent** from participants, a concept that was revolutionary at the time and has since become a cornerstone of modern research ethics.

The Code was not legally binding, but it set the groundwork for future ethical guidelines and regulations. It was one of the first documents to outline specific standards for ethical medical research, and it was largely motivated by the atrocities committed by the Nazis in the name of scientific progress. The Code also emphasized the need for researchers to minimize harm to participants, stating that the risk of harm must be justified by the potential benefit of the research. This principle, too, has become a fundamental aspect of modern clinical trials.

While the Nuremberg Code was initially focused on the unethical practices of the Nazi regime, its influence quickly spread across the globe. Researchers and regulatory bodies in various countries began to adopt its principles, and it has since been recognized as one of the most important documents in the history of medical ethics. Though later documents, such as the **Declaration of Helsinki**, would expand on its guidelines, the Nuremberg Code remains a foundational document in the development of ethical standards for clinical research.

9.1.2 Ethical Principles Established by the Nuremberg Code

The **Nuremberg Code** laid out 10 key principles that continue to guide ethical clinical research today. One of the most important of these principles is the requirement for **voluntary informed consent**, meaning that participants must be fully aware of the nature of the study, its potential risks, and their right to withdraw at any time. This was a direct response to the Nazi experiments, in which prisoners were subjected to harmful procedures without any form of consent. The Code also established the need for research to be conducted with the **aim of benefiting society**, emphasizing that scientific progress must not come at the expense of human dignity or safety.

Another key principle of the Nuremberg Code is the requirement to minimize harm and ensure that the risks involved in the research are justified by the potential benefits. This principle is closely tied to the idea of **beneficence**, which later became one of the core ethical guidelines in documents like the **Belmont Report**. The Nuremberg Code also asserts that researchers must be **qualified** to conduct their studies, and that studies should be discontinued if it becomes clear that they pose undue risk to participants. These principles ensure that the safety and well-being of research subjects remain the highest priority throughout the course of the study.

The Code also emphasized that human experimentation should be conducted only when no alternative methods (such as animal studies) are available. Moreover, it stressed that the degree of risk should never exceed the humanitarian importance of the problem the research seeks to address. By setting these ethical boundaries, the Nuremberg Code sought to prevent the kind of reckless and dangerous research that had characterized the Nazi experiments. These principles continue to be fundamental in modern ethical discussions surrounding clinical research.

9.1.3 Impact on Modern Clinical Research Ethics

The influence of the **Nuremberg Code** on modern clinical research ethics cannot be overstated. It was the first document to clearly articulate the need for **informed consent**, a principle that is now considered a legal and ethical requirement in most countries. The Code's insistence on protecting the rights and well-being of research participants has been reflected in subsequent ethical guidelines, such as the **Declaration of Helsinki** and the **Belmont Report**, which have expanded on the Nuremberg Code's basic principles and provided more detailed frameworks for ensuring ethical research practices.

One of the most significant impacts of the Nuremberg Code is the establishment of **Institutional Review Boards (IRBs)**, also known as **Ethics Committees**, which are now mandatory for most clinical trials. These committees are responsible for reviewing research proposals to ensure that they adhere to ethical standards and that participants are adequately protected from harm. The formation of IRBs was a direct response to the abuses that occurred during the Nazi experiments, and their presence helps to ensure that clinical research is conducted in an ethical and responsible manner.

The principles of the Nuremberg Code also laid the groundwork for international ethical guidelines, influencing regulatory bodies like the **World Medical Association (WMA)** and the **International Conference on Harmonisation (ICH)**. Today, the Code's emphasis on voluntary participation, the minimization of harm, and the importance of societal benefit are embedded in the laws and regulations that govern clinical research worldwide. While the Nuremberg Code may have been born out of tragedy, its legacy has shaped the ethical framework that ensures the protection of human subjects in research today.

9.2 The Thalidomide Study and Its Impact

9.2.1 Overview of the Thalidomide Disaster

The **Thalidomide disaster** of the 1950s and 1960s remains one of the most infamous examples of the dangers of insufficient drug testing and inadequate regulatory oversight. Thalidomide was originally marketed as a **sedative and treatment for morning sickness** in pregnant women, but its devastating side effects were not initially recognized. Thousands of babies were born with severe birth defects, such as **phocomelia** (limb malformations), because the drug had not been adequately tested for safety during pregnancy. The extent of the damage caused by Thalidomide was widespread, affecting families across Europe, Canada, and other parts of the world, and it brought to light the critical need for rigorous testing and ethical standards in clinical research.

The Thalidomide tragedy occurred partly because the drug was marketed without adequate safety testing, particularly for its effects on pregnant women. Regulatory agencies at the time did not have stringent requirements for clinical trials, allowing the drug to be sold without proper evidence of its safety. The disaster became a turning point in the field of clinical research, prompting governments and regulatory agencies to overhaul their drug approval processes. In many countries, including the United States, new regulations were introduced to ensure that drugs were thoroughly tested for safety and efficacy before being approved for market use.

This tragedy also highlighted the critical role of **pharmacovigilance**, the process of monitoring the safety of drugs after they have been approved and marketed. The Thalidomide disaster demonstrated that even after a drug is approved, it is essential to continue monitoring its effects, particularly in vulnerable populations such as pregnant women. This led to the establishment of more robust post-marketing surveillance systems, designed to detect adverse effects that may not have been evident during initial trials.

9.2.2 Changes in Regulations Following Thalidomide

In the wake of the Thalidomide disaster, significant changes were made to **drug regulation and clinical trial practices** around the world. In the United States, the **Kefauver-Harris Amendment** to the **Food, Drug, and Cosmetic Act** was passed in 1962, which required drug manufacturers to provide substantial evidence of both safety and efficacy through well-controlled clinical trials before a drug could be marketed. This marked a major shift from the previous system, where drugs could be marketed without robust clinical data supporting their safety. The **U.S. Food and Drug Administration (FDA)** gained new powers to oversee clinical trials and enforce these regulations, ensuring that future drugs would undergo more stringent testing before being made available to the public.

Similar regulatory reforms were adopted in Europe and other parts of the world. The **European Medicines Agency (EMA)** and other national regulatory bodies strengthened their requirements for clinical trials, particularly for drugs that would be used by vulnerable populations such as pregnant women. These changes aimed to prevent future tragedies like Thalidomide by ensuring that all drugs were tested rigorously in a controlled and ethical manner. One key lesson from Thalidomide was the importance of including all relevant populations in clinical trials to fully understand the risks and benefits of a drug.

These regulatory changes also led to the development of new ethical guidelines, such as the **Declaration of Helsinki**, which emphasized the need for ethical oversight and the protection of vulnerable populations in clinical research. Today, these guidelines form the foundation of ethical clinical research, ensuring that drugs are tested rigorously and that participants are fully informed about the potential risks and benefits of participating in a clinical trial.

9.2.3 Lessons Learned in Clinical Research Ethics

The Thalidomide disaster left an indelible mark on the field of **clinical research ethics**, highlighting the dangers of rushing drugs to market without sufficient testing and oversight. One of the key lessons learned was the importance of **informed consent**, ensuring that participants in clinical trials are fully aware of the potential risks associated with the study. In the case of Thalidomide, pregnant women were not informed of the possible dangers the drug posed to their unborn children, a failure that led to thousands of tragic outcomes. Modern clinical research now places a strong emphasis on informed consent, making sure that participants have all the information they need to make an educated decision about whether to participate.

Another crucial lesson was the need for **comprehensive testing**, particularly for drugs intended for use in vulnerable populations such as pregnant women. The Thalidomide disaster underscored the importance of conducting rigorous preclinical and clinical trials to assess the safety of drugs in all relevant populations before they are approved for market use. Today, regulatory agencies require that drugs undergo extensive testing in animals and humans, including specific studies to assess their effects on pregnancy and fetal development, before they can be approved for use in pregnant women.

Finally, the Thalidomide tragedy demonstrated the importance of **post-marketing surveillance** in detecting and responding to adverse drug reactions that may not be evident during initial clinical trials. The disaster prompted the development of more robust pharmacovigilance systems, ensuring that drugs continue to be monitored for safety even after they have been approved for use. This ongoing surveillance is essential for protecting patients and preventing future tragedies like Thalidomide, where unforeseen side effects can cause widespread harm.

9.3 The Nazi Trials and Their Ethical Legacy

9.3.1 Ethical Violations During Nazi Medical Experiments

The **Nazi medical experiments** during World War II represent some of the most egregious violations of ethical standards in the history of medicine. These experiments were conducted on concentration camp prisoners without their consent and often involved extreme forms of torture, mutilation, and in many cases, death. The experiments covered a wide range of areas, including hypothermia studies, infectious disease research, and surgical procedures, many of which had no scientific merit and were designed to cause suffering. For example, some prisoners were subjected to freezing temperatures to study hypothermia, while others were exposed to infectious diseases or underwent forced surgeries without anesthesia. The human subjects had no autonomy or choice, and the cruelty of these experiments shocked the world when they were revealed after the war.

These experiments were carried out under the guise of scientific advancement, but they were largely motivated by Nazi ideology, which dehumanized certain populations and justified their exploitation for research. The **Nuremberg Trials** brought these horrific practices to light, leading to the prosecution of many doctors and researchers involved in the experiments. The trials not only sought justice for the victims but also served as a catalyst for establishing new ethical guidelines to prevent such atrocities from happening again. The sheer scale of the ethical violations committed during the Nazi medical experiments made it clear that a framework was needed to protect human subjects in research and to ensure that science is conducted with integrity and respect for human dignity.

The legacy of these experiments forced the global medical community to confront the darker side of scientific research and to recognize the need for ethical oversight in clinical trials. The ethical violations committed during the Nazi era underscored the importance of obtaining **informed consent**, ensuring **voluntary participation**, and minimizing harm to research subjects. These principles would later form the basis of modern ethical guidelines, including the **Nuremberg Code**, which was developed in direct response to the atrocities committed during the war.

9.3.2 Contributions to Global Ethics Standards

The **Nuremberg Trials**, which exposed the horrors of Nazi medical experimentation, were instrumental in shaping the global standards for research ethics. The trials resulted in the **Nuremberg Code**, a foundational document that established key principles for conducting ethical medical research. Among its most important contributions was the emphasis on **voluntary informed consent** as an essential requirement for all human subjects research. This principle ensures that participants are fully aware of the risks involved in a study and are free to choose whether or not to participate without any coercion. The concept of informed consent, which was severely violated during the Nazi experiments, became central to the ethical conduct of research following the Nuremberg Trials.

The Nuremberg Code also introduced the idea that researchers have a moral obligation to minimize harm and ensure that the potential benefits of the research justify the risks involved. This principle, known as **beneficence**, is now a key component of many modern ethical frameworks, including the **Belmont Report** and the **Declaration of Helsinki**. The emphasis on minimizing harm was particularly important in light of the Nazi experiments, which often caused immense suffering and had no therapeutic or scientific value. The Nuremberg Code made it clear that research must prioritize the well-being of participants and must not be conducted simply for the sake of scientific curiosity or political agendas.

The ethical standards established by the Nuremberg Code have since been adopted and expanded upon by international organizations, including the **World Medical Association (WMA)** and the **World Health Organization (WHO)**. These organizations have worked to ensure that the lessons learned from the Nazi experiments are not forgotten and that human subjects are protected from exploitation in all future research endeavors. The ethical legacy of the Nazi Trials continues to influence clinical research regulations worldwide, ensuring that the rights and dignity of research participants are upheld at all times.

9.3.3 The Role of the Trials in Shaping Clinical Trial Regulations

The **Nuremberg Trials** played a pivotal role in shaping modern clinical trial regulations by highlighting the need for strict ethical oversight in medical research. One of the key outcomes of the trials was the establishment of formal processes for ethical review, including the development of **Institutional Review Boards (IRBs)**, which are now a standard requirement for clinical trials worldwide. IRBs are responsible for reviewing research proposals to ensure that they meet ethical standards and that participants are adequately protected from harm. This system of oversight was developed in direct response to the lack of accountability and oversight that allowed the Nazi experiments to occur. By requiring independent review and approval of clinical trials, IRBs help ensure that research is conducted ethically and responsibly.

The trials also contributed to the development of stricter regulatory frameworks for clinical research. In many countries, including the United States and the European Union, regulatory agencies such as the **FDA** and **EMA** now require that clinical trials meet rigorous ethical and scientific standards before they can proceed. These agencies have established guidelines that ensure trials are conducted in a way that protects participants and ensures the validity of the research. For example, researchers must demonstrate that their studies are designed to minimize risks, that participants provide informed consent, and that the research has the potential to benefit society. These regulations, which were influenced by the lessons of the Nuremberg Trials, help to ensure that clinical trials are conducted with the highest ethical standards.

Moreover, the ethical principles established during the Nuremberg Trials continue to influence international agreements on research ethics, such as the **Declaration of Helsinki** and the **International Conference on Harmonisation (ICH)** guidelines. These documents build on the foundation laid by the Nuremberg Code, providing detailed guidance on how to conduct ethical research in a global context. By incorporating the lessons of the past into modern regulations, the legacy of the Nuremberg Trials ensures that future clinical trials are conducted with respect for human rights and a commitment to ethical standards.

9.4 The Tuskegee Syphilis Study

9.4.1 The Tuskegee Syphilis Study: A Case of Unethical Research

The **Tuskegee Syphilis Study**, conducted between 1932 and 1972 in the United States, is one of the most notorious examples of unethical research in modern history. The study involved 600 African American men, 399 of whom had syphilis, while the remaining 201 served as a control group. The men were told they were receiving free medical care for their "bad blood," a term used to describe various illnesses, but they were never informed that they had syphilis or that they were being used as part of a study to observe the natural progression of the disease. Worse still, when **penicillin** became the standard treatment for syphilis in the 1940s, the researchers withheld this life-saving treatment from the participants, allowing them to suffer and die from the disease without their knowledge or consent.

The Tuskegee study is a stark example of the **violation of informed consent**, as the participants were never made aware of the true nature of the study or the risks involved. They were not given the option to receive proper treatment, nor were they informed about the available cure. Instead, they were subjected to unethical experimentation under the guise of receiving medical care. This deception caused immense harm to the participants and their families, as many of the men passed the disease to their spouses, and some of their children were born with congenital syphilis.

The unethical nature of the study was compounded by the fact that it targeted a vulnerable population—poor African American men with limited access to healthcare. The study took advantage of their socio-economic status and lack of medical knowledge, perpetuating systemic racism in the healthcare system. The revelations about the Tuskegee Syphilis Study in 1972 shocked the nation and led to widespread public outrage, ultimately resulting in significant reforms in the way clinical research is conducted.

9.4.2 Long-Term Effects on Minority Groups and Trust in Research

The Tuskegee Syphilis Study had long-lasting effects on minority groups in the United States, particularly African Americans, many of whom developed a deep mistrust of the medical and research communities as a result of the study's unethical conduct. The fact that the U.S. government had sanctioned the study, and that it continued for 40 years without intervention, fueled suspicions that medical research often exploited minority populations for unethical purposes. This mistrust extended beyond the study itself, affecting how minority communities viewed healthcare professionals, medical institutions, and clinical research as a whole. Many African Americans became hesitant to participate in clinical trials or to seek medical care, fearing they might be subjected to similar abuses.

The legacy of the Tuskegee Syphilis Study has been particularly damaging in the context of public health initiatives and medical advancements. For example, efforts to recruit minority populations into clinical trials have often faced resistance due to lingering suspicions stemming from the Tuskegee study. This mistrust has led to the **underrepresentation of minority groups in clinical trials**, which has significant implications for the development of treatments and drugs that are effective across diverse populations. Without adequate representation, the results of clinical trials may not be generalizable to all racial and ethnic groups, potentially leading to health disparities in the effectiveness of new treatments.

Efforts have been made to rebuild trust between minority communities and the medical research field. Public apologies, such as the one issued by President Bill Clinton in 1997, and the establishment of **Institutional Review Boards (IRBs)** have helped ensure that clinical research today is conducted ethically and with respect for the rights of participants. However, the scars left by the Tuskegee Syphilis Study remain, and the medical community continues to face challenges in overcoming the legacy of mistrust that the study has created. Addressing this mistrust is crucial for ensuring that all populations have equal access to the benefits of medical research.

9.4.3 Ethical Reforms in Clinical Research Post-Tuskegee

The exposure of the Tuskegee Syphilis Study led to a series of critical reforms in the field of clinical research, aimed at preventing future ethical violations and ensuring the protection of research participants. One of the most significant outcomes of the Tuskegee scandal was the establishment of the **National Research Act of 1974**, which mandated the creation of **Institutional Review Boards (IRBs)** to oversee all research involving human subjects. IRBs are responsible for reviewing research protocols to ensure that they meet ethical standards, that participants provide informed consent, and that the risks involved are minimized. This oversight mechanism has become a cornerstone of ethical research, helping to prevent the kinds of abuses that occurred during the Tuskegee study.

Another major reform was the development of the **Belmont Report** in 1979, which outlined three fundamental ethical principles to guide human subjects research: **Respect for Persons, Beneficence**, and **Justice**. These principles emphasize the importance of informed consent, the need to maximize benefits while minimizing harm, and the fair distribution of the risks and benefits of research across all segments of society. The Belmont Report has had a profound influence on the ethical standards that govern clinical research today, ensuring that the rights and dignity of participants are protected.

The Tuskegee study also prompted significant changes in the way the U.S. government regulates clinical research. Today, federal agencies such as the **Office for Human Research Protections (OHRP)** and the **FDA** are tasked with enforcing ethical standards in clinical trials, ensuring that research is conducted responsibly and with full transparency. These reforms have helped restore some degree of trust in the medical research community, though the legacy of Tuskegee continues to remind us of the importance of maintaining strict ethical standards in all aspects of clinical research.

9.5 The Belmont Report

9.5.1 Core Principles: Respect for Persons, Beneficence, Justice

The **Belmont Report**, published in 1979, is a seminal document in the history of clinical research ethics, outlining three fundamental principles that guide the ethical conduct of research involving human subjects: **Respect for Persons, Beneficence**, and **Justice**. The principle of **Respect for Persons** emphasizes the importance of treating individuals as autonomous agents who have the right to make informed decisions about their participation in research. This principle requires that participants give **informed consent**, fully understanding the risks and benefits of the study before agreeing to take part. For individuals with diminished autonomy, such as children or the mentally ill, the Belmont Report stresses the need for additional protections to ensure their safety and well-being in research contexts.

The principle of **Beneficence** requires researchers to maximize the potential benefits of the research while minimizing the risks to participants. This principle is closely linked to the idea of doing no harm and ensuring that the well-being of the research subjects is prioritized. For example, in a clinical trial, researchers must carefully balance the need for scientific advancement with the ethical obligation to protect participants from unnecessary harm. The third principle, **Justice**, focuses on the fair distribution of the benefits and burdens of research. It seeks to prevent the exploitation of vulnerable populations by ensuring that all groups, regardless of race, gender, or socioeconomic status, have equal access to the benefits of research and are not disproportionately burdened by its risks.

9.5.2 Application of Belmont Principles to Clinical Research

The principles outlined in the **Belmont Report** have had a profound impact on how clinical research is conducted, providing a clear ethical framework that has been integrated into regulatory guidelines and research practices worldwide. **Informed consent**, a key element of the Respect for Persons principle, has become a legal and ethical requirement for all clinical trials.

Researchers must provide participants with comprehensive information about the study, including its purpose, procedures, risks, and benefits, and must ensure that participants voluntarily agree to take part without coercion. The Belmont Report's emphasis on **Beneficence** has also led to stricter safety protocols in clinical trials, with researchers required to minimize risks and ensure that the potential benefits of the study outweigh any potential harm.

The principle of **Justice** has influenced how researchers select participants for clinical trials, emphasizing the need for fair inclusion of diverse populations. In the past, clinical research often excluded certain groups, such as women, minorities, and the elderly, leading to a lack of data on how treatments affect these populations. The Belmont Report has helped to address these disparities by promoting the inclusion of all relevant groups in clinical research and ensuring that the risks and benefits of research are distributed equitably. This principle has also led to the development of ethical review boards, such as **Institutional Review Boards (IRBs)**, which are tasked with reviewing research proposals to ensure that they meet the ethical standards set out in the Belmont Report. These boards play a critical role in protecting the rights and well-being of research participants.

9.6 The Declaration of Helsinki

9.6.1 Introduction to the Declaration of Helsinki

The **Declaration of Helsinki**, first adopted by the **World Medical Association (WMA)** in 1964, is one of the most important international documents governing the ethics of clinical research. It was created in response to the ethical violations that occurred during World War II, particularly the Nazi medical experiments, and sought to provide clear guidelines for conducting medical research involving human subjects. The Declaration has since been revised several times, with the most recent update in 2013, reflecting the evolving nature of clinical research and the need to adapt ethical standards to new challenges. It serves as a comprehensive framework that emphasizes the need for **informed consent**, the protection of vulnerable populations, and the importance of ensuring that the benefits of research outweigh the risks.

One of the key contributions of the Declaration of Helsinki is its emphasis on the well-being of research participants as the primary consideration in any clinical trial. It asserts that the interests of science and society should never take precedence over the rights and safety of individual participants. The Declaration also requires that all research involving human subjects be subjected to independent **ethical review** by a committee, such as an **Institutional Review Board (IRB)**, to ensure that the study is ethically sound and that participants are adequately protected. These guidelines have had a profound impact on global research practices, influencing both national regulations and the policies of international organizations such as the **World Health Organization (WHO)** and the **International Conference on Harmonisation (ICH)**.

9.6.2 Key Ethical Guidelines from the Declaration

The **Declaration of Helsinki** outlines several key ethical guidelines that have become integral to the conduct of modern clinical research. One of the most important of these guidelines is the requirement for **informed consent**. According to the Declaration, participants must be fully informed about the nature of the study, its objectives, the procedures involved, and the potential risks and benefits. This ensures that participants can make an autonomous decision about whether to participate, free from coercion or undue influence. Additionally, the Declaration emphasizes that consent must be obtained in writing, and participants must be informed of their right to withdraw from the study at any time without facing any negative consequences.

Another critical guideline from the Declaration is the protection of **vulnerable populations**, such as children, pregnant women, and individuals with mental disabilities. These groups are considered to be at greater risk of exploitation in research, and the Declaration of Helsinki mandates that they receive special protections to ensure that their participation is both ethical and voluntary. The Declaration also stresses the importance of conducting research that has a favorable **risk-benefit ratio**, meaning that the potential benefits of the research must outweigh the risks to participants. Researchers are required to continuously monitor the safety of participants throughout the study and to terminate the research if it becomes clear that the risks are too great. These guidelines have been instrumental in promoting ethical research practices and protecting the rights of research participants worldwide.

Review Questions

1. How did the Thalidomide disaster influence global drug regulations?
2. What were the ethical violations in the Nazi medical experiments, and how did they contribute to modern research ethics?
3. How did the Tuskegee Syphilis Study impact minority groups' trust in medical research?
4. What are the core principles of the Belmont Report, and how do they apply to clinical research today?
5. Explain the relevance of the Declaration of Helsinki in modern clinical trials.
6. How have historical ethical violations shaped the ethical guidelines we follow today?
7. What lessons were learned from historical unethical studies, and how do they influence current regulations?

CHAPTER TEN

The Belmont Report and Declaration of Helsinki

10.1 Historical Context of the Belmont Report

10.1.1 Development of the Belmont Report
The **Belmont Report** was developed in 1979 by the **National Commission for the Protection of Human Subjects of Biomedical and Behavioral Research** in the United States. It was commissioned in response to growing concerns about unethical practices in clinical research, especially following the exposure of the **Tuskegee Syphilis Study**. The development of the Belmont Report marked a significant turning point in research ethics, as it sought to address the lack of formal ethical guidelines that had previously allowed for abuses in human subjects research. It provided a clear framework for conducting ethical research and protecting participants' rights. The report was named after the Belmont Conference Center, where the discussions took place, and it has since become one of the most influential documents in the field of clinical research ethics.

The creation of the Belmont Report was motivated by the need to establish universal principles that could be applied across various types of research involving human subjects. The report was developed through a series of meetings, public hearings, and consultations with experts in ethics, law, medicine, and science. The commission worked to distill the fundamental ethical issues involved in research and to provide guidelines that could be easily understood and implemented by researchers. The focus was on protecting individuals who participate in research while promoting scientific advancement in a way that respects human dignity. The principles laid out in the report—**Respect for Persons, Beneficence**, and **Justice**—have since become the cornerstone of research ethics worldwide.

The Belmont Report was groundbreaking not only because of its content but also because of the collaborative process that led to its development. It brought together stakeholders from diverse fields to ensure that the guidelines it proposed were both practical and ethically sound. This collaborative approach helped to ensure that the report was widely accepted and implemented across a broad range of research disciplines. The report's recommendations were incorporated into federal regulations governing human subjects research, and they continue to serve as the ethical foundation for research oversight today.

10.1.2 The Belmont Report as a Response to Unethical Research

The **Belmont Report** was developed as a direct response to unethical research practices that had taken place over the preceding decades, most notably the **Tuskegee Syphilis Study**. This study, which ran from 1932 to 1972, involved the deliberate withholding of treatment from African American men with syphilis, even after penicillin became widely available as a cure. The participants were misled about the nature of the study and were not provided with adequate information to give informed consent. The public outcry that followed the exposure of the study in the 1970s prompted widespread calls for reform in the way clinical research was conducted, leading to the creation of the National Commission and, eventually, the Belmont Report.

The Tuskegee Syphilis Study was just one of several cases of unethical research that came to light during this period. Other notorious examples include the **Willowbrook Hepatitis Study**, in which mentally disabled children were deliberately infected with hepatitis to study the progression of the disease, and the **Milgram Experiment**, which subjected participants to psychological distress without their full understanding of the study's nature. These studies, and others like them, highlighted the need for clear ethical guidelines to protect research participants from harm and to ensure that they were treated with dignity and respect. The Belmont Report was developed in response to these concerns, providing a framework that could prevent such abuses from occurring in the future.

The ethical principles outlined in the Belmont Report were designed to address the specific issues that had arisen in previous unethical studies. For example, the principle of **Respect for Persons** was developed to ensure that individuals have the right to make informed decisions about whether to participate in research, a right that had been violated in studies like

Tuskegee and Willowbrook. Similarly, the principle of **Beneficence** was introduced to ensure that researchers take steps to minimize harm and maximize benefits to participants, addressing the disregard for participant welfare that had characterized many earlier studies.

10.1.3 Ongoing Relevance of Belmont Principles

The principles outlined in the **Belmont Report** continue to be highly relevant in modern clinical research. Despite advancements in medical technology and changes in the regulatory landscape, the fundamental ethical issues addressed by the Belmont Report remain the same. Informed consent, risk-benefit analysis, and the fair selection of research subjects are still critical concerns in clinical trials and other types of research involving human participants. The Belmont principles are embedded in the regulations that govern research in the United States, including the **Common Rule**, which provides guidelines for the protection of human subjects and requires that all research funded by federal agencies adhere to these ethical standards.

In recent years, the growing complexity of clinical research, particularly in areas like **genomics, biobanking**, and **artificial intelligence**, has raised new ethical questions that the Belmont principles help to address. For example, the principle of **Respect for Persons** is critical in ensuring that participants in genomic studies understand how their genetic information will be used and that they have the option to withdraw their data if they choose. Similarly, the principle of **Justice** ensures that the benefits of research are shared equitably across different populations, preventing the exploitation of vulnerable groups. These principles provide a strong ethical foundation that can be applied to new and emerging areas of research.

The **global nature of clinical research** today also underscores the ongoing relevance of the Belmont Report. As research increasingly involves participants from different countries and cultural backgrounds, the need for universal ethical standards becomes even more important. The Belmont principles have been adopted in various forms by international organizations and regulatory agencies, ensuring that the rights and welfare of research participants are protected regardless of where the research takes place. While new ethical challenges will undoubtedly continue to arise, the core principles of the Belmont Report provide a framework that can guide ethical decision-making in a wide range of research contexts.

10.2 Core Ethical Principles of the Belmont Report

10.2.1 Respect for Persons: Informed Consent and Autonomy

The principle of **Respect for Persons** is one of the three core ethical principles outlined in the Belmont Report and serves as the foundation for the concept of **informed consent**. This principle emphasizes the need to treat individuals as autonomous agents who have the right to make decisions about their participation in research based on full and accurate information. Informed consent is the process by which researchers provide potential participants with detailed information about the study, including its purpose, procedures, risks, and benefits, allowing individuals to make an informed choice about whether to participate. Participants must be free to withdraw from the study at any time without facing any negative consequences, and they must be given adequate time and support to consider their decision.

Autonomy is central to the concept of Respect for Persons, as it recognizes the right of individuals to make decisions about their own lives, free from coercion or undue influence. In clinical research, this means that participants must not be pressured or manipulated into taking part in a study, and they must be provided with all the information they need to understand the potential risks and benefits of the research. For vulnerable populations, such as children or individuals with cognitive impairments, additional protections must be in place to ensure that their rights are respected, and that their participation in research is truly voluntary.

10.2.2 Beneficence: Risk-Benefit Assessment in Research

The principle of **Beneficence** requires researchers to maximize the potential benefits of their research while minimizing the risks to participants. This principle is grounded in the ethical obligation to "do no harm" and to ensure that the well-being of research subjects is always the primary concern. In practice, this means that researchers must carefully design their studies to minimize potential harm, whether physical, psychological, or emotional. For example, in a clinical trial testing a new drug, researchers must ensure that the drug is likely to be safe for participants and that any risks are outweighed by the potential benefits of the treatment.

One of the key elements of Beneficence is the **risk-benefit analysis**, which is conducted during the planning stages of a study to assess whether the potential benefits of the research justify the risks involved. This analysis takes into account factors such as the likelihood of adverse events, the severity of those events, and the potential benefits to participants and society as a whole. If the risks are deemed too high or if the benefits are not clear, the study may be modified or rejected by an **Institutional Review Board (IRB)**. This process ensures that research is conducted in a manner that protects participants and promotes the advancement of science in an ethically responsible way.

10.2.3 Justice: Fair Selection of Research Subjects

The principle of **Justice** in the Belmont Report focuses on the fair and equitable selection of research participants, ensuring that no group is unfairly burdened or excluded from the benefits of research. This principle was developed in response to historical examples of exploitation in clinical research, such as the Tuskegee Syphilis Study, in which African American men were disproportionately affected by unethical research practices. Justice requires that researchers ensure the fair distribution of the risks and benefits of research across all groups in society. This means that vulnerable populations, such as the poor or marginalized communities, should not be disproportionately targeted for high-risk studies simply because they are easier to recruit.

Conversely, Justice also requires that all populations, including women, minorities, and older adults, be adequately represented in clinical research so that the benefits of new treatments and therapies are available to everyone. In the past, certain groups were often excluded from clinical trials, leading to a lack of data on how new treatments might affect them. This has been a particular issue for women and minority groups, who may respond differently to treatments than the populations traditionally included in clinical trials. The principle of Justice ensures that research is conducted in a way that benefits all members of society and that no group is unfairly excluded from the potential benefits of scientific advancements.

10.3 mplementation of the Belmont Principles

10.3.1 Informed Consent Processes

The implementation of **informed consent** is one of the most critical applications of the Belmont Report's principle of **Respect for Persons**. In clinical research, informed consent requires that participants be provided with comprehensive information about the study, including its objectives, procedures, risks, benefits, and their right to withdraw at any time. This process is not a one-time event but a continuous dialogue between the researcher and the participant, ensuring that consent is truly informed and voluntarily given. The information must be presented in a way that is understandable to participants, taking into account their level of education and comprehension. In cases involving vulnerable populations, such as children or cognitively impaired individuals, special measures must be taken to ensure that their participation is ethically sound, including obtaining consent from a legal guardian or using simplified explanations tailored to the participant's understanding.

Ensuring that informed consent is properly obtained and documented is a responsibility shared by both researchers and **Institutional Review Boards (IRBs)**. IRBs are tasked with reviewing the informed consent forms and processes to ensure that they meet ethical standards. In some cases, particularly in studies with minimal risk, informed consent procedures may be streamlined, but they must always prioritize the autonomy and rights of the participant. Informed consent is also an ongoing process, meaning that participants should be regularly updated if new information arises during the study that could affect their willingness to continue participating. This ensures transparency and maintains trust between researchers and participants, which is vital for ethical research.

10.3.2 Ensuring Beneficence in Clinical Research

To ensure **beneficence** in clinical research, investigators must carefully assess the **risk-benefit ratio** of their studies, ensuring that the potential benefits to participants and society outweigh any risks involved. The Belmont Report emphasizes that research should not expose participants to unnecessary harm, and all risks must be minimized as much as possible. This principle guides the design of clinical trials, where researchers must anticipate and mitigate any potential risks, such as adverse drug reactions or invasive procedures. For example, a study testing a new chemotherapy drug must carefully balance the potential therapeutic benefits against the known risks of toxicity, and participants must be fully informed of these risks as part of the consent process.

IRBs play a crucial role in ensuring beneficence by reviewing study protocols before a trial begins, assessing whether the risks are justified by the expected benefits. They also monitor ongoing trials to ensure that the safety of participants is upheld, and if serious adverse events occur, the study may be modified or halted. Researchers are also responsible for ongoing safety monitoring, which includes reporting any unexpected harms to the IRB and adjusting the study design to prevent further risks. By adhering to the principle of beneficence, researchers not only protect participants from harm but also enhance the ethical validity of their studies, ensuring that scientific progress is achieved without compromising human well-being.

10.4 The Declaration of Helsinki: Overview

10.4.1 Background and History of the Declaration

The **Declaration of Helsinki** was developed by the **World Medical Association (WMA)** in 1964 as a direct response to the ethical violations that occurred during World War II, particularly the Nazi medical experiments. It was created to provide a more comprehensive ethical framework for conducting medical research involving human subjects, building on earlier guidelines such as the **Nuremberg Code**. While the Nuremberg Code addressed basic ethical principles, the Declaration of Helsinki expanded on these, offering more detailed guidance on informed consent, risk management, and the rights of research participants. Over the years, the Declaration has been revised multiple times to reflect changes in medical research practices and emerging ethical challenges. The most recent version was adopted in 2013, further strengthening its role as a global standard for ethical research.

The Declaration of Helsinki is notable for its emphasis on the **well-being of research participants** over the interests of science or society. It states that the safety, dignity, and rights of individuals participating in clinical trials must always take precedence, even if this limits the potential benefits of the research. This principle has had a profound influence on national and international regulations governing clinical research, including the guidelines used by the **FDA, EMA,** and **CDSCO**. The Declaration has also shaped the ethical standards for pharmaceutical companies, academic institutions, and research organizations worldwide, making it one of the most influential documents in the history of medical ethics.

10.4.2 Role of the World Medical Association in Its Development

The **World Medical Association (WMA)** played a central role in the development and ongoing revisions of the Declaration of Helsinki. As a global organization representing physicians from over 100 countries, the WMA sought to create an ethical framework that would apply to medical research worldwide, regardless of regional differences in regulations or practices. The WMA's commitment to upholding high ethical standards in medicine is reflected in the Declaration's emphasis on protecting the rights and welfare of research participants. The WMA recognized that advances in medical science must be pursued without compromising the dignity or safety of individuals, and the Declaration was designed to ensure that these ethical principles were universally upheld.

Since its initial adoption, the WMA has overseen several revisions of the Declaration to address new challenges in clinical research, such as the increasing globalization of trials and the emergence of new technologies. These revisions have strengthened the Declaration's guidelines on informed consent, the protection of vulnerable populations, and the ethical responsibilities of researchers. The WMA continues to play a critical role in promoting the Declaration of Helsinki as a standard for ethical research, encouraging countries and organizations to adopt its principles and incorporate them into their own regulatory frameworks. This ongoing commitment has helped to ensure that the Declaration remains relevant and effective in safeguarding the rights of research participants in an ever-evolving scientific landscape.

10.5 Key Ethical Guidelines in the Declaration of Helsinki

10.5.1 Informed Consent in Human Research

One of the most important ethical guidelines in the **Declaration of Helsinki** is the requirement for **informed consent** in human research. The Declaration states that every participant in a clinical trial must be fully informed about the nature of the study, including its purpose, risks, benefits, and the procedures involved. Participants must give their voluntary consent without any form of coercion, and they should be made aware that they have the right to withdraw from the study at any time, without facing any consequences. This ensures that individuals maintain autonomy over their participation in research, aligning with the principle of **Respect for Persons** as outlined in the Belmont Report.

Informed consent must be obtained in writing, and researchers have a responsibility to ensure that participants fully understand the information provided, particularly in cases where complex medical terminology or procedures are involved. For vulnerable populations, such as children or those with cognitive impairments, additional safeguards must be in place, including obtaining consent from legal guardians or using simplified explanations to facilitate understanding. The Declaration of Helsinki has had a significant impact on the way informed consent is handled in clinical research, setting a global standard that has been integrated into national and international regulations governing medical research.

10.5.2 Clinical Research Must Prioritize Subject Safety

The **Declaration of Helsinki** emphasizes that the safety of research participants must always take precedence over the potential benefits of scientific advancement. This aligns with the principle of **Beneficence**, which requires researchers to minimize harm and ensure that the risks involved in a study are justified by the potential benefits. The Declaration stipulates that researchers must conduct a thorough risk assessment before beginning a study, considering both the likelihood and severity of potential harms. If at any point during the study it becomes clear that the risks outweigh the benefits, the trial must be modified or terminated to protect participants from further harm.

In addition to pre-trial risk assessments, the Declaration requires that researchers implement ongoing **safety monitoring** throughout the course of the study. This includes regular reporting of adverse events and a commitment to adjusting the study protocol if necessary to minimize risks. By placing the safety of research participants at the forefront, the Declaration of Helsinki has helped to establish rigorous safety standards in clinical trials, ensuring that human subjects are protected from unnecessary harm. These guidelines have been incorporated into global regulatory frameworks, influencing the ethical review processes carried out by IRBs and other oversight bodies.

10.6 Influence of the Belmont Report and Declaration of Helsinki on Modern Regulations

10.6.1 Integration of These Documents into Global Regulatory Frameworks

Both the **Belmont Report** and the **Declaration of Helsinki** have been instrumental in shaping modern regulatory frameworks for clinical research. In the United States, the ethical principles of the Belmont Report were integrated into the **Common Rule**, which governs all federally funded research involving human subjects. The Common Rule includes requirements for informed consent, risk-benefit analysis, and the protection of vulnerable populations, all of which are derived from the Belmont

Report's principles of **Respect for Persons, Beneficence,** and **Justice.** Similarly, the **Declaration of Helsinki** has influenced the regulations governing clinical research in many countries, including the guidelines set forth by the **European Medicines Agency (EMA)** and the **Central Drugs Standard Control Organization (CDSCO)** in India.

The integration of these ethical documents into global regulatory frameworks has helped to standardize the conduct of clinical trials, ensuring that research participants are protected regardless of where the study is conducted. For example, both the Belmont Report and the Declaration of Helsinki emphasize the importance of informed consent and the need for independent ethical review of research protocols. These principles are now universally accepted as fundamental to the ethical conduct of research and have been incorporated into the regulatory requirements of many countries. The influence of these documents extends beyond national borders, shaping the ethical standards of international clinical trials and ensuring that research is conducted in a manner that respects human dignity and protects the welfare of participants.

10.6.2 Comparative Analysis: Belmont Report vs. Declaration of Helsinki

While both the **Belmont Report** and the **Declaration of Helsinki** provide essential ethical guidelines for clinical research, there are some differences in their focus and scope. The Belmont Report is primarily concerned with ethical principles specific to research in the United States, particularly in the context of federally funded studies. It emphasizes three core principles—**Respect for Persons, Beneficence,** and **Justice**—which provide a broad ethical framework for conducting research. In contrast, the Declaration of Helsinki is an international document developed by the **World Medical Association (WMA)**, and its guidelines are designed to apply to medical research globally. While both documents share common principles, such as the importance of informed consent and risk-benefit assessment, the Declaration of Helsinki places a stronger emphasis on the **well-being of research participants** as the primary consideration in all clinical trials.

Another key difference is the **scope of application**. The Belmont Report is more focused on the ethical issues surrounding human subjects research in the United States, while the Declaration of Helsinki covers a broader range of issues, including the ethical responsibilities of researchers, the protection of vulnerable populations, and the importance of transparency in reporting research results. The Declaration has been revised multiple times to address new ethical challenges in global clinical research, while the Belmont Report has remained largely unchanged since its publication in 1979. Despite these differences, both documents have had a profound influence on the development of modern research ethics and continue to guide the ethical conduct of clinical trials worldwide.

Review Questions

1. What led to the development of the Belmont Report?
2. Explain the three core ethical principles outlined in the Belmont Report.
3. How do the Belmont principles apply to the informed consent process in clinical trials?
4. What role did the World Medical Association play in developing the Declaration of Helsinki?
5. What are the key ethical guidelines outlined in the Declaration of Helsinki?
6. How do the Belmont Report and the Declaration of Helsinki influence global regulatory frameworks?
7. How do these ethical guidelines ensure the protection of human subjects in clinical trials?
8. Compare and contrast the ethical principles of the Belmont Report with those of the Declaration of Helsinki.

CHAPTER ELEVEN

The Origin of ICH-GCP Guidelines

11.1 The International Conference on Harmonization (ICH)

11.1.1 Formation and Goals of ICH

The **International Conference on Harmonization (ICH)** was formed in 1990 as a collaborative effort between regulatory authorities and pharmaceutical industries from Europe, Japan, and the United States. The main goal of ICH is to harmonize the technical and regulatory requirements for the registration of pharmaceuticals across these regions. Before the formation of ICH, the differing regulatory standards in various countries often created barriers to the global development of new medicines. ICH was designed to streamline the drug approval process by aligning the requirements for safety, efficacy, and quality, making it easier for pharmaceutical companies to develop new drugs and bring them to international markets without undergoing redundant testing.

The ICH operates through the creation of **guidelines** that address key aspects of the drug development process, including clinical trials, manufacturing practices, and safety evaluations. By aligning these standards, the ICH aims to reduce the time and cost involved in bringing new medicines to market while maintaining high standards for patient safety and drug efficacy. The formation of the ICH was driven by the recognition that patients worldwide would benefit from more efficient drug development processes and better access to life-saving medications. The **ICH Guidelines** continue to be updated and expanded, addressing new challenges in the global pharmaceutical industry.

11.1.2 Role in International Regulatory Harmonization

The role of ICH in **regulatory harmonization** has been transformative for the pharmaceutical industry. By establishing a unified set of standards, the ICH has facilitated the approval of new drugs across multiple countries, significantly reducing the need for duplicative regulatory reviews and clinical trials. This has not only saved time and resources for pharmaceutical companies but has also accelerated patients' access to new treatments. The ICH's work has focused on harmonizing three key areas: **quality, safety**, and **efficacy**. Each of these areas is governed by specific guidelines that outline the requirements for drug development, clinical testing, and manufacturing practices.

For regulatory bodies, the harmonization process has simplified the task of reviewing new drug applications, as the guidelines provide a consistent framework that can be applied across different regions. This harmonization also supports the **mutual recognition agreements** between regulatory agencies, enabling them to rely on the assessments conducted by their counterparts in other countries. The ICH's efforts have expanded beyond its original members, with many other countries adopting ICH guidelines as part of their regulatory frameworks, further extending the impact of regulatory harmonization on a global scale.

11.2 Good Clinical Practice (GCP) Guidelines Overview

11.2.1 Key Principles of GCP

The **Good Clinical Practice (GCP)** guidelines provide a standardized framework for the ethical and scientific conduct of clinical trials involving human participants. These guidelines were developed to ensure that clinical trials are conducted in a way that protects the rights, safety, and well-being of trial participants, while also ensuring that the data generated from these trials are credible and reliable. The core principles of GCP include obtaining **informed consent** from all participants, ensuring that trials are designed and conducted according to sound scientific principles, and maintaining transparency and integrity throughout the trial process. These principles apply to everyone involved in the trial, including the investigators, sponsors, and ethics committees.

Another critical aspect of GCP is the requirement for **quality assurance** and **data integrity**. This ensures that the results of the clinical trials can be trusted by regulatory authorities, the scientific community, and the public.

Trials must be carefully monitored to ensure compliance with the study protocol, and any deviations must be reported and addressed. The GCP guidelines emphasize the need for accurate record-keeping and rigorous data management processes to prevent fraud, misconduct, or errors that could compromise the validity of the trial results.

11.2.2 Regulatory Compliance and GCP

Regulatory compliance is a fundamental component of the GCP guidelines. All clinical trials conducted under GCP must comply with the regulations set by the relevant authorities in the countries where the trial is conducted. For example, in the United States, clinical trials must adhere to the guidelines established by the **FDA**, while in the European Union, the **EMA** oversees compliance with GCP standards. These regulatory bodies have the authority to inspect clinical trial sites and audit trial records to ensure that GCP is being followed. Non-compliance can result in penalties, including the rejection of trial data, delays in drug approval, or even legal action.

Adhering to GCP is not only an ethical obligation but also a legal requirement in many countries. Pharmaceutical companies and clinical research organizations (CROs) are responsible for ensuring that all aspects of the trial, from planning and execution to data analysis and reporting, meet the standards set forth by GCP. This includes ensuring that all trial staff are trained in GCP principles and that robust systems are in place for monitoring compliance. The GCP guidelines also require that any adverse events or **serious adverse events (SAEs)** be promptly reported to the regulatory authorities, ensuring that participant safety is monitored throughout the trial.

11.3 Development of the ICH-GCP Guidelines

11.3.1 Historical Context for GCP Development

The development of the **ICH-GCP guidelines** was largely motivated by the need to address the ethical and scientific challenges that had emerged in clinical research. Prior to the creation of these guidelines, there were several well-documented instances of unethical practices in clinical trials, such as the **Tuskegee Syphilis Study** and the **Thalidomide disaster**. These events exposed the vulnerabilities of research participants and underscored the need for stringent ethical oversight in clinical research. The ICH-GCP guidelines were developed in the 1990s as part of a broader effort to harmonize clinical trial practices and ensure that all trials, regardless of where they are conducted, adhere to the same ethical and scientific standards.

The ICH-GCP guidelines were shaped by existing ethical frameworks, including the **Declaration of Helsinki** and the **Belmont Report**, which had established principles for the protection of human subjects in research. However, the ICH-GCP guidelines expanded on these principles by incorporating detailed requirements for the conduct of clinical trials, focusing on areas such as investigator responsibilities, sponsor oversight, and data management. The historical context of these guidelines reflects a growing recognition of the need for global standards to ensure the integrity of clinical research and the protection of participants in an increasingly international research environment.

11.3.2 Key Milestones in the Creation of ICH-GCP

The creation of the **ICH-GCP guidelines** involved several key milestones that helped shape the guidelines into their current form. One of the most significant milestones was the first **International Conference on Harmonization** in 1990, where regulatory authorities and industry representatives from Europe, Japan, and the United States came together to address the challenges of global clinical trials. This meeting laid the groundwork for the development of GCP guidelines by identifying the need for a unified approach to the ethical and scientific conduct of clinical trials. Another important milestone was the **adoption of the ICH E6 guideline** in 1996, which formalized the GCP standards and provided a comprehensive framework for conducting clinical trials.

The ongoing revision and updating of the ICH-GCP guidelines represent another important milestone. As clinical research evolves, particularly with the advent of new technologies such as digital health tools and artificial intelligence, the ICH has continued to update the GCP guidelines to ensure that they remain relevant and effective. For example, recent revisions have focused on improving the management of **data integrity**, the use of **electronic records**, and the ethical implications of new research methodologies. These updates reflect the ICH's commitment to maintaining high standards in clinical research, even as the field undergoes significant technological and regulatory changes.

11.4 Core Principles of ICH-GCP Guidelines

11.4.1 Roles and Responsibilities of the Investigator

One of the most critical roles in a clinical trial is that of the **investigator**, who is responsible for the overall conduct of the study at a specific site. According to the **ICH-GCP guidelines**, the investigator must ensure that the trial is conducted in compliance with the approved protocol, GCP standards, and applicable regulatory requirements. The investigator is also tasked with ensuring that the rights, safety, and well-being of participants are protected throughout the study. This includes obtaining **informed consent** from participants, maintaining accurate trial records, and promptly reporting any adverse events or deviations from the protocol to the appropriate authorities. The investigator is the central figure in ensuring that ethical standards are upheld in the trial.

In addition to protecting participants, the investigator is responsible for ensuring the scientific integrity of the trial. This includes maintaining the **credibility of the data** collected during the study by ensuring that all procedures are followed meticulously and that any issues are addressed in a timely manner. For example, if an investigator discovers that a participant is experiencing unexpected side effects, they must investigate the cause and determine whether adjustments to the trial are necessary. The investigator must also maintain transparent communication with the sponsor and other stakeholders, providing regular updates on the trial's progress and any challenges encountered.

Furthermore, investigators must ensure that all personnel involved in the trial are adequately trained in GCP principles and are qualified to carry out their responsibilities. This includes the supervision of medical staff, data managers, and any other individuals directly involved in the clinical trial. By fulfilling these responsibilities, the investigator plays a crucial role in upholding the **ethical and scientific rigor** of the clinical research process, ensuring that the study is both valid and ethically sound.

11.4.2 Responsibilities of the Sponsor

The **sponsor** of a clinical trial is typically a pharmaceutical company, biotechnology firm, or research institution that is responsible for initiating, managing, and financing the study. Under the **ICH-GCP guidelines**, the sponsor has several key responsibilities, including the design and management of the trial, ensuring compliance with regulatory standards, and overseeing the protection of participants. One of the sponsor's primary roles is to develop a trial protocol that outlines the study's objectives, methodology, and procedures. The sponsor must also ensure that the protocol is approved by relevant **ethics committees** or **Institutional Review Boards (IRBs)** before the trial can begin.

Another major responsibility of the sponsor is to monitor the progress of the trial through **ongoing oversight** and periodic reviews. The sponsor may appoint **Contract Research Organizations (CROs)** to carry out certain trial functions, but the ultimate responsibility for ensuring GCP compliance lies with the sponsor. This includes verifying that the investigators and trial sites are adhering to the protocol and that any adverse events are promptly reported and addressed. Additionally, the sponsor is responsible for maintaining records of all **clinical trial data**, ensuring that the information is complete, accurate, and verifiable, and making these records available to regulatory authorities when necessary.

The sponsor must also ensure that the trial's financial and logistical aspects are well-managed. This includes securing funding for the trial, providing appropriate **compensation** to participants, and ensuring that trial supplies, such as investigational products, are delivered to trial sites in a timely and secure manner. By fulfilling these responsibilities, the sponsor ensures that the clinical trial is conducted efficiently, ethically, and in accordance with GCP standards. The sponsor's role is critical in coordinating the various elements of the trial and ensuring that the study is properly executed from start to finish.

11.4.3 Protection of Human Subjects in Research

The protection of **human subjects** is at the heart of the ICH-GCP guidelines, and it is one of the fundamental principles that guides all aspects of clinical research. The guidelines emphasize that the **rights, safety, and well-being of trial participants** must always take precedence over the interests of science and society. This principle is operationalized through a variety of safeguards, including informed consent, ongoing safety monitoring, and the ethical review of trial protocols by independent committees. Informed consent ensures that participants are fully aware of the risks and benefits of participating in a study and that they have the opportunity to withdraw from the trial at any time without facing penalties.

The **ethical oversight** provided by IRBs or ethics committees is another crucial element in protecting participants. These committees review trial protocols to ensure that they are scientifically sound and ethically justified, focusing on minimizing risks to participants. They also monitor the trial as it progresses, ensuring that any new risks that emerge are addressed promptly. The ICH-GCP guidelines also require that any **serious adverse** events (SAEs) that occur during the trial are reported to the appropriate authorities, ensuring that participants' safety is continuously evaluated throughout the study.

Additionally, the guidelines mandate that trials must be designed to minimize unnecessary harm. This includes conducting **preclinical studies** to assess the potential risks of the investigational product before it is tested on humans. It also involves the careful selection of participants to ensure that vulnerable populations, such as children or individuals with impaired decision-making capacity, are only included in studies when absolutely necessary and when additional protections are in place. Through these measures, the ICH-GCP guidelines ensure that human subjects are not exploited in the pursuit of scientific knowledge and that their participation in clinical trials is conducted with the highest ethical standards.

11.5 ICH-GCP Guidelines and Regulatory Compliance

11.5.1 Compliance Requirements for Clinical Trials

Compliance with **ICH-GCP guidelines** is a legal and ethical requirement for all clinical trials involving human subjects. These guidelines provide a framework that ensures the ethical conduct of trials while also ensuring that the data generated is credible and reliable. **Regulatory authorities** in various regions, such as the **FDA** in the United States, the **EMA** in Europe, and the **CDSCO** in India, have adopted ICH-GCP guidelines as part of their regulatory frameworks. Compliance with these guidelines involves adhering to strict protocols for the design, conduct, monitoring, and reporting of clinical trials. Any deviations from the protocol or GCP standards must be documented and justified, and regulatory bodies have the authority to audit clinical trial sites to ensure compliance.

The penalties for non-compliance can be severe, ranging from the rejection of clinical trial data to **fines, legal action**, or restrictions on future research activities. Pharmaceutical companies and other sponsors are particularly incentivized to ensure that trials are conducted according to GCP standards, as failure to do so can result in delays in drug approval or even the rejection of a drug application by regulatory agencies. For investigators and clinical trial sites, non-compliance with GCP guidelines can lead to reputational damage and the potential loss of funding or future trial opportunities. As a result, both sponsors and investigators are keenly aware of the importance of maintaining GCP compliance throughout the entire trial process.

To facilitate compliance, many organizations implement **internal audits** and quality control measures to identify and address any issues before they escalate. These internal checks, combined with external audits by regulatory authorities, help to ensure that clinical trials meet the highest standards of quality and integrity. By following the GCP guidelines, researchers not only protect participants but also enhance the **scientific validity** of their research, ensuring that the results of clinical trials can be trusted by regulators, healthcare professionals, and the broader scientific community.

11.5.2 Integration into Regional Regulations: FDA, EMA, CDSCO

The **ICH-GCP guidelines** have been fully integrated into the regulatory frameworks of major drug regulatory agencies around the world, including the **FDA** (Food and Drug Administration) in the United States, the **EMA** (European Medicines Agency) in the European Union, and the **CDSCO** (Central Drugs Standard Control Organization) in India. This integration ensures that clinical trials conducted in these regions adhere to uniform ethical and scientific standards, making it easier for pharmaceutical companies to navigate the regulatory requirements of multiple countries. For example, a clinical trial that complies with ICH-GCP standards in the United States will likely meet the regulatory requirements of the EMA and CDSCO, facilitating the **international approval process** for new drugs and treatments.

The harmonization of regulatory standards through ICH-GCP has been particularly beneficial for **multinational clinical trials**, where a single trial may involve participants and trial sites in multiple countries. Prior to the development of ICH-GCP, clinical trials often had to be adapted to meet the specific requirements of each regulatory agency, leading to inefficiencies and increased costs. By aligning their regulations with ICH-GCP, agencies such as the FDA, EMA, and CDSCO have made it easier for companies to conduct **global clinical trials**, reducing the need for redundant studies and allowing for faster approval of new medicines. This has led to more efficient drug development processes and quicker access to innovative therapies for patients worldwide.

Despite the harmonization efforts, there are still some regional differences in the implementation of GCP guidelines. For instance, the FDA places a strong emphasis on **data integrity** and the use of **electronic records** in clinical trials, while the EMA may have additional requirements for the protection of participants in **pediatric or geriatric trials**. However, these differences are relatively minor, and the core principles of GCP remain consistent across all regions. This allows sponsors to design trials that are **globally applicable**, ensuring that the results can be used to support regulatory submissions in multiple countries.

11.5.3 Monitoring and Audits for GCP Compliance

Ensuring **GCP compliance** in clinical trials requires rigorous monitoring and regular audits, both by the sponsor and by regulatory authorities. Sponsors typically establish a comprehensive **monitoring plan** at the outset of a clinical trial, outlining how the trial will be overseen to ensure that it adheres to the approved protocol and GCP guidelines. This monitoring includes regular site visits, where trained monitors review trial records, interview trial staff, and ensure that procedures are being followed correctly. Any deviations from the protocol are documented and addressed, and corrective actions are implemented as needed. Monitors also verify that the **informed consent process** is being properly conducted and that participants' safety is being prioritized at all times.

In addition to sponsor-led monitoring, regulatory authorities may conduct **GCP audits** to ensure that trials are being conducted in compliance with local and international regulations. These audits can be routine, or they may be triggered by specific concerns, such as reports of serious adverse events or data discrepancies. During an audit, inspectors review all aspects of the trial, including the study design, data management processes, and participant safety protocols. They may also interview trial staff and participants to ensure that the trial is being conducted ethically and in accordance with GCP standards. If any issues are identified during an audit, the trial may be halted or modified, and the sponsor may be required to submit a corrective action plan to address the deficiencies.

For sponsors and investigators, maintaining GCP compliance through monitoring and audits is essential for ensuring the **validity of trial data** and protecting participants. Failure to comply with GCP standards can lead to serious consequences, including the rejection of trial data by regulatory authorities or legal penalties. Regular audits and careful monitoring help to identify potential problems early in the trial process, allowing sponsors to make necessary adjustments and maintain compliance. By adhering to GCP guidelines and maintaining transparency through monitoring and audits, clinical trials can be conducted with integrity, ensuring that the results are both scientifically sound and ethically responsible.

11.6 The Role of ICH-GCP in Multinational Clinical Trials

11.6.1 Harmonizing Standards for Global Trials

The **ICH-GCP guidelines** have played a pivotal role in the harmonization of standards for clinical trials conducted across multiple countries. Before the development of these guidelines, clinical trials in different regions had to adhere to distinct and often incompatible regulations, creating challenges for pharmaceutical companies seeking to conduct global studies. The ICH-GCP guidelines have helped to standardize the **ethical and scientific framework** for conducting clinical trials, ensuring that trials in Europe, Japan, the United States, and other regions are conducted in a consistent and transparent manner. This harmonization has made it easier for companies to conduct multinational trials, reducing the need for duplicative studies and allowing for the faster development of new medicines.

By providing a common set of standards, the ICH-GCP guidelines also ensure that the **data generated** in one country is accepted by regulatory authorities in other regions, facilitating the global approval of new drugs. For example, a clinical trial conducted in the United States that complies with ICH-GCP guidelines can be used to support a regulatory submission to the **European Medicines Agency (EMA)** or the **Central Drugs Standard Control Organization (CDSCO)** in India. This reduces the need for companies to conduct separate trials in each country, saving time and resources while ensuring that the trial data is valid and reliable. As a result, the ICH-GCP guidelines have become the **global standard** for conducting clinical trials, with many countries adopting these guidelines as part of their national regulations.

The harmonization of clinical trial standards through ICH-GCP has also facilitated the recruitment of **diverse populations** into trials, enabling companies to test new medicines in a wider range of patient groups. This is particularly important in today's globalized world, where medicines are developed and marketed internationally. By ensuring that trials are conducted according to the same standards regardless of location, the ICH-GCP guidelines help to ensure that the results are applicable to a global patient population. This contributes to the development of more effective treatments that are tailored to the needs of different regions and patient groups, improving access to new medicines around the world.

11.6.2 Challenges in Implementing ICH-GCP Across Regions

While the **ICH-GCP guidelines** have been widely adopted as the global standard for clinical trials, their implementation across different regions can present significant challenges. One of the key difficulties in implementing GCP guidelines globally is the variation in **regulatory infrastructure** and capacity across countries. While countries like the United States and those in the European Union have well-established regulatory frameworks and experienced staff to oversee clinical trials, other regions may lack the necessary resources and expertise to fully implement and monitor compliance with GCP standards. This can lead to inconsistencies in how the guidelines are applied, particularly in **low- and middle-income countries** where clinical trials are increasingly being conducted.

Another challenge is the **cultural and ethical differences** that may affect how GCP guidelines are interpreted and implemented in different regions. For example, obtaining informed consent may be more complex in regions where literacy rates are low or where there are cultural norms that affect the decision-making process. In some cases, local regulations may conflict with ICH-GCP guidelines, particularly with respect to **participant protection** and **data management**. Sponsors and investigators conducting multinational trials must navigate these differences carefully, ensuring that trials are conducted ethically and in compliance with both local regulations and GCP standards. This often requires additional training for trial staff and collaboration with local regulatory authorities to address any discrepancies.

The logistical challenges of conducting **multinational trials** can also complicate the implementation of GCP guidelines. For example, coordinating trial activities across multiple sites in different countries requires careful planning and communication to ensure that all sites follow the same protocols and standards. Differences in time zones, language barriers, and variations in healthcare infrastructure can make it difficult to maintain consistency across trial sites. Additionally, the complexity of managing **data collection and reporting** across regions can introduce challenges in ensuring that the trial data is accurate, complete, and compliant with GCP standards. Addressing these challenges requires strong oversight and effective coordination between sponsors, investigators, and regulatory authorities to ensure that the trial is conducted according to GCP guidelines.

11.6.3 Case Studies of Multinational Trials and GCP Compliance

Several **multinational clinical trials** have highlighted both the benefits and challenges of implementing ICH-GCP guidelines in diverse regions. One well-known case is the development of **COVID-19 vaccines**, where global trials were conducted across multiple countries to rapidly test the safety and efficacy of the vaccines. These trials, conducted by companies such as **Pfizer, Moderna,** and **AstraZeneca,** involved thousands of participants from different countries, with trial sites spanning continents. The ICH-GCP guidelines were instrumental in ensuring that these trials were conducted according to uniform ethical and scientific standards, allowing for the rapid approval of the vaccines in multiple countries. Despite the logistical challenges of conducting trials during a pandemic, the harmonization of GCP standards helped to streamline the process and ensure that the data generated was accepted by regulatory authorities worldwide.

However, the implementation of GCP guidelines in multinational trials has also exposed some of the **challenges** that arise when conducting trials in regions with varying levels of regulatory oversight. For instance, trials conducted in low- and middle-income countries have sometimes faced criticism for not adequately protecting vulnerable populations or for failing to ensure fully informed consent. In one case, a multinational trial testing an HIV prevention treatment faced allegations of **ethical violations** when it was discovered that some participants were not fully informed about the risks of the study. This highlighted the need for stronger oversight and better communication between trial sponsors, local investigators, and regulatory authorities to ensure compliance with GCP guidelines in all regions.

Despite these challenges, the overall success of multinational trials conducted under GCP guidelines demonstrates the value of **harmonizing ethical and scientific standards** across regions. The case of the **Zika virus vaccine trials** provides another example of how ICH-GCP guidelines facilitated the rapid development of a vaccine that was tested in multiple countries, including the United States, Brazil, and other parts of Latin America. These trials benefited from the standardized protocols and ethical guidelines provided by ICH-GCP, which helped to ensure that the results were accepted by regulatory authorities in multiple countries, leading to faster approval and distribution of the vaccine. These case studies demonstrate both the strengths and challenges of implementing GCP guidelines in a global research environment, highlighting the importance of ongoing efforts to harmonize clinical trial standards worldwide.

Review Questions

1. What was the purpose of the International Conference on Harmonization (ICH), and how did it contribute to clinical research regulations?
2. What are the key principles of Good Clinical Practice (GCP)?
3. Discuss the historical context behind the development of the ICH-GCP guidelines.
4. What responsibilities do investigators have under GCP guidelines?
5. How do sponsors ensure compliance with GCP during clinical trials?
6. How do the ICH-GCP guidelines protect human subjects in clinical research?
7. Explain the role of GCP in the conduct of multinational clinical trials.
8. What challenges do clinical trial teams face in complying with GCP guidelines?

CHAPTER TWELVE

Ethics of Randomized Clinical Trials

12.1 Importance of Randomization in Clinical Trials

12.1.1 Why Randomization is Critical

Randomization is one of the most critical elements in the design of clinical trials because it helps to ensure that the study results are both reliable and unbiased. In a randomized trial, participants are assigned to either the experimental group (receiving the treatment being tested) or the control group (receiving either a placebo or standard treatment) based purely on chance, without any influence from researchers or participants. This method eliminates **selection bias**, where certain characteristics could influence the outcome of the study if participants were deliberately placed in one group or another. Randomization ensures that the characteristics of participants, such as age, gender, or disease severity, are evenly distributed across both groups, making the trial results more generalizable and valid.

The ethical importance of randomization lies in its ability to create **equipoise**, a state of uncertainty in which neither the researchers nor the participants know which treatment is more effective. This ensures that no participant is knowingly assigned to a treatment group that is expected to perform worse, upholding ethical standards of fairness. Without randomization, there is a risk that researchers might unconsciously or deliberately influence the assignment of participants, potentially compromising the study's integrity and leading to skewed results. Thus, randomization is not just a statistical tool but a fundamental ethical principle in clinical research.

Randomization is particularly important in large-scale **randomized controlled trials (RCTs)**, where the sample size is large enough to provide statistically significant results. By ensuring that the groups are balanced, randomization allows researchers to isolate the effect of the intervention being studied and draw more accurate conclusions about its efficacy. In trials without randomization, confounding variables might influence the outcome, making it difficult to determine whether the treatment itself or other factors were responsible for the observed effects. Therefore, randomization is crucial for the ethical and scientific rigor of clinical trials.

12.1.2 Randomization Methods and Techniques

There are several methods of **randomization**, each with its own advantages and considerations. The most common method is **simple randomization**, where each participant has an equal chance of being assigned to any group, similar to flipping a coin. While simple randomization is easy to implement, it can sometimes lead to unequal group sizes, especially in smaller trials, which can reduce the statistical power of the study. To address this, researchers often use **block randomization**, where participants are divided into blocks, ensuring that each group has the same number of participants at the end of the trial. This method is particularly useful in smaller studies where maintaining balance between the groups is crucial.

Another method is **stratified randomization**, which is used when researchers want to ensure that certain characteristics, such as age, gender, or disease stage, are evenly distributed across the groups. In this method, participants are first grouped based on a characteristic (such as male and female) and then randomized within each group. This helps to control for confounding variables and ensures that the study results are not skewed by differences in participant characteristics. Stratified randomization is especially important in trials where certain characteristics could influence the outcome, such as trials involving different age groups or disease severities.

A more advanced technique is **adaptive randomization**, which adjusts the probability of assigning participants to a group based on the results observed so far in the trial. For example, if early results suggest that one treatment is performing significantly better, the randomization process may assign more participants to that group. While this method can enhance **ethical decision-making**, as fewer participants are exposed to less effective treatments, it also introduces statistical complexities and the potential for bias if not carefully managed. Each randomization method has its strengths and weaknesses, and the choice depends on the specific goals and design of the trial.

12.1.3 Reducing Bias through Randomization

One of the primary reasons for using **randomization** in clinical trials is its ability to reduce or eliminate **bias**, particularly **selection bias** and **allocation bias**. Bias can occur when the characteristics of participants influence their assignment to one group or another, which can skew the study's results. For instance, if younger, healthier participants are systematically placed in the treatment group, while older or sicker participants are placed in the control group, the results may falsely suggest that the treatment is more effective than it truly is. Randomization ensures that such characteristics are evenly distributed, making the groups comparable and reducing the risk of bias.

Randomization also helps to prevent **confounding**, where factors unrelated to the treatment could influence the outcome of the trial. Confounding variables, such as socioeconomic status, lifestyle, or genetic factors, could impact the participants' response to the treatment. By randomly assigning participants to groups, researchers can ensure that these confounding factors are distributed equally between the experimental and control groups. This allows the researchers to isolate the effect of the treatment being studied, leading to more accurate and trustworthy results.

While randomization is an effective tool for reducing bias, it must be properly implemented to ensure its success. Poor randomization techniques, such as using non-random methods like assigning participants based on their birth date or the order of enrollment, can introduce bias into the trial. **Blinding**, which is often used in conjunction with randomization, further helps to reduce bias by ensuring that neither the participants nor the researchers know which group the participants have been assigned to. This combination of randomization and blinding is essential for maintaining the integrity and ethical conduct of clinical trials.

12.2 Blinding in Randomized Trials

12.2.1 Single-Blind vs. Double-Blind Studies

Blinding is a critical method used in clinical trials to reduce **bias** and ensure the integrity of the study. In a **single-blind trial**, only the participants are unaware of whether they are receiving the experimental treatment or the control (which could be a placebo or an existing treatment). This helps to eliminate **placebo effects**, where participants might experience changes in their condition simply because they believe they are receiving a new treatment, even if they are actually in the control group. The purpose of single-blind studies is to prevent participants' expectations from influencing the results, as this could skew the outcomes.

On the other hand, **double-blind trials** are more comprehensive in reducing bias. In these trials, neither the participants nor the investigators know which participants are receiving the experimental treatment and which are in the control group. This method prevents both **performance bias** and **observer bias**, as the researchers' expectations about the effectiveness of the treatment cannot influence how they interact with the participants or how they interpret the results. Double-blind studies are considered the **gold standard** in clinical trial design, as they provide the highest level of protection against bias, making the results more reliable and valid.

Despite the advantages of both single- and double-blind trials, there are some situations where blinding is not feasible. For example, in surgical trials or trials involving physical therapies, it may be impossible to blind participants or investigators because the nature of the intervention is obvious. In these cases, researchers must take additional steps to minimize bias, such as using **objective outcome measures** or relying on independent assessors who are not involved in the treatment. Both single-blind and double-blind studies are valuable tools in randomized clinical trials, each with its own strengths depending on the context of the research.

12.2.2 Ethical Implications of Blinding

The use of **blinding** in clinical trials carries important **ethical implications**, particularly in terms of protecting participants' rights and ensuring transparency in the research process. One of the key ethical concerns related to blinding is the issue of **informed consent**. Participants must be fully informed about the nature of the study, including the fact that they may be randomly assigned to either the treatment or control group and that they will not know which group they are in. While participants are made aware of the possibility of receiving a placebo or alternative treatment, the lack of transparency due to blinding can sometimes lead to **discomfort or uncertainty**, especially in trials where the outcome could have a significant impact on the participant's health.

Blinding can also raise ethical questions about the **right to treatment**. In trials where participants are blinded to whether they are receiving the active treatment or a placebo, there is a risk that some participants might not receive potentially life-saving treatments if they are placed in the control group. This is particularly controversial in **life-threatening conditions** or in cases where an effective standard treatment is already available. In such scenarios, ethical guidelines often require that the trial design ensures participants are not denied access to necessary care, and researchers may need to offer participants the option of receiving the experimental treatment after the study concludes if it proves to be effective.

Additionally, blinding can lead to **mistrust** among participants if they feel that the lack of transparency violates their autonomy or if they experience adverse effects without knowing whether these are due to the treatment or the placebo. Researchers must balance the need for **scientific rigor** with the ethical obligation to respect participants' autonomy and ensure that they are not exposed to unnecessary harm. Ethical oversight by **Institutional Review Boards (IRBs)** is essential in ensuring that the use of blinding is justified and that participants' rights are protected throughout the study.

12.2.3 Challenges in Maintaining Blinding

Maintaining **blinding** throughout the course of a clinical trial can be challenging, especially in longer studies or those involving complex interventions. One of the most common challenges is the **unintentional unblinding** of participants or researchers. For instance, if the treatment group experiences noticeable side effects that are not present in the control group, participants or investigators may be able to deduce which group the participants are in, compromising the integrity of the study. This can lead to **observer bias**, where researchers may consciously or unconsciously alter their behavior or assessment of the participants based on their knowledge of the group assignment.

Another challenge arises in studies that involve **multiple interventions** or frequent contact between participants and the research team. In such cases, it becomes increasingly difficult to maintain blinding as participants may ask questions or seek clues about their treatment status. To mitigate this, researchers must ensure that all trial personnel are thoroughly trained in maintaining blinding procedures and that any interactions with participants are carefully managed to avoid unblinding. In double-blind trials, it is also important to have **objective measures** in place to assess outcomes, such as using laboratory tests or independent evaluators who are not involved in the trial.

In some trials, particularly those involving **medical devices** or **surgical procedures**, maintaining blinding may be technically impossible. In these situations, alternative methods must be used to ensure that bias is minimized. For example, using an independent data monitoring committee to assess the trial's progress and safety can help maintain objectivity. Moreover, researchers can use **partial blinding** or **masked data** in their analysis to ensure that even if blinding is compromised at certain stages of the trial, the final results remain reliable and unbiased. Overcoming these challenges requires careful planning, rigorous oversight, and a commitment to the ethical conduct of the trial.

12.3 Ethical Challenges in Randomized Controlled Trials (RCTs)

12.3.1 The Concept of Equipoise

The concept of **equipoise** is fundamental to the ethical justification of conducting **randomized controlled trials (RCTs)**. Equipoise refers to a genuine state of uncertainty or balance regarding the relative merits of the treatment being tested versus the control or alternative treatments. In other words, researchers must be uncertain whether the new treatment is better or worse than the current standard of care or placebo, creating a situation where it is ethically permissible to randomly assign participants to different groups. If equipoise does not exist, assigning participants to a treatment known to be less effective or harmful would be ethically unjustifiable, as it would violate the principle of **beneficence**.

The challenge with maintaining equipoise is that, over time, researchers may begin to form opinions about the effectiveness of the treatment as the trial progresses. This can lead to ethical dilemmas, particularly if early data suggests that one treatment is clearly superior. In such cases, continuing to assign participants to the less effective treatment would violate the ethical obligation to **maximize benefits** and **minimize harm**. To address this, researchers must carefully design trials with mechanisms such as **interim analyses**, where the data is reviewed at pre-specified intervals to determine if the trial should be stopped early for ethical reasons.

Equipoise also plays a crucial role in ensuring that participants are not being exposed to unnecessary risks. For example, if a trial tests a new drug against a placebo in a condition for which an effective treatment already exists, this could be considered ethically questionable, as it would mean withholding known treatment from participants. In such cases, researchers must justify the use of a placebo or alternative treatment by demonstrating that there is genuine uncertainty about the relative benefits of the new intervention. By maintaining equipoise, RCTs can uphold ethical standards and ensure that participants are not subjected to undue harm.

12.3.2 Ensuring Informed Consent in RCTs

Informed consent is a critical component of any clinical trial, but it presents unique challenges in the context of **randomized controlled trials (RCTs)**. In an RCT, participants must be fully informed that they will be randomly assigned to one of several treatment groups, which could include a new treatment, a standard treatment, or a placebo. This means that participants must understand the implications of randomization, including the fact that they will not have control over which treatment they receive and that there is a possibility they will not receive the experimental treatment. Providing this information in a clear and understandable manner is essential for ensuring that participants can make an informed decision about whether to take part in the study.

One of the key ethical challenges in obtaining informed consent for RCTs is ensuring that participants truly comprehend the **randomization process**. Studies have shown that many participants struggle to understand the concept of randomization, often assuming that they will receive the treatment that is best suited for their condition. This misunderstanding can undermine the validity of informed consent, as participants may not be fully aware of the risks and benefits associated with their participation in the trial. To address this, researchers must use clear, non-technical language when explaining the trial to participants and provide opportunities for participants to ask questions and seek clarification before consenting to participate.

In addition to explaining randomization, researchers must also ensure that participants understand the potential risks and benefits of the trial, including the possibility of receiving a placebo or a treatment that may be less effective than the standard of care. This can be particularly challenging in **placebo-controlled trials**, where participants may feel disappointed or anxious about the possibility of receiving an inactive treatment. Researchers must carefully balance the need for scientific rigor with the ethical obligation to protect participants' **autonomy** and **well-being**, ensuring that the informed consent process is transparent, respectful, and fully compliant with ethical standards.

12.3.3 Ethical Considerations in Randomizing Patients to Placebo

Randomizing patients to receive a **placebo** in clinical trials is one of the most ethically contentious practices in **randomized controlled trials (RCTs)**. Placebos are often used as a control group to test the effectiveness of a new treatment, especially in conditions where no standard treatment exists. While placebo-controlled trials can provide valuable data, they raise ethical concerns about withholding potentially beneficial treatments from participants, particularly in trials involving serious or life-threatening conditions. The ethical justification for using a placebo hinges on the principle of **equipoise**, which requires genuine uncertainty about whether the new treatment is better than no treatment or existing therapies.

One of the primary ethical concerns with placebo use is the **potential harm** to participants who are randomized to the placebo group, especially if an effective treatment is already available. For example, in a trial testing a new drug for a condition like cancer or heart disease, assigning participants to a placebo group could mean denying them access to a treatment that could improve their survival or quality of life. In such cases, ethical guidelines often recommend that placebos should only be used when there is no established effective treatment, or when withholding treatment does not pose a significant risk to participants' health. Researchers must carefully weigh the risks and benefits of using a placebo and ensure that participants are fully informed about the possibility of receiving an inactive treatment.

In response to these ethical concerns, many clinical trials now use **active control groups** instead of placebos. In an active control trial, the experimental treatment is compared to an existing standard treatment rather than a placebo. This approach addresses the ethical dilemma of withholding treatment while still providing valuable data about the relative effectiveness of the new intervention. However, active control trials also have limitations, as they may require larger sample sizes and more complex statistical analyses. Researchers must consider these factors when designing trials and ensure that the chosen methodology aligns with both ethical and scientific principles.

12.4 The Role of Placebos in Clinical Trials

12.4.1 Ethical Justification for Placebo Use

The use of **placebos** in clinical trials has long been debated from an ethical standpoint, particularly when it comes to balancing the need for rigorous scientific evidence with the obligation to protect participants. Placebos are often used to establish a baseline or control group in trials, against which the efficacy of a new treatment can be measured. The ethical justification for placebo use is grounded in the principle of **equipoise**, where genuine uncertainty exists about whether the new treatment is better than no treatment at all. When no established treatment exists, placebos provide a scientifically valid comparison, ensuring that any observed effects in the experimental group can be attributed to the treatment itself, rather than external factors or psychological effects.

However, the ethical use of placebos must be carefully considered in the context of the **potential risks** to participants. Placebo-controlled trials can only be justified when withholding treatment does not pose serious harm to participants. For example, using a placebo in a trial for a mild condition, such as the common cold, may be acceptable because the risks to participants are minimal. On the other hand, using a placebo in a trial for a life-threatening condition, where an effective treatment already exists, would be ethically questionable. In such cases, denying participants access to the standard treatment in favor of a placebo may violate the ethical principles of **beneficence** and **non-maleficence**.

To address these concerns, ethical guidelines, including those from the **Declaration of Helsinki**, recommend that placebos should only be used when no proven treatment exists or when withholding treatment poses no additional risk to the participants. Researchers must ensure that participants are fully informed about the possibility of receiving a placebo and must justify the use of placebos based on the scientific necessity of obtaining unbiased data. Ultimately, the ethical use of placebos must balance the need for robust scientific evidence with the imperative to protect participants from unnecessary harm.

12.4.2 Controversies and Limitations of Placebo-Controlled Trials

The use of **placebo-controlled trials** continues to be a topic of ethical controversy, particularly in fields where effective treatments already exist. One of the main criticisms of placebo-controlled trials is that they may expose participants to **unnecessary risks** by withholding effective treatments. For instance, in trials for conditions like cancer, cardiovascular disease, or HIV, using a placebo may deprive participants of life-saving therapies, which raises serious ethical concerns. Critics argue that it is unethical to randomize participants to a placebo group when a treatment that could alleviate suffering or prolong life is available, even if the new treatment being tested is expected to offer superior outcomes.

Another limitation of placebo-controlled trials is the **ethical challenge of informed consent**. While participants must be informed about the possibility of receiving a placebo, understanding the full implications of this can be difficult. Many participants may mistakenly believe they will receive some form of treatment or assume that the researchers will act in their best interests. This misunderstanding can compromise the validity of the informed consent process, as participants may not fully appreciate the risks involved in receiving a placebo. This is particularly problematic in **vulnerable populations**, such as those with limited healthcare access, who may be more inclined to participate in trials out of desperation for any form of care.

Despite these controversies, placebo-controlled trials remain a powerful tool for generating **unbiased evidence** about the efficacy of new treatments. By eliminating the placebo effect and providing a clear comparison group, they allow researchers to determine whether the benefits of a new treatment are real or simply the result of participants' expectations. However, to address the ethical challenges, researchers are increasingly exploring **alternative trial designs**, such as using **active control groups** or employing adaptive trial designs that minimize the duration of placebo exposure. These approaches offer a compromise that maintains scientific rigor while minimizing ethical concerns.

12.4.3 Alternatives to Placebos: Active Control Groups

In response to the ethical challenges posed by placebo-controlled trials, many researchers are turning to **active control groups** as an alternative. In an active control trial, the new treatment is compared to an existing standard treatment, rather than a placebo. This design addresses the ethical concern of withholding treatment from participants, as all participants receive some form of care, ensuring that no one is left untreated. Active control trials are particularly useful in fields where effective treatments already exist, as they allow researchers to assess whether the new treatment offers any significant advantages over the current standard of care.

One of the key benefits of using an active control group is that it maintains the **ethical principle of beneficence**, ensuring that participants are not exposed to unnecessary harm. In conditions where effective treatments are available, randomizing participants to a placebo group may violate this principle, as it denies them access to proven therapies. By using an active control group, researchers can ensure that participants receive care that is consistent with current medical standards, while still generating valuable data about the relative efficacy of the new treatment. This approach also helps to build **trust** between participants and researchers, as participants are more likely to feel that their well-being is being prioritized.

However, active control trials are not without their challenges. One of the main limitations is that they often require **larger sample sizes** and more complex statistical analyses compared to placebo-controlled trials. This is because the differences between the new treatment and the standard treatment may be smaller than the differences between a treatment and a placebo, making it harder to detect a statistically significant effect. Additionally, active control trials may be less suitable for conditions where no established treatment exists, as there would be no clear comparator group. Despite these limitations, active control trials offer an ethically robust alternative to placebo-controlled designs, particularly in fields where withholding treatment would be unethical.

12.5 Balancing Risk and Benefit in RCTs

12.5.1 Risk-Benefit Assessment in Randomized Trials

A thorough **risk-benefit assessment** is one of the cornerstones of ethical research, especially in the context of **randomized controlled trials (RCTs)**. Before a trial begins, researchers must carefully evaluate the potential risks to participants against the potential benefits, both to the participants and to society. This assessment is crucial for ensuring that the trial is ethically justifiable and that participants are not exposed to unnecessary harm. Risks in an RCT can include side effects from the experimental treatment, the possibility of receiving a placebo instead of active treatment, or the psychological and physical burdens associated with trial procedures. Benefits can include the direct therapeutic effects of the experimental treatment, as well as the broader contribution to scientific knowledge.

In conducting a risk-benefit assessment, researchers must consider several factors, including the **severity of the condition** being treated, the availability of alternative therapies, and the likelihood that the new treatment will offer significant benefits. In trials for life-threatening conditions, the **tolerance for risk** may be higher, as participants may be willing to accept greater risks in the hope of receiving a potentially life-saving treatment. Conversely, in trials for conditions that are less serious or where effective treatments already exist, the tolerance for risk is lower, and the justification for exposing participants to new risks must be stronger. This delicate balance is central to the ethical conduct of clinical trials and must be carefully monitored throughout the study.

The **Institutional Review Board (IRB)** or ethics committee plays a key role in overseeing the risk-benefit assessment. The IRB reviews the trial protocol to ensure that the potential benefits outweigh the risks and that appropriate measures are in place to minimize harm. This includes ensuring that participants are fully informed of the risks involved and that their **informed consent** is obtained before they enroll in the trial. Regular monitoring during the trial helps to ensure that the risk-benefit ratio remains favorable, and any significant changes in the risks or benefits can prompt the trial to be modified or halted if necessary.

12.5.2 Mitigating Risks to Participants

One of the primary responsibilities of researchers in an **RCT** is to **mitigate risks** to participants, ensuring that their safety and well-being are protected throughout the study. This involves implementing a range of strategies to reduce the likelihood of harm, such as designing the trial to include **appropriate exclusion criteria** that prevent individuals who are at high risk from participating. For example, in a trial testing a new drug with potential cardiovascular side effects, participants with pre-existing heart conditions may be excluded to avoid unnecessary harm. Similarly, researchers may monitor participants closely for adverse effects, adjusting the treatment or dosage as needed to minimize risk.

Another key strategy for mitigating risks is the use of **data and safety monitoring boards (DSMBs)**, which are independent committees responsible for overseeing the safety of participants during the trial. DSMBs regularly review the data generated by the trial, paying close attention to any adverse events or **serious adverse events (SAEs)** that may indicate increased risk to participants. If the DSMB determines that the risks are outweighing the potential benefits, it can recommend modifying the trial protocol or even stopping the trial altogether. This ensures that participants are not exposed to unnecessary harm and that the trial remains ethically sound.

In addition to safety monitoring, researchers must also ensure that participants are adequately informed about the risks and benefits of the trial through a **robust informed consent process**. This includes providing clear, non-technical information about the potential risks, as well as ensuring that participants have the opportunity to ask questions and make an informed decision about whether to participate. By actively mitigating risks and prioritizing participant safety, researchers can conduct RCTs in a manner that upholds the highest ethical standards and ensures the well-being of all participants.

12.5.3 Institutional Review Board (IRB) Roles in Risk Management

The **Institutional Review Board (IRB)** plays a crucial role in ensuring that the risks and benefits of **randomized controlled trials (RCTs)** are carefully managed throughout the study. As an independent body, the IRB is responsible for reviewing and approving all aspects of the trial protocol before the study can begin, with a particular focus on the **risk-benefit assessment**. The IRB ensures that the trial is ethically justified, that the risks to participants are minimized, and that any potential benefits outweigh the risks. This review process includes evaluating the study design, the informed consent process, and the procedures in place for monitoring participant safety.

In addition to its role in **initial protocol review**, the IRB has an ongoing responsibility to monitor the trial as it progresses. This includes conducting regular reviews of the data to ensure that the risk-benefit ratio remains favorable and that participants are not being exposed to undue harm. If new risks emerge during the trial, such as unexpected side effects or **adverse events**, the IRB may require modifications to the study design or even recommend halting the trial if the risks become too great. This continuous oversight ensures that the trial remains ethically sound and that participant safety is maintained at all times.

The IRB also plays a key role in overseeing the **informed consent process**, ensuring that participants are fully informed about the potential risks and benefits of the trial before they agree to participate. The IRB reviews the informed consent forms and ensures that they are written in clear, non-technical language that participants can understand. By ensuring that participants are fully informed and that the risks are managed appropriately, the IRB helps to uphold the ethical integrity of the trial and protect the rights and well-being of all participants involved.

12.6 Legal and Regulatory Aspects of Randomized Trials

12.6.1 Regulatory Requirements for RCTs

Regulatory requirements for randomized controlled trials (RCTs) are designed to ensure the ethical conduct of research involving human participants while maintaining the integrity and validity of the data collected. In many countries, these requirements are enforced by regulatory authorities such as the **FDA** in the United States, the **EMA** in Europe, and the **CDSCO** in India. Before a clinical trial can commence, it must be approved by the relevant regulatory body, which reviews the study protocol to ensure it meets the necessary ethical and scientific standards. This includes evaluating the trial's objectives, design, and methodology, as well as the proposed methods for recruiting and protecting participants.

In addition to pre-trial approvals, regulatory agencies require that sponsors adhere to specific reporting and monitoring obligations throughout the duration of the trial. This includes ongoing reporting of adverse events, regular updates on the trial's progress, and final reports summarizing the study's findings. Regulatory agencies may also conduct **inspections** of trial sites to ensure compliance with Good Clinical Practice (GCP) guidelines and other regulatory standards. Non-compliance with these regulatory requirements can result in significant penalties, including the rejection of trial data, suspension of the trial, or legal repercussions for the sponsors or investigators involved.

Furthermore, international harmonization efforts, such as those led by the **International Conference on Harmonization (ICH)**, have established standardized regulatory requirements that facilitate the conduct of multinational trials. These harmonized guidelines help to ensure that trials conducted across different countries maintain consistent ethical and scientific standards, streamlining the regulatory process and improving access to new treatments for patients worldwide. As a result, understanding and complying with regulatory requirements is critical for the successful conduct of RCTs and for protecting the rights and safety of participants.

12.6.2 Informed Consent Documentation

Informed consent documentation is a crucial legal and ethical requirement in randomized controlled trials (RCTs) that ensures participants are fully aware of the nature of the study and their rights as participants. The informed consent process involves providing participants with detailed information about the trial, including its purpose, procedures, potential risks and benefits, and the possibility of being assigned to a placebo or control group. This information must be conveyed clearly and understandably, using non-technical language, to facilitate participant comprehension. The documentation must also include a statement affirming that participation is voluntary, and that participants can withdraw from the study at any time without penalty.

The informed consent form serves as a formal record of this process and must be reviewed and approved by the **Institutional Review Board (IRB)** or ethics committee before the trial begins. Regulatory authorities require that the informed consent form accurately reflects the information provided to participants and is updated as needed to reflect any changes in the trial or new risks that may emerge. Proper documentation of informed consent is essential for protecting the rights of participants and ensuring compliance with ethical and legal standards. It also helps to build trust between researchers and participants, as individuals who feel informed and respected are more likely to participate in clinical research.

In cases where vulnerable populations are involved, such as children or individuals with cognitive impairments, additional measures must be taken to ensure that informed consent is obtained ethically. This may involve obtaining consent from a legal guardian or using simplified explanations to ensure understanding. Researchers must be particularly diligent in these situations, as vulnerable populations may be more susceptible to coercion or exploitation. Ensuring that informed consent is thoroughly documented and ethically obtained is fundamental to the integrity of RCTs and the protection of participant rights.

12.6.3 Ethical Approvals and Ongoing Safety Monitoring

Before a randomized controlled trial (RCT) can begin, it must undergo an ethical approval process involving review by an **Institutional Review Board (IRB)** or ethics committee. This independent body assesses the study protocol to ensure that it complies with ethical standards and protects the rights and welfare of participants. The IRB evaluates various aspects of the trial, including the risk-benefit ratio, informed consent processes, and the adequacy of participant protections. Ethical approval is crucial for ensuring that the study is designed to uphold the highest ethical standards and that any potential risks to participants are minimized.

Ongoing safety monitoring is another essential component of ethical oversight during the course of an RCT. As the trial progresses, the IRB is responsible for continuously reviewing data related to participant safety and welfare, including reports of any adverse events or serious adverse events (SAEs) that may arise. This monitoring allows the IRB to identify potential safety concerns early and take necessary actions to protect participants, such as modifying the study protocol or halting the trial if significant risks are detected. The importance of ongoing safety monitoring cannot be overstated, as it ensures that the rights and well-being of participants remain the top priority throughout the study.

In addition to IRB oversight, regulatory agencies often require sponsors to submit regular safety reports and updates on the trial's progress. This provides an additional layer of oversight and ensures that regulatory authorities are informed about any developments that may impact participant safety or the validity of the trial results. By adhering to rigorous ethical approval processes and ongoing safety monitoring, researchers can conduct RCTs in a manner that is both scientifically sound and ethically responsible, ultimately leading to the advancement of medical knowledge while safeguarding the rights and welfare of participants.

Review Questions

1. Why is randomization important in clinical trials?
2. Explain the difference between single-blind and double-blind studies and their ethical implications.
3. What is the concept of equipoise, and why is it critical to randomized controlled trials (RCTs)?
4. Discuss the ethical challenges associated with placebo-controlled trials.
5. What role do Institutional Review Boards (IRBs) play in ensuring ethical conduct in RCTs?
6. How is risk-benefit analysis conducted in RCTs?
7. How does blinding help in reducing bias in clinical trials?
8. What ethical issues arise in the use of placebo when effective treatments are already available?

CHAPTER THIRTEEN

The Role of Placebo in Clinical Trials

13.1 Understanding Placebo-Controlled Trials

13.1.1 Definition of Placebo and Placebo Effect

A **placebo** is defined as a substance or treatment that has no therapeutic effect, often used as a control in clinical trials to evaluate the effectiveness of new drugs. The **placebo effect** refers to the phenomenon where participants experience a perceived improvement in their condition after receiving a placebo, solely due to their expectations or beliefs about the treatment. This effect highlights the power of the mind in influencing physical symptoms, which can complicate the interpretation of trial results. In essence, the placebo serves as a critical control that allows researchers to determine whether the actual treatment has a genuine pharmacological effect beyond what might be achieved through psychological factors.

The understanding of the placebo effect is crucial for designing effective clinical trials. Researchers must ensure that any observed benefits in the experimental group can be attributed to the active treatment rather than to the participants' expectations. By comparing the results of participants receiving the new treatment against those receiving a placebo, investigators can more accurately assess the true efficacy of the drug. This differentiation is particularly important in conditions with subjective symptoms, such as pain or anxiety, where patient perception plays a significant role in reporting outcomes. Understanding the dynamics of placebos is essential for both ethical trial design and accurate scientific evaluation.

13.1.2 Types of Placebo-Controlled Studies

There are several types of **placebo-controlled studies** that researchers can employ, each designed to answer specific research questions while minimizing bias. One common design is the **parallel-group study**, where participants are randomly assigned to either the treatment group or the placebo group, and both groups are treated simultaneously over a predetermined period. This design allows for a direct comparison of the effects of the treatment against the placebo, providing clear insights into its efficacy. Another design is the **crossover study**, where participants receive both the active treatment and the placebo in a sequential manner, allowing each participant to serve as their own control. This design can enhance the power of the trial by reducing variability caused by differences between participants.

Another important type of placebo-controlled trial is the **active comparator trial**, where the new treatment is compared to an existing standard treatment rather than a placebo. This design is especially relevant in therapeutic areas where effective treatments are available, as it addresses ethical concerns about withholding effective therapy. While not strictly placebo-controlled, this design allows researchers to evaluate whether the new treatment is superior, inferior, or equivalent to existing therapies. The choice of study design ultimately depends on the research objectives, the condition being treated, and the ethical considerations surrounding placebo use.

13.1.3 Importance of Placebo in Drug Evaluation

The use of a placebo in drug evaluation is critical for establishing the **safety and efficacy** of new treatments. Placebo-controlled trials provide a rigorous methodology for determining whether a new drug has effects beyond those attributable to psychological factors or spontaneous recovery. By controlling for the placebo effect, researchers can confidently attribute any observed benefits or adverse effects directly to the active treatment being studied. This clarity is essential for regulatory approval processes, as it provides the necessary evidence to support claims of efficacy and safety made by pharmaceutical companies when submitting new drug applications to authorities like the **FDA** or **EMA**.

Additionally, placebos help to enhance the **scientific validity** of clinical trials by minimizing bias. They serve as a baseline against which the experimental treatment can be measured, allowing for more accurate interpretations of trial outcomes. The use of placebos also aids in the assessment of long-term treatment effects, as researchers can evaluate how patients fare after treatment discontinuation compared to those who did not receive the active treatment. Ultimately, the use of placebo in drug evaluation is a cornerstone of evidence-based medicine, ensuring that new therapies are proven to be effective and safe before they are made available to the public.

13.2 Ethical Considerations of Placebo Use

13.2.1 Informed Consent and Placebo Deception

Informed consent is a fundamental ethical principle in clinical trials, and it takes on added complexity when placebos are involved. Participants must be adequately informed about the possibility of receiving a placebo as part of the trial, and they should understand that this means they may not receive the experimental treatment. This requirement is crucial because it respects the autonomy of participants and ensures that their consent is based on a clear understanding of what participation entails. Researchers have the ethical obligation to provide this information in a manner that is both comprehensible and transparent, allowing participants to make informed decisions about their involvement in the study.

However, the issue of **placebo deception** can arise in trials where participants are not informed about the use of a placebo, particularly if the trial aims to measure the efficacy of a treatment against a placebo. While some argue that withholding this information is necessary to avoid bias in the participants' responses, this approach raises significant ethical concerns. Deceiving participants can erode trust between researchers and participants, leading to long-term implications for the integrity of clinical research. Ethical guidelines generally recommend that researchers strive for transparency, ensuring that participants are informed about the nature of the study while also discussing the scientific rationale for using a placebo. Balancing the need for scientific rigor with the ethical obligation to inform participants is a delicate yet essential task in the design of placebo-controlled trials.

The ethical complexities of informed consent and placebo deception necessitate careful consideration and oversight. Institutional Review Boards (IRBs) play a crucial role in evaluating the ethical implications of using placebos in trials and ensuring that participants are adequately informed about what their participation entails. Researchers must engage in an open dialogue with IRBs and adhere to established ethical guidelines to safeguard participants' rights. Ultimately, the ethical management of informed consent and the use of placebos is critical for maintaining the integrity of clinical research and ensuring the protection of participants' autonomy and well-being.

13.2.2 Placebo Use in Vulnerable Populations

The use of placebos in clinical trials raises particular ethical concerns when it involves **vulnerable populations**, such as children, the elderly, or individuals with cognitive impairments. Vulnerable groups may have limited capacity to provide informed consent or may be more susceptible to coercion, making it imperative for researchers to take extra precautions when enrolling these individuals in placebo-controlled studies. Ethical guidelines stipulate that additional safeguards must be implemented to protect these populations, ensuring that they are not exposed to unnecessary risks or denied effective treatments that could improve their health.

In trials involving vulnerable populations, researchers must clearly communicate the risks and benefits of participating in the study, including the possibility of being assigned to a placebo group. It is essential that caregivers or legal guardians provide consent for individuals who may not be able to do so independently. Researchers should also consider the ethical implications of withholding treatment from these individuals, especially if they have serious medical conditions for which effective therapies are available. The ethical obligation to provide the best possible care must be balanced with the need to generate reliable scientific data, creating a complex ethical landscape for researchers working with vulnerable populations.

To address these ethical challenges, researchers must be vigilant in their adherence to ethical guidelines and actively seek to engage with vulnerable populations in a respectful and inclusive manner. This includes providing additional information and support throughout the trial and ensuring that participants understand their rights, including the right to withdraw at any time without repercussions. By prioritizing the ethical treatment of vulnerable populations and being transparent about the use of placebos, researchers can help maintain trust and protect the rights of all participants in clinical trials.

13.2.3 Ethical Guidelines for Placebo Use

Ethical guidelines regarding the use of placebos in clinical trials are essential for ensuring that research is conducted responsibly and with respect for participants' rights. The **Declaration of Helsinki** and the **ICH-GCP**

guidelines both provide frameworks that outline when and how placebos can be ethically employed in clinical research. These guidelines specify that the use of placebos is acceptable when no effective treatment exists, or when withholding treatment does not pose a significant risk to participants. Researchers are expected to justify the use of a placebo and to ensure that participants are fully informed about the potential for receiving a placebo as part of the study.

Additionally, ethical guidelines emphasize the importance of maintaining transparency throughout the informed consent process. Participants must be made aware of their rights, including the right to withdraw from the study at any time without facing any penalties or loss of benefits. Researchers are also responsible for ensuring that participants are not placed at undue risk by being assigned to a placebo group, particularly in cases where effective treatments are available. Ongoing safety monitoring and ethical oversight by IRBs are crucial components of this process, as they help to ensure that the trial remains ethically sound and that participant welfare is prioritized throughout the study.

By adhering to established ethical guidelines regarding placebo use, researchers can conduct trials that not only generate valuable scientific data but also uphold the highest standards of ethical conduct. These guidelines foster an environment of respect and transparency, promoting trust between researchers and participants. Ultimately, ethical guidelines for placebo use are designed to balance the need for rigorous scientific inquiry with the ethical obligation to protect the rights and well-being of all individuals involved in clinical research.

13.3 Controversies Surrounding Placebo-Controlled Trials

13.3.1 Is Placebo Use Ethical When Effective Treatment Exists?
The ethical implications of using placebos in clinical trials are hotly debated, especially when effective treatments are already available for the condition being studied. Critics argue that assigning participants to a placebo group in such situations is unethical, as it withholds potentially beneficial treatment from individuals who may be in urgent need of care. This concern is particularly prominent in trials for serious or life-threatening conditions, such as cancer or severe depression, where effective therapies are already established. In these cases, participants randomized to a placebo may experience unnecessary suffering or deterioration in their health status,

raising significant ethical questions about the appropriateness of such trial designs.

Proponents of placebo-controlled trials argue that they are essential for rigorously assessing the efficacy of new treatments. They assert that the placebo effect must be accounted for to accurately determine whether a new intervention is genuinely effective beyond the psychological and physiological effects of participants' expectations. In situations where an existing treatment exists, ethical guidelines suggest that the use of a placebo can only be justified if withholding treatment does not pose significant risks to the participants. Therefore, researchers must demonstrate that there is genuine uncertainty regarding the relative efficacy of the treatments being compared and ensure that participants are fully informed about the potential risks of participating in the study.

The controversy surrounding placebo use in the presence of effective treatments calls for careful ethical scrutiny and robust justification. To navigate this ethical landscape, researchers may opt for designs that involve **active comparators** rather than placebos, allowing for a direct comparison between the new treatment and existing therapies. Ultimately, the use of placebos in clinical trials must prioritize the ethical principles of **beneficence, non-maleficence**, and respect for participants' autonomy, ensuring that research is conducted responsibly and ethically.

13.3.2 Balancing Scientific Rigor with Patient Welfare

In the context of placebo-controlled trials, striking a balance between **scientific rigor** and **patient welfare** is a critical ethical challenge. On one hand, the integrity of clinical research relies on the ability to generate valid and reliable data regarding the efficacy of new treatments. Placebos are an important tool in achieving this goal, as they help researchers determine whether the observed effects of a treatment are genuinely attributable to the intervention itself or if they arise from other factors, including the placebo effect. However, the requirement to adhere to rigorous scientific standards must not come at the expense of participants' health and well-being.

The ethical challenge arises when the scientific need for a placebo is pitted against the ethical obligation to provide the best possible care to participants. For example, in trials for conditions with available treatments, using a placebo may compromise patient welfare by denying them access to effective therapies. This tension necessitates careful ethical deliberation and consultation with ethics committees to ensure that participant safety and well-being are not sacrificed for the sake of scientific inquiry.

Researchers must also communicate openly with participants about the rationale for using a placebo and the potential risks involved in participating in the study.

Ultimately, the balance between scientific rigor and patient welfare requires ongoing dialogue among researchers, ethics committees, and regulatory authorities. By prioritizing patient safety while striving to uphold the integrity of clinical research, investigators can design trials that are both scientifically valid and ethically sound. This commitment to ethical principles not only protects participants but also enhances the credibility of the research, fostering public trust in clinical trials.

13.3.3 Alternatives to Placebo Controls

In light of the ethical controversies surrounding the use of placebos, researchers are increasingly exploring **alternatives to placebo controls** in clinical trials. One of the most prominent alternatives is the use of **active control groups**, where the experimental treatment is compared directly to an existing standard treatment rather than a placebo. This approach allows for a more ethical design when effective therapies are available, ensuring that all participants receive some form of treatment while still allowing researchers to assess the efficacy of the new intervention. Active control trials help to uphold ethical standards while still providing valuable data on the effectiveness of new treatments.

Another alternative to traditional placebo-controlled trials is the use of **waitlist control designs**. In this design, participants on the waitlist receive the experimental treatment after the trial concludes, allowing them to benefit from the new intervention while still providing a control group for comparison. This design can help mitigate ethical concerns associated with withholding effective treatment, particularly in trials involving psychological or behavioral interventions. Waitlist control designs enable researchers to gather robust data on treatment efficacy while ensuring that all participants eventually receive access to the intervention.

Researchers are also considering **pragmatic trial designs**, which are designed to evaluate the effectiveness of interventions in real-world settings. These trials often involve comparisons between existing treatment options rather than strict placebo controls, making them more ethically acceptable in certain contexts. Pragmatic trials focus on the practical implications of treatments and aim to provide insights into how new therapies will perform in everyday clinical practice. By exploring these alternative designs, researchers can address ethical concerns while continuing to advance medical knowledge and improve patient care.

13.4 Placebo Effect and Its Implications

13.4.1 Mechanisms of the Placebo Effect

The **placebo effect** is a complex phenomenon that illustrates the profound influence of the mind on physical health. It occurs when participants experience real improvements in their condition after receiving a placebo, which has no therapeutic effect. Several mechanisms are thought to underlie the placebo effect, including **psychological factors** such as expectation, conditioning, and individual beliefs about the treatment. For instance, when patients believe they are receiving an effective treatment, their expectations can lead to physiological changes, such as the release of endorphins or other neurochemicals, which can alleviate symptoms. This highlights the significant role that the **mind-body connection** plays in the healing process.

Another important mechanism contributing to the placebo effect is **classical conditioning**, where patients learn to associate specific cues—such as taking a pill or visiting a clinic—with positive health outcomes. Over time, these associations can trigger physiological responses similar to those produced by actual treatments, resulting in measurable improvements in symptoms. The placebo effect is also influenced by various contextual factors, including the patient-provider relationship, the setting in which treatment is administered, and the overall treatment experience. Understanding these mechanisms is crucial for researchers, as it enables them to design studies that account for the potential impact of the placebo effect on treatment outcomes.

Recognizing the placebo effect is essential not only for the design of clinical trials but also for interpreting their results. In drug evaluation, distinguishing between the actual therapeutic effects of a drug and the placebo effect is vital for establishing the drug's efficacy. Researchers must account for the placebo effect when analyzing trial outcomes, especially in conditions where psychological factors play a significant role in symptom presentation. By studying the mechanisms of the placebo effect, researchers can gain insights into how patients respond to treatments, leading to improved strategies for optimizing therapeutic interventions.

13.4.2 Impact on Clinical Trial Outcomes

The placebo effect can significantly impact the outcomes of clinical trials, often complicating the assessment of a new treatment's efficacy. In trials where participants exhibit strong placebo responses, it may be challenging to determine whether observed improvements are due to the active treatment or simply the result of participants' expectations and beliefs. This variability can mask the true therapeutic effects of a drug, leading to potentially misleading conclusions about its effectiveness. As a result, researchers must carefully consider the design and analysis of trials to account for the placebo effect and ensure that it does not confound the results.

The impact of the placebo effect is particularly pronounced in conditions characterized by subjective symptoms, such as pain, anxiety, or depression. In these cases, participants may report improvements in their condition after receiving a placebo, complicating the interpretation of trial outcomes. To address this challenge, researchers often employ methods such as **blinding** and **randomization** to minimize bias and control for the placebo effect. Additionally, they may use objective measures to assess outcomes, such as physiological markers or biomarkers, which are less susceptible to the influence of the placebo effect. By implementing these strategies, researchers can better isolate the true effects of the treatment being studied.

Understanding the implications of the placebo effect on clinical trial outcomes is essential for designing effective studies and interpreting their results. By recognizing the power of the mind in shaping health outcomes, researchers can improve trial designs and analysis strategies to yield more accurate assessments of new treatments. Ultimately, addressing the impact of the placebo effect is crucial for advancing evidence-based medicine and ensuring that patients receive the most effective therapies.

13.4.3 Minimizing Placebo Effect in Drug Efficacy Studies

Minimizing the influence of the **placebo effect** in drug efficacy studies is a significant challenge that researchers face when designing clinical trials. To accurately assess the true therapeutic effects of a treatment, it is essential to implement strategies that mitigate the impact of participants' expectations and beliefs. One approach is to utilize **placebo-controlled designs**, where participants are randomly assigned to either the treatment or placebo group. This randomization helps ensure that any observed effects can be attributed to the active treatment rather than the psychological influence of the placebo. By creating a balanced comparison, researchers can gain insights into the true efficacy of the drug.

Another strategy to minimize the placebo effect is to use **objective outcome measures** that are less susceptible to participant bias. For instance, in trials for pain relief, researchers may include physiological assessments, such as changes in biomarker levels or imaging studies, alongside subjective measures like self-reported pain scores. By incorporating objective data, researchers can better determine whether the treatment has a measurable effect beyond that of the placebo. Additionally, ensuring that trial personnel involved in participant assessments are blinded to group assignments can help prevent any potential biases in outcome reporting, further enhancing the integrity of the results.

Education and awareness about the placebo effect also play a role in minimizing its influence on clinical trial outcomes. Researchers can educate participants about the possibility of receiving a placebo and the nature of the trial while emphasizing the importance of unbiased reporting of symptoms. This transparency can help manage participants' expectations and reduce the likelihood of exaggerated placebo responses. By employing these strategies, researchers can improve the reliability of drug efficacy studies, ensuring that they generate meaningful data that accurately reflects the therapeutic effects of new treatments.

13.5 Designing Placebo-Controlled Trials

13.5.1 Placebo Selection and Administration

The selection and administration of a **placebo** are critical components in the design of placebo-controlled trials, as these factors can significantly impact the study's validity and the interpretation of results. Researchers must choose a placebo that closely resembles the active treatment in terms of appearance, administration route, and regimen to minimize participants' ability to discern their group assignment. For instance, if the experimental drug is a capsule, the placebo should also be a capsule with similar size, color, and texture. This similarity is crucial for maintaining **blinding**, as it helps to ensure that any observed effects can be attributed to the active treatment rather than participants' expectations about receiving a specific intervention.

The administration of the placebo must also mimic that of the active treatment to ensure that participants have a consistent experience throughout the trial. This includes maintaining the same schedule of dosing and providing the same level of support and monitoring to both treatment and placebo groups. It is essential for researchers to ensure that participants are unaware of their group assignment to prevent biases related to expectations or beliefs about the treatment. Proper training of trial personnel in administering the placebo and monitoring participants is also vital to uphold the integrity of the trial. Ultimately, careful selection and administration of the placebo are critical for reducing bias and enhancing the validity of the trial's findings.

13.5.2 Blinding in Placebo-Controlled Trials

Blinding is a fundamental aspect of designing placebo-controlled trials, as it helps to prevent bias and ensures the integrity of the study results. In a double-blind trial, neither the participants nor the investigators know which individuals are receiving the active treatment and which are receiving the placebo. This lack of knowledge minimizes the risk of **observer bias**, where the expectations or beliefs of investigators could influence their assessments of participants' responses to treatment. By maintaining blinding throughout the study, researchers can ensure that any differences observed between the groups are attributable to the treatment itself rather than external influences.

Implementing effective blinding can be challenging, especially in longer trials or those involving multiple interventions. Researchers must develop robust protocols to maintain blinding and must be prepared to address any potential breaches of blinding that may occur during the trial. For instance, if participants begin to experience noticeable side effects that are characteristic of the active treatment, they may infer their group assignment, compromising the integrity of the trial. To mitigate these risks, researchers can utilize independent data monitoring committees to oversee the trial and ensure that blinding is upheld throughout the study. By prioritizing effective blinding, researchers can enhance the validity of the findings and maintain the ethical integrity of the trial.

13.5.3 Statistical Considerations in Placebo-Controlled Studies

Statistical considerations are crucial in the design and analysis of placebo-controlled studies, as they determine how data will be interpreted and whether the trial can draw valid conclusions about the efficacy of the treatment. One of the primary statistical considerations is the **sample size**, which must be adequately powered to detect a statistically significant difference between the treatment and placebo groups. Calculating the appropriate sample size requires considering factors such as the expected effect size, the variability of the outcome measures, and the desired level of statistical significance. Underestimating the necessary sample size can lead to **Type II errors**, where a potentially effective treatment appears ineffective simply because the study was not adequately powered to detect its effects.

Another important statistical aspect is the method of analyzing the data collected during the trial. Researchers must decide whether to employ **intention-to-treat (ITT)** analysis or per-protocol analysis. ITT analysis involves including all participants in the groups to which they were originally assigned, regardless of whether they completed the trial or adhered to the treatment protocol. This approach helps to preserve the benefits of randomization and reduces bias in the analysis. In contrast, per-protocol analysis only includes participants who completed the trial according to the study protocol, which may lead to biased results if dropouts or non-compliance are related to treatment outcomes. Selecting the appropriate statistical approach is essential for accurately interpreting the results and ensuring that they reflect the true efficacy of the treatment.

Furthermore, researchers must be aware of potential **confounding variables** that could impact the results of the trial. Randomization typically helps to control for these confounders; however, it is still important to identify and account for any variables that may influence the outcomes. Using stratification or multivariable analysis techniques can help researchers better control for these factors in their analyses. By carefully considering these statistical factors in the design and analysis of placebo-controlled studies, researchers can enhance the validity and reliability of their findings, ensuring that they contribute meaningfully to the evidence base in clinical research.

13.6 Placebo-Controlled Trials in Global Regulatory Frameworks

13.6.1 FDA and EMA Guidelines on Placebo Use

Regulatory bodies such as the **FDA** (Food and Drug Administration) in the United States and the **EMA** (European Medicines Agency) in Europe have established guidelines regarding the use of placebos in clinical trials. These guidelines emphasize the importance of conducting trials ethically while ensuring that they are scientifically rigorous. Both agencies recognize that placebos can be valuable tools in determining the efficacy of new treatments, particularly when no effective therapies exist. The FDA allows the use of placebo controls in trials for conditions where standard treatments are not available, provided that the research adheres to ethical principles and safeguards participant welfare.

The EMA also supports the use of placebo controls but places a strong emphasis on the need for scientific justification when effective treatments are available. According to EMA guidelines, trials involving placebos should ensure that the use of a placebo does not compromise the health and well-being of participants. In cases where effective treatments exist, researchers must demonstrate that the trial design is essential for addressing specific scientific questions and that the potential benefits of the research outweigh the risks associated with withholding treatment. By establishing these guidelines, both the FDA and EMA aim to protect participants while advancing the development of new therapies.

Regulatory agencies continue to assess and update their guidelines on placebo use in response to evolving ethical considerations and emerging evidence from clinical research. This dynamic nature of regulatory frameworks ensures that they remain aligned with current scientific practices while addressing public concerns regarding the ethical implications of placebo-controlled trials. Researchers must remain informed about these evolving guidelines to ensure compliance and uphold ethical standards in their studies.

13.6.2 Ethical Requirements for Placebo Trials Across Regions
Ethical requirements for placebo trials can vary significantly across different regions and countries, reflecting local cultural attitudes, healthcare practices, and regulatory environments. In many countries, ethical guidelines dictate that placebos should only be used when no effective treatments are available, or when withholding treatment does not pose significant risks to participants. For instance, in regions where standard treatments are readily accessible, the ethical justification for using a placebo becomes more complex, requiring researchers to demonstrate that the trial design is necessary for addressing specific scientific questions. This diversity in ethical requirements necessitates careful consideration by researchers conducting multinational trials to ensure compliance with local regulations while maintaining the integrity of the study.

Moreover, the **cultural context** surrounding healthcare can influence how placebo use is perceived. In some cultures, patients may have different expectations regarding treatment, which can affect their willingness to accept the possibility of receiving a placebo. Researchers must be sensitive to these cultural differences and consider how they may impact the informed consent process and participant recruitment. Engaging local stakeholders and ethics committees can help ensure that the trial design respects cultural norms while also adhering to ethical standards. By navigating these ethical requirements and cultural considerations, researchers can conduct placebo trials that are both scientifically valid and ethically responsible.

The challenges of aligning ethical requirements across regions underscore the importance of **international collaboration** in clinical research. Organizations like the **International Conference on Harmonization (ICH)** work to harmonize guidelines and promote ethical standards in clinical trials worldwide. By fostering collaboration and communication among regulatory bodies, researchers can work toward establishing more uniform ethical frameworks for placebo trials. This will help ensure that all participants, regardless of their geographic location, are treated with respect and fairness, and that the integrity of clinical research is upheld across borders.

13.6.3 Case Studies on the Success and Challenges of Placebo-Controlled Trials

Case studies of **placebo-controlled trials** offer valuable insights into both the successes and challenges associated with this study design. One notable example is the **clinical trials for the antidepressant medication Prozac (fluoxetine)**, which were conducted in the late 1980s. In these trials, participants receiving Prozac experienced significantly greater improvements in depressive symptoms compared to those assigned to a placebo. The success of these trials not only provided strong evidence for the efficacy of Prozac but also helped to establish the importance of placebo-controlled designs in assessing the effectiveness of psychiatric medications. These findings contributed to a better understanding of how effective pharmacological treatments can alter the course of mental health conditions.

However, placebo-controlled trials have also faced challenges and criticisms. The **Antidepressant Versus Placebo Controlled Trial (AVERT)**, which aimed to evaluate the efficacy of a new antidepressant, encountered significant ethical concerns when early results suggested that the placebo group was experiencing similar rates of improvement as those receiving the active treatment. Critics argued that continuing to assign participants to a placebo group, given the emerging evidence of comparable outcomes, was ethically questionable. This situation prompted a reevaluation of the trial design and raised important questions about maintaining equipoise in the face of changing evidence.

These case studies highlight the importance of ethical oversight and adaptability in the design and conduct of placebo-controlled trials. They serve as a reminder that while placebos can be essential tools for establishing the efficacy of new treatments, researchers must remain vigilant in ensuring that participant welfare is prioritized and that the ethical implications of using placebos are thoroughly addressed. By learning from past experiences and implementing best practices, researchers can continue to advance medical knowledge while adhering to the highest ethical standards.

Review Questions

1. Define placebo and describe the placebo effect.
2. What are the ethical considerations of using placebo in clinical trials?
3. When is it ethically justifiable to use a placebo in a clinical trial?
4. Discuss the controversies surrounding placebo-controlled trials when effective treatment options exist.
5. How does the placebo effect impact the outcome of clinical trials?
6. What are the alternatives to placebo controls in clinical research?
7. What are the challenges of maintaining blinding in placebo-controlled trials?
8. How do regulatory bodies such as the FDA and EMA view placebo-controlled trials?

CHAPTER FOURTEEN

Ethical Considerations for Special Populations

14.1 Special Populations in Clinical Research

14.1.1 Definition of Special Populations (Children, Elderly, Pregnant Women)

Special populations in clinical research refer to groups of individuals who may have different vulnerabilities or ethical considerations due to their specific characteristics or circumstances. This includes children, the elderly, and pregnant women, among others. Each of these groups presents unique challenges and considerations in clinical trials. For instance, children are often underrepresented in clinical research, despite being affected by many medical conditions that require effective treatment. Their physiological and psychological differences necessitate careful consideration when designing studies, as the effects of medications can vary significantly from those in adults.

The elderly population also represents a special group in clinical research due to age-related physiological changes, comorbidities, and polypharmacy, which can affect drug metabolism and response. This population often faces barriers to participation, such as cognitive impairments or mobility issues, which can complicate recruitment and retention efforts in clinical trials. Pregnant women are another special population, as ethical considerations regarding fetal exposure to investigational drugs create unique challenges. Regulatory bodies often mandate that clinical trials involving pregnant women provide clear justifications for their inclusion and ensure that both maternal and fetal risks are adequately assessed.

Given these complexities, it is vital to adopt a tailored approach when conducting research involving special populations. Ethical considerations must be at the forefront of study design to ensure that the rights and welfare of participants are protected. Regulatory frameworks and guidelines provide a necessary foundation for researchers, ensuring that trials involving special populations are conducted ethically and responsibly. This requires ongoing collaboration between researchers, ethics committees, and regulatory authorities to establish clear protocols that address the unique needs of these vulnerable groups.

Ultimately, understanding the definition and characteristics of special populations is crucial for fostering ethical clinical research practices. By recognizing the unique challenges associated with recruiting and conducting studies in these populations, researchers can develop more effective and inclusive trial designs. This commitment to ethical research practices not only promotes the welfare of participants but also enhances the quality and applicability of the research findings.

14.1.2 Ethical Challenges in Recruiting Special Populations

Recruiting special populations for clinical research poses significant **ethical challenges** that must be carefully navigated to protect participants' rights and well-being. One major challenge is the potential for **coercion** or undue influence when seeking consent from vulnerable individuals. For example, children may not fully understand the implications of participating in a clinical trial, making it essential for researchers to obtain informed consent from parents or guardians while also ensuring that the child's assent is sought wherever possible. This dual consent process can be complex, as it requires balancing the child's best interests with parental authority.

Another ethical concern is the risk of **exploitation** in special populations, particularly in economically disadvantaged groups. Researchers must be vigilant to ensure that participation in clinical trials does not become a means of financial gain for the sponsors at the expense of vulnerable individuals. There is a responsibility to provide fair compensation for participation while ensuring that financial incentives do not unduly influence individuals' decisions to enroll in studies. This is particularly important in populations that may feel compelled to participate due to financial hardships, as it raises significant ethical concerns about voluntariness and autonomy.

Moreover, the representation of special populations in clinical research is often inadequate, leading to a lack of generalizability of findings. For example, clinical trials may disproportionately involve young, healthy adults, making it challenging to understand how new treatments may affect children, the elderly, or pregnant women. This underrepresentation raises ethical questions about the obligation to include diverse populations in research to ensure that findings are applicable to the broader population. Researchers must prioritize inclusivity and strive to recruit participants from special populations while addressing the ethical complexities involved.

Ultimately, addressing the ethical challenges of recruiting special populations requires a multifaceted approach that prioritizes participant welfare, informed consent, and inclusivity. Researchers must engage with ethics committees, patient advocacy groups, and community representatives to develop strategies for ethical recruitment that respect the rights and dignity of all individuals involved. By doing so, they can ensure that clinical research is conducted responsibly and ethically, leading to better health outcomes for diverse populations.

14.1.3 Regulatory Guidelines for Research on Special Populations

Regulatory guidelines play a crucial role in ensuring the ethical conduct of research involving special populations. Agencies such as the **FDA**, **EMA**, and **ICH** have established specific regulations and recommendations to guide researchers in addressing the unique considerations associated with these groups. For example, the **ICH E11 guidelines** specifically address the ethical and scientific considerations for pediatric studies, emphasizing the need for appropriate study designs that are tailored to the developmental stages of children. These guidelines outline the importance of minimizing risks, maximizing potential benefits, and ensuring that the welfare of child participants is prioritized throughout the research process.

In addition to pediatric populations, regulatory bodies also recognize the unique considerations involved in studying the elderly and pregnant women. For instance, the FDA has provided guidelines on conducting research in the elderly, focusing on the need to account for age-related physiological changes and comorbidities that may affect drug efficacy and safety. Similarly, regulations surrounding research involving pregnant women require that potential risks to both the mother and fetus be thoroughly assessed before conducting trials. These guidelines aim to ensure that the ethical principles of beneficence, non-maleficence, and respect for autonomy are upheld while advancing medical knowledge and developing new treatments.

Researchers must familiarize themselves with these regulatory guidelines and ensure that their study designs align with the established ethical standards. Engaging with regulatory authorities early in the research process can help clarify any uncertainties regarding the inclusion of special populations and ensure that the trials are designed in compliance with applicable regulations. By adhering to regulatory guidelines, researchers can conduct studies that not only generate meaningful data but also prioritize the rights and welfare of participants, fostering trust and integrity in clinical research.

14.2 Clinical Trials in Children

14.2.1 Pediatric-Specific Ethical Concerns

Conducting clinical trials involving children raises unique **ethical concerns** that researchers must navigate carefully to protect this vulnerable population. One of the primary concerns is the **capacity of children to provide informed consent**. Unlike adults, children may lack the cognitive ability to fully understand the implications of participating in a trial, including potential risks and benefits. As such, obtaining informed consent requires careful consideration of how information is presented to both the child and their parents or guardians. The ethical obligation to ensure that children are adequately informed, while also respecting parental authority, creates a complex dynamic that researchers must address.

Another significant ethical concern is the risk of **exploitation** of child participants in clinical research. Children are particularly vulnerable to coercion, especially when parents or guardians may feel pressure to enroll their children in studies for the potential benefits of new treatments. This concern is amplified in economically disadvantaged populations, where the prospect of receiving free healthcare or compensation may unduly influence decisions about participation. To safeguard against exploitation, researchers must implement robust ethical safeguards, including transparent communication about the nature of the study, as well as emphasizing the voluntariness of participation.

Additionally, researchers must consider the **potential risks** associated with pediatric trials. Children are not simply small adults; their developing bodies may respond differently to medications and treatments, necessitating specific considerations for dosing, safety, and monitoring. Researchers must ensure that risks are minimized and that any potential benefits are clearly communicated to participants and their families. This includes the need for age-appropriate protocols that take into account children's unique physiological and psychological needs, ensuring that their welfare remains the top priority throughout the research process.

14.2.2 Assent and Consent in Pediatric Trials

In pediatric clinical trials, obtaining both **assent** from the child and informed consent from a parent or guardian is essential. **Informed consent** involves securing permission from the parent or guardian, ensuring that they understand the study's purpose, procedures, risks, and benefits. This process is crucial for respecting the autonomy of parents and their role in making decisions about their child's participation in research. Parents must be adequately informed about the trial and feel confident in their decision to allow their child to participate, recognizing that their child's welfare is paramount.

Assent, on the other hand, refers to the process of obtaining agreement from the child to participate in the study, even if they are not legally able to provide full informed consent. Researchers should strive to engage children in the decision-making process in an age-appropriate manner, ensuring that they understand the study's nature and implications to the best of their ability. The assent process can vary based on the child's age and maturity, requiring researchers to adapt their communication strategies accordingly. For younger children, this may involve simple explanations and assurances, while older children may engage in more detailed discussions about their participation.

The ethical obligation to obtain both assent and consent underscores the need for researchers to foster an environment of trust and respect in pediatric trials. Researchers must be sensitive to the emotional and psychological aspects of participation and ensure that children feel comfortable expressing their feelings about the study. By prioritizing the rights and welfare of child participants through a thoughtful assent process, researchers can uphold ethical standards while generating valuable data that contribute to improved treatments for pediatric populations.

14.2.3 Regulatory Requirements for Pediatric Studies (ICH E11)

Regulatory bodies recognize the importance of addressing the unique considerations involved in conducting clinical trials with children, leading to the establishment of specific guidelines such as **ICH E11**. These guidelines provide a framework for designing pediatric studies that are both ethically sound and scientifically rigorous. The ICH E11 guidelines emphasize the necessity of conducting trials that are appropriate for the developmental stages of children, ensuring that study designs are tailored to meet their specific needs and vulnerabilities. This includes considerations for dosing, administration routes, and potential side effects, which may differ significantly from those in adults.

In addition to addressing ethical and scientific considerations, the ICH E11 guidelines stress the importance of involving children and their families in the research process. Engaging with stakeholders can enhance the design of pediatric studies by ensuring that protocols reflect the perspectives and preferences of both parents and children. The guidelines also advocate for minimizing risks and maximizing potential benefits, emphasizing that participation in clinical research should provide meaningful opportunities for pediatric patients to access new therapies that may not be available otherwise.

Regulatory authorities require that pediatric studies adhere to the principles outlined in ICH E11 when submitting trial protocols for approval. This includes demonstrating compliance with ethical standards for obtaining consent and assent, as well as providing a thorough justification for the study's design and objectives. By following these regulatory requirements, researchers can conduct pediatric trials that are ethically responsible and contribute to the development of safe and effective treatments for children.

14.3 Clinical Trials in Pregnant and Lactating Women

14.3.1 Ethical Issues in Research with Pregnant Women

Conducting clinical trials involving **pregnant women** presents unique ethical challenges that require careful consideration. One of the primary concerns is the potential risk to both the mother and the developing fetus. Ethical guidelines emphasize the necessity of protecting the welfare of both parties, as pregnant women may be at increased risk for adverse effects from experimental treatments. This heightened risk necessitates a thorough evaluation of the safety and efficacy of any intervention prior to conducting trials in this population. Ethical principles, such as **beneficence, non-maleficence**, and **justice**, must guide the design and execution of research involving pregnant participants to ensure that their rights and well-being are prioritized.

Another ethical issue is the historical context surrounding the exclusion of pregnant women from clinical research. Historically, regulatory authorities have recommended limiting their participation due to concerns about potential fetal harm and the difficulties associated with obtaining informed consent. As a result, this exclusion has led to a significant gap in knowledge regarding the safety and efficacy of medications during pregnancy, leaving healthcare providers with limited evidence to guide treatment decisions. Researchers must navigate the delicate balance between ensuring the safety of pregnant women and the ethical obligation to generate the necessary data to inform clinical practice. Engaging with obstetricians, ethicists, and representatives from advocacy groups can help researchers develop protocols that prioritize the ethical considerations surrounding the inclusion of pregnant women in clinical trials.

14.3.2 Risk-Benefit Analysis for Trials Involving This Group

Conducting a comprehensive **risk-benefit analysis** is critical when designing clinical trials involving pregnant women. This analysis involves weighing the potential benefits of the research—such as improved treatments for pregnant women and enhanced understanding of drug safety during pregnancy—against the possible risks to both the mother and the fetus. It is essential for researchers to carefully assess the potential impacts of the intervention being studied, including any known risks associated with the drug, the potential for adverse fetal outcomes, and the mother's health status. The ultimate goal is to ensure that the potential benefits justify the risks involved in the study.

Moreover, conducting research in this population requires special attention to the informed consent process. Pregnant women must be provided with clear, comprehensive information about the study, including its purpose, procedures, potential risks, and the implications for both themselves and their unborn child. Researchers must communicate any uncertainties regarding the effects of the intervention during pregnancy, as well as the potential consequences of not participating in the study. This transparency is essential for ensuring that pregnant women can make informed decisions about their participation, understanding both the potential benefits and risks associated with the trial. Engaging in an open dialogue with participants can foster trust and ensure that their autonomy is respected throughout the research process.

14.3.3 Regulatory Guidelines for Including Pregnant Women in Trials

Regulatory guidelines play a crucial role in shaping the conduct of clinical trials involving **pregnant women**. Organizations such as the **FDA** and **EMA** have established specific recommendations for including pregnant women in research, reflecting a growing recognition of the need to better understand the effects of medications during pregnancy. The **FDA** has developed guidelines that emphasize the importance of evaluating drug safety and efficacy in pregnant populations, particularly for conditions that disproportionately affect women during pregnancy. These guidelines underscore the necessity of conducting thorough risk assessments and ensuring that potential benefits are clearly communicated to participants.

The **ICH E6 and E11 guidelines** also address the ethical and scientific considerations for including pregnant women in clinical trials. These guidelines emphasize the importance of obtaining informed consent, ensuring that the rights of both the mother and the fetus are protected throughout the study. They also highlight the need for conducting adequate preclinical studies to assess the safety of the intervention prior to enrolling pregnant women. Regulatory bodies encourage researchers to seek input from **ethics committees** and obstetric specialists when designing studies that involve this population. By adhering to these regulatory guidelines, researchers can ensure that they conduct trials involving pregnant women responsibly, ethically, and in accordance with established standards.

14.4 Research in the Elderly

14.4.1 Challenges in Studying Older Populations

Studying older populations in clinical trials presents a variety of **challenges** that researchers must navigate to ensure ethical and scientifically valid outcomes. One major challenge is the **heterogeneity** within the elderly population, which encompasses a wide range of ages, health statuses, and comorbidities. This variability can complicate the recruitment process, as participants may have different responses to treatments due to their unique health profiles. Moreover, the presence of multiple chronic conditions is common among older adults, which can increase the risk of adverse effects and complicate the interpretation of trial results. Researchers must take these factors into account when designing studies to ensure that they can accurately assess the efficacy and safety of new interventions.

Another significant challenge in researching older populations is related to **cognitive impairments** that may affect participants' ability to provide informed consent. Many elderly individuals may experience conditions such as dementia or other cognitive decline, which can impair their understanding of the trial's purpose, risks, and benefits. This raises ethical concerns about their capacity to provide valid informed consent and underscores the need for additional safeguards when enrolling these individuals in clinical trials. Researchers may need to engage caregivers or legally authorized representatives in the consent process to ensure that the rights and welfare of vulnerable participants are adequately protected.

Additionally, older adults may face barriers to participation in clinical trials due to physical limitations, transportation issues, or a lack of access to healthcare resources. These challenges can result in lower enrollment rates among older populations, leading to an underrepresentation of this group in clinical research. Researchers must actively seek to address these barriers by developing flexible trial designs that accommodate the needs of older participants and promote accessibility. This may include offering transportation assistance, conducting remote assessments, or implementing home visits to facilitate participation. By addressing these challenges, researchers can enhance the representation of older populations in clinical trials and generate data that is more relevant to their healthcare needs.

14.4.2 Special Ethical Considerations for Geriatric Studies

When conducting clinical trials involving older adults, researchers must navigate a range of **ethical considerations** to ensure that the rights and welfare of participants are prioritized. One key ethical issue is the need to obtain informed consent from older adults, many of whom may have cognitive impairments that impact their decision-making abilities. Researchers must be diligent in assessing participants' capacity to consent and may need to involve caregivers or legally authorized representatives when necessary. This dual-consent process emphasizes the importance of respecting both the autonomy of older adults and the rights of their guardians while ensuring that participants fully understand the nature of the trial and their role in it.

Another ethical consideration is the potential for **exploitation** of older adults in research. Vulnerable populations, including the elderly, may be more susceptible to coercion or undue influence, particularly if they perceive participation in clinical trials as a means of obtaining care or financial benefits. Researchers must establish safeguards to protect against exploitation, such as providing clear and transparent information about the study's risks and benefits, ensuring that participation is truly voluntary, and allowing participants the option to withdraw from the trial at any time without penalty. Upholding ethical standards is vital for fostering trust between researchers and older participants, ultimately contributing to more successful and ethically sound research.

Furthermore, researchers must consider the broader societal implications of their studies involving older adults. The results of geriatric studies can significantly impact healthcare policy and practice, influencing treatment recommendations and guidelines for managing chronic conditions in the elderly. As such, researchers have a responsibility to ensure that their studies are designed to generate valid and reliable data that accurately reflect the needs and responses of older populations. By conducting ethical and rigorous research, investigators can contribute to improving healthcare outcomes for the elderly while maintaining the highest ethical standards.

14.4.3 Regulatory Requirements for Geriatric Research (ICH E7)

The importance of including older populations in clinical trials has led to the establishment of regulatory requirements specifically aimed at **geriatric research**. The **ICH E7 guidelines** address the need for studies involving the elderly to ensure that their unique characteristics and health needs are adequately considered. These guidelines emphasize the necessity of designing trials that are appropriate for older populations, taking into account factors such as **polypharmacy**, comorbidities, and age-related physiological changes that can affect drug metabolism and response. By adhering to these guidelines, researchers can improve the relevance and applicability of trial findings for the elderly.

Regulatory authorities also emphasize the importance of obtaining informed consent from older participants while considering their capacity to provide valid consent. The ICH E7 guidelines recommend using simplified consent processes and providing additional support to ensure that older adults understand the implications of their participation. This may include using clear and accessible language, engaging family members in discussions, and allowing ample time for questions. The goal is to foster an environment in which older participants feel comfortable making informed decisions about their involvement in research.

Furthermore, the regulatory framework for geriatric research includes provisions for ongoing safety monitoring to protect older participants throughout the study. Researchers are encouraged to implement robust monitoring processes to identify and address any adverse events promptly. This oversight is especially critical in studies involving older adults, who may have different responses to treatments compared to younger populations. By complying with regulatory requirements and prioritizing the ethical conduct of geriatric research, researchers can contribute to a growing body of evidence that informs the development of safe and effective treatments for older adults.

14.5 Vulnerable Populations and Clinical Research

14.5.1 Identifying Vulnerable Populations in Research

Identifying **vulnerable populations** in clinical research is a critical first step in ensuring ethical and responsible study design. Vulnerable populations may include groups such as children, the elderly, pregnant women, individuals with cognitive impairments, economically disadvantaged individuals, and those from minority or marginalized communities. Each of these groups may face unique challenges that can impact their capacity to provide informed consent, their access to healthcare, and their ability to participate in research without coercion or exploitation. Recognizing these vulnerabilities is essential for researchers to tailor their approaches and protect the rights and well-being of these individuals.

To effectively identify vulnerable populations, researchers must conduct thorough **community assessments** and engage with stakeholders, including community leaders, healthcare providers, and patient advocacy groups. These assessments can provide valuable insights into the specific needs, barriers, and concerns of vulnerable groups, allowing researchers to design studies that are culturally sensitive and inclusive. Additionally, regulatory bodies and ethics committees often provide guidance on identifying vulnerable populations and may require researchers to demonstrate that they have considered these factors in their study designs. By proactively identifying and addressing the needs of vulnerable populations, researchers can foster trust and enhance the ethical conduct of clinical research.

14.5.2 Safeguards for Protecting Vulnerable Participants

Implementing **safeguards** for protecting vulnerable participants in clinical research is essential to uphold ethical standards and ensure participant welfare. One of the primary safeguards is the establishment of robust **informed consent processes** that take into account the unique needs and capacities of vulnerable individuals. Researchers must ensure that participants are fully informed about the study, including its purpose, risks, benefits, and their rights. When working with populations that may have cognitive impairments or limited understanding, such as children or individuals with mental disabilities, researchers should involve caregivers or legally authorized representatives in the consent process to ensure that participants' rights are upheld.

Another key safeguard is the implementation of **independent oversight** through ethics committees or Institutional Review Boards (IRBs). These bodies play a crucial role in reviewing research proposals involving vulnerable populations to ensure that appropriate protections are in place. They assess the study design, informed consent processes, and risk-benefit analyses to ensure that the rights and welfare of vulnerable participants are prioritized. Additionally, ongoing monitoring during the trial helps identify any emerging ethical concerns, enabling timely interventions to protect participants as needed.

Researchers can also adopt flexible trial designs that accommodate the needs of vulnerable populations. This may include simplifying study procedures, offering transportation assistance, or providing support services to help participants navigate the research process. By actively addressing barriers to participation and implementing safeguards, researchers can help ensure that vulnerable individuals can participate in clinical research safely and ethically.

14.5.3 Ethical Guidelines for Conducting Research in Vulnerable Groups

Ethical guidelines for conducting research in vulnerable groups are established to protect participants and promote ethical research practices. Various organizations and regulatory bodies, including the **World Health Organization (WHO)** and the **Belmont Report**, have developed guidelines that outline the ethical principles applicable to vulnerable populations. These guidelines emphasize the importance of **respect for persons**, **beneficence**, and **justice** in research involving vulnerable groups. For instance, they highlight the need to ensure that individuals are treated with dignity, that their autonomy is respected, and that the risks associated with research participation are minimized.

One key aspect of these guidelines is the requirement for researchers to obtain informed consent from vulnerable participants while ensuring that the consent process is tailored to their specific needs. This may involve simplifying information, providing additional support, and ensuring that participants understand the implications of their involvement. Ethical guidelines also stress the importance of conducting thorough risk-benefit analyses to ensure that vulnerable populations are not exploited and that the potential benefits of research outweigh the risks involved.

Furthermore, the guidelines advocate for the inclusion of representatives from vulnerable populations in the research planning and oversight process. By engaging these communities in discussions about research design and ethical considerations, researchers can foster trust and ensure that the study addresses the needs and perspectives of those directly impacted. Adhering to ethical guidelines not only helps protect vulnerable participants but also enhances the credibility and integrity of clinical research.

14.6 Case Studies on Ethical Issues in Special Population Research

14.6.1 Case Study: Pediatric Trials in Oncology
The inclusion of children in clinical trials for oncology presents significant ethical challenges, as evidenced by various case studies. Pediatric oncology trials aim to evaluate new treatments for childhood cancers, which often differ from adult cancers in terms of biology and treatment response. Ethical concerns arise when balancing the need for effective treatments with the potential risks associated with experimental therapies. For instance, in a notable case study involving a new chemotherapeutic agent, researchers faced ethical dilemmas regarding the informed consent process. Many parents were eager to enroll their children in trials for promising new therapies, but the potential risks and unknown long-term effects created tension in the consent process.

Additionally, the trial's design required careful consideration of how to convey complex information about treatment protocols, potential side effects, and the impact of the trial on the child's quality of life. The involvement of child advocacy groups helped facilitate the informed consent process, ensuring that parents and guardians were well-informed and that the children's voices were considered in the decision-making. The case highlighted the importance of transparency and effective communication when conducting research involving pediatric populations, emphasizing that the welfare of the child must remain the top priority.

Furthermore, the results of pediatric oncology trials often provide critical insights into treatment efficacy and safety for childhood cancers. The ethical responsibility to conduct rigorous research in this population is underscored by the lack of existing data on treatment options tailored specifically for children. Successful trials have led to the development of more effective therapies, improving survival rates and outcomes for young patients. This case study illustrates the delicate balance researchers must maintain between advancing medical knowledge and protecting the rights and well-being of vulnerable pediatric populations.

14.6.2 Case Study: HIV Research in Pregnant Women

Research involving **HIV-infected pregnant women** presents a complex array of ethical considerations, as highlighted in various case studies. One significant study aimed to assess the safety and efficacy of antiretroviral therapies (ART) during pregnancy. This research was vital, as untreated HIV can lead to serious complications for both the mother and the unborn child. However, the ethical implications of including pregnant women in such studies raised important questions regarding fetal safety and the need for informed consent. Many women were understandably concerned about potential risks to their babies and whether participation would affect their access to effective treatments.

To address these concerns, researchers implemented comprehensive informed consent processes that clearly outlined the potential benefits and risks associated with participation. Additionally, the involvement of obstetricians and maternal-fetal medicine specialists in the study design helped ensure that both maternal and fetal welfare were prioritized. As a result, the study provided critical insights into the effects of ART during pregnancy, ultimately contributing to the development of safer treatment protocols for HIV-infected pregnant women.

The results of this research have had far-reaching implications, as they have informed clinical guidelines for managing HIV in pregnant women and have contributed to the significant reduction of mother-to-child transmission rates. This case study highlights the importance of conducting ethical research that prioritizes the health and safety of both mothers and their infants while generating valuable data to guide clinical practice.

14.6.3 Lessons Learned and Guidelines Development

The examination of case studies involving ethical issues in special population research provides valuable lessons that can inform the development of guidelines and best practices. One key takeaway is the necessity of **engaging stakeholders**, including community members, patient advocates, and healthcare providers, throughout the research process. By involving these groups, researchers can better understand the unique needs and concerns of special populations, leading to more ethical and inclusive trial designs. This engagement can also foster trust and improve recruitment and retention rates among vulnerable participants, ultimately enhancing the validity of the research findings.

Additionally, the case studies underscore the importance of ongoing **ethical training** for researchers and trial personnel. Understanding the ethical complexities associated with conducting research in special populations is essential for maintaining high ethical standards. Training programs can help researchers navigate issues related to informed consent, participant welfare, and risk-benefit assessments while providing the necessary tools to ensure that ethical considerations are integrated into study designs.

Moreover, the insights gained from these case studies can contribute to the refinement of existing ethical guidelines and regulations. By addressing gaps in the current frameworks and emphasizing the need for tailored approaches to special populations, researchers can help shape the future of clinical research. Ultimately, the lessons learned from these experiences can lead to more effective and ethically sound research practices, fostering advancements in medical knowledge while prioritizing the rights and welfare of all participants involved.

Review Questions

1. Who are considered "special populations" in clinical research, and why do they require special ethical considerations?
2. What are the key ethical concerns in conducting clinical trials in children?
3. How is assent and consent obtained in pediatric trials?
4. What are the ethical challenges in conducting trials with pregnant and lactating women?
5. Discuss the special considerations required in geriatric clinical research.
6. How do regulatory guidelines, such as ICH E7 and E11, address research in special populations?
7. What are the ethical challenges in recruiting vulnerable populations for clinical trials?
8. How can ethical safeguards be implemented to protect vulnerable populations in research?

CHAPTER FIFTEEN

Institutional Review Boards (IRB) and Independent Ethics Committees (IEC)

15.1 Introduction to IRBs and IECs

15.1.1 Role and Purpose of IRBs/IECs

Institutional Review Boards (IRBs) and **Independent Ethics Committees (IECs)** play a crucial role in the oversight of clinical research, ensuring that the rights and welfare of research participants are protected. The primary purpose of these committees is to review and approve research protocols before they can be initiated, ensuring that ethical standards are upheld throughout the research process. IRBs/IECs assess the scientific validity of proposed studies, evaluate the risk-benefit ratio, and ensure that informed consent processes are adequate and transparent. This oversight is vital for maintaining public trust in the research process and ensuring that studies are conducted responsibly and ethically.

Moreover, IRBs/IECs are tasked with ongoing monitoring of approved trials to ensure compliance with ethical and regulatory standards. They conduct regular reviews of participant safety data, evaluate any adverse events, and assess whether any changes to the research protocol are necessary. This continuous oversight helps to identify potential ethical concerns early and ensures that researchers are held accountable for adhering to the highest ethical standards throughout the duration of the study. By safeguarding the rights and welfare of participants, IRBs/IECs play a pivotal role in promoting ethical research practices and enhancing the integrity of clinical trials.

15.1.2 Historical Context: Development of Ethics Committees

The establishment of **ethics committees** such as IRBs and IECs can be traced back to the need for ethical oversight in research, particularly in the wake of historical abuses in medical research. The **Nuremberg Code** (1947), born from the trials of Nazi doctors, underscored the importance of voluntary consent and the ethical treatment of human subjects in research. Following this, the **Declaration of Helsinki** (1964) further established ethical principles for medical research involving human subjects, promoting the need for ethical review processes. These foundational documents highlighted the necessity for independent oversight to protect research participants from exploitation and harm.

The modern conception of IRBs and IECs emerged in response to these ethical imperatives. In the 1970s, the **U.S. National Commission for the Protection of Human Subjects of Biomedical and Behavioral Research** recommended the establishment of IRBs to provide ethical oversight for research funded by the federal government. This initiative led to the implementation of federal regulations requiring IRB review for all research involving human participants. In parallel, IECs developed globally, particularly in Europe, to address ethical considerations in research and ensure that participant rights were prioritized. The evolution of these committees reflects the growing recognition of the need for ethical oversight in research, leading to the establishment of robust frameworks that govern the conduct of clinical trials today.

15.1.3 Global Differences in IRBs/IECs

While the fundamental principles guiding IRBs and IECs are consistent across many countries, there are notable **global differences** in their structures, functions, and regulatory frameworks. In the United States, IRBs are primarily governed by federal regulations set forth by the **FDA** and **Office for Human Research Protections (OHRP)**, which dictate the composition, responsibilities, and review processes for these committees. In contrast, many European countries have established IECs that operate under the **European Medicines Agency (EMA)** guidelines, which emphasize the need for independent ethical review and participant protection while adhering to local laws and regulations.

Additionally, the composition of IRBs and IECs can vary significantly across regions. In some countries, IRBs may consist predominantly of scientific experts, while IECs may include a broader representation of community members, ethicists, and laypersons. This diversity can enhance the ethical review process by incorporating a wider range of perspectives and values, ensuring that the interests and concerns of various stakeholders are considered. Furthermore, the cultural context and societal attitudes toward research can influence the functioning of IRBs and IECs, affecting how ethical issues are prioritized and addressed.

The differences in IRB and IEC structures and functions underscore the importance of understanding the local regulatory environment when conducting international research. Researchers must be aware of the specific requirements and expectations of the ethics committees in each country to ensure compliance and uphold ethical standards. By fostering collaboration and communication among IRBs and IECs globally, researchers can promote best practices and enhance the ethical conduct of clinical trials worldwide.

15.2 Composition and Structure of IRBs/IECs

15.2.1 Members and Their Roles

The composition of **Institutional Review Boards (IRBs)** and **Independent Ethics Committees (IECs)** is designed to ensure a balanced representation of expertise, perspectives, and interests. Typically, these committees include members from diverse backgrounds, including scientists, healthcare professionals, ethicists, legal experts, and community representatives. This diversity is essential for conducting thorough ethical reviews, as it brings a variety of viewpoints to the decision-making process. Scientific members contribute their expertise in research methodology and clinical practice, while non-scientific members, including ethicists and community advocates, provide valuable insights into ethical considerations and participant welfare.

Each member of the IRB or IEC plays a specific role in the review process. The chairperson typically leads meetings, ensuring that discussions remain focused and that all members have an opportunity to voice their opinions. Members are responsible for critically evaluating research protocols, assessing potential risks and benefits, and ensuring that ethical standards are upheld throughout the study. The presence of lay members is particularly important, as they can represent the views and concerns of the community, ensuring that the committee remains connected to the populations it serves. This collaborative approach enhances the quality of ethical review and fosters public trust in the research process.

15.2.2 Importance of Diversity in IRB/IEC Membership

The importance of **diversity** in IRB and IEC membership cannot be overstated. Diverse committees are better equipped to identify and address ethical issues, as they bring a range of experiences, backgrounds, and perspectives to the review process. For instance, members from various cultural, social, and economic backgrounds can offer insights into the potential impact of research on different communities. This diversity helps ensure that the rights and welfare of all participants, particularly those from marginalized or vulnerable populations, are adequately protected throughout the research process.

Moreover, diverse IRBs and IECs can enhance the credibility and legitimacy of the ethical review process. When the composition of these committees reflects the diversity of the populations being studied, it fosters greater public confidence in the ethical oversight of clinical research. Community representatives can act as liaisons between researchers and participants, facilitating communication and trust. By prioritizing diversity in their membership, IRBs and IECs can ensure that their decisions are informed by a comprehensive understanding of the ethical implications of the research they review.

In addition to enhancing ethical review, diversity in IRB and IEC membership can also contribute to better research outcomes. Studies have shown that diverse teams are more innovative and effective at problem-solving. By incorporating a range of perspectives, IRBs and IECs can identify potential ethical issues that may have been overlooked by more homogenous groups. This collaborative approach not only strengthens the ethical review process but also contributes to the overall quality and rigor of clinical research.

15.2.3 Structure of an Effective IRB/IEC

The structure of an effective **Institutional Review Board (IRB)** or **Independent Ethics Committee (IEC)** is essential for its functionality and success in overseeing ethical research practices. An effective committee typically consists of a well-defined hierarchy, including a chairperson, vice-chair, and several members representing various fields of expertise. The chairperson plays a pivotal role in guiding discussions, ensuring that all perspectives are heard, and facilitating decision-making processes. Additionally, the vice-chair provides support in the chair's absence and may take on specific responsibilities related to protocol review or member recruitment.

An effective IRB or IEC also relies on clearly defined operating procedures that outline how meetings are conducted, how protocols are reviewed, and how decisions are made. These procedures should include guidelines for the frequency of meetings, the process for submitting research protocols, and criteria for ethical evaluation. Ensuring transparency and accountability in decision-making processes is vital for maintaining public trust and fostering collaboration between researchers and ethics committees. Regular training and professional development for IRB/IEC members are also essential to keep them informed about evolving ethical standards and regulatory requirements, ensuring that they remain well-equipped to address complex ethical dilemmas.

Furthermore, the integration of technology can enhance the efficiency and effectiveness of IRBs and IECs. Utilizing electronic submission systems can streamline the protocol review process, allowing members to access documents and data more efficiently. Technology can also facilitate communication between committee members, ensuring timely and effective discussions. By adopting a structured approach and embracing technological advancements, IRBs and IECs can improve their functionality and contribute to the ethical oversight of clinical research in a meaningful way.

15.3 Roles and Responsibilities of IRBs/IECs

15.3.1 Reviewing and Approving Clinical Trial Protocols

One of the primary responsibilities of **Institutional Review Boards (IRBs)** and **Independent Ethics Committees (IECs)** is the thorough review and approval of clinical trial protocols. This process is vital for ensuring that research studies are designed ethically and scientifically. During the review process, committees evaluate various aspects of the protocol, including the study objectives, methodology, recruitment strategies, and informed consent processes. The goal is to identify any potential ethical concerns or risks to participants and ensure that these issues are adequately addressed before the trial can proceed.

In addition to assessing the overall design of the study, IRBs and IECs also consider the **risk-benefit ratio** associated with the research. They evaluate whether the potential benefits of the study justify the risks participants may face. This assessment requires careful consideration of the health status of the population being studied, the nature of the intervention, and the potential for adverse events. By conducting a thorough review, IRBs and IECs play a crucial role in protecting the rights and welfare of participants while promoting ethical research practices.

15.3.2 Ongoing Monitoring of Approved Trials

Beyond the initial review and approval of clinical trial protocols, IRBs and IECs have a responsibility to conduct ongoing monitoring of approved studies. This includes reviewing safety data, evaluating any reported adverse events, and assessing whether the research continues to comply with ethical standards and regulatory requirements. Continuous oversight is essential for identifying potential issues that may arise during the course of the trial, ensuring that participant safety remains a top priority.

During the monitoring process, IRBs and IECs may request updates from researchers on trial progress, including recruitment rates, changes to the protocol, and any emerging safety concerns. This oversight allows committees to intervene promptly if ethical issues arise or if participant welfare is compromised. Furthermore, ongoing monitoring fosters a collaborative relationship between researchers and ethics committees, ensuring that researchers receive the necessary guidance and support to conduct their studies ethically.

15.3.3 Ensuring Compliance with Ethical and Legal Standards

Another crucial role of IRBs and IECs is to ensure that clinical research complies with established **ethical** and **legal standards**. This responsibility encompasses a broad range of activities, including reviewing research proposals to ensure they adhere to ethical principles, federal and state regulations, and institutional policies. By maintaining a high standard of ethical oversight, IRBs and IECs help to protect the rights and welfare of participants and foster public trust in the research process.

Compliance monitoring is an ongoing process that requires IRBs and IECs to stay informed about changes in regulations and best practices. They must regularly update their policies and procedures to reflect new ethical guidelines and legal requirements. Additionally, IRBs and IECs often provide education and training to researchers to ensure they understand the ethical considerations involved in conducting research and the importance of adhering to compliance standards. By proactively promoting ethical conduct and compliance, IRBs and IECs contribute to the integrity and credibility of clinical research.

15.4 The Approval Process: How IRBs/IECs Function

15.4.1 Protocol Submission and Review Processes
The approval process for clinical trials begins with the **submission of the research protocol** to an Institutional Review Board (IRB) or Independent Ethics Committee (IEC). Researchers must provide a comprehensive and detailed description of their study, including the objectives, methodology, participant recruitment strategies, informed consent procedures, and data analysis plans. This submission must also include any relevant background information and prior research findings that support the proposed study. The clarity and thoroughness of this submission are critical, as they provide the foundation for the IRB/IEC's evaluation of the ethical implications of the research.

Upon receiving the protocol, the IRB/IEC initiates a multi-step review process. This process often involves the distribution of the protocol to committee members for preliminary evaluation. Members are typically given a specific timeframe to review the materials and identify any ethical concerns or issues that require further discussion. The committee may convene to discuss the protocol in detail during scheduled meetings, allowing members to voice their opinions, ask questions, and provide input. This collaborative approach to protocol review fosters a thorough examination of the study's ethical considerations, ensuring that multiple perspectives are considered before a decision is made.

Following the initial discussions, the IRB/IEC may request additional information or modifications from the researchers to address any identified concerns. This iterative process of feedback and revision ensures that the protocol aligns with ethical standards and adequately protects the rights and welfare of participants. Once the IRB/IEC is satisfied with the protocol, it proceeds to the final review and approval stage, which culminates in a formal decision regarding the study's ethical acceptability. This approval is essential before researchers can initiate participant recruitment and begin the study.

15.4.2 Communication Between Researchers and IRBs/IECs
Effective communication between researchers and IRBs/IECs is essential for ensuring a smooth and efficient review process. Open lines of communication help to clarify expectations, address questions, and facilitate a collaborative relationship between researchers and ethics committees. Before submitting a protocol, researchers are often encouraged

to engage in **pre-submission consultations** with IRB/IEC members to discuss their study design, potential ethical concerns, and any specific regulatory requirements. This preliminary dialogue can help researchers tailor their protocols to align with the committee's expectations, ultimately expediting the review process.

Once a protocol is submitted, ongoing communication is crucial for addressing any issues that may arise during the review. IRBs and IECs may communicate with researchers to request clarifications or modifications to the protocol, ensuring that all ethical concerns are adequately addressed. Researchers should be prepared to respond promptly to these requests, providing the necessary information or revisions in a timely manner. Maintaining clear and open communication throughout the review process helps to build trust and fosters a collaborative environment, ultimately contributing to more efficient and effective ethical oversight.

Moreover, after a protocol is approved, ongoing communication remains important throughout the trial. IRBs/IECs may require regular updates on the study's progress, including participant recruitment rates, adverse events, and any modifications to the protocol. Researchers should be proactive in keeping the ethics committee informed, ensuring transparency and accountability in their research practices. This ongoing dialogue not only helps to maintain compliance with ethical standards but also supports the overall integrity of the research process.

15.4.3 Decision-Making and Approval Timelines

The decision-making process of IRBs and IECs is critical in determining the timeline for study approval. Upon submission of the protocol, the committee typically has a specified period to conduct its review, often ranging from a few weeks to several months, depending on the complexity of the study and the committee's workload. The timeline for approval is influenced by various factors, including the thoroughness of the submitted protocol, the level of detail provided, and any requests for additional information or revisions. Simple studies may receive expedited reviews, while more complex protocols may require multiple rounds of discussion and feedback before reaching a final decision.

Once the IRB/IEC completes its review, it issues a formal decision regarding the protocol's approval. This decision may include recommendations for modifications, stipulations for monitoring, or conditions for ongoing oversight. In some cases, the committee may reject the protocol if it raises significant ethical concerns that cannot be adequately addressed. Researchers must be prepared for the possibility of revision and resubmission, which can extend the overall timeline for initiating the study. Effective planning and communication can help mitigate delays and ensure that the research progresses smoothly.

It is essential for researchers to factor in the approval timelines when designing their study timelines and budgets. Delays in receiving IRB/IEC approval can impact project timelines, funding, and participant recruitment efforts. By engaging with the ethics committee early in the process and maintaining clear communication, researchers can enhance the efficiency of the review and approval process. Understanding the intricacies of IRB/IEC decision-making and timelines is vital for successful clinical trial management and ensures that studies are conducted in compliance with ethical standards.

15.5 Ongoing Safety Monitoring by IRBs/IECs

15.5.1 Adverse Event Reporting and Review

One of the critical responsibilities of Institutional Review Boards (IRBs) and Independent Ethics Committees (IECs) is the ongoing **monitoring of participant safety** during clinical trials, which includes the review of adverse events (AEs). Adverse events refer to any untoward medical occurrences that arise during the course of the study, whether or not they are related to the treatment being administered. IRBs and IECs require researchers to implement robust reporting mechanisms for AEs to ensure that any potential safety concerns are promptly identified and addressed. This proactive approach allows the committee to assess whether the benefits of the research continue to outweigh the risks as the trial progresses.

When researchers report adverse events, IRBs and IECs carefully evaluate the nature, severity, and frequency of these events in relation to the study intervention. They consider whether the reported AEs are consistent with known side effects of the treatment or if they indicate unexpected safety concerns. This review process is essential for determining whether modifications to the study protocol, such as increased monitoring, participant withdrawal, or even study suspension, are necessary to protect the health and safety of participants. By maintaining vigilance in the review of adverse event data, IRBs and IECs play a vital role in safeguarding participants throughout the duration of the trial.

Additionally, the monitoring of adverse events must be coupled with clear communication between researchers and the ethics committee. Researchers are typically required to report serious adverse events (SAEs) immediately to ensure timely oversight by the IRB/IEC. This collaborative relationship fosters an environment of transparency and accountability, enabling the committee to make informed decisions regarding the ongoing safety and ethical conduct of the study. The commitment to thorough adverse event reporting and review is essential for ensuring the welfare of participants and maintaining the integrity of clinical research.

15.5.2 Periodic Safety Updates and Continuing Review

IRBs and IECs are tasked with conducting **periodic safety reviews** of approved clinical trials to ensure the ongoing protection of participants. This process involves reviewing safety updates, including reports of adverse events, interim analysis results, and any new findings that may impact the risk-benefit assessment of the study. These periodic reviews are essential for identifying any emerging safety concerns and evaluating the continued ethical appropriateness of the research. Depending on the level of risk involved and the complexity of the trial, IRBs and IECs may require updates on a quarterly or annual basis, ensuring that they remain informed about the trial's safety profile.

Continuing review processes not only assess participant safety but also evaluate the progress of the study. IRBs and IECs examine whether the study is adhering to the approved protocol, whether recruitment targets are being met, and whether there have been any significant deviations from the original study design. This ongoing oversight ensures that researchers remain accountable for maintaining ethical standards and following established guidelines throughout the trial's duration. If concerns are identified during the continuing review process, the IRB/IEC may request corrective actions or modifications to the protocol, reinforcing the importance of ethical conduct in clinical research.

The commitment to conducting regular safety updates and continuing reviews reflects the dynamic nature of clinical research and the need for ethical oversight to adapt to emerging data. By prioritizing participant safety through ongoing monitoring, IRBs and IECs contribute to the credibility and integrity of clinical trials, fostering public trust in the research process.

15.5.3 Responsibilities of IRBs/IECs in Trial Suspension or Termination

IRBs and IECs hold critical responsibilities regarding the **suspension or termination of clinical trials** when ethical concerns arise or participant safety is compromised. If an IRB or IEC identifies significant risks, unexpected adverse events, or ethical violations during their reviews, they have the authority to halt the study to protect participants. This decision is not taken lightly and requires thorough consideration of the available data and potential impacts on the participants involved in the trial. The ability to suspend or terminate a study is a vital safeguard that underscores the IRB/IEC's commitment to prioritizing the welfare of participants over research objectives.

In addition to their authority to suspend trials, IRBs and IECs are responsible for ensuring that participants are appropriately informed about any changes to the study's status. This includes providing clear communication regarding the reasons for suspension, any necessary follow-up procedures, and potential implications for participants' health. Moreover, when a trial is terminated, IRBs and IECs must ensure that participants receive appropriate care and support, facilitating their transition to alternative treatment options if necessary. This compassionate approach is essential for maintaining the trust of participants and the broader community.

The responsibilities of IRBs and IECs in managing trial suspension or termination highlight the importance of ethical oversight in clinical research. By taking decisive action when ethical concerns arise, these committees play a crucial role in safeguarding participants' rights and well-being. The commitment to prioritizing participant safety reflects the ethical principles that underpin the conduct of clinical research, fostering public trust and confidence in the research process.

15.6 Regulatory Framework Governing IRBs/IECs

15.6.1 FDA, EMA, and CDSCO Regulations for IRBs/IECs

The regulatory framework governing **Institutional Review Boards (IRBs)** and **Independent Ethics Committees (IECs)** is shaped by guidelines established by various regulatory bodies, including the **FDA** (U.S. Food and Drug Administration), **EMA** (European Medicines Agency), and **CDSCO** (Central Drugs Standard Control Organization in India). Each of these agencies has set forth specific regulations that outline the responsibilities and functions of IRBs/IECs, ensuring that ethical standards are upheld in clinical research. For example, the FDA mandates that all clinical trials involving human subjects be reviewed by an IRB before they can commence, emphasizing the need for ethical oversight to protect participant rights and welfare.

The EMA also requires that all clinical trials conducted within the European Union adhere to ethical review standards established by competent authorities and independent ethics committees. The regulations ensure that IRBs/IECs assess protocols based on ethical principles, scientific validity, and participant safety. Similarly, the CDSCO has developed guidelines that govern the functioning of ethics committees in India, emphasizing the need for independent review of clinical trials to enhance participant protection. These regulatory frameworks reflect a global commitment to promoting ethical research practices and safeguarding the rights of participants in clinical trials.

Moreover, these regulatory agencies regularly update their guidelines to adapt to advancements in research methodologies and ethical considerations. It is essential for IRBs and IECs to remain informed about these changes to ensure compliance with evolving standards. By adhering to regulatory requirements established by the FDA, EMA, and CDSCO, IRBs and IECs contribute to the ethical conduct of clinical research and foster public trust in the research process.

15.6.2 International Guidelines: ICH-GCP

International guidelines, such as the **International Conference on Harmonization's Good Clinical Practice (ICH-GCP)** guidelines, play a pivotal role in shaping the regulatory landscape for IRBs and IECs worldwide. The ICH-GCP guidelines provide a comprehensive framework for ensuring that clinical trials are conducted ethically and that the rights, safety, and well-being of participants are protected. These guidelines outline the roles and responsibilities of IRBs and IECs in the ethical review process, emphasizing the importance of independent oversight in clinical research.

By adhering to the ICH-GCP guidelines, IRBs and IECs can promote harmonization in ethical standards across different countries and regions. The guidelines encourage collaboration between regulatory authorities, researchers, and ethics committees to establish best practices for ethical review processes. This global perspective is particularly important in today's increasingly interconnected world, where clinical trials often involve multinational collaborations. By following the principles outlined in

ICH-GCP, IRBs and IECs can enhance the quality and integrity of clinical research while ensuring that ethical standards are consistently applied.

Furthermore, the adoption of ICH-GCP guidelines helps facilitate the acceptance of clinical trial data across borders, making it easier for researchers to share findings and for regulatory agencies to evaluate new treatments. By providing a standardized approach to ethical review and oversight, ICH-GCP guidelines support the advancement of medical research while prioritizing participant protection.

15.6.3 Case Studies of IRB/IEC Failures and Their Consequences

Examining case studies of **IRB and IEC failures** provides valuable insights into the critical importance of ethical oversight in clinical research. One notable case involved a clinical trial that failed to adequately address the risks associated with the experimental intervention, leading to severe adverse events among participants. The IRB involved in the study did not perform thorough reviews of the protocol or monitor ongoing safety data effectively. As a result, several participants experienced serious complications, prompting a regulatory investigation and significant public backlash against the institution conducting the trial. This case underscores the necessity of diligent oversight and highlights the potential consequences of failing to uphold ethical standards.

Another case study illustrates the challenges associated with the lack of diversity within an IRB. An ethics committee that predominantly consisted of members from a single demographic failed to recognize the unique ethical considerations relevant to a study involving a marginalized population. This lack of perspective led to inadequate risk assessments and the approval of a protocol that did not sufficiently protect the rights and welfare of the participants. The resulting ethical breaches led to mistrust within the community and raised significant questions about the committee's credibility. This example emphasizes the importance of diverse representation in IRBs and IECs to ensure that a wide range of perspectives is considered in the ethical review process.

These case studies demonstrate that failures in IRB and IEC oversight can have serious repercussions for participants, researchers, and the broader community. By learning from these experiences, regulatory bodies and ethics committees can refine their practices and guidelines to prevent similar issues from occurring in the future. Ensuring rigorous ethical oversight and accountability in clinical research is essential for protecting participant rights and maintaining public trust in the research process.

Review Questions

1. What is the role of Institutional Review Boards (IRBs) and Independent Ethics Committees (IECs) in clinical trials?
2. How have IRBs/IECs evolved historically, and why are they essential for ethical oversight in research?
3. What is the composition of an IRB/IEC, and why is diversity in membership important?
4. Describe the process of submitting a clinical trial protocol to an IRB/IEC.
5. How do IRBs/IECs monitor ongoing clinical trials for safety?
6. What are the responsibilities of IRBs/IECs in ensuring ethical and legal compliance in research?
7. Discuss the challenges IRBs/IECs face in decision-making for clinical trials.
8. How do regulatory frameworks govern IRBs/IECs across different regions?

CHAPTER SIXTEEN

Data Safety Monitoring Boards (DSMB)

16.1 Introduction to Data Safety Monitoring Boards

16.1.1 Purpose and Role of DSMBs in Clinical Trials

Data Safety Monitoring Boards (DSMBs) are independent groups established to oversee the safety of participants in clinical trials. Their primary purpose is to ensure that the rights and welfare of participants are protected while the study is ongoing. DSMBs are responsible for monitoring the accumulating data during a trial, with a focus on participant safety, treatment efficacy, and overall trial integrity. By evaluating the safety data, including adverse events and serious adverse events, DSMBs can identify potential risks associated with the intervention being tested, allowing for timely recommendations to ensure participant safety.

The role of DSMBs is especially critical in large, multi-center trials where the potential for unforeseen risks is heightened. They provide an additional layer of oversight, ensuring that researchers are accountable for the ethical conduct of the trial. DSMBs operate independently from the trial sponsor and investigators, which helps to eliminate conflicts of interest and promote impartiality in their evaluations. This independence is vital for maintaining public trust in clinical research, as it assures stakeholders that participant safety is the foremost priority throughout the study.

Moreover, DSMBs have the authority to recommend the continuation, modification, or termination of a trial based on their safety assessments. Their recommendations are grounded in rigorous analysis of interim data, allowing them to make informed decisions that balance the potential benefits of the intervention against the risks to participants. This proactive approach to monitoring ensures that any emerging safety concerns are addressed promptly, ultimately contributing to the ethical conduct of clinical trials and the responsible advancement of medical knowledge.

16.1.2 Legal and Ethical Significance of DSMBs

The establishment of Data Safety Monitoring Boards (DSMBs) carries significant legal and ethical implications for clinical research. Legally, DSMBs are seen as an essential component of the ethical oversight framework mandated by regulatory authorities. Both the **FDA** and **EMA** recognize the importance of DSMBs in monitoring participant safety, particularly in trials involving higher risks. Regulatory guidelines often require the inclusion of DSMBs in certain types of studies, particularly those involving vulnerable populations or novel interventions with uncertain safety profiles. This legal recognition underscores the critical role that DSMBs play in safeguarding participants and ensuring compliance with ethical standards.

From an ethical perspective, the presence of DSMBs enhances the credibility of clinical trials. Their independent oversight reinforces the ethical principle of **beneficence**, ensuring that researchers are committed to maximizing benefits while minimizing potential harms to participants. Furthermore, DSMBs embody the principle of **transparency**, as their assessments and recommendations are grounded in objective analysis of the data collected throughout the trial. This transparency is vital for maintaining the trust of participants, researchers, and the public, as it demonstrates a commitment to ethical research practices.

The ethical significance of DSMBs extends to their ability to identify potential ethical concerns early in the research process. By reviewing interim data, DSMBs can identify any emerging trends related to participant safety that may warrant immediate action. This proactive approach allows for timely interventions, such as modifying the trial protocol or halting the study altogether if necessary. By serving as independent monitors, DSMBs play a vital role in promoting ethical standards in clinical research and protecting the rights and welfare of participants.

16.1.3 Formation and Selection of DSMB Members

The formation and selection of members for Data Safety Monitoring Boards (DSMBs) are crucial to their effectiveness and credibility. DSMBs are typically composed of individuals with diverse expertise, including clinical researchers, biostatisticians, ethicists, and subject matter experts relevant to the trial's focus. The inclusion of members from various backgrounds helps ensure that the board can comprehensively evaluate safety data, consider ethical implications, and provide informed recommendations based on their collective knowledge and experience.

The selection process for DSMB members is designed to promote **independence** and **objectivity**. Members should have no conflicts of interest with the study sponsor or investigators, as this independence is essential for maintaining the integrity of the monitoring process. Regulatory agencies often provide guidelines for the selection of DSMB members, emphasizing the need for a transparent process that ensures appropriate expertise and impartiality. Moreover, the inclusion of community representatives or patient advocates can enhance the board's perspective and ensure that participant interests are adequately represented in decision-making.

Once the DSMB is formed, members must be adequately trained on their roles and responsibilities, as well as the ethical and legal frameworks governing clinical research. Training helps to ensure that all members understand the significance of their oversight role and are equipped to evaluate the trial's safety data effectively. By establishing a well-structured DSMB with qualified and independent members, researchers can enhance the ethical oversight of clinical trials and promote participant safety throughout the study.

16.2 Structure and Composition of DSMBs

16.2.1 Members and Their Expertise
The composition of a Data Safety Monitoring Board (DSMB) is critical to its function and effectiveness. Members are typically selected based on their expertise and experience in relevant fields, such as clinical medicine, biostatistics, epidemiology, and ethics. Having a diverse range of expertise within the DSMB ensures that the board can comprehensively evaluate safety data and make informed decisions regarding trial continuation or modification. For instance, a clinical expert can provide insights into the medical implications of the findings, while a biostatistician can analyze the data's statistical significance and interpret the results accurately.

In addition to technical expertise, it is essential for DSMB members to possess strong ethical grounding. This ethical perspective is vital for guiding the board's discussions and decisions about participant safety, risk assessment, and ethical conduct. Members should be familiar with relevant regulatory guidelines and ethical standards, such as those outlined in the **ICH-GCP** guidelines. By ensuring that DSMB members possess both technical expertise and ethical awareness, the board can provide robust oversight and accountability throughout the clinical trial.

Furthermore, it is important for DSMBs to include lay members or community representatives when appropriate. Including individuals from diverse backgrounds can enhance the board's ability to evaluate how research findings may affect various populations. This inclusivity ensures that the voices of patients and community members are heard, fostering trust and transparency in the research process. By comprising a well-rounded DSMB with members who bring different perspectives, the board can make more informed and ethically sound decisions.

16.2.2 Importance of an Independent DSMB

The **independence** of Data Safety Monitoring Boards (DSMBs) is paramount for ensuring the integrity and credibility of clinical trials. Independent DSMBs operate without any conflicts of interest that could compromise their objectivity, which is essential for maintaining public trust in the research process. Their ability to provide impartial oversight allows them to focus solely on participant safety and the ethical conduct of the trial. By being independent from the trial sponsor and investigators, DSMBs can critically assess the safety and efficacy data without bias, ensuring that their recommendations are grounded in ethical principles and scientific evidence.

Moreover, the independence of DSMBs fosters accountability in clinical research. When researchers know that an independent board is monitoring the trial, they are more likely to adhere to ethical standards and prioritize participant safety. This oversight can act as a deterrent to unethical practices, ensuring that the research is conducted transparently and responsibly. The presence of an independent DSMB is also a crucial factor in gaining the confidence of regulatory agencies, as it demonstrates a commitment to ethical oversight and participant protection.

The role of an independent DSMB becomes particularly significant in trials involving vulnerable populations or higher-risk interventions. In these cases, the need for objective oversight is amplified, as the potential for adverse outcomes may be greater. Independent DSMBs provide an additional layer of protection, ensuring that any emerging safety concerns are promptly addressed and that participants are not placed at undue risk. By prioritizing independence in the structure and function of DSMBs, researchers can enhance the ethical conduct of clinical trials and promote the welfare of all participants involved.

16.2.3 Criteria for Appointing DSMB Members

The criteria for appointing members to Data Safety Monitoring Boards (DSMBs) are essential for ensuring that the board is equipped to fulfill its responsibilities effectively. First and foremost, members should possess relevant expertise in their respective fields, including clinical practice, biostatistics, ethics, and epidemiology. This expertise is crucial for enabling the DSMB to conduct thorough evaluations of safety data and provide informed recommendations based on their findings. The selection process should prioritize individuals who have a track record of conducting high-quality research and a demonstrated understanding of ethical considerations in clinical trials.

Another important criterion is the absence of conflicts of interest. DSMB members must be independent from the trial sponsor and investigators to ensure that their decisions are impartial and free from external pressures. This independence is critical for maintaining the credibility of the DSMB and fostering trust in the research process. To uphold this principle, the appointment process should include a thorough review of potential members' affiliations and financial interests. Transparency in this process is vital to prevent any undue influence on the board's decision-making.

Additionally, diversity in the composition of DSMB members is an essential criterion for appointment. The board should reflect a range of perspectives and experiences to enhance its ability to assess the ethical implications of the trial and evaluate participant safety. Including members from various demographic backgrounds, professional disciplines, and cultural perspectives can enrich discussions and lead to more comprehensive evaluations of trial data. By considering these criteria in the appointment of DSMB members, researchers can establish effective boards that contribute to the ethical oversight of clinical research.

16.3 Responsibilities of DSMBs

16.3.1 Safety Monitoring and Risk-Benefit Analysis

One of the primary responsibilities of Data Safety Monitoring Boards (DSMBs) is the continuous **monitoring of safety** throughout the course of clinical trials. This involves the evaluation of data related to adverse events, serious adverse events, and any other safety concerns that may arise as the study progresses. DSMBs are tasked with assessing the overall risk-benefit ratio associated with the intervention being tested, ensuring that the potential benefits to participants justify any risks they may encounter. This ongoing evaluation is essential for protecting the welfare of participants and maintaining ethical standards in clinical research.

In addition to safety monitoring, DSMBs also play a crucial role in conducting regular **risk-benefit analyses**. As new data emerges, the board must assess whether the risk of harm to participants remains acceptable in light of the potential benefits of the study. This analysis is particularly important in studies involving vulnerable populations or higher-risk interventions, where the potential for adverse outcomes may be greater. DSMBs have the authority to recommend modifications to the trial protocol or even halt the study if they determine that the risks outweigh the benefits. Their commitment to participant safety underscores the ethical importance of their role in clinical trials.

Moreover, DSMBs are responsible for fostering transparency in the monitoring process. By providing clear communication regarding their findings and recommendations, they can enhance the accountability of researchers and build public trust in the clinical research process. This transparency is essential for ensuring that stakeholders, including participants, sponsors, and regulatory agencies, are informed about the trial's safety profile and any emerging concerns. Ultimately, the responsibilities of DSMBs in safety monitoring and risk-benefit analysis are vital for maintaining the ethical conduct of clinical research and protecting the rights and welfare of participants.

16.3.2 Review of Interim Data and Decision-Making

Another critical responsibility of Data Safety Monitoring Boards (DSMBs) is the **review of interim data** collected during the course of clinical trials. This interim analysis provides essential insights into the safety and efficacy of the intervention being tested, allowing DSMBs to assess whether the trial should continue, be modified, or terminated. The board analyzes data from participant outcomes, adverse events, and any other relevant information to determine the overall safety profile of the study. This ongoing evaluation enables the board to make informed recommendations based on real-time data, ensuring that participant safety remains a top priority.

The decision-making process for DSMBs is collaborative, with members engaging in thorough discussions about the interim findings and their implications. During these discussions, the board considers various factors, including the severity and frequency of adverse events, the overall progress of the trial, and the potential benefits of the intervention. This collective approach to decision-making ensures that diverse perspectives are considered, leading to more comprehensive assessments of the data. Once the board reaches a consensus, they communicate their recommendations to the researchers, outlining any necessary actions that must be taken to address safety concerns or ethical considerations.

The ability to review interim data and make timely decisions is particularly important in the context of ongoing trials involving vulnerable populations or novel interventions. By conducting regular evaluations, DSMBs can identify potential safety issues early, allowing researchers to take proactive measures to mitigate risks. This commitment to vigilant oversight is essential for maintaining the integrity of the research process and ensuring that participants are not exposed to unnecessary harm. Ultimately, the responsibilities of DSMBs in reviewing interim data and making informed decisions are critical for the ethical conduct of clinical trials.

16.3.3 Advising on Trial Continuation, Modification, or Termination

Data Safety Monitoring Boards (DSMBs) are tasked with the important responsibility of advising researchers on the **continuation, modification, or termination** of clinical trials based on their ongoing safety assessments and interim data reviews. After evaluating the accumulated data, the DSMB may recommend that a trial continue as planned, suggesting that the benefits outweigh the risks. This recommendation provides reassurance to both researchers and participants that the study is proceeding ethically and safely. Conversely, if safety concerns arise or if the data indicate a lack of efficacy, the DSMB may advise modifications to the trial protocol, such as altering dosing regimens or implementing additional safety monitoring measures.

In some cases, the DSMB may determine that the risks associated with the trial have become unacceptable, leading them to recommend termination. This recommendation is never taken lightly, as it has significant implications for participants and the research community. If a trial is terminated, the DSMB is responsible for ensuring that participants are informed about the decision, the reasons for termination, and any follow-up care or alternative treatment options available to them. The ability of DSMBs to make such recommendations reinforces the ethical framework within which clinical research operates, prioritizing participant welfare above all else.

Moreover, the guidance provided by DSMBs can significantly impact the future direction of clinical research. When a trial is terminated or modified based on safety concerns, it prompts further investigation into the underlying issues, contributing to a broader understanding of the intervention's safety profile. These insights can inform future research designs, improve ethical oversight, and enhance participant safety in subsequent trials. The role of DSMBs in advising on trial continuation, modification, or termination is vital for ensuring that clinical research is conducted responsibly and ethically, ultimately promoting the welfare of participants and the integrity of the research process.

16.4 DSMB Processes and Decision-Making

16.4.1 Data Review and Interim Analysis

The **data review process** is a critical component of the functions carried out by Data Safety Monitoring Boards (DSMBs) in clinical trials. As independent entities, DSMBs are tasked with evaluating safety and efficacy data collected during the trial. This evaluation is typically conducted through **interim analyses**, where the DSMB reviews data at predefined intervals to assess participant safety, treatment effectiveness, and the overall conduct of the study. The interim analysis provides an opportunity for the DSMB to make data-driven recommendations regarding the continuation of the trial, modifications to the protocol, or even its termination, depending on the emerging safety profile and treatment efficacy.

Interim analyses serve several important functions. Firstly, they help to identify any concerning trends in adverse events or treatment responses that may not have been evident in early phases of the trial. For example, if a significant number of serious adverse events are observed among participants receiving a particular treatment, the DSMB can evaluate whether these events are related to the intervention. Secondly, these analyses allow the DSMB to assess the overall progress of the study in terms of recruitment and data collection, ensuring that the trial remains on track to meet its objectives. The independent evaluation of interim data not only protects participants but also maintains the integrity of the research process by promoting accountability.

Additionally, the data review process involves careful consideration of statistical methods and analyses used to interpret the interim data. DSMBs rely on statistical experts to provide insights into the significance of the findings and guide decision-making. The use of appropriate statistical techniques is vital for ensuring that the conclusions drawn from interim analyses are valid and reliable. By conducting thorough data reviews and interim analyses, DSMBs can ensure that clinical trials are conducted ethically, prioritizing participant safety and well-being while advancing medical knowledge.

16.4.2 How DSMBs Make Recommendations

Making recommendations is one of the most significant roles of Data Safety Monitoring Boards (DSMBs) in clinical trials. After conducting data reviews and interim analyses, DSMBs may recommend various actions based on their assessments. Recommendations can include the continuation of the trial as planned, modifications to the study protocol, or termination of the trial if safety concerns arise. The decision-making process involves a collaborative discussion among board members, where they evaluate the safety and efficacy data, consider ethical implications, and weigh the potential risks and benefits associated with the intervention.

The process of making recommendations is guided by several key principles. Firstly, DSMBs prioritize participant safety above all else. If there is any indication that the risks of the intervention outweigh the benefits, the board is obligated to recommend changes or termination. Secondly, the DSMB considers the integrity of the study. They must evaluate whether the study design can adequately answer the research questions in light of the emerging data. This requires a nuanced understanding of the study's objectives and the potential impact of the board's recommendations on the validity of the trial's outcomes.

The recommendations made by DSMBs are typically communicated to the study sponsors and investigators, along with a rationale for their decisions. This transparency is essential for fostering trust and collaboration between the DSMB and the research team. In some cases, the board may recommend conducting additional safety analyses or enhancing participant monitoring protocols to address identified concerns. Ultimately, the recommendations from DSMBs play a vital role in shaping the course of clinical trials and ensuring that ethical standards are upheld throughout the research process.

16.4.3 Frequency and Scheduling of DSMB Meetings

The **frequency and scheduling of DSMB meetings** are critical aspects of their operational framework, impacting the effectiveness of their oversight. DSMBs typically convene at predefined intervals to review interim data and discuss participant safety and trial progress. The frequency of these meetings can vary depending on the nature of the trial, the level of risk involved, and regulatory requirements. For example, high-risk trials may necessitate more frequent meetings, while lower-risk studies might require less frequent oversight. This adaptability allows DSMBs to maintain vigilant oversight while balancing resource allocation.

Meeting schedules should be planned in advance, with clear timelines established for data review and decision-making. These timelines help ensure that DSMBs remain proactive in their evaluations and can promptly address any emerging safety concerns. In addition to regularly scheduled meetings, DSMBs may also hold emergency meetings if critical safety issues arise that require immediate attention. Such flexibility in scheduling ensures that the board can respond quickly to any potential risks, reinforcing the commitment to participant safety and ethical research practices.

The effectiveness of DSMB meetings relies not only on their frequency but also on the preparation and organization of the discussions. Comprehensive materials, including interim data reports, safety summaries, and relevant background information, should be provided to board members in advance to facilitate informed discussions. This preparation allows members to engage meaningfully during meetings and contributes to efficient decision-making. By establishing a structured and well-coordinated meeting schedule, DSMBs can effectively fulfill their oversight responsibilities and promote ethical conduct in clinical trials.

16.5 Ethical Issues Related to DSMBs

16.5.1 Conflict of Interest Concerns

One of the primary ethical issues surrounding Data Safety Monitoring Boards (DSMBs) is the potential for **conflicts of interest** among board members. Conflicts of interest can arise when members have financial or professional ties to the study sponsor, researchers, or competing interests that may compromise their impartiality. For example, a board member who has previously collaborated with the trial sponsor may be perceived as biased in their evaluations, potentially undermining the integrity of the DSMB's oversight. To mitigate these concerns, it is essential for DSMBs to implement strict guidelines for member selection and to conduct thorough conflict-of-interest assessments prior to appointments.

Transparency is also crucial in addressing conflict of interest concerns. DSMBs should require members to disclose any financial or professional relationships that may influence their decision-making. This transparency helps maintain public trust in the research process and reinforces the integrity of the DSMB's recommendations. If conflicts are identified, the affected member may need to recuse themselves from specific discussions or decisions related to the trial, ensuring that the board's evaluations remain objective and unbiased. By prioritizing conflict-of-interest management, DSMBs can uphold their ethical responsibilities and protect participant welfare throughout the research process.

Furthermore, the governance of DSMBs should include mechanisms for ongoing monitoring of conflicts of interest throughout the duration of the trial. This may involve regular updates from members regarding any changes in their professional affiliations or financial interests that could influence their impartiality. By fostering a culture of transparency and accountability, DSMBs can effectively address conflict-of-interest concerns and maintain the credibility of their oversight.

16.5.2 Transparency and Confidentiality in DSMB Operations

The ethical management of **transparency and confidentiality** is crucial in the operations of Data Safety Monitoring Boards (DSMBs). Transparency is essential for building trust in the clinical research process, as it ensures that stakeholders, including participants and regulatory bodies, are informed about the board's activities and decisions. However, this transparency must be balanced with the need for confidentiality, particularly regarding sensitive data related to participant safety and trial outcomes. Striking this balance is vital for maintaining participant privacy while ensuring that ethical standards are upheld.

One way to achieve transparency is through regular communication with researchers and stakeholders about the DSMB's findings and recommendations. However, sensitive data, such as individual participant information and specific adverse event details, should be handled with the utmost care to protect confidentiality. DSMBs must develop clear protocols for disseminating information to ensure that only aggregated or anonymized data is shared publicly. This approach allows the board to communicate important findings while safeguarding participant privacy and complying with ethical standards.

Moreover, maintaining confidentiality within the DSMB itself is essential for fostering open discussions among members. Board members must feel free to express their opinions and concerns without fear of repercussions or external scrutiny. To facilitate this environment, DSMBs should establish clear guidelines regarding the handling of confidential information and ensure that all members understand their responsibilities in protecting participant privacy. By prioritizing both transparency and confidentiality, DSMBs can effectively navigate ethical challenges while maintaining the integrity of clinical research oversight.

16.5.3 DSMBs in Placebo-Controlled Trials

Data Safety Monitoring Boards (DSMBs) play a vital role in overseeing **placebo-controlled trials**, which often raise unique ethical considerations. In these trials, participants are randomly assigned to receive either the experimental treatment or a placebo, which can sometimes create ethical dilemmas, particularly if effective treatment options exist. DSMBs must carefully evaluate the ethical implications of using a placebo, ensuring that participants are not subjected to unnecessary risks and that the research adheres to established ethical standards.

The responsibilities of DSMBs in placebo-controlled trials include closely monitoring safety data to identify any emerging risks associated with the placebo group. If significant adverse events occur, the DSMB must assess whether the benefits of the trial still outweigh the risks for participants receiving the placebo. This monitoring is particularly crucial in studies involving vulnerable populations, where the ethical implications of withholding effective treatment can be significant. The DSMB's ability to provide recommendations for trial modifications or termination in response to emerging safety concerns reinforces the importance of ethical oversight in these complex studies.

Additionally, the DSMB must ensure that the informed consent process is robust and transparent. Participants should be made aware of the possibility of receiving a placebo and the potential implications for their health. The DSMB's oversight ensures that participants are adequately informed, thus respecting their autonomy and promoting ethical research practices. By addressing the unique challenges associated with placebo-controlled trials, DSMBs contribute to the ethical conduct of clinical research while safeguarding participant welfare.

16.6 DSMB Case Studies and Lessons Learned

16.6.1 Case Studies of DSMBs Intervening in Trials
Examining case studies of Data Safety Monitoring Boards (DSMBs) intervening in clinical trials provides valuable insights into their critical role in safeguarding participant safety and ethical research practices. In one notable case, a DSMB monitoring a trial for a novel cancer treatment identified a concerning trend of serious adverse events among participants receiving the experimental intervention. The board's thorough review of interim data revealed a higher-than-expected rate of adverse reactions, prompting them to recommend a temporary halt to participant enrollment and additional safety assessments. This intervention not only protected the participants but also provided researchers with an opportunity to reassess the treatment's safety profile before proceeding.

In another case study, a DSMB overseeing a trial for a new vaccine against a viral infection detected early signals of inadequate immune response among trial participants. The DSMB's proactive analysis of the interim data revealed that the vaccine formulation was less effective than anticipated, raising concerns about its potential use in broader populations. Acting on this information, the DSMB recommended modifications to the trial design, including adjustments to the dosing schedule and additional safety monitoring. The prompt intervention not only improved the trial's chances of success but also reinforced the importance of ongoing safety assessments in clinical research.

These case studies highlight the importance of DSMBs in ensuring the ethical conduct of clinical trials and the protection of participants. By intervening when safety concerns arise, DSMBs can prevent potential harm and guide researchers in making informed decisions about the continuation or modification of studies. Their independent oversight enhances the credibility of clinical research and fosters public trust in the scientific process.

16.6.2 Impact of DSMB Decisions on Trial Outcomes
The decisions made by Data Safety Monitoring Boards (DSMBs) can significantly influence the outcomes of clinical trials, shaping the direction of research and the development of new treatments. When DSMBs recommend modifications to trial protocols or halt studies due to safety concerns, their interventions can lead to the reassessment of treatment

strategies and the implementation of more effective measures to protect participants. For instance, a DSMB's recommendation to pause a trial for additional safety monitoring can prompt researchers to gather more data, refine their methodologies, and ensure that participant welfare remains a top priority.

Furthermore, DSMB decisions can have broader implications for the research community and regulatory agencies. For example, when a DSMB identifies serious safety concerns related to a specific intervention, their recommendations can lead to changes in clinical guidelines or regulations governing the use of that treatment. Such decisions help ensure that new therapies are safe and effective before they are introduced to the market. Additionally, the transparency of DSMB decisions contributes to a culture of accountability and ethical responsibility in clinical research, reinforcing the importance of participant safety and informed decision-making.

The impact of DSMB decisions extends beyond individual trials; they can also influence the public perception of clinical research as a whole. When DSMBs intervene to protect participants, it fosters public trust in the research process, assuring the community that ethical standards are being upheld. Conversely, negative outcomes resulting from a failure to act on safety concerns can undermine public confidence in research. Therefore, the effectiveness of DSMBs in making timely and informed decisions is crucial for the ethical conduct of clinical trials and the advancement of medical knowledge.

16.6.3 Lessons Learned for Future DSMB Operations

The examination of case studies involving Data Safety Monitoring Boards (DSMBs) offers valuable lessons that can inform and enhance their future operations. One key lesson is the importance of **clear communication** among DSMB members, researchers, and regulatory agencies. Effective communication ensures that all stakeholders are informed about safety concerns, interim findings, and recommendations for trial modifications. Establishing robust communication protocols can facilitate timely decision-making and foster collaboration between researchers and DSMBs, ultimately enhancing the ethical oversight of clinical trials.

Another significant takeaway is the necessity of **ongoing training and education** for DSMB members. As clinical research methodologies evolve and ethical standards adapt, it is essential for DSMB members to stay informed about the latest developments in their respective fields. Regular training sessions can equip members with the knowledge and skills needed to conduct thorough reviews, make informed recommendations, and navigate complex ethical dilemmas. By investing in the professional development of DSMB members, organizations can strengthen the effectiveness and credibility of their oversight.

Additionally, case studies highlight the value of including diverse perspectives within DSMBs. Incorporating members with varied backgrounds and expertise can lead to more comprehensive evaluations of trial data and enhance the board's ability to address ethical considerations effectively. Emphasizing diversity in the selection of DSMB members can improve decision-making processes and contribute to the overall integrity of clinical research oversight.

Lastly, the importance of a well-defined operational framework for DSMBs cannot be overstated. Clear guidelines regarding their responsibilities, decision-making processes, and reporting requirements are essential for ensuring accountability and transparency in their operations. By establishing and adhering to these frameworks, DSMBs can effectively fulfill their oversight responsibilities and promote ethical conduct in clinical trials.

Review Questions

1. What is the role of Data Safety Monitoring Boards (DSMB) in clinical trials?
2. Why is the independence of DSMBs crucial for maintaining ethical standards in clinical trials?
3. What are the responsibilities of DSMBs in safety monitoring and decision-making during clinical trials?
4. How do DSMBs review interim data to make recommendations about continuing or modifying a trial?
5. What are the key considerations for selecting members of a DSMB?
6. What ethical concerns can arise in DSMB operations, such as conflicts of interest?
7. How do DSMBs function in placebo-controlled trials?
8. What are some examples of DSMBs intervening in trials, and what lessons were learned?

CHAPTER SEVENTEEN

Informed Consent Process and Documentation

17.1 Importance of Informed Consent in Clinical Research

17.1.1 Definition and Ethical Foundations of Informed Consent

Informed consent is a foundational ethical principle in clinical research that ensures participants are fully aware of the nature, purpose, risks, and potential benefits of a study before agreeing to participate. This process is rooted in the ethical principles of **autonomy, beneficence,** and **justice**. Autonomy emphasizes the right of individuals to make informed decisions regarding their participation in research, ensuring that they have the capacity to understand the information provided and the implications of their choices. Beneficence requires researchers to prioritize the well-being of participants, minimizing risks while maximizing potential benefits. Lastly, justice ensures that the selection of participants is fair and equitable, preventing exploitation of vulnerable populations.

The ethical foundations of informed consent are further reinforced by various regulatory frameworks and guidelines, including the **Declaration of Helsinki** and the **Belmont Report**. These documents outline the necessity of informed consent as a protective measure for human subjects, emphasizing the need for transparency and respect for participants' rights. By obtaining informed consent, researchers demonstrate their commitment to ethical conduct, fostering trust between investigators and participants and promoting the integrity of the research process.

17.1.2 Historical Evolution of Informed Consent

The concept of informed consent has evolved significantly over time, shaped by historical events and ethical advancements in medical research.

The roots of informed consent can be traced back to the **Nuremberg Code** established after World War II, which emphasized the necessity of voluntary consent in medical experimentation. The atrocities committed during the war highlighted the importance of protecting human subjects and the need for ethical guidelines in research. Following the Nuremberg Code, the **Declaration of Helsinki** further developed the principles of informed consent, providing comprehensive guidelines for obtaining consent from participants in medical research.

Throughout the latter half of the 20th century, the ethical requirements for informed consent became increasingly formalized in response to various controversial studies, such as the **Tuskegee Syphilis Study**. This unethical research, which involved deceiving participants about their treatment status, led to significant public outcry and prompted calls for stronger ethical oversight in research. As a result, regulatory bodies began to establish clearer requirements for informed consent, including the necessity of disclosing relevant information to participants and ensuring that consent is given freely and without coercion.

In recent years, the evolution of informed consent has also been influenced by advancements in technology and changing societal expectations. The rise of patient autonomy and advocacy has further highlighted the need for meaningful consent processes that empower individuals to make informed choices about their participation in research. Today, informed consent is viewed not only as a legal requirement but also as a fundamental ethical obligation, reflecting a commitment to respecting the rights and dignity of all research participants.

17.1.3 Key Principles Underlying Informed Consent

The key principles underlying informed consent encompass a range of ethical considerations that guide the process of obtaining consent from research participants. First and foremost is the principle of **autonomy**, which emphasizes the right of individuals to make informed decisions regarding their participation in research. This principle requires that participants are provided with comprehensive information about the study, allowing them to understand the risks, benefits, and procedures involved before agreeing to participate. Autonomy also necessitates that consent is obtained voluntarily, without coercion or undue influence.

Another important principle is **disclosure**, which refers to the obligation of researchers to provide participants with all relevant information needed to make an informed decision. This includes details about the study's purpose, the nature of the interventions, potential risks and side effects, and any alternative treatments available. The information must be presented in a clear and understandable manner, taking into account the participants' varying levels of comprehension and literacy. Effective disclosure helps participants evaluate their options and make informed choices that align with their values and preferences.

Beneficence is also a critical principle in informed consent, requiring researchers to prioritize the welfare of participants. Researchers must ensure that the potential benefits of the study outweigh the risks involved. This principle aligns with ethical standards aimed at protecting participants from harm and ensuring that research is conducted in a manner that promotes their well-being. Finally, the principle of **justice** emphasizes the fair selection of participants in research, ensuring that no group is unduly burdened by the risks of the study while others receive its benefits. By adhering to these key principles, researchers can uphold ethical standards in clinical research and promote a culture of respect and transparency in the informed consent process.

17.2 Components of the Informed Consent Process

17.2.1 Disclosure of Information to Participants

The **disclosure of information** is a critical component of the informed consent process in clinical research. Researchers are obligated to provide participants with comprehensive details about the study, including its purpose, methodology, duration, potential risks, and anticipated benefits. This information should be conveyed clearly and concisely, avoiding technical jargon to ensure that participants fully understand what participation entails. Effective disclosure empowers individuals to make informed decisions about their involvement in research and reinforces the ethical principle of autonomy.

Moreover, the information disclosed must be tailored to the specific needs and characteristics of the participant population. For instance, individuals from diverse cultural backgrounds may require culturally sensitive explanations to ensure that they grasp the significance of the research and its potential implications for their health. Researchers should also consider participants' varying levels of education and literacy when developing their disclosure materials. This attention to the diversity of the participant population enhances the informed consent process and ensures that all individuals can engage meaningfully in decision-making regarding their participation.

In addition to initial disclosure, researchers should provide participants with updated information throughout the course of the study, particularly if new risks or benefits emerge. This ongoing communication helps to maintain transparency and ensures that participants remain informed about any changes that may affect their decision to continue in the study. By prioritizing thorough and effective disclosure, researchers can foster trust and respect between themselves and study participants, ultimately enhancing the integrity of the research process.

17.2.2 Comprehension and Voluntary Participation

Comprehension is a key aspect of the informed consent process, ensuring that participants not only receive information but also understand it fully. Researchers must assess participants' comprehension through various means, such as asking questions or providing opportunities for discussion, to confirm that they grasp the details of the study and their rights as participants. The informed consent process should facilitate an open dialogue where participants feel comfortable asking questions or seeking clarification. This interactive approach enhances participants' understanding and helps to ensure that their consent is informed.

Voluntary participation is another fundamental principle of informed consent, emphasizing that individuals must choose to participate without coercion or undue influence. Researchers must be cautious not to exert pressure on potential participants, whether through financial incentives, social expectations, or the authority of the research team. Ensuring voluntary participation requires that individuals are free to withdraw from the study at any point without facing negative consequences or loss of access to treatment. This principle upholds the ethical obligation to respect participants' autonomy and individual rights, reinforcing their agency in the decision-making process.

To support comprehension and voluntary participation, researchers should provide ample time for potential participants to consider their decision before consenting. This may involve allowing individuals to reflect on the information provided or discussing it with family members or trusted advisors. By prioritizing comprehension and voluntary participation in the informed consent process, researchers can foster an ethical environment that respects participants' rights and promotes their well-being throughout the study.

17.2.3 Documentation of Consent

The **documentation of consent** is a crucial element of the informed consent process in clinical research. Proper documentation serves as a record that participants have been informed about the study and have voluntarily agreed to participate. This documentation typically includes a signed informed consent form that outlines the key information provided to participants, including the study's purpose, procedures, risks, benefits, and confidentiality measures. Having a written record of consent not only protects participants' rights but also serves as evidence that the researchers have complied with ethical and regulatory requirements.

In addition to the signed consent form, researchers should consider providing participants with a copy of the document for their records. This practice reinforces the commitment to transparency and allows participants to refer back to the information as needed. It also fosters a sense of ownership and empowerment, as participants can review their rights and responsibilities throughout the course of the study.

Moreover, it is important for researchers to ensure that the documentation process is conducted ethically and sensitively. For instance, researchers should be mindful of any potential barriers to understanding that participants may face, such as language differences or cognitive impairments. In such cases, researchers may need to employ additional strategies, such as providing consent forms in multiple languages or using simplified language to enhance comprehension. By prioritizing thorough documentation and ethical practices in the informed consent process, researchers can ensure that participants are adequately informed and their rights are protected throughout the study.

17.3 Informed Consent in Vulnerable Populations

17.3.1 Special Considerations for Children, Elderly, and Incapacitated Individuals

Informed consent processes must account for the unique needs and vulnerabilities of certain populations, including children, the elderly, and incapacitated individuals. Each of these groups presents specific challenges in obtaining meaningful informed consent, necessitating tailored approaches that prioritize their rights and well-being. For children, consent is typically obtained from parents or legal guardians, while the child's assent may also be sought if they are of sufficient age and understanding. Researchers must ensure that parents are fully informed about the study's risks and benefits, while also fostering an environment where the child's voice is considered, encouraging them to express their feelings about participation.

For elderly individuals, the informed consent process must address potential cognitive impairments and varying levels of health literacy. Researchers should ensure that information is conveyed in clear, accessible language, and consider utilizing additional support tools, such as visual aids or simplified explanations, to enhance understanding. It is also important to assess whether elderly participants can provide informed consent independently or if a legally authorized representative should be involved. This consideration is crucial for respecting their autonomy while safeguarding their rights.

Incapacitated individuals, such as those with severe cognitive disabilities or mental health challenges, present further ethical dilemmas in the informed consent process. In these cases, obtaining consent from a legally authorized representative is necessary to protect the individual's rights and welfare. Researchers must engage with representatives sensitively, ensuring that they understand the study and can advocate for the best interests of the incapacitated individual. Ethical guidelines for research involving vulnerable populations emphasize the need for additional protections and considerations to uphold the principles of autonomy, beneficence, and justice, ensuring that research is conducted ethically and responsibly.

17.3.2 Obtaining Informed Consent from Legally Authorized Representatives

When conducting research involving individuals who are unable to provide informed consent due to incapacity, obtaining consent from a **legally authorized representative (LAR)** becomes necessary. The process for obtaining consent from an LAR is guided by ethical and legal standards that ensure the rights and welfare of the participant are prioritized. Researchers must ensure that the LAR is fully informed about the study's purpose, risks, benefits, and procedures, just as they would for the participant themselves. Clear communication is crucial in this process to foster understanding and trust.

In some cases, the determination of who qualifies as a legally authorized representative can vary depending on local laws and institutional policies. For example, family members, legal guardians, or designated healthcare proxies may serve as LARs, but researchers must verify their authority to make decisions on behalf of the participant. It is essential for researchers to understand and comply with the specific legal requirements in their jurisdiction to ensure the informed consent process is conducted appropriately.

Additionally, obtaining consent from an LAR does not exempt researchers from their ethical obligation to respect the wishes of the incapacitated individual, if they can be expressed. Whenever possible, researchers should strive to involve the individual in discussions about participation, seeking their preferences and opinions. This approach enhances the ethical integrity of the research and affirms the dignity and autonomy of the participant, even in the context of incapacity.

17.3.3 Ethical Dilemmas in Obtaining Consent from Vulnerable Populations

Obtaining informed consent from vulnerable populations often presents complex ethical dilemmas that require careful consideration and sensitivity. One significant ethical challenge arises from the inherent power dynamics between researchers and vulnerable participants, which can create an environment where individuals feel pressured to participate in research. For instance, economically disadvantaged individuals may be more inclined to accept participation due to potential financial incentives, which can compromise their ability to provide truly informed consent. Researchers must remain vigilant to ensure that participants are not coerced or unduly influenced by external factors when making their decisions.

Another ethical dilemma relates to the capacity of vulnerable populations to understand and engage with the informed consent process. Researchers must carefully assess whether individuals have the cognitive ability to comprehend the information provided and appreciate the implications of their participation. This assessment is especially critical when working with populations that may have cognitive impairments, such as individuals with intellectual disabilities or severe mental health conditions. Researchers should prioritize clear communication and, when necessary, employ additional tools or resources to enhance comprehension and support informed decision-making.

Additionally, the ethical implications of conducting research on vulnerable populations extend to the potential risks associated with participation. Researchers must carefully consider whether the benefits of the research outweigh the risks for these groups. Ethical guidelines emphasize the need for enhanced protections for vulnerable populations, such as increased monitoring and oversight during the research process. By addressing these ethical dilemmas and prioritizing participant rights and welfare, researchers can uphold the ethical standards essential to the conduct of clinical research involving vulnerable populations.

17.4 Patient Information Sheet and Informed Consent Form

17.4.1 Key Elements of a Patient Information Sheet (PIS)

A **Patient Information Sheet (PIS)** is a crucial document provided to potential participants in a clinical trial, designed to inform them about the study and help them make an informed decision regarding their participation. The key elements of a PIS include the study's purpose, the procedures involved, potential risks and benefits, and information about the confidentiality of participant data. It is essential that the PIS is written in clear and accessible language, avoiding technical jargon that may confuse or mislead participants. This clarity enhances understanding and empowers individuals to engage meaningfully in the informed consent process.

Additionally, the PIS should outline the rights of participants, including the right to withdraw from the study at any time without penalty. It is also beneficial to include contact information for the research team and ethics committee, allowing participants to ask questions or voice concerns about the study. By providing comprehensive information in the PIS, researchers demonstrate their commitment to transparency and respect for participant autonomy. Furthermore, a well-structured PIS can foster trust between participants and researchers, contributing to a more ethical research environment.

17.4.2 Designing the Informed Consent Form (ICF)

The **Informed Consent Form (ICF)** is a formal document that participants sign to indicate their agreement to participate in a clinical trial. Designing an effective ICF requires careful attention to detail and adherence to ethical and regulatory standards. The ICF should include all key information outlined in the PIS, presented in a structured format that is easy for participants to navigate. Important components of the ICF include a clear explanation of the study purpose, a description of the procedures involved, a discussion of potential risks and benefits, and assurances of confidentiality regarding personal data.

Moreover, the language used in the ICF should be clear, concise, and easily understandable for the target population. Researchers should consider the literacy levels and cultural backgrounds of participants when crafting the ICF. Utilizing plain language and avoiding complex medical terminology can enhance comprehension and ensure that participants fully understand the information being presented. Additionally, the ICF should provide space for participants to ask questions and express any concerns they may have about the study, fostering an environment of open communication.

Furthermore, the ICF should explicitly state the participant's right to withdraw from the study at any time, without any consequences to their care. This emphasis on participant rights is crucial for upholding ethical standards in clinical research. By prioritizing clarity and participant engagement in the design of the ICF, researchers can enhance the informed consent process and promote ethical conduct in clinical trials.

17.4.3 Language and Cultural Considerations in the Consent Form

When designing the Informed Consent Form (ICF), it is vital to consider the **language** and **cultural** backgrounds of the intended participants. The use of culturally appropriate language can significantly impact participants' understanding and engagement with the informed consent process. Researchers should strive to present information in a language that is familiar and accessible to participants, ensuring that they can grasp the key elements of the study without confusion. This may involve translating the ICF into multiple languages or using culturally relevant examples to convey complex concepts.

Additionally, cultural considerations extend beyond language to encompass the beliefs, values, and practices of diverse populations. Researchers should be aware of cultural sensitivities that may affect participants' perceptions of clinical research. For example, some cultures may prioritize collective decision-making over individual autonomy, necessitating discussions about informed consent that respect these values. Researchers should engage with community representatives or cultural experts to develop an ICF that resonates with the target population and effectively communicates the study's objectives.

Furthermore, it is essential to conduct comprehension assessments during the consent process to ensure that participants fully understand the information provided in the ICF. Researchers may use teach-back methods, where participants explain the study back to the researcher in their own words, to gauge comprehension. This iterative process allows for adjustments to be made in real-time, enhancing the overall effectiveness of the informed consent process. By prioritizing language and cultural considerations in the ICF, researchers can promote inclusivity and ensure that all participants are empowered to make informed decisions about their involvement in clinical research.

17.5 Regulatory Requirements for Informed Consent

17.5.1 FDA, EMA, and CDSCO Guidelines
Regulatory requirements for informed consent in clinical research are established by key regulatory bodies, including the **U.S. Food and Drug Administration (FDA), the European Medicines Agency (EMA)**, and the **Central Drugs Standard Control Organization (CDSCO)** in India. Each of these agencies provides comprehensive guidelines outlining the essential elements of informed consent and the obligations of researchers in obtaining it. For example, the FDA requires that informed consent be obtained prior to enrolling participants in a study and emphasizes the necessity of clear and comprehensive information to facilitate informed decision-making. This ensures that participants are fully aware of what their participation entails, including any risks and potential benefits.

The EMA has similar guidelines, stressing the importance of transparency in the informed consent process. Their regulations require that participants receive clear and understandable information about the study, along with an explanation of their rights as research participants. The EMA's focus on ethical considerations aligns with its commitment to protecting the rights and welfare of trial participants. Meanwhile, the CDSCO also mandates that informed consent be obtained in compliance with national regulations, ensuring that Indian participants are protected and that ethical standards are upheld in clinical research.

These regulatory guidelines underscore the necessity of thorough documentation of the informed consent process, which should include written consent forms that capture participants' agreement to participate in the study. Compliance with these guidelines not only safeguards participant rights but also reinforces the ethical integrity of clinical research. Researchers must remain vigilant in adhering to the specific requirements set forth by regulatory authorities to maintain compliance and ensure the ethical conduct of their studies.

17.5.2 GCP Requirements for Informed Consent
Good Clinical Practice (GCP) guidelines outline specific requirements for obtaining informed consent in clinical trials. GCP emphasizes the ethical obligation of researchers to ensure that participants are adequately

informed about the study and its implications before providing consent. According to GCP guidelines, informed consent must be obtained voluntarily, without any coercion or undue influence. Researchers are responsible for ensuring that participants comprehend the information provided, and they must be given the opportunity to ask questions and engage in discussions regarding their participation.

Additionally, GCP guidelines require that informed consent be documented properly, with signed consent forms retained as part of the trial's records. This documentation serves as a safeguard to ensure that the consent process was conducted ethically and in compliance with regulatory requirements. Researchers are also encouraged to implement processes for obtaining ongoing consent if there are significant changes to the study or if new information arises that may impact participants' willingness to continue.

Moreover, GCP guidelines highlight the importance of cultural sensitivity in the informed consent process. Researchers are urged to consider the cultural backgrounds of participants when developing consent materials, ensuring that they are appropriately tailored to meet the needs of diverse populations. By adhering to GCP requirements for informed consent, researchers can uphold ethical standards in clinical research and foster trust and respect between participants and investigators.

17.5.3 Legal Implications of Improper Consent Documentation

Improper documentation of the informed consent process can have serious legal implications for researchers and institutions involved in clinical trials. Failure to obtain valid informed consent may lead to allegations of negligence or violations of ethical standards, resulting in potential legal repercussions. In cases where participants experience adverse events related to the study, inadequate documentation can complicate liability issues and undermine the institution's defense in legal proceedings. Therefore, it is crucial for researchers to maintain meticulous records of the informed consent process to demonstrate compliance with regulatory requirements and ethical guidelines.

Additionally, legal implications may arise if consent documentation is not adequately detailed or fails to capture key elements of the informed consent process. For instance, if the consent form does not clearly outline the risks associated with the study or fails to specify participants' rights, it may be deemed invalid in a legal context. In such cases, participants could argue that they were not fully informed, potentially leading to lawsuits or regulatory investigations. Researchers should, therefore, prioritize thorough documentation practices to mitigate legal risks and protect their institutions from potential liabilities.

Moreover, the repercussions of improper consent documentation extend beyond individual cases to impact the broader research community. Inadequate adherence to informed consent standards can lead to a loss of public trust in clinical research, resulting in decreased participation rates and heightened scrutiny from regulatory agencies. To safeguard both participants' rights and the integrity of the research process, researchers must prioritize the accuracy and completeness of informed consent documentation, ensuring compliance with legal and ethical standards.

17.6 Case Studies in Informed Consent Violations

17.6.1 High-Profile Cases of Informed Consent Violations
Several high-profile cases of informed consent violations have underscored the critical importance of adhering to ethical standards in clinical research. One notable example is the **Tuskegee Syphilis Study**, in which African American men with syphilis were deceived about their diagnosis and were not provided with effective treatment, even after penicillin became widely available. This unethical study, which lasted for decades, highlighted the egregious consequences of failing to obtain informed consent and respecting participant autonomy. The fallout from this study led to widespread public outrage and significant changes in ethical regulations surrounding informed consent, emphasizing the need for transparency and accountability in research.

Another prominent case involved a clinical trial conducted by a pharmaceutical company that failed to adequately inform participants about potential risks associated with a new medication. In this instance, several participants experienced serious adverse effects that were not disclosed in the informed consent process. Legal action ensued, resulting in substantial fines for the company and increased scrutiny from regulatory agencies. This case serves as a reminder of the necessity for clear and comprehensive communication during the informed consent process, as well as the legal repercussions that can arise from inadequate disclosure.

These cases illustrate that informed consent is not merely a procedural formality but rather a fundamental ethical obligation that protects participants' rights and well-being. The lessons learned from these high-profile violations have led to a heightened focus on ethical standards in clinical research, promoting the importance of transparency, honesty, and respect for participants in the informed consent process.

17.6.2 Regulatory Responses and Consequences

In response to high-profile cases of informed consent violations, regulatory agencies have implemented stricter guidelines and oversight to enhance the ethical conduct of clinical research. Following the revelations of the Tuskegee Syphilis Study, the U.S. government established the **Office for Human Research Protections (OHRP)**, which is tasked with ensuring compliance with federal regulations regarding the protection of human subjects in research. This agency, along with the **FDA**, has emphasized the importance of informed consent as a cornerstone of ethical research practices. Regulatory bodies now require that informed consent processes be thoroughly documented, and they often mandate additional training for researchers on ethical standards and informed consent practices.

Additionally, regulatory responses to informed consent violations have included increased penalties for non-compliance. Institutions that fail to adhere to informed consent guidelines may face significant fines, loss of funding, or restrictions on conducting future research. These consequences serve as a deterrent, reinforcing the need for researchers and institutions to prioritize ethical standards and transparency in their practices. Furthermore, regulatory agencies often require independent audits of research studies to ensure compliance with informed consent requirements, adding an additional layer of oversight to protect participants.

The regulatory responses to informed consent violations have resulted in a cultural shift within the research community, emphasizing the importance of ethical conduct and participant protection. Researchers are increasingly recognizing that informed consent is not only a legal requirement but also a moral obligation that upholds the dignity and rights of individuals participating in research. This shift has contributed to a more robust ethical framework for clinical research, ultimately fostering trust between researchers and participants.

17.6.3 Lessons Learned for Enhancing Consent Practices

The examination of case studies involving informed consent violations has yielded valuable lessons that can enhance consent practices in clinical research. One key takeaway is the importance of fostering a culture of transparency and accountability in the informed consent process. Researchers must prioritize open communication with participants, ensuring they are fully informed about the study's purpose, risks, and benefits. By promoting transparency, researchers can build trust with participants, which is essential for ethical research conduct.

Another lesson learned is the necessity for ongoing education and training for researchers regarding ethical standards and informed consent practices. Comprehensive training can help researchers understand the complexities of obtaining informed consent and reinforce the importance of adhering to ethical guidelines. Regular workshops and seminars can be implemented to keep researchers informed about the latest developments in ethical standards and regulatory requirements, ensuring that they are equipped to engage effectively with participants during the consent process.

Furthermore, involving community representatives and stakeholders in the development of informed consent materials can enhance the effectiveness of consent practices. By soliciting feedback from diverse populations, researchers can create consent documents that are culturally sensitive and accessible, ultimately improving participants' understanding and engagement. This collaborative approach not only enhances the informed consent process but also reinforces the ethical commitment to respect the rights and welfare of all participants involved in clinical research.

Review Questions

1. Why is informed consent essential in clinical research, and what are its key principles?
2. How has the informed consent process evolved historically in clinical research?
3. What are the main components of the informed consent process, and how is comprehension ensured?
4. Discuss the ethical challenges of obtaining informed consent from vulnerable populations.
5. What are the key elements of a Patient Information Sheet (PIS) and an Informed Consent Form (ICF)?
6. How do regulatory bodies such as the FDA, EMA, and CDSCO enforce informed consent requirements?
7. What are some high-profile cases of informed consent violations, and what lessons were learned?
8. How can informed consent documentation be designed to account for language and cultural differences?

CHAPTER EIGHTEEN

Clinical Research Regulations in India – Schedule Y

18.1 Introduction to Schedule Y

18.1.1 Overview of Schedule Y and Its Scope

Schedule Y is a critical regulatory framework in India that governs the conduct of clinical trials and the approval of new drugs and medical devices. It is part of the **Drugs and Cosmetics Act** and outlines the requirements and guidelines for clinical research involving human participants. Schedule Y aims to ensure that clinical trials are conducted ethically, safely, and in compliance with international standards. The scope of Schedule Y encompasses various aspects of clinical research, including trial design, participant recruitment, informed consent, data management, and reporting of adverse events.

The regulations stipulated in Schedule Y are designed to protect the rights and welfare of participants while promoting the ethical conduct of research. By establishing clear guidelines for researchers and sponsors, Schedule Y helps foster public trust in the clinical research process. The framework applies to all phases of clinical trials, from early-stage studies to post-marketing surveillance, ensuring a comprehensive approach to the ethical oversight of clinical research in India.

18.1.2 Key Objectives and Significance for Indian Clinical Trials

The key objectives of Schedule Y include ensuring participant safety, promoting ethical research practices, and establishing a robust regulatory framework for clinical trials in India. One of the primary goals is to protect the rights and welfare of participants by mandating rigorous informed consent processes, comprehensive risk assessments, and ongoing safety monitoring. These requirements are essential for minimizing potential harm to participants and ensuring that their rights are respected throughout the research process.

Schedule Y also plays a significant role in enhancing the credibility of clinical trials conducted in India. By aligning Indian regulations with international standards, Schedule Y facilitates the acceptance of clinical trial data by global regulatory authorities. This alignment is particularly important for sponsors seeking approval for new drugs or medical devices in multiple countries. The regulations outlined in Schedule Y contribute to the overall growth of the clinical research industry in India, attracting both domestic and international sponsors to conduct trials in the country.

18.1.3 Evolution of Schedule Y

The evolution of Schedule Y reflects the changing landscape of clinical research in India and the increasing emphasis on ethical standards and participant protection. Initially introduced in 2005, Schedule Y has undergone several revisions to address emerging challenges and align with global best practices. The Indian government recognized the need for a comprehensive regulatory framework to govern clinical trials, especially as the country became a significant player in the global clinical research arena.

Revisions to Schedule Y have included enhancements to the informed consent process, stricter requirements for ethical oversight, and improved guidelines for data management and reporting. These changes have been informed by the experiences and feedback from stakeholders in the clinical research community, including researchers, regulatory authorities, and ethics committees. The ongoing evolution of Schedule Y demonstrates a commitment to promoting ethical research practices while ensuring participant safety and welfare in clinical trials.

18.2 Regulatory Approval Process in India

18.2.1 Steps Involved in Obtaining Trial Approval

The regulatory approval process for clinical trials in India involves several key steps that researchers and sponsors must navigate to ensure compliance with Schedule Y and other relevant regulations. The process typically begins with the submission of a **Clinical Trial Application (CTA)** to the **Central Drugs Standard Control Organization (CDSCO)**. The CTA must include comprehensive information about the study, including the trial protocol, investigator's brochure, and informed consent documents. This submission initiates the review process by regulatory authorities to assess the scientific validity, ethical considerations, and safety aspects of the proposed study.

Once the CTA is submitted, the CDSCO conducts a thorough evaluation of the application, which includes reviewing the study design, risk assessments, and the qualifications of the investigators involved. This evaluation process can take several weeks, during which the CDSCO may request additional information or clarification from the sponsor. If the application meets all regulatory requirements, the CDSCO grants approval for the trial to commence. Additionally, researchers must obtain approval from an independent ethics committee (IEC) to ensure that the study adheres to ethical standards and protects participant rights.

Throughout the approval process, researchers must remain in communication with regulatory authorities and ethics committees, addressing any concerns raised during the review. Timely and transparent communication can facilitate a smoother approval process and help to build trust with regulatory agencies. Overall, understanding the steps involved in obtaining trial approval is crucial for researchers and sponsors to navigate the regulatory landscape effectively and ensure compliance with ethical standards.

18.2.2 Key Regulatory Bodies: CDSCO and DCGI

The **Central Drugs Standard Control Organization (CDSCO)** is the primary regulatory body overseeing clinical trials and drug approvals in India. As part of the Ministry of Health and Family Welfare, CDSCO is responsible for ensuring the safety, efficacy, and quality of drugs and medical devices used in clinical research. The organization plays a critical role in reviewing Clinical Trial Applications (CTAs), monitoring ongoing trials, and enforcing compliance with regulatory requirements outlined in Schedule Y. By conducting thorough evaluations, CDSCO helps to protect participant rights and ensure that research is conducted ethically.

Within CDSCO, the **Drug Controller General of India (DCGI)** is the key authority responsible for granting approvals for new drugs and overseeing the regulatory processes related to clinical trials. The DCGI evaluates the safety and efficacy data submitted in the CTA and makes decisions regarding trial approval and post-marketing surveillance. The role of the DCGI is particularly significant in the context of safeguarding public health, as they assess the potential risks and benefits associated with new treatments. By ensuring that clinical trials adhere to rigorous ethical and scientific standards, the DCGI plays a vital role in advancing medical research while prioritizing participant safety.

In addition to CDSCO and DCGI, various state regulatory authorities may also be involved in overseeing clinical trials at the regional level. This multi-tiered regulatory structure allows for comprehensive oversight and monitoring of clinical research activities across the country. Researchers and sponsors must familiarize themselves with the roles and responsibilities of these regulatory bodies to ensure compliance with the established guidelines and facilitate the approval process for clinical trials.

18.2.3 Differences Between Drug and Device Trials

While both drug and device trials fall under the purview of Schedule Y, there are important differences in the regulatory processes and requirements for obtaining approval for these two types of interventions. For drug trials, the approval process primarily focuses on assessing the safety, efficacy, and pharmacokinetics of the investigational product. Researchers must provide detailed information regarding the drug's mechanism of action, dosage, potential side effects, and clinical trial design. The CDSCO evaluates this information rigorously to determine whether the drug meets the necessary safety and efficacy standards before granting approval for human trials.

In contrast, device trials often require a different set of considerations due to the unique nature of medical devices. The regulatory framework for devices may emphasize safety and performance characteristics rather than pharmacological effects. For example, when conducting trials for medical devices, researchers may need to demonstrate that the device performs as intended, poses minimal risks, and has appropriate design specifications. This may involve conducting bench tests, preclinical studies, and clinical evaluations to establish the device's safety and efficacy.

Additionally, the approval timelines and documentation requirements may differ between drug and device trials. While drug trials typically involve a more extensive regulatory review, device trials may have streamlined processes for certain low-risk devices, allowing for faster approvals. Researchers must be aware of these differences and ensure that they adhere to the specific regulatory requirements associated with their type of trial to facilitate a successful approval process.

18.3 Requirements for Clinical Trial Applications (CTA)

18.3.1 Documents Required for CTA Submissions

Submitting a **Clinical Trial Application (CTA)** in India involves providing a comprehensive set of documents to regulatory authorities, including the **Central Drugs Standard Control Organization (CDSCO)**. These documents are essential for enabling the CDSCO to evaluate the proposed trial's scientific validity, safety, and ethical considerations. Among the key documents required for a CTA are the **clinical trial protocol**, which outlines the study design, objectives, methodology, and statistical analysis plan. The protocol must provide sufficient detail to allow reviewers to assess the feasibility and ethical implications of the trial.

Another critical document in the CTA submission is the **Investigator's Brochure (IB)**. The IB contains essential information about the investigational product, including its pharmacological properties, known risks, and relevant preclinical and clinical data. This document serves as a comprehensive resource for investigators and ethics committees, facilitating informed decision-making throughout the trial. Additionally, the CTA must include participant consent forms, which outline the rights and responsibilities of participants and detail the informed consent process.

Other supporting documents may include a detailed description of the trial site, the qualifications of the principal investigator, and any previous regulatory approvals for the investigational product. Researchers must also provide a risk management plan and data management strategies to ensure that participant safety is prioritized throughout the trial. By ensuring that all required documents are meticulously prepared and submitted, researchers can facilitate a smoother approval process and demonstrate their commitment to ethical research practices.

18.3.2 Role of the Investigator's Brochure (IB)

The **Investigator's Brochure (IB)** is a pivotal document in the clinical trial process, serving as a comprehensive reference for investigators and regulatory authorities. The IB is designed to provide essential information about the investigational product, including its pharmacological properties, preclinical data, and any previous clinical trial results. This document plays a critical role in helping investigators understand the safety profile of the product, potential risks, and the scientific rationale for the proposed study. By presenting a clear and concise summary of relevant data, the IB supports informed decision-making throughout the trial.

The IB also serves as a key component of the Clinical Trial Application (CTA) submitted to the **Central Drugs Standard Control Organization**

(CDSCO). Regulatory authorities rely on the information contained in the IB to evaluate the safety and efficacy of the investigational product, assess the risk-benefit ratio, and determine whether the trial meets ethical standards. As such, the IB must be regularly updated to reflect new findings and emerging data, ensuring that investigators and regulatory bodies have access to the most current information. This ongoing updating process is vital for maintaining the integrity of the research and protecting participant welfare.

Moreover, the IB serves as a resource for ethics committees during their review of the clinical trial protocol. It provides essential context for understanding the proposed study's objectives and methodology, enabling ethics committees to assess whether the trial aligns with ethical standards and participant rights. By prioritizing the development of a thorough and well-organized Investigator's Brochure, researchers can enhance the informed consent process and facilitate compliance with regulatory requirements throughout the clinical trial.

18.3.3 Essential Elements of a Clinical Trial Protocol

The **Clinical Trial Protocol** is a foundational document that outlines the study design, objectives, methodology, and analytical plans for a clinical trial. It serves as a comprehensive roadmap for researchers and regulatory authorities, detailing every aspect of the study to ensure that it is conducted consistently and ethically. Essential elements of a clinical trial protocol include the study's objectives, which define the research questions the trial aims to address. These objectives guide the overall design and provide clarity on the trial's purpose.

Another critical component of the protocol is the **study design**, which outlines the methodology, including the types of participants, randomization procedures, treatment assignments, and statistical analysis plans. Detailed descriptions of the study population, inclusion and exclusion criteria, and participant recruitment strategies are essential for ensuring that the trial is adequately powered to detect meaningful differences. The protocol should also address safety monitoring plans, detailing how adverse events will be reported and managed throughout the study.

Additionally, the protocol must include information about the informed consent process, ensuring that participants will be adequately informed about the study's risks and benefits. This element emphasizes the importance of ethical conduct and participant protection in clinical research. By incorporating these essential elements into the Clinical Trial Protocol, researchers can ensure that their study is methodologically sound, ethically conducted, and compliant with regulatory requirements, ultimately contributing to the advancement of medical knowledge.

18.4 Ethical Considerations in Indian Clinical Trials

18.4.1 Informed Consent Requirements Under Schedule Y

Informed consent is a fundamental ethical requirement in clinical trials, ensuring that participants are adequately informed about the study and willingly agree to participate. Under **Schedule Y**, specific guidelines dictate the process of obtaining informed consent in Indian clinical trials. Researchers must provide participants with comprehensive information regarding the study's objectives, procedures, potential risks, benefits, and their rights as participants. This information must be presented in a language that is clear and comprehensible to the participants, allowing them to make informed decisions regarding their involvement in the study.

Schedule Y also emphasizes the necessity for ongoing informed consent, particularly in long-term studies where new risks may emerge. Researchers are required to ensure that participants remain informed throughout the trial and that they can withdraw their consent at any time without facing any penalties or loss of access to necessary medical care. This ongoing communication is essential for maintaining ethical standards and protecting participant autonomy throughout the research process. By adhering to the informed consent requirements set forth in Schedule Y, researchers demonstrate their commitment to ethical conduct and the protection of participants in clinical trials.

18.4.2 Role of Ethics Committees (ECs)

Ethics Committees (ECs) play a crucial role in the oversight of clinical trials in India, ensuring that studies are conducted ethically and that participant rights are protected. As mandated by Schedule Y, every clinical trial must obtain approval from an independent EC before commencing. The primary function of ECs is to review the trial protocol, informed consent documents, and recruitment strategies to assess whether they comply with ethical standards and regulatory requirements. This review process helps to identify potential ethical concerns and ensures that the study design prioritizes participant safety and welfare.

Moreover, ECs are responsible for ongoing monitoring of approved trials to ensure continued compliance with ethical guidelines throughout the study's duration. This monitoring may include periodic reviews of safety data and reports of adverse events, as well as assessments of any amendments to the trial protocol. By fulfilling these oversight responsibilities, ECs contribute significantly to fostering a culture of ethical research in India. Their independent assessments not only enhance participant protection but also promote public trust in the integrity of clinical trials.

18.4.3 Participant Protection in Indian Trials

Participant protection is a cornerstone of ethical clinical research, and Schedule Y outlines several measures to safeguard the rights and welfare of individuals involved in clinical trials. Researchers are required to implement robust safety monitoring protocols to identify and address potential risks associated with the investigational product or study procedures. This includes the establishment of Data Safety Monitoring Boards (DSMBs) to oversee participant safety and conduct regular reviews of trial data to ensure that risks remain acceptable.

Additionally, Schedule Y emphasizes the importance of protecting vulnerable populations, including children, pregnant women, and individuals with cognitive impairments. Special ethical considerations must be taken into account when conducting research involving these groups, ensuring that their rights are upheld and that appropriate safeguards are in place. For instance, informed consent from legally authorized representatives may be necessary for incapacitated individuals, and the assent of minors must also be sought wherever possible.

Furthermore, participant anonymity and confidentiality are paramount in Indian clinical trials. Researchers must implement measures to protect personal data and ensure that sensitive information is not disclosed without participant consent. By prioritizing participant protection through ethical oversight and adherence to regulatory requirements, clinical researchers in India can contribute to a safer and more trustworthy research environment.

18.5 Safety Monitoring and Reporting Requirements

18.5.1 Adverse Event Reporting in Indian Clinical Trials

Adverse event reporting is a critical aspect of ensuring participant safety in clinical trials. Schedule Y outlines specific requirements for the timely reporting and management of adverse events (AEs) that may occur during the course of a study. Researchers are obligated to closely monitor participants for any AEs and to document these occurrences systematically. Adverse events can range from minor side effects to serious health complications, and researchers must establish a robust reporting mechanism to capture all relevant data.

In India, the reporting of AEs is required to follow a standardized format, detailing the nature of the event, its severity, and any actions taken in response. This standardized approach ensures consistency and facilitates the collection of meaningful safety data that can be reviewed by regulatory authorities and ethics committees. The timely reporting of AEs not only helps protect the safety of participants but also contributes to the overall understanding of the investigational product's safety profile.

Furthermore, researchers must communicate serious adverse events (SAEs) to the **Central Drugs Standard Control Organization (CDSCO)** within stipulated timelines. This communication is essential for enabling regulatory authorities to assess the safety of the investigational product and take necessary actions if warranted. By adhering to the adverse event reporting requirements outlined in Schedule Y, researchers demonstrate their commitment to participant safety and ethical research practices.

18.5.2 Guidelines for Serious Adverse Event (SAE) Reporting

Reporting serious adverse events (SAEs) is a critical component of safety monitoring in clinical trials. SAEs are defined as events that result in death, hospitalization, persistent or significant disability, or any other important medical event that requires intervention. Schedule Y mandates that researchers must report all SAEs to the relevant regulatory authorities, including the **CDSCO**, promptly and within specified timelines. This requirement ensures that regulatory bodies are informed of any significant safety concerns that may arise during the trial.

The SAE reporting process must include comprehensive documentation that outlines the nature of the event, its relationship to the investigational product, and any corrective actions taken. Researchers are responsible for conducting thorough investigations of SAEs to determine their causality and to implement appropriate measures to protect participant safety. This may involve modifying the trial protocol, enhancing monitoring procedures, or, in some cases, halting participant enrollment.

Moreover, the guidelines for SAE reporting emphasize the importance of communication with participants regarding any potential risks associated with the study. Researchers must keep participants informed about the results of investigations into SAEs and any necessary precautions that should be taken. By adhering to the SAE reporting guidelines established in Schedule Y, researchers contribute to the ethical oversight of clinical trials and the safeguarding of participant well-being.

18.5.3 Post-Marketing Surveillance Under Schedule Y

Post-marketing surveillance is an essential component of the regulatory framework for ensuring the safety of drugs and medical devices after they have been approved for public use. Schedule Y outlines the requirements for conducting post-marketing surveillance to monitor the safety and effectiveness of products in real-world settings. This surveillance aims to identify any potential long-term effects, rare adverse events, or issues that may not have been evident during clinical trials.

Researchers and sponsors are required to implement comprehensive post-marketing surveillance programs, which may include ongoing monitoring of adverse events, periodic safety update reports, and active surveillance of patient populations. These programs are crucial for collecting data on the real-world performance of drugs and medical devices and for identifying any emerging safety signals. Additionally, regulatory authorities, such as the **CDSCO**, play a vital role in overseeing post-marketing surveillance and ensuring compliance with established guidelines.

By emphasizing post-marketing surveillance, Schedule Y reinforces the commitment to participant safety and the ethical conduct of clinical research. This ongoing monitoring helps ensure that any safety concerns are promptly addressed and that the benefits of approved products continue to outweigh their risks. The data collected through post-marketing surveillance can also inform future research and regulatory decisions, contributing to the overall advancement of medical knowledge and public health.

18.6 Amendments and Updates to Schedule Y

18.6.1 Major Updates to Schedule Y

Since its initial introduction, Schedule Y has undergone several significant updates to address the evolving landscape of clinical research in India. These updates reflect the increasing complexity of clinical trials, advancements in medical science, and the need for enhanced participant protection. Notable revisions have included the introduction of stricter guidelines for informed consent, emphasizing the importance of transparency and clarity in communication with participants. Additionally, updates have strengthened requirements for monitoring and reporting adverse events, ensuring that safety remains a top priority throughout the research process.

Another major update to Schedule Y has involved the integration of international best practices into the Indian regulatory framework. This alignment with global standards, such as those set by the **International Conference on Harmonization (ICH)** and **Good Clinical Practice (GCP)** guidelines, aims to enhance the credibility of clinical research conducted in India. By adopting these standards, Schedule Y facilitates the acceptance of clinical trial data by international regulatory agencies, promoting India's position as a hub for clinical research.

Moreover, recent updates have also focused on improving the regulatory approval process for clinical trials, streamlining submission procedures and reducing timelines for approval. These changes reflect a commitment to fostering an environment that supports innovation in clinical research while maintaining rigorous ethical and safety standards. By continuously updating Schedule Y, Indian regulatory authorities demonstrate their responsiveness to the needs of the research community and their dedication to promoting ethical practices in clinical trials.

18.6.2 Future Directions for Indian Clinical Research Regulations
Looking ahead, the future of clinical research regulations in India is poised for further evolution as the country continues to emerge as a significant player in the global research landscape. One potential direction is the continued emphasis on participant protection and ethical oversight. As clinical trials become more complex and involve diverse populations, there will be a growing need for regulations that address the unique challenges associated with conducting research in vulnerable groups. Future updates to Schedule Y may focus on enhancing protections for these populations, ensuring that their rights and welfare are prioritized in research endeavors.

Additionally, the integration of digital technologies and data analytics into clinical research may drive regulatory changes in the coming years. The increasing use of electronic health records, telemedicine, and real-world evidence in clinical trials necessitates updates to regulatory frameworks to accommodate these innovations. Future regulations may need to address issues related to data privacy, security, and the ethical implications of using digital tools in research. By embracing advancements in technology while maintaining ethical standards, Indian regulatory authorities can promote the responsible conduct of clinical research.

Furthermore, ongoing collaboration between regulatory bodies, researchers, and industry stakeholders will be essential for shaping the future of clinical research regulations in India. Engaging in dialogue with these groups can help identify emerging trends, address challenges, and develop effective strategies for promoting ethical research practices. By fostering a collaborative approach, Indian regulators can ensure that the regulatory framework remains adaptive and responsive to the needs of the research community and the evolving landscape of clinical research.

18.6.3 Comparison with International Regulations

Comparing Schedule Y with international regulations reveals both similarities and differences in the oversight of clinical trials. Like many global regulatory frameworks, Schedule Y emphasizes the importance of informed consent, ethical conduct, and participant protection. The regulations align closely with the principles outlined in international guidelines, such as the **Declaration of Helsinki** and **ICH-GCP**, reflecting a commitment to maintaining high ethical standards in clinical research.

However, there are also notable differences in the regulatory processes and requirements between Schedule Y and international regulations. For example, while the FDA and EMA have established clear pathways for expedited approvals for specific populations or conditions, Schedule Y may have different criteria and timelines for trial approvals. Additionally, the approach to post-marketing surveillance and reporting requirements can vary between India and other countries, influencing how safety data is monitored and managed after a product's approval.

Understanding these differences is essential for researchers and sponsors operating in the global clinical research landscape. By comparing and contrasting Schedule Y with international regulations, stakeholders can identify areas for improvement and work towards harmonizing practices. Ultimately, fostering alignment between Indian regulations and international standards can enhance the credibility of clinical trials conducted in India and promote the ethical conduct of research on a global scale.

Review Questions

1. What is the purpose of Schedule Y in the context of clinical research regulations in India?
2. Describe the steps involved in obtaining regulatory approval for a clinical trial in India.
3. What are the key documents required for Clinical Trial Applications (CTA) in India?
4. How does Schedule Y address the role of ethics committees in Indian clinical trials?
5. What are the reporting requirements for adverse events in Indian clinical trials under Schedule Y?
6. How does post-marketing surveillance work under Schedule Y?
7. What major updates have been made to Schedule Y in recent years?
8. How does Schedule Y compare with international regulations for clinical research?

CHAPTER NINETEEN

USA Clinical Research Regulations (FDA)

19.1 Overview of the FDA's Role in Clinical Research

19.1.1 Introduction to the FDA and Its Regulatory Authority

The **U.S. Food and Drug Administration (FDA)** plays a critical role in the regulation of clinical research, ensuring that new drugs, biologics, and medical devices are safe and effective for public use. Established in 1906, the FDA's mission is to protect public health by regulating the safety and efficacy of food products, drugs, medical devices, cosmetics, and tobacco. The agency has the authority to oversee clinical trials, review applications for new drugs and devices, and enforce compliance with federal regulations governing research involving human subjects. This regulatory oversight is essential for maintaining public trust in the medical and scientific communities.

The FDA's authority in clinical research is derived from the **Federal Food, Drug, and Cosmetic (FD&C) Act**, which grants the agency the power to set standards for the testing and approval of new medical products. Under this act, the FDA has established a comprehensive regulatory framework that governs the conduct of clinical trials. This framework includes guidelines for obtaining informed consent from participants, requirements for the submission of clinical trial applications, and procedures for monitoring the safety of products during and after clinical trials. By enforcing these regulations, the FDA aims to safeguard the rights and welfare of participants and ensure the scientific integrity of clinical research.

In addition to its regulatory functions, the FDA also plays a role in educating researchers and sponsors about the requirements and expectations for conducting clinical trials. Through guidance documents, workshops, and outreach programs, the agency provides valuable resources to help stakeholders navigate the complexities of the regulatory landscape. This commitment to education and transparency fosters collaboration between the FDA and the research community, ultimately enhancing the quality and safety of clinical trials conducted in the United States.

19.1.2 Key Objectives of FDA Clinical Trial Oversight

The FDA's oversight of clinical trials is driven by several key objectives aimed at protecting public health and ensuring the ethical conduct of research. One of the primary objectives is to assess the safety and efficacy of new medical products before they can be marketed to the public. The FDA evaluates clinical trial data to determine whether the benefits of a new drug or device outweigh the associated risks. This evaluation process is crucial for preventing harmful products from reaching consumers and for ensuring that only safe and effective treatments are available in the market.

Another important objective of FDA oversight is to uphold the rights and welfare of research participants. The agency mandates that informed consent must be obtained from all participants, ensuring they are fully aware of the risks, benefits, and procedures involved in the study. The FDA also requires that clinical trials adhere to ethical standards, including the establishment of independent **Institutional Review Boards (IRBs)** to review study protocols and monitor participant safety. By prioritizing participant protection, the FDA fosters an ethical research environment and enhances public trust in clinical trials.

Additionally, the FDA aims to facilitate innovation in the development of new medical products while maintaining rigorous safety standards. The agency provides pathways for expedited approvals of promising therapies, such as **Breakthrough Therapy Designation** and **Fast Track Designation**, which allow for faster access to new treatments for serious conditions. By balancing the need for innovation with the imperative of safety, the FDA plays a pivotal role in advancing medical research and improving public health outcomes.

19.1.3 FDA Organizational Structure Relevant to Clinical Research

The FDA's organizational structure is designed to support its regulatory functions and ensure effective oversight of clinical research. At the helm of the FDA is the **Commissioner**, who oversees the agency's various centers and offices. The most relevant of these is the **Center for Drug Evaluation and Research (CDER)**, which is responsible for evaluating new drugs and their clinical trial data. CDER plays a crucial role in reviewing Investigational New Drug (IND) applications and New Drug Applications (NDAs), providing guidance on study design, data requirements, and regulatory compliance.

In addition to CDER, the **Center for Biologics Evaluation and Research (CBER)** oversees the regulation of biological products, including vaccines and blood products. CBER's responsibilities encompass the review of clinical trials for biologics, ensuring that these products are safe and effective for public use. The **Center for Devices and Radiological Health (CDRH)** is another critical component of the FDA, focusing on the regulation of medical devices. CDRH evaluates clinical trial data related to the safety and performance of devices, ensuring compliance with regulatory standards before products can be marketed.

Furthermore, the FDA has established various offices and divisions within these centers to specialize in different aspects of clinical research oversight. For instance, the **Office of Good Clinical Practice** (OGCP) is responsible for promoting compliance with GCP regulations and providing guidance on the ethical conduct of clinical trials. This office also works to educate researchers and stakeholders about the importance of adhering to regulatory requirements. By fostering collaboration and communication across its organizational structure, the FDA enhances its ability to oversee clinical research effectively and ensure participant safety.

19.2 New Drug Application (NDA) Processes

19.2.1 NDA 505(b)(1): New Drug Approval Process

The **New Drug Application (NDA) 505(b)(1)** process is a comprehensive pathway through which a pharmaceutical company submits an application to the **U.S. Food and Drug Administration (FDA)** for approval of a new drug that has not previously been marketed in the United States. This process requires the submission of extensive data demonstrating the drug's safety and efficacy based on clinical trials. The NDA must include detailed information on the drug's chemistry, pharmacology, clinical study results, labeling, and proposed use. This robust data collection is essential to ensure that the drug meets the FDA's stringent standards for safety and effectiveness before it can be made available to the public.

The review process for NDA 505(b)(1) applications is rigorous and thorough. Once the application is submitted, the FDA conducts a comprehensive evaluation that includes assessing clinical trial data, inspecting manufacturing facilities, and reviewing proposed labeling to ensure it accurately reflects the drug's indications and risks. The FDA may also hold advisory committee meetings to seek external expertise and public input regarding the application. Upon completion of the review process, the FDA will either approve the NDA, request additional information, or deny the application based on safety or efficacy concerns. This meticulous approval process is critical for safeguarding public health and ensuring that new therapies are both safe and effective for consumers.

19.2.2 NDA 505(b)(2): Approval Based on Existing Data

The **NDA 505(b)(2)** process provides a flexible pathway for drug approval that allows for the submission of applications based on data not developed by the applicant. This can include published literature, studies conducted outside of the U.S., or data submitted in previous applications. The NDA 505(b)(2) process is particularly beneficial for companies seeking to bring modifications to existing drugs, such as new formulations, dosage forms, or indications. By leveraging existing data, this pathway can significantly reduce the time and resources required for drug development, enabling quicker access to new therapies for patients.

The approval process under NDA 505(b)(2) still requires the submission of sufficient evidence to demonstrate the drug's safety and efficacy. The FDA assesses the submitted data to determine whether it meets the necessary standards for approval. This pathway also allows for flexibility in addressing specific regulatory requirements, as the FDA may grant approval based on a combination of existing data and new clinical trials tailored to the modified drug. This hybrid approach facilitates innovation while maintaining rigorous safety standards, allowing for the efficient development of new therapies that build upon established drug profiles.

19.2.3 Abbreviated New Drug Application (ANDA) 505(j): Generic Drug Approval

The **Abbreviated New Drug Application (ANDA) 505(j)** process is designed specifically for the approval of generic drugs. This pathway allows pharmaceutical companies to seek approval for a generic version of an already marketed brand-name drug without the need to conduct extensive clinical trials demonstrating safety and efficacy. Instead, ANDA applicants must demonstrate that their generic drug is **bioequivalent** to the reference listed drug (RLD), meaning it delivers the same active ingredient in the same dosage form and achieves similar drug concentrations in the bloodstream.

The ANDA submission must include data demonstrating bioequivalence, along with information regarding the drug's manufacturing processes, quality controls, and labeling. The FDA rigorously reviews the application to ensure that the generic drug meets all regulatory standards before granting approval. This process not only facilitates competition in the pharmaceutical market but also helps to lower drug costs for consumers, improving access to essential medications. The ANDA 505(j) pathway is a critical component of the FDA's efforts to promote generic drug utilization, thereby enhancing public health and healthcare affordability.

19.3 Investigational New Drug (IND) Applications

19.3.1 Requirements for IND Submissions

An **Investigational New Drug (IND)** application is a request submitted to the FDA to begin clinical trials with an unapproved drug or to conduct research on a previously approved drug for a new indication. The IND submission process is critical for ensuring that the proposed clinical trials meet safety and ethical standards. To initiate the IND process, researchers must provide detailed information about the drug's pharmacological properties, the results of preclinical studies, and the proposed clinical trial design. This includes the study's objectives, methodologies, participant selection criteria, and statistical analysis plans.

Additionally, the IND application must contain a comprehensive **Investigator's Brochure (IB)**, which provides essential information about the drug, including its chemical composition, mechanisms of action, and prior research findings. The IB serves as a key resource for investigators and ethics committees, helping them understand the rationale for the proposed clinical study. Importantly, the IND must also include a plan for monitoring participant safety, which is vital for protecting human subjects during the research process. The thorough preparation and submission of an IND application is crucial for gaining FDA approval and ensuring that clinical trials are conducted ethically and responsibly.

19.3.2 Clinical Trials Under IND Status

Once an IND application is approved by the FDA, the sponsor can initiate clinical trials to evaluate the safety and efficacy of the investigational drug.

The clinical trials conducted under IND status are typically conducted in phases, beginning with Phase I trials that focus primarily on assessing safety and tolerability in a small group of healthy volunteers. Subsequent phases involve larger populations and aim to evaluate the drug's effectiveness and further monitor its safety profile. The progression through these phases is designed to generate robust data that informs the regulatory decision-making process.

Throughout the course of the clinical trials, the FDA continues to monitor the safety of participants. Researchers are required to report any adverse events or serious adverse events (SAEs) promptly to the FDA, ensuring that any potential risks are addressed in a timely manner. Additionally, the FDA may require periodic progress reports detailing the study's outcomes and any modifications to the trial protocol. This oversight is essential for maintaining participant safety and upholding the integrity of the clinical research process. By conducting well-designed clinical trials under IND status, researchers can contribute to the advancement of medical knowledge and the development of new therapeutic options.

19.3.3 Responsibilities of the Sponsor and Investigator

In the context of IND applications, both the sponsor and the investigator have distinct yet interrelated responsibilities to ensure the successful conduct of clinical trials. The **sponsor**, typically a pharmaceutical company or research organization, is responsible for overseeing the entire research process, from the development of the investigational drug to the completion of clinical trials. This includes ensuring compliance with regulatory requirements, managing trial logistics, and providing the necessary funding and resources. The sponsor must also maintain communication with the FDA throughout the trial, submitting required reports and addressing any safety concerns that arise during the study.

On the other hand, the **investigator** is responsible for the direct conduct of the clinical trial, ensuring that it is carried out in accordance with the approved protocol and ethical guidelines. Investigators must obtain informed consent from participants and ensure that they understand the study's risks and benefits. Additionally, investigators are responsible for monitoring participant safety and reporting any adverse events to the sponsor and regulatory authorities. Effective communication between the sponsor and investigator is vital for the successful execution of the trial, as both parties must work collaboratively to navigate challenges and ensure the ethical conduct of research.

In summary, the responsibilities of both the sponsor and investigator are integral to the IND process, with each party playing a crucial role in safeguarding participant rights and ensuring the integrity of the clinical research. Their collaborative efforts contribute to advancing medical science and enhancing the safety and efficacy of new therapies.

19.4 FDA Guidance for Industry

19.4.1 Acceptance of Foreign Clinical Studies

The FDA recognizes the increasing globalization of clinical research and the need to accept data from foreign clinical studies as part of the regulatory process. The **acceptance of foreign clinical studies** allows sponsors to leverage data generated outside the United States when seeking approval for new drugs or devices. To ensure that these foreign studies meet U.S. standards, the FDA requires that they comply with Good Clinical Practice (GCP) guidelines and be conducted in a manner consistent with U.S. regulations. This includes ensuring that the rights and welfare of participants are protected, informed consent is obtained, and that the studies are appropriately monitored.

When foreign clinical studies are submitted as part of an application, the FDA reviews the data to assess its reliability and relevance to the U.S. population. Factors such as the study design, patient population, and methodologies used in the foreign trials are evaluated to determine whether they provide sufficient evidence to support the drug's safety and efficacy for the intended use in the U.S. This acceptance of foreign clinical studies not only streamlines the drug approval process but also facilitates access to potentially beneficial therapies for U.S. patients.

Furthermore, the FDA encourages collaboration with international regulatory authorities to harmonize standards for clinical research. By promoting consistency in regulatory requirements and expectations, the FDA aims to enhance the quality of clinical data generated globally and support the timely approval of new medical products. This collaborative approach ultimately benefits patients by facilitating access to innovative treatments and ensuring that the regulatory processes remain aligned with global best practices.

19.4.2 FDA Good Clinical Practice (GCP) Guidelines

The **FDA Good Clinical Practice (GCP) guidelines** establish essential standards for the design, conduct, and monitoring of clinical trials in the

United States. GCP aims to ensure the ethical and scientific quality of clinical research while protecting the rights and welfare of participants. The guidelines emphasize the importance of obtaining informed consent, conducting thorough risk assessments, and implementing appropriate monitoring procedures to safeguard participant safety throughout the study.

GCP guidelines also require that clinical trial protocols are developed and adhered to rigorously, outlining the study's objectives, methodologies, and data analysis plans. Researchers are obligated to report any adverse events promptly and to ensure that trial data is collected, managed, and analyzed with integrity. By adhering to GCP guidelines, researchers demonstrate their commitment to ethical research practices and the protection of participant rights, contributing to the overall credibility and reliability of clinical research findings.

Moreover, the FDA provides guidance documents that elaborate on GCP principles and offer practical advice for researchers and sponsors conducting clinical trials. These documents serve as valuable resources for understanding regulatory expectations and ensuring compliance with GCP standards. By promoting adherence to GCP, the FDA helps maintain public trust in clinical research and enhances the quality of data generated through these studies.

19.4.3 Key FDA Guidance Documents for Clinical Trials

The FDA publishes a range of **guidance documents** that provide critical information and recommendations for conducting clinical trials. These documents cover various aspects of clinical research, including trial design, statistical considerations, safety monitoring, and regulatory compliance. Some key guidance documents address specific issues, such as the **FDA's Guidance on Adaptive Designs for Clinical Trials**, which outlines the principles and considerations for implementing adaptive trial methodologies. These designs allow for modifications to the trial based on interim data, enhancing the efficiency and effectiveness of clinical research.

Another important guidance document is the **FDA's Guidance on Good Clinical Practice**, which outlines the expectations for ethical conduct and the protection of human subjects in clinical research. This document serves as a comprehensive resource for researchers, offering insights into best practices for obtaining informed consent, conducting safety assessments, and maintaining compliance with regulatory requirements. By providing clear and accessible guidance, the FDA helps researchers navigate the complexities of clinical trials while ensuring that participant safety and ethical standards are prioritized.

Furthermore, the FDA's guidance documents are regularly updated to reflect emerging scientific knowledge, technological advancements, and changes in regulatory requirements. Researchers and sponsors are encouraged to stay informed about these updates and to incorporate the latest recommendations into their trial designs and practices. By doing so, they can enhance the quality and reliability of clinical research while ensuring compliance with FDA expectations.

19.5 FDA Safety Reporting Requirements

19.5.1 IND Safety Reporting
Safety reporting under an **Investigational New Drug (IND)** application is a critical component of the clinical trial process, designed to protect participants and ensure the integrity of the research. The FDA mandates that sponsors report any adverse events that occur during clinical trials involving an IND to ensure timely monitoring of the investigational drug's safety profile. The reporting requirements include both routine reports of adverse events and expedited reports for serious adverse events (SAEs) that may pose significant risks to participants.

The IND safety reporting process requires sponsors to submit an **Adverse Event Report (AER)** that includes comprehensive information about the adverse event, such as the nature of the event, its severity, the participant's medical history, and any actions taken in response. This data is essential for assessing the safety of the investigational drug and determining whether any changes to the trial protocol or monitoring procedures are necessary. Furthermore, the FDA expects sponsors to maintain open lines of communication regarding safety concerns, allowing for proactive management of risks throughout the clinical trial process.

By implementing stringent safety reporting requirements, the FDA aims to protect participants from potential harm and ensure that any safety signals are promptly addressed. This emphasis on safety reporting fosters a culture of accountability and ethical conduct in clinical research, reinforcing the FDA's commitment to safeguarding public health.

19.5.2 Serious Adverse Event (SAE) Reporting Requirements
Serious Adverse Events (SAEs) are defined as any undesirable experiences associated with the use of an investigational drug that result in significant medical consequences, such as hospitalization, disability, or death. The FDA

has established specific requirements for the reporting of SAEs that occur during clinical trials under IND status. Sponsors are required to report SAEs to the FDA within a defined time frame, typically within 7 days for life-threatening events and 15 days for all other serious events. This timely reporting is critical for facilitating the FDA's evaluation of the safety of the investigational drug and for making informed regulatory decisions.

In addition to reporting SAEs to the FDA, sponsors must also provide detailed information about the nature of the event, its relationship to the investigational product, and any corrective actions taken. The FDA reviews these reports to identify any potential safety concerns and assess whether the risk-benefit profile of the investigational drug remains acceptable. If a pattern of SAEs emerges, the FDA may require sponsors to conduct additional safety analyses, modify trial protocols, or even suspend enrollment in the trial. By enforcing stringent SAE reporting requirements, the FDA aims to protect participants and ensure that any potential risks associated with the investigational drug are adequately managed.

Moreover, effective communication between sponsors and investigators is essential for ensuring that all SAEs are reported accurately and promptly. Investigators are responsible for monitoring participants closely and reporting any serious events to the sponsor immediately. This collaborative approach enhances the safety monitoring process and supports the ethical conduct of clinical research, ultimately benefiting both participants and the integrity of the research.

19.5.3 Post-Marketing Safety Surveillance

Post-marketing safety surveillance is a vital aspect of the FDA's commitment to ensuring the ongoing safety of drugs and medical devices after they have been approved for public use. Once a drug receives market approval, the FDA mandates that sponsors continue to monitor its safety through various surveillance activities. This includes collecting and analyzing reports of adverse events from healthcare providers, patients, and other stakeholders to identify any potential safety signals that may emerge after the drug is widely used.

The FDA employs several mechanisms to facilitate post-marketing safety surveillance, including the **MedWatch** system, which allows healthcare professionals and the public to report adverse events, product defects, and safety concerns related to FDA-regulated products. These reports are invaluable for detecting trends and patterns that may indicate a need for further investigation or regulatory action. Additionally, the FDA may require post-marketing studies or risk evaluation and mitigation strategies (REMS) to further assess the long-term safety and effectiveness of a drug.

Furthermore, the FDA collaborates with other regulatory agencies, healthcare providers, and industry stakeholders to enhance post-marketing surveillance efforts. By sharing data and insights, the FDA aims to improve the understanding of a drug's safety profile and address any emerging safety concerns proactively. This commitment to continuous safety monitoring underscores the FDA's dedication to protecting public health and ensuring that approved medical products remain safe and effective for consumers over time.

19.6 FDA Audits and Inspections

19.6.1 FDA Audit Process

The FDA audit process is a crucial component of the agency's regulatory oversight of clinical trials and drug development activities. These audits are conducted to assess compliance with federal regulations, including those outlined in Good Clinical Practice (GCP) guidelines, the Federal Food, Drug, and Cosmetic Act, and other applicable laws. The audit process typically begins with the FDA notifying the sponsor or investigator of the impending inspection. This notification may include details about the specific aspects of the trial that will be examined, enabling the site to prepare adequately.

During the audit, FDA inspectors will review trial documentation, including participant consent forms, study protocols, and records of adverse events. The inspectors will also assess the adequacy of training and qualifications of personnel involved in the trial. This comprehensive examination allows the FDA to determine whether the trial was conducted in accordance with ethical standards and regulatory requirements. If any discrepancies or non-compliance issues are identified, the FDA may issue a Form 483, detailing the observations made during the audit and requiring corrective actions to be implemented.

After the audit, the FDA may conduct follow-up inspections to ensure that the identified issues have been resolved. The agency may also require the submission of additional documentation or corrective action plans to address any deficiencies noted during the audit. This proactive approach helps to maintain the integrity of clinical research and fosters a culture of compliance within the research community.

19.6.2 Key Areas of Focus During FDA Inspections

During FDA inspections, several key areas are closely scrutinized to ensure compliance with regulatory requirements and the ethical conduct of clinical trials. One primary focus is the **informed consent process**, where inspectors assess whether participants were adequately informed about the study and their rights before enrollment. This includes reviewing consent forms and documentation to verify that they meet the necessary criteria outlined in FDA regulations. Inspectors may also conduct interviews with participants to gauge their understanding of the study and their willingness to participate.

Another critical area of focus during FDA inspections is the **monitoring of adverse events**. Inspectors review how adverse events are reported, documented, and managed throughout the trial. They assess the protocols in place for monitoring participant safety and evaluate whether appropriate measures were taken in response to adverse events. Additionally, the integrity of the data collected during the trial is scrutinized, with inspectors examining the accuracy and completeness of study records, data entry processes, and any data management practices.

Finally, the qualifications and training of investigators and study personnel are assessed to ensure that they possess the necessary expertise to conduct the trial ethically and effectively. Inspectors may review training records, certifications, and investigator qualifications to verify compliance with FDA standards. By focusing on these key areas, FDA inspections aim to uphold the highest standards of safety, efficacy, and ethical conduct in clinical research.

19.6.3 Common Findings and Responses to FDA Audits

Common findings during FDA audits can vary widely, but they typically highlight areas of non-compliance or deficiencies in trial conduct. Some frequent observations include inadequate documentation of informed consent, failures in adverse event reporting, and discrepancies between the study protocol and actual practices. For example, auditors may find that consent forms lack essential information about potential risks or that participants were not properly informed of their rights, leading to concerns about the ethical conduct of the trial.

In response to these findings, sponsors and investigators are generally required to implement corrective action plans to address the identified issues. This may involve revising informed consent documents to ensure clarity and compliance, enhancing training for study personnel on regulatory requirements, or implementing more robust monitoring procedures for adverse events. Additionally, the FDA may require follow-up inspections to verify that corrective actions have been effectively implemented.

Ultimately, the goal of the FDA audit process is not only to identify areas of non-compliance but also to promote continuous improvement in clinical research practices. By addressing the findings from audits and responding proactively, researchers can enhance the quality and integrity of their studies, contributing to the overall advancement of safe and effective medical treatments. The collaborative relationship between the FDA and the research community is essential for maintaining high standards of ethical conduct and participant protection in clinical trials.

Review Questions

1. What is the role of the FDA in regulating clinical research in the USA?
2. Explain the difference between NDA 505(b)(1), NDA 505(b)(2), and ANDA 505(j).
3. What are the key requirements for submitting an Investigational New Drug (IND) application to the FDA?
4. How does the FDA ensure compliance with Good Clinical Practice (GCP)?
5. What are the FDA's safety reporting requirements during clinical trials?
6. How does the FDA conduct audits and inspections of clinical trials?
7. What challenges do sponsors face during the FDA's regulatory approval process?
8. Discuss the importance of post-marketing safety surveillance under FDA guidelines.

CHAPTER TWENTY

Clinical Research Regulations in the European Union (EMA)

20.1 Introduction to the European Medicines Agency (EMA)

20.1.1 Role and Responsibilities of the EMA

The **European Medicines Agency (EMA)** plays a pivotal role in the regulation of medicinal products within the European Union (EU). Established in 1995, the EMA is responsible for the scientific evaluation, supervision, and safety monitoring of medicines in the EU. Its primary aim is to ensure that all medications are safe, effective, and of high quality, thereby protecting public health across member states. The EMA provides a centralized regulatory process for the approval of new medicines, which allows for the swift and efficient access to safe treatments for patients throughout Europe.

The agency also contributes to the ongoing monitoring of medicines once they are on the market. This involves collecting and analyzing data on adverse reactions and conducting periodic safety reviews to ensure that the benefits of a drug continue to outweigh its risks. The EMA also provides scientific advice and guidance to companies developing new therapies, helping to shape the design of clinical trials and the overall regulatory strategy. This collaborative approach fosters innovation in drug development while maintaining rigorous safety and efficacy standards.

Additionally, the EMA works closely with national regulatory authorities, ensuring that regulatory processes are harmonized across EU member states. This cooperation enhances the agency's ability to respond effectively to emerging health threats, such as infectious disease outbreaks or public health emergencies. Through its comprehensive regulatory framework and commitment to transparency, the EMA plays a crucial role in promoting public confidence in the safety and effectiveness of medicines.

20.1.2 EMA's Regulatory Framework for Clinical Trials

The regulatory framework established by the EMA for clinical trials is designed to ensure the ethical conduct of research while promoting the rapid development of new therapies. This framework includes several key regulations and directives that govern the design, conduct, and oversight of clinical trials throughout the EU. The EMA requires that all clinical trials comply with **Good Clinical Practice (GCP)** guidelines, which set forth standards for the design, conduct, performance, monitoring, auditing, and reporting of clinical trials. GCP guidelines ensure that the rights, safety, and well-being of trial participants are protected and that data generated during the study is credible and accurate.

A significant part of the EMA's regulatory framework is the **Clinical Trials Regulation (EU) No 536/2014**, which aims to streamline the approval process for clinical trials and improve transparency and cooperation among member states. This regulation outlines the requirements for obtaining authorization to conduct clinical trials, including the submission of a detailed clinical trial application, ethical approvals from relevant ethics committees, and the establishment of a clinical trial register to provide public access to trial information. This approach facilitates the sharing of information among regulatory authorities and helps to prevent unnecessary duplication of trials.

Furthermore, the EMA emphasizes the importance of safety monitoring during clinical trials, requiring sponsors to implement robust risk management plans to identify and mitigate potential risks to participants. This regulatory framework not only supports the ethical conduct of clinical trials but also enhances the overall quality of clinical research conducted in the EU, ultimately leading to safer and more effective medicinal products for patients.

20.1.3 Structure and Key Committees of the EMA

The EMA is structured to facilitate its diverse functions in drug regulation and public health protection. At the core of the agency is the **Management Board**, which oversees its activities and ensures that it operates effectively and efficiently. The Management Board consists of representatives from EU member states, the European Commission, and the European Parliament. This composition allows for balanced governance and ensures that the interests of all stakeholders are considered in decision-making processes.

Supporting the Management Board are several scientific committees that focus on specific areas of drug evaluation and regulation. Notable among these is the **Committee for Medicinal Products for Human Use (CHMP)**, which is responsible for evaluating applications for human medicines. The CHMP reviews the data submitted in marketing authorization applications and provides scientific opinions to the European Commission regarding drug approval. Another important committee is the **Pharmacovigilance Risk Assessment Committee (PRAC)**, which assesses and monitors the safety of medicines once they are authorized for use, ensuring that any safety concerns are promptly addressed.

In addition to these committees, the EMA also collaborates with various working groups and stakeholder forums to engage with the pharmaceutical industry, healthcare professionals, and patient organizations. This collaborative approach fosters transparency and encourages the incorporation of diverse perspectives in regulatory decision-making. By maintaining a well-structured organization and actively involving stakeholders, the EMA enhances its ability to fulfill its mission of protecting public health and promoting the safe and effective use of medicines across the EU.

20.2 EU Directives on Clinical Trials

20.2.1 Overview of Directive 2001/20/EC

The **EU Directive 2001/20/EC** is a landmark piece of legislation that established the framework for the conduct of clinical trials in the European Union. This directive was implemented to harmonize the regulatory requirements for clinical trials across member states, ensuring that trials are conducted ethically and safely while promoting the free movement of goods and services within the EU. The directive sets forth essential guidelines for the design, approval, and conduct of clinical trials, outlining the obligations of sponsors, investigators, and ethics committees.

One of the key aspects of Directive 2001/20/EC is the emphasis on obtaining informed consent from trial participants. The directive mandates that participants must be adequately informed about the nature of the trial, potential risks, and benefits before agreeing to participate. This requirement reflects the ethical principles underpinning clinical research and ensures that participants can make informed decisions about their involvement. Additionally, the directive requires that clinical trials be conducted in compliance with Good Clinical Practice (GCP) standards, which set the framework for the ethical and scientific conduct of research involving human subjects.

Furthermore, the directive introduced provisions for the protection of vulnerable populations, including children, pregnant women, and individuals with diminished capacity. It recognizes the need for additional safeguards to protect these groups during clinical trials, emphasizing the importance of ethical considerations in the design and implementation of studies. Overall, Directive 2001/20/EC has played a vital role in shaping the regulatory landscape for clinical trials in the EU, promoting high standards of ethics and safety while facilitating research and innovation.

20.2.2 Requirements for Clinical Trial Approval in the EU

Obtaining approval for clinical trials in the EU involves a comprehensive process that requires adherence to the stipulations outlined in Directive 2001/20/EC and subsequent regulations. The approval process begins with the submission of a **Clinical Trial Application (CTA)** to the relevant national regulatory authority in the member state where the trial will be conducted. The application must include detailed information about the trial design, objectives, methodology, and participant population. Additionally, it must provide evidence of compliance with ethical standards, including documentation of informed consent processes and the involvement of ethics committees in the review of the trial protocol.

Once the CTA is submitted, the regulatory authority conducts a thorough evaluation of the application to assess its scientific validity and ethical compliance. This review process may involve collaboration with other member states, particularly if the trial is conducted in multiple countries. The regulatory authority assesses whether the proposed trial adheres to GCP guidelines and whether the risks to participants are justified by the potential benefits of the research. If the application meets all regulatory requirements, approval is granted, allowing the trial to commence.

Moreover, the approval process may also involve ongoing oversight during the trial, including the submission of periodic progress reports and safety updates to the regulatory authority. This requirement ensures that any emerging safety concerns are promptly addressed and that participant welfare remains a priority throughout the study. By adhering to these requirements for clinical trial approval, researchers contribute to the ethical and responsible conduct of research in the EU, promoting public trust in the clinical research process.

20.2.3 Differences Between EU and FDA Regulations

While both the **European Union (EU)** and the **U.S. Food and Drug Administration (FDA)** aim to ensure the safety and efficacy of clinical trials and medical products, there are notable differences in their regulatory approaches. One of the primary distinctions lies in the approval processes for clinical trials. In the EU, the process involves a centralized system where clinical trial applications must be submitted to national regulatory authorities, which may then engage in collaboration with other member states for trials conducted across multiple countries. In contrast, the FDA operates a more centralized approach, where all clinical trial applications are submitted to the FDA directly, allowing for a streamlined process.

Additionally, the requirements for informed consent and participant protections may vary between the two regulatory frameworks. While both the EU and FDA emphasize the importance of informed consent, the EU's regulations often mandate more detailed disclosures and a more comprehensive consent process, especially for vulnerable populations. This reflects the EU's commitment to protecting participant rights and welfare, which is reinforced through additional oversight by ethics committees.

Furthermore, the post-marketing surveillance systems differ in their structure and scope. In the EU, post-marketing surveillance is regulated under the **Pharmacovigilance Directive**, which emphasizes the ongoing monitoring of drug safety through mandatory reporting of adverse events. The FDA also has robust post-marketing surveillance requirements but operates through a different framework, with a strong focus on continuous monitoring and the ability to mandate safety labeling changes or product recalls based on emerging safety data. Understanding these differences is essential for researchers and sponsors conducting clinical trials in both jurisdictions, as it impacts regulatory compliance and the overall conduct of clinical research.

20.3 EudraLex and Volume 3 Guidelines

20.3.1 Overview of EudraLex

EudraLex is the collection of laws, regulations, and guidelines governing medicinal products in the European Union. It provides a comprehensive legal framework that ensures the safety, efficacy, and quality of drugs throughout their lifecycle, from development to marketing. The EudraLex framework is essential for facilitating the regulatory processes associated with clinical trials, providing clear directives on the responsibilities of stakeholders involved in drug development, including sponsors, investigators, and regulatory authorities.

EudraLex is structured into various volumes, each addressing specific aspects of drug regulation and clinical research. This structured approach allows for clarity and ease of access to the relevant guidelines for all parties involved. For instance, **Volume 1** pertains to the regulatory framework for medicinal products, while **Volume 3** focuses specifically on guidelines for human medicinal products, including those related to clinical trials. This comprehensive framework not only streamlines the approval process for new drugs but also enhances collaboration among member states, ensuring that clinical research is conducted uniformly across the EU.

Furthermore, EudraLex facilitates transparency in the regulatory process by providing public access to information regarding ongoing clinical trials and their results. The EudraCT database is a key component of this transparency initiative, allowing stakeholders to view information about clinical trials conducted in the EU. By promoting openness and accountability, EudraLex helps to build public trust in the clinical research process and the safety of medicinal products available in the market.

20.3.2 Volume 3: Scientific Guidelines for Human Medicinal Products

Volume 3 of EudraLex is specifically dedicated to scientific guidelines for human medicinal products, outlining the regulatory framework for conducting clinical trials and the requirements for marketing authorization. This volume encompasses various aspects of clinical research, including the design and conduct of clinical trials, data management, and the ethical considerations involved in research with human participants. It serves as a vital resource for researchers, regulatory authorities, and ethics committees, providing essential information on the expectations for compliance with EU regulations.

One of the key components of Volume 3 is the emphasis on adherence to **Good Clinical Practice (GCP)** guidelines, which set the standards for the ethical conduct of clinical trials. The guidelines specify the roles and responsibilities of sponsors, investigators, and ethics committees, ensuring that participant rights and welfare are prioritized throughout the research process. Additionally, Volume 3 addresses the requirements for trial protocols, including detailed descriptions of study design, statistical analysis plans, and risk management strategies.

Moreover, Volume 3 provides guidance on the requirements for submitting clinical trial applications and the information needed for regulatory review. This includes the necessary documentation to support the trial's scientific validity, safety assessments, and ethical considerations. By outlining these requirements clearly, Volume 3 helps streamline the approval process for clinical trials and ensures that researchers are well-informed about the expectations for compliance with EU regulations.

20.3.3 Key Regulations for Clinical Trials in Europe

Key regulations governing clinical trials in Europe are integral to maintaining high standards of safety, efficacy, and ethical conduct in research involving human subjects. In addition to the provisions outlined in Directive 2001/20/EC, the **Clinical Trials Regulation (EU) No. 536/2014** plays a pivotal role in establishing a harmonized framework for conducting clinical trials across the EU. This regulation aims to enhance the transparency, safety, and efficiency of clinical research while ensuring that participant rights are protected throughout the trial process.

One of the essential aspects of these regulations is the requirement for comprehensive risk assessments and safety monitoring throughout clinical trials. Sponsors must implement robust risk management plans, detailing how they will monitor and address potential safety issues that may arise during the study. Furthermore, the regulations require the establishment of independent ethics committees (ECs) to review trial protocols and ensure that studies are conducted ethically and in compliance with GCP standards.

Additionally, the regulations emphasize the importance of data integrity and transparency in clinical trials. Sponsors are obligated to ensure that trial data is collected, managed, and reported accurately, with provisions for auditing and oversight by regulatory authorities. These requirements contribute to the overall credibility and reliability of clinical research findings, enhancing public trust in the safety and efficacy of new medical products. By adhering to these key regulations, researchers and sponsors in Europe can ensure the ethical conduct of clinical trials while contributing to the advancement of medical knowledge and public health.

20.4 Annual Safety Report (ASR) and Pharmacovigilance

20.4.1 Requirements for Annual Safety Reports

The **Annual Safety Report (ASR)** is a critical component of the pharmacovigilance framework in the European Union, designed to monitor the safety of medicinal products and ensure that any emerging risks are promptly addressed. Under the regulations established by the European Medicines Agency (EMA), sponsors are required to submit ASRs for clinical trials on a yearly basis. These reports must summarize all safety data collected during the reporting period, including adverse events, serious adverse events (SAEs), and any new information regarding the safety profile of the investigational product.

The ASR should also include a comprehensive analysis of the benefit-risk balance of the product, highlighting any significant changes in safety data that may impact the ongoing clinical trial. This requirement emphasizes the importance of continual monitoring and evaluation of participant safety throughout the study's duration. The ASR serves as a critical communication tool between the sponsor and regulatory authorities, ensuring that any safety concerns are promptly reviewed and addressed. By providing a transparent account of safety data, the ASR helps maintain the integrity of the clinical trial process and reinforces the commitment to protecting participant welfare.

In addition to the summary of safety data, the ASR must also outline any actions taken in response to identified safety issues, such as changes to the trial protocol, updated informed consent forms, or modifications to participant monitoring procedures. The timely submission of ASRs is essential for maintaining compliance with EU regulations and fostering a culture of safety in clinical research. By adhering to these reporting requirements, sponsors demonstrate their dedication to participant safety and the ethical conduct of clinical trials.

20.4.2 Role of the Qualified Person for Pharmacovigilance (QPPV)

The **Qualified Person for Pharmacovigilance (QPPV)** plays a vital role in ensuring the safety and efficacy of medicinal products in the European Union. Designated by the marketing authorization holder, the QPPV is responsible for overseeing the pharmacovigilance activities related to a specific product or portfolio of products. This includes the management of safety data, ensuring compliance with regulatory requirements, and maintaining a thorough understanding of the safety profile of the product.

One of the primary responsibilities of the QPPV is to ensure that all adverse events and safety reports are collected, analyzed, and reported accurately and promptly to regulatory authorities. This involves close collaboration with clinical trial teams, data management personnel, and regulatory affairs professionals to facilitate the effective monitoring of product safety. The QPPV is also responsible for ensuring that pharmacovigilance systems are in place and functioning properly, allowing for the systematic collection and evaluation of safety data.

In addition to these operational responsibilities, the QPPV serves as a key liaison between the company and regulatory authorities, providing expert guidance on safety issues and regulatory compliance. The QPPV's expertise is crucial for interpreting safety data and making informed decisions regarding product labeling, risk management strategies, and the need for additional studies or safety evaluations. By fulfilling these responsibilities, the QPPV plays a critical role in safeguarding public health and enhancing the safety of medicinal products on the market.

20.4.3 Pharmacovigilance in the European Union

Pharmacovigilance in the European Union is a systematic approach to monitoring the safety of medicinal products after they have been authorized for public use. The EMA oversees the pharmacovigilance system in collaboration with national regulatory authorities, ensuring that safety data is collected, analyzed, and acted upon effectively. The primary objective of pharmacovigilance is to identify and evaluate adverse events and potential safety signals associated with medications, thereby safeguarding public health and ensuring that the benefits of a product continue to outweigh its risks.

The EU pharmacovigilance framework is governed by several regulations and directives, including **Regulation (EU) No. 1235/2010**, which amended the pharmacovigilance legislation to enhance safety monitoring processes. This regulation emphasizes the importance of continuous safety monitoring and requires marketing authorization holders to implement risk management plans for their products. These plans outline strategies for minimizing risks and ensuring that appropriate measures are in place to address safety concerns.

Furthermore, the EU has established various databases and systems for collecting safety data, such as the **EudraVigilance** database, which allows for the reporting and analysis of suspected adverse reactions across the EU. This centralized system enables regulatory authorities to detect trends and patterns in safety data, facilitating timely interventions when necessary. By maintaining a robust pharmacovigilance system, the EU aims to promote the safe and effective use of medicines, ultimately improving patient safety and public health outcomes.

20.5 ISO 14155 and Medical Device Clinical Trials in the EU

20.5.1 Overview of ISO 14155: GCP for Medical Device Trials

ISO 14155 is an international standard that outlines Good Clinical Practice (GCP) principles specifically for clinical trials of medical devices. It provides a framework for conducting ethical and scientifically sound clinical research while ensuring the safety and rights of participants. ISO 14155 serves as a vital guideline for manufacturers, researchers, and regulatory authorities involved in the development and evaluation of medical devices in the European Union. This standard emphasizes the importance of maintaining high-quality data integrity throughout the clinical trial process.

One of the key aspects of ISO 14155 is its focus on the design and execution of clinical trials. The standard outlines essential requirements for trial protocols, including the need for clear objectives, participant eligibility criteria, and detailed methodologies for data collection and analysis. By providing these guidelines, ISO 14155 helps ensure that medical device trials are conducted consistently and rigorously, enhancing the reliability of the results. Furthermore, the standard highlights the importance of informed consent and participant safety, requiring that researchers prioritize the well-being of subjects throughout the trial process.

ISO 14155 also emphasizes the need for proper documentation and reporting of trial results, which is crucial for regulatory submissions and post-market surveillance. By adhering to the principles outlined in ISO 14155, researchers can ensure compliance with both regulatory requirements and ethical standards, ultimately contributing to the successful evaluation and approval of medical devices within the EU.

20.5.2 Requirements for Clinical Investigation of Medical Devices

Conducting clinical investigations of medical devices in the EU involves adhering to a comprehensive set of regulatory requirements that align with ISO 14155 and EU directives. Before initiating a clinical trial, sponsors must obtain approval from relevant regulatory authorities, including the **European Medicines Agency (EMA)** or national competent authorities, as well as ethical approval from an independent ethics committee. This approval process ensures that the proposed study meets ethical standards and that participant rights and welfare are prioritized.

The clinical investigation must be designed to gather sufficient data to demonstrate the safety and performance of the medical device. This includes establishing a clear protocol that outlines the study objectives, design, methodology, and analysis plan. Key considerations in the protocol include participant selection criteria, sample size, and statistical methods for analyzing the data. Additionally, sponsors must implement robust monitoring procedures to track participant safety throughout the study, including mechanisms for reporting adverse events and serious adverse events (SAEs).

Furthermore, post-study obligations are essential to ensure that the safety and efficacy of the medical device continue to be evaluated even after the clinical investigation has concluded. This may involve conducting post-market surveillance and reporting any emerging safety signals or concerns to regulatory authorities. By fulfilling these requirements, sponsors can contribute to the responsible development and evaluation of medical devices in the EU, enhancing patient safety and public trust in new medical technologies.

20.5.3 Key Differences Between Drug and Device Trial Regulations

While both drug and medical device trials are subject to rigorous regulatory oversight, there are notable differences in the regulatory frameworks governing their conduct in the EU. One of the primary distinctions lies in the regulatory approval processes for clinical trials. Drug trials are primarily regulated under the **Clinical Trials Regulation (EU) No. 536/2014** and the **European Medicines Agency (EMA)**, whereas medical device trials are governed by **ISO 14155** and specific medical device regulations.

Another significant difference is the level of scrutiny applied to preclinical data requirements. For drugs, extensive preclinical testing is often required to establish safety and efficacy before moving to clinical trials. In contrast, medical devices may be subject to different preclinical requirements depending on their classification (Class I, II, or III) and the associated risks. This classification influences the regulatory pathway and the depth of clinical data required for approval.

Moreover, the approach to post-market surveillance also differs between drugs and devices. While both require ongoing monitoring, medical device regulations may place more emphasis on real-world performance and post-marketing studies, particularly for high-risk devices. This divergence in regulatory focus reflects the unique considerations associated with the development and evaluation of drugs versus medical devices, emphasizing the need for tailored regulatory approaches that address the specific characteristics and risks of each category.

20.6 Case Studies in EU Clinical Trials

20.6.1 Successful Clinical Trials Conducted Under EMA Guidelines

Numerous clinical trials conducted under the auspices of the **European Medicines Agency (EMA)** have successfully led to the approval of innovative therapies and medical products. One notable example is the clinical development of the drug **Imatinib** (Gleevec), which revolutionized the treatment of chronic myeloid leukemia (CML). Conducted in compliance with EMA guidelines, the clinical trials demonstrated Imatinib's effectiveness in targeting specific cancer cells, resulting in significant improvements in patient outcomes. The successful approval of Imatinib underscores the importance of adhering to rigorous regulatory standards in clinical research and the impact of well-conducted trials on patient care.

Another successful case is the clinical trial program for the vaccine against **COVID-19**. Several vaccines, including those developed by Pfizer-BioNTech and Moderna, underwent expedited clinical trials following EMA guidelines, enabling rapid access to effective vaccines during the pandemic. The trials employed innovative designs and adaptive methodologies to evaluate safety and efficacy swiftly while adhering to GCP principles. The successful and timely approval of these vaccines illustrates the EMA's ability to facilitate the development of critical therapies while maintaining high standards for safety and efficacy.

These case studies demonstrate how adherence to EMA guidelines and regulations can lead to successful clinical trials that not only advance medical knowledge but also significantly improve patient care. The collaborative efforts of researchers, regulatory authorities, and industry stakeholders are essential for driving innovation in clinical research while ensuring the safety and efficacy of new therapies.

20.6.2 Challenges Faced in Multinational EU Trials

Conducting multinational clinical trials within the EU presents a unique set of challenges that can impact the efficiency and effectiveness of the research process. One significant challenge is the diversity of regulatory requirements across member states. Although the EMA promotes harmonization, variations in national regulations, ethical review processes, and local requirements can complicate trial initiation and execution. This disparity can lead to delays in approvals, requiring sponsors to navigate a complex landscape of regulatory submissions and communications with multiple national authorities.

Another challenge is managing cultural and linguistic differences among participant populations in various countries. Researchers must ensure that study materials, including informed consent forms and patient information sheets, are translated accurately and culturally adapted to meet the needs of diverse populations. Failure to address these differences may lead to misunderstandings or mistrust, ultimately affecting participant recruitment and retention in the trial. Effective communication and engagement with local communities are essential for overcoming these barriers and fostering participant trust.

Furthermore, logistical challenges related to trial management can arise in multinational settings. Coordinating data collection, monitoring procedures, and adverse event reporting across multiple sites can be complex, requiring robust systems and processes to ensure consistency and compliance with regulatory requirements. Despite these challenges, multinational EU trials can provide valuable insights into the safety and efficacy of new therapies across diverse populations, contributing to the advancement of medical science and public health.

Review Questions

1. What is the role of the European Medicines Agency (EMA) in clinical research regulation?
2. How do EU Directives 2001/20/EC govern clinical trials in Europe?
3. What is the purpose of EudraLex Volume 3 guidelines, and how do they impact clinical trials?
4. What are the requirements for submitting Annual Safety Reports (ASR) in the EU?
5. How does ISO 14155 apply to clinical trials involving medical devices in the EU?
6. What is the role of the Qualified Person for Pharmacovigilance (QPPV) in the EU?
7. How do EMA regulations differ from those of the FDA in the USA?
8. What lessons have been learned from case studies of EMA-regulated clinical trials?

CHAPTER TWENTY-ONE

Good Clinical Practice (GCP) Guidelines – ICH E6

21.1 Introduction to ICH and the ICH E6 GCP Guidelines

21.1.1 History and Purpose of the ICH

The **International Council for Harmonisation of Technical Requirements for Pharmaceuticals for Human Use (ICH)** was established in 1990 as a collaborative effort among regulatory authorities and the pharmaceutical industry from Europe, Japan, and the United States. The primary aim of the ICH is to promote uniformity in the regulatory requirements for the development and approval of new medicines across these regions. Historically, the need for harmonization arose from the recognition that different countries had varying regulatory standards, which often resulted in delays in bringing new therapies to market. By developing guidelines that streamline the regulatory process, the ICH seeks to ensure that patients worldwide have timely access to safe and effective medicines.

The ICH guidelines cover various aspects of drug development, including quality, safety, efficacy, and multidisciplinary topics. The establishment of the ICH has significantly enhanced cooperation among regulatory authorities and the pharmaceutical industry, fostering a shared understanding of the principles that govern drug development. By promoting the adoption of common regulatory standards, the ICH aims to reduce duplication of efforts and improve the efficiency of the clinical trial process, ultimately benefiting public health.

21.1.2 Development of the ICH E6 Guidelines

The **ICH E6 Good Clinical Practice (GCP) guidelines** were developed as part of the ICH's commitment to ensuring the ethical conduct of clinical trials and the integrity of data generated during research. First adopted in 1996, the ICH E6 guidelines provide a comprehensive framework for conducting clinical trials involving human subjects, emphasizing the need for high ethical standards and regulatory compliance. The guidelines were created to reflect best practices in clinical research and to align with existing regulatory requirements in member regions.

The development of the ICH E6 guidelines involved extensive collaboration among various stakeholders, including regulatory authorities, industry representatives, and clinical researchers. This collaborative approach ensured that the guidelines would be practical, relevant, and adaptable to different regulatory environments. The guidelines have undergone revisions over the years to incorporate new scientific knowledge, technological advancements, and evolving regulatory landscapes, further solidifying their relevance in the context of modern clinical research.

Today, the ICH E6 GCP guidelines are recognized globally as the gold standard for conducting clinical trials. They provide essential guidance on various aspects of trial conduct, including the responsibilities of sponsors and investigators, the protection of trial participants, and the integrity of data collection and management. By adhering to these guidelines, researchers can contribute to the ethical and scientifically sound conduct of clinical trials, ultimately enhancing the credibility of research findings.

21.1.3 Scope and Objectives of GCP

The scope of the ICH E6 GCP guidelines encompasses all aspects of the conduct of clinical trials involving human subjects, from the planning stages through to data analysis and reporting. The primary objectives of GCP are to ensure the protection of participants' rights, safety, and well-being while maintaining the integrity and reliability of trial data. This comprehensive framework sets forth the essential principles that must be followed by sponsors, investigators, and ethics committees throughout the clinical trial process.

One of the key objectives of GCP is to establish clear roles and responsibilities for all parties involved in the clinical trial. This includes defining the responsibilities of sponsors in ensuring compliance with regulatory requirements and ethical standards, as well as outlining the roles of investigators in conducting trials ethically and safely. GCP also emphasizes the importance of obtaining informed consent from participants, ensuring they are fully aware of the study's risks and benefits before agreeing to participate. By setting these standards, GCP aims to promote public trust in the clinical research process and enhance the credibility of the data generated.

Additionally, GCP provides guidance on the management of clinical trial data, ensuring that data is collected, analyzed, and reported accurately and transparently. This focus on data integrity is crucial for regulatory submissions and for making informed decisions about the safety and efficacy of new therapies. Overall, the scope and objectives of the ICH E6 GCP guidelines are essential for fostering ethical conduct and scientific rigor in clinical trials, ultimately benefiting public health and patient safety.

21.2 Key Principles of ICH-GCP E6 Guidelines

21.2.1 Responsibilities of the Sponsor

The sponsor plays a crucial role in the conduct of clinical trials, with significant responsibilities outlined in the ICH E6 GCP guidelines. Primarily, the sponsor is responsible for the design, initiation, and management of the clinical trial, ensuring that it complies with all regulatory requirements and ethical standards. This includes the obligation to prepare and submit the clinical trial protocol for approval, obtain necessary regulatory authorizations, and ensure adequate funding and resources are allocated for the trial.

Furthermore, the sponsor must ensure that the trial is conducted in compliance with GCP guidelines and that appropriate oversight is in place to monitor participant safety. This includes the establishment of mechanisms for reporting adverse events and ensuring that data is collected and managed accurately. The sponsor is also responsible for maintaining communication with regulatory authorities, providing updates on trial progress, and submitting safety reports as required. By fulfilling these responsibilities, the sponsor contributes to the ethical conduct and scientific integrity of the clinical trial.

Another important aspect of the sponsor's responsibilities is ensuring that investigators are adequately trained and qualified to conduct the trial. This involves providing investigators with the necessary resources and support, as well as facilitating ongoing education regarding regulatory requirements and best practices in clinical research. By promoting a culture of compliance and accountability among investigators, sponsors play a pivotal role in ensuring the success of clinical trials and the protection of participants.

21.2.2 Roles and Duties of the Investigator

The investigator holds a critical role in the conduct of clinical trials, with specific responsibilities outlined in the ICH E6 GCP guidelines. The primary duty of the investigator is to ensure that the trial is conducted ethically and in accordance with the approved protocol and regulatory requirements. This includes obtaining informed consent from all participants, ensuring they are fully aware of the study's nature, risks, and benefits before agreeing to participate. The investigator must also ensure that participants understand their rights and can withdraw from the study at any time without penalty.

Additionally, the investigator is responsible for the safety and well-being of trial participants throughout the study. This involves closely monitoring participants for adverse events and responding promptly to any safety concerns that arise during the trial. The investigator must maintain accurate and comprehensive records of all trial-related activities, including data collection, participant interactions, and adverse event reporting. These records are essential for ensuring the integrity of the trial data and for facilitating regulatory reviews.

Furthermore, the investigator must communicate effectively with the sponsor, providing regular updates on trial progress and any emerging safety issues. This collaboration is vital for ensuring compliance with regulatory requirements and for maintaining participant safety. By fulfilling these responsibilities, the investigator plays a key role in upholding the ethical conduct of clinical trials and contributing to the advancement of medical research.

21.2.3 Protection of Human Subjects in Clinical Research

The protection of human subjects is a fundamental principle embedded in the ICH E6 GCP guidelines, reflecting the ethical commitment to prioritize participant rights and welfare in clinical trials. One of the primary mechanisms for protecting participants is the requirement for informed consent, which ensures that individuals are adequately informed about the study's nature, risks, and potential benefits before enrolling. Informed consent is not merely a formality; it is a continuous process that requires open communication between researchers and participants throughout the trial.

Additionally, the ICH E6 GCP guidelines emphasize the importance of conducting risk assessments and implementing appropriate safeguards to mitigate potential risks to participants. This includes establishing monitoring procedures to track adverse events and ensuring that participants receive timely medical care in the event of an adverse reaction. Ethics committees play a vital role in this process by reviewing trial protocols to ensure that they comply with ethical standards and that participant protections are in place.

Moreover, the guidelines call for the inclusion of vulnerable populations in clinical trials to be approached with caution. Special considerations must be made when enrolling individuals who may be at greater risk, such as children, pregnant women, or those with cognitive impairments. By establishing these protections, the ICH E6 GCP guidelines aim to foster an ethical research environment that upholds the dignity and rights of all participants, ultimately enhancing public trust in the clinical research process.

21.3 Investigator's Responsibilities Under GCP

21.3.1 Ensuring Informed Consent

One of the fundamental responsibilities of the investigator under the ICH E6 GCP guidelines is to ensure that informed consent is obtained from all participants involved in the clinical trial. Informed consent is a process that provides potential participants with the information necessary to make an educated decision about their involvement in the study. The investigator must ensure that participants are adequately informed about the purpose of the trial, the procedures involved, potential risks and benefits, and their rights as participants. It is essential that this information is presented clearly and comprehensibly, taking into consideration the participants' background and comprehension level.

Furthermore, the informed consent process is not a one-time event but an ongoing dialogue throughout the study. Investigators must be available to address any questions or concerns that participants may have, ensuring that they fully understand the implications of their involvement in the trial. If there are any changes to the study protocol or new risks identified during the trial, the investigator is obligated to update participants and obtain renewed consent as necessary. By prioritizing informed consent, investigators uphold the ethical principles of respect for persons and autonomy, fostering trust between researchers and participants.

21.3.2 Conduct of the Clinical Trial According to the Protocol

The investigator has the critical responsibility of conducting the clinical trial strictly according to the approved study protocol. The protocol outlines the study's objectives, methodologies, participant eligibility criteria, and data collection methods. Adhering to the protocol ensures that the trial is conducted systematically and consistently, allowing for valid and reliable data collection. Any deviations from the protocol must be documented and justified, as they can impact the integrity of the study results.

In addition to following the protocol, the investigator must maintain accurate and complete records of all trial-related activities, including participant enrollment, data collection, and adverse event reporting. This documentation is essential for regulatory compliance and for ensuring the credibility of the trial data. The investigator must also regularly communicate with the sponsor and report any issues that may arise during the trial, such as recruitment challenges or safety concerns. By conducting the trial according to the protocol and maintaining thorough documentation, the investigator plays a pivotal role in upholding the scientific integrity of the research.

21.3.3 Reporting Requirements and Safety Monitoring

Another essential responsibility of the investigator is to ensure compliance with reporting requirements and to implement effective safety monitoring throughout the clinical trial. Investigators must promptly report adverse events and serious adverse events to the sponsor, following the established protocols for safety reporting. This includes providing detailed information about the nature and severity of the events, as well as any actions taken in response to the events. Timely reporting is critical for maintaining participant safety and for allowing the sponsor to evaluate the safety profile of the investigational product.

Moreover, the investigator is responsible for monitoring participant safety throughout the study. This includes conducting regular assessments of participant health, addressing any emerging safety concerns, and ensuring that appropriate medical care is provided in the event of an adverse reaction. By implementing robust safety monitoring procedures, the investigator contributes to the ethical conduct of the trial and the protection of participant welfare. This ongoing commitment to safety monitoring is a fundamental aspect of the investigator's role under GCP, reinforcing the importance of prioritizing participant rights and safety in clinical research.

21.4 Sponsor's Responsibilities Under GCP

21.4.1 Trial Management, Data Handling, and Record Keeping

The sponsor plays a critical role in the management of clinical trials, and under the ICH E6 GCP guidelines, they bear significant responsibilities regarding trial management, data handling, and record-keeping. Effective trial management involves establishing clear communication channels among all stakeholders, including investigators, study personnel, and regulatory authorities. The sponsor must develop comprehensive trial plans that outline study objectives, methodologies, and timelines, ensuring that all parties involved understand their roles and responsibilities throughout the trial process.

Data handling is another vital aspect of the sponsor's responsibilities. The sponsor must ensure that all data collected during the trial is accurate, complete, and securely maintained. This involves implementing robust data management systems that facilitate the efficient collection, processing, and storage of trial data. Additionally, sponsors are required to maintain meticulous records of all trial-related activities, including participant recruitment, consent processes, and data collection methods. Proper record-keeping is essential for regulatory compliance and for ensuring the integrity and credibility of the trial findings.

Moreover, the sponsor must ensure that all documentation related to the clinical trial is readily accessible for monitoring and auditing purposes. This includes maintaining a Trial Master File (TMF) that houses all essential documents related to the study. By fulfilling these responsibilities, the sponsor contributes to the overall success of the clinical trial, ensuring that it is conducted ethically and in compliance with GCP standards.

21.4.2 Monitoring and Auditing the Clinical Trial

Monitoring and auditing are crucial components of the sponsor's responsibilities under GCP. The sponsor must implement systematic monitoring processes to ensure that the trial is conducted according to the approved protocol and regulatory requirements. This monitoring involves regular site visits, data verification, and assessments of participant safety and compliance with ethical standards. By conducting thorough monitoring, sponsors can identify potential issues early on and take corrective actions to mitigate risks to participants and ensure the integrity of the trial data.

In addition to monitoring, the sponsor must conduct internal audits to assess compliance with GCP guidelines and standard operating procedures. Audits provide an opportunity to evaluate the effectiveness of the monitoring process and to ensure that all aspects of the trial are being conducted in accordance with regulatory requirements. The findings from these audits should be documented and analyzed to identify areas for improvement. By maintaining a proactive approach to monitoring and auditing, sponsors can enhance the overall quality of the clinical trial and contribute to the ethical conduct of research.

Furthermore, it is essential for sponsors to foster a culture of compliance and accountability among trial personnel. This includes providing ongoing training and resources to ensure that all staff members understand GCP principles and their responsibilities in maintaining compliance. By promoting a culture of transparency and integrity, sponsors can enhance the credibility of the clinical trial and build trust with regulatory authorities and participants alike.

21.4.3 Reporting Safety Information to Regulatory Authorities

Under the ICH E6 GCP guidelines, sponsors have a paramount responsibility to report safety information to regulatory authorities promptly. This includes the submission of safety reports related to adverse events, serious adverse events, and any other safety concerns that may arise during the clinical trial. The timely reporting of safety information is essential for protecting participants and ensuring that any emerging risks associated with the investigational product are adequately addressed.

The sponsor must establish clear protocols for the reporting of safety information, including the criteria for determining the severity and relationship of adverse events to the investigational product. This process involves careful documentation and analysis of all reported events to identify potential safety signals and trends. In addition, sponsors must ensure that they are compliant with the specific reporting requirements set forth by regulatory authorities in the regions where the trial is conducted.

Furthermore, effective communication with regulatory authorities is crucial during the safety reporting process. Sponsors should maintain open lines of communication to address any concerns that regulatory authorities may have regarding the safety profile of the investigational product. By adhering to these reporting requirements and maintaining transparent communication, sponsors play a vital role in upholding participant safety and ensuring the ethical conduct of clinical trials.

21.5 Clinical Trial Protocol Development

21.5.1 Key Components of a GCP-Compliant Protocol
The development of a clinical trial protocol is a critical step in the planning and execution of clinical research, as it outlines the study's objectives, design, methodology, and analysis plan. A GCP-compliant protocol must include several key components, including a clear statement of the study's objectives and hypotheses. This clarity ensures that all stakeholders understand the purpose of the trial and what it aims to achieve, guiding the research team throughout the study.

Additionally, the protocol should detail the study design, including participant selection criteria, randomization methods, and the specific interventions to be administered. This information is essential for ensuring that the trial is conducted systematically and ethically. Furthermore, the protocol must outline the data collection and management procedures, specifying how data will be recorded, analyzed, and reported. By including these essential components, the protocol serves as a comprehensive roadmap for the clinical trial, promoting compliance with GCP standards and enhancing the overall quality of the research.

Moreover, the protocol must incorporate safety monitoring plans, detailing how adverse events will be monitored, reported, and managed throughout the trial. This is particularly important for ensuring participant safety and complying with regulatory requirements. By adhering to GCP principles during protocol development, researchers can establish a solid foundation for the successful conduct of the clinical trial, ultimately contributing to the generation of credible and reliable data.

21.5.2 Protocol Amendments and Ethical Approvals
As clinical trials progress, it may become necessary to make amendments to the original protocol to address emerging findings, logistical challenges, or changes in regulatory requirements. Protocol amendments must be carefully considered and documented, ensuring that any changes made do not compromise participant safety or the integrity of the trial. Under GCP guidelines, sponsors are required to submit all protocol amendments to the relevant regulatory authorities and ethics committees for approval before implementing any changes.

The process of obtaining ethical approvals for protocol amendments is crucial, as it ensures that the revised study design continues to uphold the rights and welfare of participants. Ethics committees must review the proposed amendments to assess their impact on participant safety, informed consent processes, and the overall ethical conduct of the trial. This rigorous review process is essential for maintaining public trust in clinical research and ensuring that ethical standards are upheld.

Additionally, it is important for researchers to communicate any protocol amendments clearly and transparently to all study personnel and participants. This may involve updating informed consent documents and providing participants with information about any changes that may affect their involvement in the trial. By maintaining open communication and adhering to regulatory requirements for protocol amendments, researchers can ensure that the clinical trial remains compliant with GCP standards and that participant safety is prioritized throughout the research process.

21.5.3 Challenges in Protocol Design and Implementation

Designing and implementing a clinical trial protocol can pose significant challenges for researchers. One of the primary difficulties is balancing scientific rigor with practical considerations, such as participant recruitment, retention, and compliance with regulatory requirements. Researchers must carefully consider the trial design, including sample size, randomization methods, and endpoints, to ensure that the study is both feasible and capable of generating meaningful results. Striking this balance is critical for the success of the trial and for ensuring that it adheres to GCP standards.

Additionally, logistical challenges may arise during the implementation phase, particularly when conducting trials across multiple sites or in diverse populations. Coordinating communication and data collection among various study sites can be complex, requiring robust data management systems and effective oversight. Researchers must also navigate cultural and regional differences that may impact participant recruitment and retention. To address these challenges, investigators must engage in thorough planning and collaboration with all stakeholders, including sponsors, regulatory authorities, and site personnel.

Moreover, researchers must be prepared to adapt to unforeseen challenges that may arise during the trial, such as changes in regulatory requirements or unexpected safety concerns. Flexibility and responsiveness are essential qualities for researchers, allowing them to make timely decisions and implement necessary adjustments while maintaining compliance with GCP guidelines. By proactively addressing these challenges, researchers can enhance the quality and credibility of the clinical trial and contribute to the advancement of medical knowledge.

21.6 GCP Compliance and Monitoring

21.6.1 Monitoring and Auditing Clinical Trials for GCP Compliance

Monitoring and auditing are essential components of ensuring compliance with Good Clinical Practice (GCP) guidelines during clinical trials. Monitoring involves ongoing oversight of the trial's conduct to verify that it adheres to the approved protocol, regulatory requirements, and ethical standards. Sponsors are responsible for implementing a monitoring plan that outlines the frequency and methods of monitoring visits, ensuring that all aspects of the trial are assessed systematically. This may include site visits, data verification, and assessments of participant safety and adherence to study procedures.

Auditing, on the other hand, is a more formal and comprehensive evaluation of the trial's compliance with GCP standards. Audits can be conducted by the sponsor's internal quality assurance team or by external auditors and typically involve a detailed review of trial documentation, data management practices, and participant records. The findings from these audits are critical for identifying any areas of non-compliance and implementing corrective actions as necessary. By maintaining robust monitoring and auditing processes, researchers can enhance the quality and integrity of the clinical trial and ensure that participant rights and safety are upheld.

Furthermore, effective monitoring and auditing contribute to building trust between researchers, participants, and regulatory authorities. Transparency in these processes allows stakeholders to have confidence in the trial's conduct and the reliability of the data generated. Continuous oversight also ensures that any safety concerns are promptly identified and addressed, reinforcing the commitment to ethical research practices and participant protection.

21.6.2 Addressing Non-Compliance Issues

Addressing non-compliance issues is a crucial aspect of maintaining GCP compliance in clinical trials. When non-compliance is identified, it is essential for sponsors and investigators to take immediate action to rectify the situation. This may involve conducting a root cause analysis to determine the underlying factors contributing to the non-compliance and developing a corrective action plan to address these issues. The plan should outline specific steps to be taken, timelines for implementation, and responsibilities assigned to relevant personnel.

Effective communication is key in addressing non-compliance issues. Sponsors must inform all stakeholders, including regulatory authorities and ethics committees, of any instances of non-compliance and the actions being taken to resolve them. This transparency not only helps to maintain trust but also demonstrates the commitment of the research team to uphold GCP standards and prioritize participant safety. Additionally, providing training and resources to study personnel can help prevent similar issues from arising in the future, fostering a culture of compliance and accountability within the research team.

Moreover, ongoing monitoring and audits can help ensure that corrective actions are implemented effectively and that compliance is maintained moving forward. This proactive approach to addressing non-compliance issues reinforces the importance of ethical conduct in clinical research and contributes to the overall integrity of the study.

21.6.3 Regulatory Actions for GCP Violations

Regulatory authorities have established specific actions that may be taken in response to violations of GCP guidelines during clinical trials. When significant non-compliance issues are identified, regulatory authorities may issue a **Form 483** or other formal notices to the sponsor or investigator, outlining the specific violations and requesting a response. These notices serve as a warning and may lead to further regulatory scrutiny, including additional inspections or audits.

In more severe cases of GCP violations, regulatory authorities may impose sanctions, such as suspending or terminating the clinical trial, revoking the trial's approval, or taking legal action against the sponsor or investigator. These actions aim to protect participant safety and maintain the integrity of the clinical research process. Regulatory authorities may also require sponsors to implement corrective actions and submit progress reports to demonstrate compliance with GCP standards moving forward.

Moreover, repeated violations or a history of non-compliance can result in significant reputational damage for the sponsor or investigator, impacting future research opportunities and collaborations. By recognizing the serious consequences of GCP violations and proactively addressing compliance issues, researchers can contribute to the ethical conduct of clinical trials and enhance public trust in the clinical research process.

Review Questions

1. What was the purpose of establishing the ICH E6 Good Clinical Practice (GCP) guidelines?
2. What are the core principles of the ICH E6 GCP guidelines, and how do they ensure ethical conduct in clinical trials?
3. Describe the key responsibilities of the sponsor under the ICH-GCP guidelines.
4. What are the main responsibilities of an investigator according to GCP?
5. How do GCP guidelines protect human subjects participating in clinical trials?
6. What are the key components of a GCP-compliant clinical trial protocol?
7. How do monitoring and auditing ensure GCP compliance in clinical trials?
8. What actions are taken in response to GCP non-compliance during a clinical trial?

CHAPTER TWENTY-TWO

Indian Good Clinical Practice Guidelines

22.1 Overview of Indian GCP Guidelines

22.1.1 Development and Purpose of Indian GCP

The **Indian Good Clinical Practice (GCP)** guidelines were established to ensure that clinical trials conducted in India adhere to high ethical and scientific standards. Developed by the **Central Drugs Standard Control Organization (CDSCO)** and released in 2013, these guidelines align with international standards while addressing the unique aspects of conducting clinical research in India. The purpose of Indian GCP is to protect the rights and well-being of trial participants while ensuring the integrity and credibility of the data generated during the studies.

The guidelines aim to provide a framework that promotes transparency and accountability in clinical research. By establishing clear responsibilities for sponsors, investigators, and ethics committees, Indian GCP guidelines facilitate the ethical conduct of clinical trials and foster public confidence in the research process. The guidelines also seek to streamline the regulatory process for clinical trials in India, enabling researchers to conduct studies efficiently while maintaining compliance with ethical and legal requirements.

Furthermore, the Indian GCP guidelines emphasize the importance of informed consent, safety monitoring, and data integrity. These principles reflect the commitment to ensuring that clinical trials are conducted in a manner that prioritizes participant safety and promotes ethical research practices. The development of these guidelines marks a significant step forward in enhancing the quality of clinical research in India and aligning it with global best practices.

22.1.2 Comparison with ICH-GCP Guidelines

While the Indian GCP guidelines are influenced by the **International Council for Harmonisation (ICH) Good Clinical Practice (GCP)** guidelines, there are key differences that reflect the specific context of clinical research in India. One notable difference is the emphasis on obtaining informed consent, which includes provisions for cultural considerations and language barriers that may affect understanding among participants. The Indian GCP guidelines recognize the diverse populations within India and stress the importance of tailoring consent processes to accommodate these differences.

Another distinction is the regulatory framework governing clinical trials in India. The Indian GCP guidelines outline the roles and responsibilities of local regulatory authorities, such as the CDSCO, in overseeing clinical trials. This contrasts with the ICH GCP guidelines, which are designed to provide a harmonized framework applicable across multiple jurisdictions. Additionally, Indian GCP guidelines incorporate specific requirements related to the protection of vulnerable populations, reflecting the ethical considerations unique to the Indian context.

Despite these differences, both sets of guidelines share common principles, including the protection of human subjects, the importance of data integrity, and the necessity of compliance with ethical standards. By aligning with international GCP standards while addressing local considerations, the Indian GCP guidelines aim to enhance the quality and credibility of clinical research conducted in India.

22.1.3 Applicability to Clinical Trials in India

The Indian GCP guidelines apply to all clinical trials conducted in India, regardless of whether the trials are sponsored by domestic or international organizations. This broad applicability ensures that all stakeholders involved in clinical research in India adhere to the same ethical and scientific standards. The guidelines cover various aspects of trial conduct, including study design, participant recruitment, informed consent, data management, and reporting requirements.

These guidelines are particularly relevant in the context of India's growing significance in global clinical research. With a diverse population and a rich pool of potential participants, India offers unique opportunities for clinical trials, particularly in areas such as infectious diseases, oncology, and cardiology. The Indian GCP guidelines provide a framework for conducting trials that not only prioritizes participant safety but also enhances the credibility of the research findings.

Moreover, adherence to Indian GCP guidelines is essential for obtaining regulatory approval from the CDSCO for clinical trial applications. By ensuring compliance with these guidelines, sponsors and investigators can facilitate smoother regulatory processes and foster a culture of ethical research within the country. This commitment to high standards in clinical research ultimately contributes to advancing public health and improving patient outcomes in India.

22.2 Ethical Principles in Indian GCP

22.2.1 Informed Consent Requirements in India

Informed consent is a fundamental ethical principle embedded in the Indian GCP guidelines, ensuring that participants are fully aware of the nature, risks, and benefits of their involvement in clinical trials. The guidelines stipulate that obtaining informed consent is not merely a procedural formality but a continuous process that requires clear and ongoing communication between researchers and participants. Researchers must provide potential participants with comprehensive information about the study, including its objectives, procedures, potential risks, and the right to withdraw at any time without penalty.

Additionally, the Indian GCP guidelines emphasize the importance of ensuring that informed consent is obtained in a language and manner that participants can understand. This is particularly relevant in India, where diverse linguistic and cultural backgrounds may impact comprehension. Researchers must take the necessary steps to tailor consent materials and processes to the specific needs of the participant population, fostering a sense of trust and empowerment among individuals considering participation in the trial.

Moreover, special considerations must be made for vulnerable populations, including children, pregnant women, and individuals with cognitive impairments. In such cases, researchers may need to obtain consent from legally authorized representatives while ensuring that the participants' voices are still considered in the decision-making process. By prioritizing informed consent, the Indian GCP guidelines uphold the ethical principles of autonomy and respect for individuals, ultimately contributing to the integrity of clinical research in India.

22.2.2 Ethical Review by Indian Ethics Committees

The role of ethics committees in the Indian GCP guidelines is paramount for ensuring that clinical trials are conducted ethically and in compliance with regulatory standards. Ethics committees are responsible for reviewing study protocols and informed consent documents to assess the ethical implications of the research and to safeguard the rights and welfare of participants. These committees play a critical role in ensuring that the proposed research is scientifically valid and ethically sound, and they have the authority to approve, reject, or request modifications to the study protocols.

The Indian GCP guidelines outline the composition and functioning of ethics committees, emphasizing the importance of having a diverse membership that includes individuals with expertise in medicine, ethics, law, and community representation. This diversity helps to ensure that ethical considerations are evaluated from multiple perspectives, enhancing the quality of the review process. Additionally, ethics committees are required to conduct ongoing monitoring of approved trials to ensure compliance with ethical standards throughout the study.

Moreover, the guidelines stipulate that ethics committees must operate transparently and maintain proper documentation of their decisions and rationales. This transparency fosters accountability and trust in the ethical review process, reinforcing public confidence in clinical research. By ensuring that ethics committees are integral to the clinical trial process, the Indian GCP guidelines promote ethical research practices that prioritize participant rights and safety.

22.2.3 Protecting Vulnerable Populations in Indian Trials

The Indian GCP guidelines place a strong emphasis on protecting vulnerable populations participating in clinical trials. Vulnerable groups, including children, pregnant women, and individuals with limited decision-making capacity, require special ethical considerations to ensure that their rights and welfare are safeguarded throughout the research process. The guidelines emphasize that researchers must assess the risks and benefits of including these populations in clinical trials and ensure that adequate protections are in place to mitigate any potential risks.

In the case of pediatric trials, for example, researchers are required to demonstrate that the study offers direct benefits to child participants or that it is necessary for advancing pediatric knowledge. The guidelines also outline the process for obtaining informed consent from parents or guardians while ensuring that, whenever possible, the child's assent is sought, respecting their emerging autonomy. This dual approach not only safeguards the interests of vulnerable populations but also empowers them by including their perspectives in the decision-making process.

Additionally, the Indian GCP guidelines provide specific recommendations for conducting research involving pregnant women. These recommendations stress the importance of conducting a thorough risk-benefit analysis, ensuring that the potential benefits of the research outweigh any risks to both the mother and the fetus. By establishing these protections and emphasizing the ethical considerations unique to vulnerable populations, the Indian GCP guidelines promote responsible and ethical conduct in clinical research, ultimately enhancing participant safety and well-being.

22.3 Roles and Responsibilities in Indian Clinical Trials

22.3.1 Investigator Responsibilities Under Indian GCP

Investigators in Indian clinical trials have significant responsibilities under the Indian GCP guidelines, which emphasize the need for ethical conduct and regulatory compliance throughout the research process. The primary role of the investigator is to ensure that the trial is conducted according to the approved protocol, adhering to GCP principles and protecting the rights and welfare of participants. This involves obtaining informed consent from all participants, ensuring that they fully understand the nature of the trial, its risks, and their rights as participants.

Moreover, investigators are responsible for ensuring that the trial is conducted with the highest level of scientific integrity. This includes implementing robust data collection and management procedures, ensuring the accuracy and reliability of the data generated during the trial. Investigators must also monitor participants for adverse events and report any safety concerns promptly to the sponsor and ethics committee. By fulfilling these responsibilities, investigators play a crucial role in maintaining the ethical standards of clinical research and contributing to the generation of credible data.

Additionally, investigators are expected to engage in ongoing education and training to stay informed about current GCP guidelines and best practices in clinical research. This commitment to professional development is essential for ensuring that investigators are well-equipped to manage the complexities of clinical trials and navigate the regulatory landscape. By embracing their responsibilities under Indian GCP, investigators contribute to the ethical conduct of research and the advancement of medical knowledge.

22.3.2 Sponsor Responsibilities in Indian Clinical Trials

Sponsors have a critical role in the successful conduct of clinical trials in India, with specific responsibilities outlined in the Indian GCP guidelines. Primarily, sponsors are responsible for the design, management, and funding of the clinical trial. This involves developing a comprehensive trial protocol, obtaining necessary regulatory and ethical approvals, and ensuring that adequate resources are allocated for the study. The sponsor must also ensure that the trial is conducted in compliance with GCP principles and regulatory requirements, fostering a culture of accountability and transparency.

Moreover, sponsors are responsible for implementing effective monitoring and oversight mechanisms throughout the trial. This includes establishing a monitoring plan to regularly assess the conduct of the trial, participant safety, and data integrity. Sponsors must ensure that any adverse events or safety concerns are promptly reported to regulatory authorities and ethics committees, demonstrating their commitment to participant welfare and regulatory compliance. By fulfilling these responsibilities, sponsors play a vital role in upholding the ethical standards of clinical research in India.

Additionally, sponsors must ensure that investigators are adequately trained and qualified to conduct the trial. This involves providing ongoing support, resources, and training to ensure that study personnel are well-informed about regulatory requirements and best practices in clinical research. By fostering a collaborative relationship with investigators, sponsors can enhance the quality and credibility of the clinical trial, ultimately contributing to the responsible development of new therapies.

22.3.3 Role of Contract Research Organizations (CROs)

Contract Research Organizations (CROs) play a significant role in the conduct of clinical trials in India, providing essential support services to sponsors and investigators. CROs are specialized firms that offer expertise in various aspects of clinical research, including trial management, data collection, regulatory compliance, and monitoring. By partnering with CROs, sponsors can leverage their expertise to enhance the efficiency and quality of clinical trials.

One of the primary responsibilities of CROs is to assist in the planning and execution of clinical trials. This includes developing trial protocols, managing study logistics, and ensuring compliance with regulatory requirements. CROs also play a critical role in participant recruitment and retention, utilizing their networks and resources to identify and enroll suitable participants for clinical studies. By streamlining these processes, CROs help sponsors expedite the clinical trial timeline and reduce costs associated with research.

Additionally, CROs are responsible for monitoring trial conduct and ensuring compliance with GCP guidelines. This involves conducting regular site visits, verifying data accuracy, and assessing participant safety. CROs must maintain open communication with sponsors and investigators, providing updates on trial progress and any issues that may arise. By fulfilling these responsibilities, CROs contribute to the ethical conduct and scientific rigor of clinical trials in India, ultimately advancing the field of clinical research.

22.4 Regulatory Compliance in Indian GCP

22.4.1 Monitoring and Auditing for GCP Compliance in India

Regulatory compliance is a cornerstone of the Indian GCP guidelines, ensuring that clinical trials are conducted ethically and in accordance with established standards. Monitoring and auditing are vital processes that facilitate compliance, providing oversight to assess whether clinical trials are being conducted according to the approved protocol and GCP guidelines. The Central Drugs Standard Control Organization (CDSCO) mandates that sponsors implement a monitoring plan that includes regular site visits, data verification, and assessments of participant safety throughout the trial.

Monitoring activities involve comprehensive checks on trial conduct, including participant recruitment, informed consent processes, and adherence to safety protocols. This ongoing oversight allows sponsors to identify potential issues early, facilitating timely corrective actions to mitigate risks and ensure the integrity of the trial. Additionally, independent audits may be conducted to evaluate compliance with GCP standards, providing an objective assessment of trial conduct. These audits serve as a critical tool for ensuring transparency and accountability in clinical research, ultimately reinforcing public trust in the research process.

Furthermore, the importance of training and educating trial personnel on GCP principles cannot be overstated. By fostering a culture of compliance and accountability within the research team, sponsors can enhance the quality of the clinical trial and ensure that all stakeholders are committed to maintaining high ethical standards throughout the research process. Continuous monitoring and auditing, combined with robust training programs, contribute to the overall success and credibility of clinical trials conducted in India.

22.4.2 Reporting Requirements to CDSCO

Under the Indian GCP guidelines, sponsors have specific reporting requirements to the CDSCO that are crucial for maintaining regulatory compliance and participant safety. These reporting obligations include the timely submission of clinical trial data, adverse event reports, and updates on any significant changes to the trial protocol. The CDSCO requires that sponsors report serious adverse events (SAEs) within a specified timeframe to ensure prompt evaluation and appropriate responses to any emerging safety concerns.

In addition to adverse event reporting, sponsors must submit regular progress reports to the CDSCO, detailing the status of the clinical trial, participant enrollment figures, and any challenges encountered during the study. These reports allow the regulatory authority to monitor ongoing trials and assess their compliance with ethical and regulatory standards. By providing transparent and accurate information to the CDSCO, sponsors contribute to the oversight and integrity of clinical research in India.

Moreover, the Indian GCP guidelines emphasize the need for effective communication between sponsors and regulatory authorities. Timely reporting and open dialogue help to address any concerns that may arise during the trial, ensuring that participant safety remains a top priority. By adhering to these reporting requirements, sponsors demonstrate their commitment to responsible conduct and regulatory compliance in clinical research.

22.4.3 Addressing Non-Compliance and Regulatory Actions

Addressing non-compliance with Indian GCP guidelines is essential for maintaining the integrity of clinical research. When instances of non-compliance are identified, sponsors and investigators are required to take immediate corrective actions to rectify the situation. This may involve conducting thorough investigations to determine the root cause of the non-compliance and implementing measures to prevent its recurrence. The

Indian GCP guidelines stress the importance of documenting all non-compliance issues and the steps taken to address them, ensuring transparency in the research process.

Regulatory authorities, such as the CDSCO, have the authority to take action in response to significant non-compliance issues. This may include issuing warnings, conducting additional inspections, or imposing sanctions such as suspension or termination of the clinical trial. The CDSCO may also require sponsors to submit corrective action plans and progress reports to demonstrate compliance moving forward. These regulatory actions are essential for protecting participant rights and safety and maintaining public trust in the clinical research process.

Additionally, fostering a culture of compliance within research organizations is vital for addressing non-compliance issues effectively. By prioritizing GCP training and education for all personnel involved in clinical trials, organizations can enhance awareness of regulatory requirements and promote adherence to ethical standards. This proactive approach not only minimizes the risk of non-compliance but also contributes to the overall quality and credibility of clinical research in India.

22.5 Safety Reporting and Pharmacovigilance

22.5.1 Adverse Event Reporting Requirements in India

Safety reporting is a critical aspect of pharmacovigilance in clinical trials, and the Indian GCP guidelines outline specific requirements for the reporting of adverse events. Sponsors are obligated to establish comprehensive systems for collecting, analyzing, and reporting adverse events that occur during the trial. This includes promptly documenting all adverse events, determining their severity, and assessing their relationship to the investigational product. The Indian GCP guidelines emphasize the need for sponsors to report serious adverse events (SAEs) to the CDSCO within specified timelines, ensuring that regulatory authorities are informed of any potential safety concerns.

Moreover, the guidelines require sponsors to implement procedures for ongoing safety monitoring throughout the trial. This includes conducting regular safety assessments, reviewing safety data from all study sites, and identifying any emerging safety signals that may necessitate further investigation. By maintaining a proactive approach to safety reporting, sponsors can ensure that participant welfare remains a top priority and that appropriate actions are taken to mitigate risks associated with the investigational product.

Effective communication with investigators and trial sites is also essential for ensuring compliance with adverse event reporting requirements. Sponsors must provide training and resources to study personnel, enabling them to recognize and report adverse events accurately. By fostering a culture of safety and open communication, sponsors contribute to the ethical conduct of clinical trials and the protection of participant rights.

22.5.2 Pharmacovigilance and Post-Marketing Safety Monitoring

Pharmacovigilance plays a vital role in ensuring the ongoing safety and efficacy of medicinal products, both during clinical trials and after they have been approved for market use. The Indian GCP guidelines emphasize the need for sponsors to establish robust pharmacovigilance systems that enable the continuous monitoring of safety data throughout the clinical trial process. This includes conducting thorough safety assessments and data analysis to identify any potential risks or adverse effects associated with the investigational product.

Once a product is approved for marketing, the pharmacovigilance obligations continue, with sponsors required to implement post-marketing safety monitoring programs. These programs are designed to collect and analyze safety data from real-world use of the product, allowing for the identification of any new safety signals that may emerge once the product is widely used. By maintaining active pharmacovigilance efforts, sponsors can ensure that any potential safety concerns are promptly addressed and that appropriate risk management strategies are implemented.

Moreover, regulatory authorities, including the CDSCO, play a crucial role in overseeing pharmacovigilance activities in India. The CDSCO monitors adverse event reporting, assesses safety data, and provides guidance on risk management plans for approved products. By fostering collaboration between sponsors and regulatory authorities, pharmacovigilance efforts can contribute to the ongoing safety and efficacy of medicinal products, ultimately protecting public health.

22.5.3 Role of the Pharmacovigilance Program of India (PvPI)

The **Pharmacovigilance Program of India (PvPI)** plays a pivotal role in enhancing drug safety monitoring and pharmacovigilance practices across the country. Launched in 2010 by the CDSCO, the PvPI aims to improve patient safety and ensure the continuous assessment of the safety of pharmaceuticals through systematic data collection and analysis of adverse drug reactions (ADRs). The program operates by collaborating with various stakeholders, including healthcare professionals, pharmaceutical companies, and regulatory authorities, to promote a culture of safety and vigilance in the use of medications.

One of the primary objectives of the PvPI is to establish a nationwide ADR monitoring system that enables healthcare professionals to report adverse drug reactions promptly. This system facilitates the collection of valuable data that can be analyzed to identify safety signals and trends in drug use. By actively engaging healthcare professionals in the reporting process, the PvPI aims to improve the quality and completeness of safety data, ultimately contributing to informed decision-making regarding drug safety and efficacy.

Additionally, the PvPI is responsible for disseminating information about drug safety and promoting awareness among healthcare professionals and the general public. Through educational initiatives, workshops, and training programs, the program seeks to enhance the understanding of pharmacovigilance principles and the importance of ADR reporting. By fostering collaboration and transparency in drug safety monitoring, the PvPI plays a crucial role in protecting public health and ensuring that the benefits of medications continue to outweigh their risks.

22.6 Case Studies in Indian GCP Compliance

22.6.1 Examples of Successful GCP-Compliant Trials in India

Numerous clinical trials conducted in India have successfully adhered to the principles outlined in the Indian GCP guidelines, resulting in significant advancements in medical research and patient care. One notable example is the **clinical trial for the vaccine against human papillomavirus (HPV)**, which demonstrated the efficacy and safety of the vaccine in preventing cervical cancer. Conducted in compliance with GCP standards, this trial involved a diverse population across multiple sites in India, ensuring that the results were representative of the broader community.

The successful implementation of this trial not only contributed to the global understanding of HPV vaccination but also highlighted the importance of adhering to GCP guidelines in protecting participant rights and safety. By following rigorous protocols for informed consent, participant monitoring, and data management, the researchers were able to generate credible data that supported the regulatory approval of the vaccine in India. This case exemplifies the positive impact of GCP-compliant trials on public health outcomes and the importance of ethical research practices.

Another example is the **clinical trial conducted for the treatment of tuberculosis (TB)**, which is a major public health concern in India. The trial focused on evaluating the efficacy of a new drug regimen for drug-resistant TB. By adhering to Indian GCP guidelines, the researchers ensured that participant safety was prioritized throughout the trial, with robust monitoring and reporting mechanisms in place. The successful completion of this trial has contributed to the development of effective treatment options for drug-resistant TB, showcasing the vital role of GCP compliance in advancing medical science and improving patient care.

22.6.2 Challenges Faced in Implementing Indian GCP

Despite the advancements made in clinical research in India, challenges remain in the effective implementation of Indian GCP guidelines. One significant challenge is the variability in the understanding and application of GCP principles among investigators and research staff. This variability can lead to inconsistencies in trial conduct, informed consent processes, and data management practices, ultimately affecting the quality and credibility of the research. To address this challenge, it is crucial to invest in ongoing education and training programs that enhance the knowledge and skills of all personnel involved in clinical trials.

Additionally, logistical challenges may arise in conducting multicenter trials, particularly in ensuring compliance with GCP standards across diverse sites. Variations in local regulations, cultural factors, and infrastructure capabilities can complicate the implementation of standardized practices. Coordinating communication and data collection among multiple sites requires robust systems and effective oversight to maintain consistency and compliance. By fostering collaboration among investigators, sponsors, and regulatory authorities, these challenges can be addressed, ultimately enhancing the quality and integrity of clinical trials in India.

Furthermore, the rapid growth of the clinical research sector in India has led to an increasing demand for regulatory oversight and monitoring. As the number of clinical trials continues to rise, regulatory authorities face the challenge of ensuring compliance with GCP standards while facilitating timely approvals. Balancing the need for efficient regulatory processes with the imperative of participant safety is essential for fostering a sustainable clinical research environment in India. By proactively addressing these challenges, stakeholders can contribute to the responsible conduct of clinical trials and the advancement of medical science.

22.6.3 Lessons Learned from Indian Clinical Trials

The experiences gained from clinical trials conducted under Indian GCP guidelines provide valuable lessons for researchers, sponsors, and regulatory authorities. One important lesson is the significance of early engagement with regulatory authorities and ethics committees during the trial design phase. By proactively discussing trial protocols and objectives with relevant stakeholders, researchers can identify potential challenges and streamline the approval process, ultimately enhancing the efficiency of clinical trials.

Another critical lesson is the importance of transparency and effective communication throughout the research process. Maintaining open lines of communication with participants, investigators, and regulatory authorities fosters trust and ensures that safety concerns are addressed promptly. Implementing robust safety monitoring and reporting systems is essential for identifying potential risks and ensuring participant protection. These systems also enable sponsors to respond swiftly to any emerging safety signals, contributing to the overall integrity of the trial.

Finally, the experiences of Indian clinical trials underscore the need for continuous monitoring and evaluation of research practices. By learning from both successes and challenges, researchers and sponsors can enhance the quality of clinical trials and improve participant outcomes. Ultimately, these lessons contribute to advancing public health and the responsible development of new therapies in India.

Review Questions

1. How do the Indian Good Clinical Practice (GCP) guidelines compare with the ICH-GCP guidelines?
2. What are the ethical principles outlined in the Indian GCP guidelines?
3. What are the investigator's responsibilities under the Indian GCP guidelines?
4. How does the role of Contract Research Organizations (CROs) differ from the sponsor's role in Indian clinical trials?
5. How are vulnerable populations protected under the Indian GCP guidelines?
6. What are the adverse event reporting requirements in Indian clinical trials?
7. What challenges do researchers face in ensuring GCP compliance in India?
8. How does the Indian regulatory framework enforce GCP in clinical trials?

CHAPTER TWENTY-THREE

ICMR Ethical Guidelines for Biomedical Research

23.1 Overview of ICMR Guidelines

23.1.1 History and Purpose of ICMR Guidelines

The **Indian Council of Medical Research (ICMR)** has played a pivotal role in shaping ethical standards for biomedical research in India. Established in 1911, the ICMR has continuously evolved its guidelines to address the ethical considerations inherent in clinical and biomedical research. The formalization of ethical guidelines began in 2006 with the release of the "ICMR Ethical Guidelines for Biomedical Research on Human Participants," which aimed to align India's research practices with global ethical standards while addressing the unique cultural and societal contexts within the country. These guidelines serve as a framework for conducting research involving human participants, ensuring that studies are carried out ethically, responsibly, and in compliance with legal requirements.

The primary purpose of the ICMR guidelines is to protect the rights, safety, and well-being of research participants while promoting scientific integrity and credibility. By establishing clear ethical standards, the ICMR aims to foster public trust in biomedical research and enhance the quality of research conducted in India. The guidelines also emphasize the importance of informed consent, the role of ethics committees, and the need for transparency in research practices, ultimately contributing to the responsible conduct of research in the country.

23.1.2 Key Ethical Principles in ICMR Guidelines

The ICMR ethical guidelines are built upon several key ethical principles that guide the conduct of biomedical research. These principles include

respect for persons, which emphasizes the importance of obtaining informed consent and recognizing the autonomy of research participants. This principle underscores the necessity of providing potential participants with comprehensive information about the study, enabling them to make informed decisions about their involvement.

Another fundamental principle is **beneficence**, which requires researchers to prioritize the well-being of participants and maximize potential benefits while minimizing risks. Researchers are obligated to conduct risk-benefit analyses to ensure that the potential benefits of the research outweigh the risks to participants. Additionally, the principle of **justice** emphasizes the fair selection of research participants, ensuring that vulnerable populations are not exploited and that the burdens and benefits of research are distributed equitably.

These ethical principles collectively guide researchers in their decision-making processes, fostering a culture of ethical conduct in biomedical research. By adhering to these principles, researchers can ensure that their work contributes positively to the advancement of medical science while safeguarding the rights and welfare of participants.

23.1.3 Scope of ICMR Guidelines in Clinical and Biomedical Research

The ICMR ethical guidelines encompass a broad scope of clinical and biomedical research, applying to all studies involving human participants, including clinical trials, observational studies, and epidemiological research. The guidelines provide comprehensive guidance on various aspects of research, including study design, informed consent processes, the role of ethics committees, and data management practices. This holistic approach ensures that ethical considerations are integrated into every phase of the research process, from planning and implementation to reporting and dissemination of findings.

Furthermore, the guidelines emphasize the importance of context-specific considerations in research. Given India's diverse cultural, social, and economic landscape, the ICMR guidelines encourage researchers to adapt their practices to address the unique needs and perspectives of the populations involved in their studies. This adaptability is crucial for conducting ethically sound research that respects the rights and welfare of participants while generating valuable insights into health issues affecting various communities.

In summary, the ICMR ethical guidelines play a vital role in promoting ethical conduct in clinical and biomedical research in India. By providing a comprehensive framework that emphasizes respect for participants, scientific integrity, and cultural sensitivity, the guidelines contribute to the responsible advancement of medical research in the country.

23.2 Ethical Review of Biomedical Research

23.2.1 Role of Ethics Committees in India

Ethics committees play a crucial role in the ethical review of biomedical research in India, ensuring that studies involving human participants are conducted in compliance with ethical standards and regulatory requirements. These committees, often referred to as Institutional Review Boards (IRBs) or Ethics Review Committees (ERCs), are responsible for reviewing research proposals to assess their ethical implications and to safeguard the rights and welfare of participants. The composition of ethics committees typically includes a diverse group of members with expertise in medicine, ethics, law, and community representation, allowing for a comprehensive evaluation of the ethical considerations associated with the proposed research.

The primary responsibilities of ethics committees include reviewing study protocols to ensure that they adhere to ethical principles, assessing the informed consent process, and monitoring the ongoing conduct of approved studies. By conducting thorough reviews, ethics committees contribute to the protection of participants and help to maintain public trust in the research process. Moreover, the guidelines stipulate that ethics committees must operate transparently and maintain accurate records of their decisions and rationales, reinforcing accountability in the ethical review process.

Additionally, ethics committees are tasked with promoting awareness of ethical issues in biomedical research among researchers and study personnel. They provide guidance and support to investigators, helping them navigate the ethical landscape of clinical research. By fostering a culture of ethical awareness and responsibility, ethics committees play a pivotal role in ensuring that biomedical research in India is conducted with integrity and respect for participants.

23.2.2 ICMR Guidelines for Ethics Committee Operations

The ICMR guidelines outline specific requirements and best practices for the operations of ethics committees in India. These guidelines emphasize the need for ethics committees to have a clear structure and defined roles for their members, ensuring that all individuals involved in the review process are adequately qualified and trained in ethical principles and regulatory requirements. The guidelines also stress the importance of diversity within ethics committees, encouraging the inclusion of individuals from various backgrounds to provide a well-rounded perspective on the ethical considerations of research proposals.

In addition to these structural requirements, the ICMR guidelines provide detailed recommendations for the review and approval processes followed by ethics committees. This includes conducting thorough assessments of research proposals, evaluating informed consent procedures, and ensuring that appropriate safeguards are in place to protect participants, particularly vulnerable populations. The guidelines also encourage ethics committees to engage in ongoing training and capacity-building initiatives to enhance their effectiveness in evaluating ethical issues in biomedical research.

Moreover, the ICMR guidelines emphasize the importance of maintaining clear documentation of all ethics committee activities, including meeting minutes, decisions, and rationales for approvals or disapprovals. This documentation is essential for ensuring transparency and accountability in the ethical review process. By adhering to the ICMR guidelines, ethics committees can enhance their credibility and contribute to the responsible conduct of biomedical research in India.

23.2.3 Review and Approval Processes for Biomedical Research

The review and approval processes for biomedical research, as outlined in the ICMR guidelines, are designed to ensure that studies are conducted ethically and in compliance with regulatory standards. Once a research proposal is submitted to an ethics committee, the committee undertakes a comprehensive review of the protocol, focusing on various aspects, including study design, participant selection, informed consent processes, and risk-benefit assessments. The committee evaluates whether the proposed research adheres to ethical principles, regulatory requirements, and community standards.

After the review process, the ethics committee may grant approval, request modifications to the protocol, or deny approval based on ethical concerns. If modifications are required, the committee provides feedback to the researcher, allowing them to address any identified issues before resubmitting the proposal for further review. This iterative process ensures that ethical considerations are thoroughly addressed and that participant welfare is prioritized.

Additionally, the ICMR guidelines encourage ethics committees to conduct ongoing monitoring of approved studies to ensure compliance with ethical standards throughout the research process. This monitoring may involve periodic reviews, site visits, and assessments of adverse events to identify any emerging safety concerns. By maintaining an active role in the oversight of biomedical research, ethics committees contribute to the ethical conduct of studies and the protection of research participants in India.

23.3 Informed Consent Under ICMR Guidelines

23.3.1 Requirements for Obtaining Informed Consent

Informed consent is a fundamental ethical requirement in biomedical research, and the ICMR guidelines outline specific requirements for obtaining informed consent from participants. Researchers must provide comprehensive information about the study, including its objectives, procedures, potential risks, benefits, and the right to withdraw from the study at any time without penalty. This information must be presented clearly and understandably, enabling potential participants to make informed decisions about their involvement in the research.

The process of obtaining informed consent should be documented thoroughly, and researchers are encouraged to use consent forms that are simple, concise, and culturally appropriate. Informed consent must be sought before enrolling participants, and researchers should be prepared to answer any questions that individuals may have about the study. Moreover, the guidelines emphasize that informed consent is an ongoing process, and participants should be informed of any new information that may arise during the course of the study that could affect their decision to continue participation.

Furthermore, in instances where research involves vulnerable populations, additional safeguards must be implemented to ensure that informed consent is obtained ethically. This may include obtaining consent from legally authorized representatives while also seeking assent from the participants themselves, wherever appropriate. By prioritizing informed consent, the ICMR guidelines uphold the ethical principles of respect for persons and autonomy, ensuring that participants are empowered to make informed decisions regarding their involvement in clinical research.

23.3.2 Special Considerations for Vulnerable Populations

The ICMR guidelines recognize that certain populations, such as children, pregnant women, and individuals with cognitive impairments, may be particularly vulnerable in the context of biomedical research. As such, special considerations must be made when obtaining informed consent from these groups. Researchers are required to assess the potential risks and benefits of the research for vulnerable populations and to implement appropriate safeguards to protect their rights and welfare.

In the case of pediatric trials, for instance, researchers must obtain informed consent from parents or guardians while also seeking the child's assent whenever feasible. The process of obtaining assent should be adapted to the child's age, understanding, and maturity level, ensuring that their perspectives are taken into account. Additionally, for pregnant women participating in research, it is crucial to conduct thorough risk-benefit analyses to ensure that the potential benefits of the research outweigh any risks to both the mother and the fetus.

The guidelines also emphasize the need for researchers to maintain sensitivity and cultural competence when engaging with vulnerable populations. This involves tailoring the informed consent process to accommodate cultural beliefs and practices that may influence participants' understanding and acceptance of the research. By taking these considerations into account, researchers can uphold ethical standards and ensure that vulnerable populations are treated with respect and dignity throughout the research process.

23.3.3 Language and Cultural Factors in the Consent Process

Language and cultural factors play a significant role in the informed consent process, and the ICMR guidelines emphasize the importance of ensuring that consent materials are accessible and comprehensible to participants from diverse backgrounds. Researchers are required to provide informed consent documents in languages that participants understand, allowing them to grasp the nature of the study and their rights as participants. This linguistic accessibility is essential for facilitating informed decision-making and promoting participant autonomy.

Moreover, cultural factors may influence participants' perceptions of research and their willingness to engage in clinical trials. Researchers must be aware of cultural beliefs, values, and practices that may affect participants' understanding of the study and their comfort with the consent process. It is crucial to engage with local communities and stakeholders to gain insights into cultural considerations that may impact participation in research. By incorporating culturally sensitive practices into the informed consent process, researchers can build trust with participants and foster a more inclusive and respectful research environment.

Additionally, the guidelines encourage researchers to conduct thorough training for study personnel on the importance of effective communication and cultural competence in the informed consent process. This training can enhance the skills of research staff in engaging with participants, addressing their questions, and ensuring that the consent process is both ethical and respectful. By prioritizing language and cultural factors, researchers can ensure that the informed consent process aligns with ethical standards and contributes to the overall integrity of biomedical research.

23.4 Protection of Participants in Biomedical Research
23.4.1 Ensuring Participant Safety and Well-being

The protection of participants is a fundamental ethical obligation in biomedical research, and the ICMR guidelines underscore the necessity of ensuring their safety and well-being throughout the research process. Researchers are required to implement comprehensive safety monitoring protocols that include regular assessments of participant health, close monitoring for adverse effects, and prompt reporting of any safety concerns to the relevant authorities. The commitment to participant safety begins with the informed consent process, where researchers must clearly communicate potential risks and benefits associated with the study, enabling participants to make informed choices regarding their involvement.

Furthermore, researchers must be prepared to respond to any adverse events or unexpected complications that may arise during the trial. This includes having contingency plans in place to provide appropriate medical care for participants who experience adverse reactions or require additional support. The ICMR guidelines advocate for a proactive approach to participant safety, emphasizing the need for researchers to foster an environment where participants feel comfortable reporting any concerns they may have about their health or the research process.

Additionally, researchers must engage in ongoing education and training related to safety protocols and participant protection. This training should encompass topics such as recognizing signs of distress, managing adverse events, and addressing participants' emotional and psychological needs. By prioritizing the safety and well-being of participants, researchers uphold the ethical standards of biomedical research and contribute to the integrity of the study.

23.4.2 ICMR Guidelines for Adverse Event Reporting

The ICMR guidelines outline specific requirements for the reporting of adverse events (AEs) that occur during biomedical research. Researchers are obligated to establish comprehensive systems for documenting, assessing, and reporting AEs to ensure participant safety and regulatory compliance. This involves implementing protocols for the timely identification and classification of AEs, determining their severity and relationship to the investigational product, and assessing the need for immediate intervention or medical care.

Prompt reporting of serious adverse events (SAEs) to the ethics committee and the regulatory authorities is crucial for maintaining participant safety and informing ongoing risk assessments. The guidelines stipulate that researchers must report SAEs within defined timelines, allowing for swift action to mitigate any risks associated with the research. This proactive approach to adverse event reporting is essential for protecting participants and ensuring that ethical standards are upheld throughout the research process.

Moreover, the ICMR guidelines encourage researchers to maintain open communication with participants regarding adverse events. Participants should be informed about the nature of reported AEs, their implications for the study, and any potential changes to the research protocol as a result. This transparency fosters trust and reinforces participants' rights to be informed about their health and safety during the study.

23.4.3 Ethical Considerations in High-Risk Research

Research involving high-risk populations or interventions presents unique ethical challenges that require careful consideration and planning. The ICMR guidelines emphasize the importance of conducting thorough risk-benefit analyses for studies that may pose significant risks to participants. Researchers must ensure that the potential benefits of the research outweigh the risks, and they must implement strategies to minimize any identified risks to participant safety.

In high-risk research, it is essential to establish robust monitoring and oversight mechanisms to safeguard participants. This may involve forming independent data safety monitoring boards (DSMBs) to oversee the study and provide recommendations based on ongoing safety data. Additionally, researchers should engage in continuous dialogue with ethics committees to address any ethical concerns that may arise throughout the study.

Furthermore, informed consent processes must be particularly rigorous in high-risk research. Participants should be made fully aware of the potential risks and benefits associated with their involvement, and researchers must ensure that consent is obtained in a manner that respects participants' autonomy. By addressing these ethical considerations, researchers can navigate the complexities of high-risk research while prioritizing participant safety and ethical integrity.

23.5 Ethical Guidelines for Research in Special Populations
23.5.1 ICMR Guidelines for Pediatric Research

The ICMR guidelines provide specific ethical considerations for conducting research involving pediatric populations, recognizing that children are particularly vulnerable participants in clinical trials. When designing studies that include children, researchers must ensure that the research is scientifically valid and that it addresses issues relevant to pediatric health. The guidelines emphasize the importance of conducting risk-benefit assessments, ensuring that the potential benefits of the research significantly outweigh any risks to child participants.

Informed consent for pediatric research requires obtaining consent from parents or guardians, as well as seeking the assent of the child whenever feasible. The assent process involves providing age-appropriate information about the study to the child, allowing them to express their willingness to participate. This practice respects the emerging autonomy of young participants and acknowledges their right to be involved in decisions about their participation in research.

Moreover, the guidelines stress the necessity of protecting the rights and welfare of child participants throughout the research process. This includes implementing safety monitoring protocols to ensure that any adverse events are promptly addressed and reported. By adhering to the ICMR guidelines for pediatric research, researchers can uphold ethical standards and contribute to the advancement of knowledge that benefits children's health.

23.5.2 Research Involving Pregnant Women and the Elderly

The ICMR guidelines also emphasize the ethical considerations involved in conducting research with pregnant women and elderly populations. When researching pregnant women, researchers must conduct thorough risk-benefit analyses to ensure that the potential benefits of the research justify any risks to both the mother and the fetus. This includes assessing the safety of investigational products and ensuring that appropriate safeguards are in place to protect maternal and fetal health throughout the study.

Informed consent processes for pregnant women must account for the unique ethical challenges presented by their condition. Researchers should provide comprehensive information about the study, including potential risks and benefits, while also addressing any concerns that pregnant women may have about participating in research. Furthermore, the guidelines encourage researchers to engage healthcare providers to facilitate discussions around the risks and benefits of participating in research during pregnancy.

For elderly participants, the ICMR guidelines highlight the importance of considering age-related factors that may impact their ability to provide informed consent. Researchers must ensure that consent processes are accessible and that participants fully understand the nature of the study. Additionally, researchers should assess the appropriateness of study interventions for elderly participants, taking into account their specific health conditions and vulnerabilities. By prioritizing the ethical considerations surrounding research involving pregnant women and the elderly, the ICMR guidelines promote responsible and respectful conduct in biomedical research.

23.5.3 Research in Socially or Economically Disadvantaged Populations

The ICMR guidelines acknowledge the ethical complexities involved in conducting research within socially or economically disadvantaged populations. Researchers must be particularly vigilant in ensuring that the rights and welfare of these participants are protected throughout the research process. Special consideration must be given to the informed consent process, ensuring that individuals from disadvantaged backgrounds are provided with clear, understandable information about the study and that their participation is voluntary.

Moreover, the guidelines emphasize the importance of avoiding exploitation of disadvantaged populations in research. Researchers should ensure that the study design is equitable and that the burdens and benefits of participation are distributed fairly. This includes conducting risk-benefit analyses that specifically address the needs and vulnerabilities of socially disadvantaged groups, ensuring that participation in research does not further marginalize these populations.

Additionally, the ICMR guidelines encourage researchers to engage with community representatives and stakeholders when designing studies involving socially or economically disadvantaged populations. By involving these groups in the research process, researchers can gain valuable insights into the specific needs and concerns of participants, fostering trust and collaboration. This approach not only enhances the ethical conduct of research but also contributes to the generation of data that is relevant and beneficial to the communities involved.

23.6 Case Studies in ICMR-Guided Research

23.6.1 Ethical Dilemmas in Indian Biomedical Research

Case studies in Indian biomedical research often highlight ethical dilemmas that arise during the conduct of clinical trials. One notable case involved a study evaluating the efficacy of a new drug for tuberculosis (TB) among marginalized populations. Researchers faced significant challenges in obtaining informed consent from participants who were illiterate and had limited understanding of the research process. This situation raised ethical concerns regarding the adequacy of the informed consent process and the potential for exploitation of vulnerable populations.

In another instance, a clinical trial investigating the safety of a new vaccine raised questions about the risk-benefit balance, particularly when adverse events were reported among participants. The need to address these ethical dilemmas required researchers to engage with ethics committees and regulatory authorities, demonstrating the importance of adherence to the ICMR guidelines in navigating complex ethical issues. These case studies illustrate the critical need for researchers to prioritize ethical considerations in all aspects of biomedical research, ensuring that participant rights and welfare are upheld.

23.6.2 Examples of Successful Application of ICMR Guidelines

Despite the challenges faced, there are numerous examples of successful application of ICMR guidelines in Indian biomedical research. One exemplary case is the clinical trial conducted for a novel treatment for cervical cancer, which adhered to ethical principles by ensuring robust informed consent processes and rigorous safety monitoring. The trial engaged with diverse populations, providing information in multiple languages and formats to ensure that all participants understood the study and their rights.

Another successful example is the research conducted on maternal and child health, which focused on addressing health disparities in rural communities. By implementing culturally sensitive approaches and engaging local communities in the research process, the study demonstrated a commitment to ethical research practices and participant welfare. These successful applications of the ICMR guidelines not only contribute to scientific advancement but also reinforce the importance of ethical conduct in clinical research.

23.6.3 Lessons Learned from Ethical Challenges in Research

The experiences gained from ethical challenges encountered in Indian biomedical research provide valuable lessons for researchers and stakeholders. One key lesson is the importance of ongoing training and education for research personnel regarding ethical principles and the requirements outlined in the ICMR guidelines. By enhancing the understanding of ethical considerations, researchers can better navigate complex situations and prioritize participant welfare throughout the research process.

Additionally, the need for transparency and effective communication among all stakeholders is crucial. Establishing open lines of communication with participants, ethics committees, and regulatory authorities helps to address concerns promptly and fosters trust in the research process. Engaging with communities and participants can also provide valuable insights that inform the ethical conduct of research, ensuring that studies are responsive to the needs and concerns of those involved.

Finally, ongoing evaluation and adaptation of research practices are essential for improving ethical standards in biomedical research. By reflecting on past experiences and actively seeking feedback from participants and stakeholders, researchers can enhance their approaches and contribute to a culture of ethical research in India. These lessons learned serve to strengthen the integrity of biomedical research and reinforce the commitment to protecting participant rights and well-being.

Review Questions

1. What is the purpose of the ICMR Ethical Guidelines for Biomedical Research, and when were they established?
2. What ethical principles form the foundation of the ICMR guidelines?
3. How do the ICMR guidelines address the role of ethics committees in India?
4. What are the informed consent requirements under the ICMR guidelines?
5. How do the ICMR guidelines ensure the protection of participants in biomedical research, especially vulnerable populations?
6. What are the ethical guidelines for conducting research involving children and pregnant women under the ICMR guidelines?
7. Discuss the key considerations for adverse event reporting according to the ICMR guidelines.
8. What lessons have been learned from case studies in biomedical research guided by the ICMR guidelines?

CHAPTER TWENTY-FOUR

Regulatory Guidance on Efficacy and Safety (ICH Guidelines)

24.1 Overview of ICH Guidelines on Efficacy

24.1.1 ICH E4: Dose-Response Information to Support Drug Registration
The **ICH E4 guideline** provides essential recommendations for the design and interpretation of dose-response studies, which are critical for the drug registration process. Dose-response studies aim to establish the relationship between the dose of a drug and the magnitude of its therapeutic effect. This information is vital for determining the appropriate dosing regimen for the target population, thereby ensuring that the drug's efficacy is optimized while minimizing the potential for adverse effects. The guideline emphasizes the importance of using scientifically sound methodologies in designing these studies to ensure robust and reliable data.

In the context of drug registration, the ICH E4 guideline outlines the necessary considerations for conducting dose-response studies, including the selection of appropriate endpoints, statistical analysis, and the incorporation of pharmacokinetic and pharmacodynamic data. Regulatory authorities rely on this information to assess the therapeutic benefit of a new drug relative to its risks, which is critical for making informed decisions regarding market authorization. By adhering to the ICH E4 guidelines, researchers can contribute to the generation of high-quality data that supports the safe and effective use of new medications.

Additionally, the ICH E4 guideline encourages researchers to consider the variability in response among different populations, including factors such as age, sex, and comorbid conditions. Understanding these variations is crucial for determining the optimal dosing strategy for diverse patient groups. By integrating this knowledge into the design and analysis of dose-response studies, researchers can enhance the applicability of their findings and contribute to the development of more effective therapeutic interventions.

24.1.2 ICH E7: Studies in Geriatric Populations

The **ICH E7 guideline** focuses on the specific considerations required when conducting clinical trials in geriatric populations. As the elderly are often underrepresented in clinical research, the ICH E7 guideline emphasizes the need for inclusive study designs that account for the unique physiological, pharmacological, and psychosocial factors that can influence drug efficacy and safety in this demographic. This guideline aims to ensure that therapeutic interventions are appropriately evaluated for their effectiveness and safety in older adults, who may have different responses to medications compared to younger populations.

Key recommendations within ICH E7 include the necessity of conducting thorough assessments of age-related changes in pharmacokinetics and pharmacodynamics, which can impact drug absorption, distribution, metabolism, and excretion. Additionally, the guideline emphasizes the importance of considering comorbidities and polypharmacy, as many elderly individuals are likely to be taking multiple medications simultaneously. Researchers are encouraged to design studies that facilitate the assessment of these complexities, ensuring that findings are relevant and applicable to the geriatric population.

Moreover, the ICH E7 guideline underscores the importance of obtaining informed consent from geriatric participants, highlighting the need for clear communication and support during the consent process. By addressing these ethical and practical considerations, researchers can enhance the quality of clinical trials involving older adults and contribute to the development of safe and effective treatment options for this vulnerable population.

24.1.3 ICH E8: General Considerations for Clinical Trials

The **ICH E8 guideline** provides overarching principles and considerations for the conduct of clinical trials, emphasizing the importance of scientific integrity, ethical conduct, and participant safety. This guideline serves as a foundation for all aspects of clinical trial design and execution, outlining best practices that researchers should follow to ensure that studies are conducted rigorously and ethically. The ICH E8 guideline promotes a holistic approach to clinical research, encouraging researchers to consider the entire research process, from protocol development to data analysis and reporting.

Key considerations outlined in the ICH E8 guideline include the necessity of establishing clear trial objectives, ensuring appropriate study design, and selecting relevant endpoints that accurately reflect the therapeutic benefits of the investigational product. The guideline also emphasizes the importance of minimizing bias and ensuring that the study population is representative of the target patient population. By following these principles, researchers can enhance the reliability and credibility of their findings, ultimately contributing to the safe and effective use of new treatments.

Furthermore, the ICH E8 guideline addresses the importance of ensuring informed consent and participant protection throughout the trial process. Researchers are encouraged to prioritize the rights and well-being of participants, implementing measures to safeguard their safety and confidentiality. By adhering to the ICH E8 guidelines, researchers can conduct clinical trials that not only generate valuable data but also uphold the highest ethical standards in research.

24.2 Dose-Response Studies (ICH E4)

24.2.1 Purpose of Dose-Response Studies

Dose-response studies serve a critical role in the drug development process, aiming to establish the relationship between the dose of an investigational product and the magnitude of its therapeutic effect. These studies provide essential data that inform dosing recommendations, helping to optimize the therapeutic benefits while minimizing the risks of adverse effects. By understanding how different doses impact efficacy, researchers can identify the optimal dosing regimen for various patient populations, ultimately contributing to safer and more effective treatments.

The primary purpose of dose-response studies is to ascertain the therapeutic window of a drug, which is defined as the range of doses that elicits the desired therapeutic effect without producing unacceptable side effects. By carefully assessing the dose-response relationship, researchers can determine the minimum effective dose (MED) and the maximum tolerated dose (MTD), providing crucial information for regulatory submissions and clinical practice. This understanding is especially important in the context of populations with varying sensitivities to medications, such as the elderly or individuals with comorbidities.

Additionally, dose-response studies can help identify potential pharmacokinetic and pharmacodynamic interactions, enhancing the understanding of how different doses affect drug behavior within the body. By systematically evaluating these interactions, researchers can develop more tailored and effective treatment strategies, addressing the specific needs of diverse patient populations.

24.2.2 Study Design and Data Collection for Dose-Response

The design of dose-response studies is critical for obtaining reliable and interpretable results. Researchers must carefully select study designs that align with the objectives of the trial, considering factors such as randomization, blinding, and control groups. Common approaches for dose-response studies include parallel-group designs, where participants are assigned to different dose levels, and dose-escalation designs, which involve progressively increasing doses within the same participant group.

Data collection methods must be robust and systematic to accurately capture the relationship between dose and response. This includes establishing clear endpoints that reflect the therapeutic effects being measured, as well as consistent procedures for measuring outcomes. Researchers may utilize various statistical techniques to analyze dose-response data, ensuring that the findings are statistically significant and clinically meaningful.

Moreover, ongoing monitoring of participant safety during dose-response studies is essential. Researchers should implement safety monitoring protocols to assess any adverse events that may occur as a result of different dosing levels. By maintaining a rigorous approach to study design and data collection, researchers can generate high-quality evidence that informs dosing recommendations and supports regulatory approval.

24.2.3 Regulatory Submission of Dose-Response Data

Regulatory authorities require that dose-response data be submitted as part of the drug registration process to evaluate the efficacy and safety of new therapeutics. The ICH E4 guideline outlines specific requirements for the submission of dose-response data, emphasizing the importance of presenting comprehensive information that supports the conclusions drawn from the studies. This includes providing detailed descriptions of the study design, methodologies, participant demographics, and statistical analyses conducted to assess the dose-response relationship.

When preparing regulatory submissions, researchers must ensure that the dose-response data is presented in a clear and accessible format, allowing regulatory reviewers to evaluate the findings effectively. Additionally, researchers should provide context for the data, discussing its relevance to the overall safety and efficacy of the investigational product. This transparency is essential for facilitating informed decision-making by regulatory authorities, ultimately contributing to the safe and effective use of new medications.

Furthermore, the submission process may involve addressing any questions or concerns raised by regulatory authorities regarding the dose-response data. Researchers should be prepared to provide additional analyses or clarifications as needed, demonstrating their commitment to regulatory compliance and participant safety. By adhering to the regulatory requirements for the submission of dose-response data, researchers can contribute to the successful advancement of new therapeutic interventions through the drug registration process.

24.3 Studies in Special Populations (ICH E7 and E11)

24.3.1 ICH E7: Geriatric Population Studies

The **ICH E7 guideline** specifically addresses the need for clinical studies to include geriatric populations, recognizing that this demographic often exhibits unique physiological and pharmacological responses to medications. Geriatric populations frequently experience age-related changes in organ function, polypharmacy, and various comorbid conditions that can significantly affect drug efficacy and safety. As a result, it is imperative for researchers to conduct studies that assess the effects of investigational products in older adults, ensuring that therapeutic interventions are appropriately evaluated for this vulnerable group.

The ICH E7 guidelines emphasize the necessity of designing studies that account for the complexities of geriatric populations. This includes conducting thorough assessments of participants' health status, monitoring for potential adverse effects, and ensuring that study protocols reflect the specific needs of older adults. Additionally, the guidelines advocate for the inclusion of endpoints that are relevant to the geriatric population, such as quality of life measures and functional assessments. By focusing on these considerations, researchers can generate data that is applicable and meaningful for the treatment of elderly patients.

Furthermore, the ICH E7 guidelines highlight the importance of informed consent processes in geriatric studies. Researchers must ensure that older participants fully understand the study, their rights, and any associated risks. The consent process should be conducted in a manner that respects the autonomy and dignity of elderly individuals, taking into account their cognitive abilities and preferences. By adhering to the ICH E7 guidelines, researchers can contribute to the ethical conduct of geriatric studies and promote the development of effective therapies tailored to the needs of older adults.

24.3.2 ICH E11: Pediatric Population Studies

The **ICH E11 guideline** provides specific recommendations for conducting clinical studies in pediatric populations, emphasizing the importance of developing effective treatments for children. Pediatric studies present unique challenges, including the need to account for differences in pharmacokinetics and pharmacodynamics compared to adults. The ICH E11 guidelines encourage researchers to design studies that are scientifically rigorous while also being ethically sound, ensuring that the rights and welfare of child participants are prioritized.

When designing pediatric studies, researchers must consider the appropriateness of dosing regimens, endpoints, and study methodologies. The ICH E11 guidelines recommend that researchers engage in consultations with pediatric experts and stakeholders, including parents and caregivers, to gain insights into the specific needs and preferences of children. This collaborative approach helps ensure that the study design is both ethical and relevant to the pediatric population.

Additionally, the ICH E11 guidelines emphasize the importance of informed consent and assent processes in pediatric research. While parental or guardian consent is necessary, obtaining the assent of the child, when feasible, is essential for respecting their autonomy. Researchers must present information in a manner that is understandable to children, allowing them to participate meaningfully in the decision-making process. By following the ICH E11 guidelines, researchers can enhance the quality and ethical standards of pediatric clinical trials.

24.3.3 Regulatory Challenges in Special Population Studies

Conducting studies in special populations, such as geriatric and pediatric groups, presents unique regulatory challenges that researchers must navigate. Regulatory authorities often require additional documentation and justification for the inclusion of these populations in clinical trials, as they may exhibit distinct responses to treatments compared to the general population. Researchers must be prepared to provide detailed rationales for their study designs and methodologies to demonstrate compliance with regulatory expectations.

One of the significant challenges faced in special population studies is the potential for increased scrutiny from regulatory authorities regarding the ethical conduct of research. This is particularly relevant for studies involving vulnerable populations, where there may be concerns about the adequacy of informed consent processes and participant protections. Researchers must ensure that they have robust protocols in place to address these concerns and that they adhere to the ethical guidelines outlined by ICH E7 and E11.

Additionally, the complexities associated with obtaining regulatory approvals for studies in special populations can result in delays in the research timeline. Researchers must be diligent in their communications with regulatory authorities, addressing any questions or concerns raised during the approval process. By proactively addressing regulatory challenges and maintaining transparency in their research practices, researchers can contribute to the successful conduct of studies in special populations and facilitate the development of effective treatments tailored to their needs.

24.4 General Considerations for Clinical Trials (ICH E8)

24.4.1 Study Design, Conduct, and Analysis

The **ICH E8 guideline** provides comprehensive guidance on the general considerations for the design, conduct, and analysis of clinical trials. One of the primary objectives of this guideline is to ensure that clinical studies are scientifically valid and ethically sound, thereby generating credible and reliable data that can support regulatory approvals. Researchers are encouraged to develop clear study objectives and hypotheses, as these elements are critical for guiding the design of the trial and ensuring that the results are meaningful.

In terms of study design, the ICH E8 guidelines advocate for the use of robust methodologies that are appropriate for the research question being addressed. This includes considerations related to sample size, randomization, blinding, and the selection of endpoints that accurately reflect the therapeutic effects of the investigational product. The guideline emphasizes the importance of planning for data collection and analysis from the outset, ensuring that statistical methods are predefined and appropriate for the study design. By adhering to these principles, researchers can enhance the integrity and scientific rigor of their clinical trials.

Furthermore, the ICH E8 guideline underscores the necessity of conducting ongoing assessments of study conduct to ensure compliance with ethical standards and regulatory requirements. This involves monitoring participant safety and data quality throughout the trial, with mechanisms in place to address any issues that may arise. By prioritizing these general considerations, researchers can contribute to the responsible conduct of clinical trials and the advancement of medical science.

24.4.2 Importance of Quality Assurance in Clinical Trials

Quality assurance is a fundamental component of clinical trials, ensuring that research is conducted according to established standards and that the integrity of the data is maintained. The ICH E8 guideline emphasizes the need for comprehensive quality assurance processes throughout the trial lifecycle, from planning and protocol development to data collection and reporting. Implementing effective quality assurance measures helps to minimize the risk of errors, inconsistencies, and non-compliance, ultimately enhancing the credibility of the study findings.

One of the key aspects of quality assurance is the establishment of standard operating procedures (SOPs) that outline the processes and responsibilities of all individuals involved in the trial. SOPs serve as a framework for ensuring consistency and compliance with regulatory requirements and GCP guidelines. Additionally, regular training and education for study personnel are essential for maintaining high standards of quality and ensuring that all team members are knowledgeable about their roles and responsibilities.

Moreover, ongoing monitoring and auditing are critical components of a robust quality assurance framework. These activities involve regular assessments of study conduct, data integrity, and participant safety, allowing for timely identification of any issues that may arise. By prioritizing quality assurance in clinical trials, researchers can foster a culture of accountability and transparency, ultimately contributing to the successful advancement of new therapeutic interventions.

24.4.3 Regulatory Guidelines for Global Clinical Trials

As clinical trials increasingly take place on a global scale, the ICH E8 guideline emphasizes the importance of understanding and adhering to the regulatory requirements of different regions. Conducting global clinical trials presents unique challenges, including variations in regulatory frameworks, ethical standards, and cultural considerations. The ICH E8 guideline encourages researchers to consider these factors during the planning and design phases of the trial to ensure compliance with the regulatory requirements of all countries involved.

Researchers must be aware of the specific guidelines and regulations set forth by regulatory authorities in each country where the trial is conducted. This may include obtaining necessary approvals from local ethics committees and regulatory bodies, as well as adhering to reporting requirements for adverse events and safety monitoring. By understanding these regulatory guidelines, researchers can facilitate a smoother approval process and enhance the likelihood of successful study outcomes.

Furthermore, the ICH E8 guideline promotes collaboration and communication among stakeholders in global clinical trials. Engaging with regulatory authorities, ethics committees, and local investigators can provide valuable insights into the regulatory landscape and cultural nuances that may impact trial conduct. By fostering strong partnerships and open lines of communication, researchers can navigate the complexities of global clinical trials more effectively, ultimately contributing to the successful development of new therapeutics on an international scale.

24.5 Choice of Control Groups (ICH E10)

24.5.1 Types of Control Groups in Clinical Trials

The choice of control groups is a critical aspect of clinical trial design, and the ICH E10 guideline provides guidance on the various types of control groups that researchers can utilize. Control groups serve as a benchmark for evaluating the efficacy and safety of an investigational product, allowing researchers to compare the outcomes of participants receiving the treatment against those who do not. Common types of control groups include placebo controls, active controls, and historical controls.

Placebo controls are often used when evaluating the efficacy of a new treatment, allowing researchers to determine whether the observed effects are attributable to the treatment itself rather than psychological factors.

Active controls involve comparing the investigational product to an established treatment, providing insights into relative effectiveness. Historical controls utilize data from previous studies to establish a comparison group, although this approach may be subject to biases and confounding factors. By carefully selecting the appropriate control group, researchers can enhance the validity and reliability of their study findings.

The choice of control group also influences the ethical considerations of the trial. Researchers must ensure that participants in the control group are treated ethically and that their rights are upheld. This includes providing adequate information about the study, obtaining informed consent, and ensuring that participants are not subjected to undue risk or harm. By aligning the choice of control groups with ethical principles and regulatory guidelines, researchers can contribute to the integrity of clinical trials.

24.5.2 Ethical Considerations in Choosing Control Groups

The ethical considerations surrounding the choice of control groups in clinical trials are paramount, as they directly impact participant welfare and informed consent. One of the key ethical dilemmas arises when considering the use of placebo controls, particularly in situations where effective treatments exist. Researchers must carefully weigh the potential benefits of using a placebo against the ethical obligation to provide participants with the best available treatment. The principle of **beneficence** mandates that researchers act in the best interest of participants, which may complicate the decision to use placebo controls in certain contexts.

In cases where placebo controls are deemed necessary, researchers should ensure that participants are fully informed about the nature of the study and the potential risks involved. This includes transparent communication regarding the possibility of receiving a placebo instead of an active treatment. By obtaining informed consent that clearly outlines the use of control groups, researchers uphold the ethical principle of **respect for persons** and empower participants to make informed decisions about their involvement in the research.

Additionally, researchers must consider the implications of using active controls in clinical trials. While active controls may be ethically preferable in certain situations, they can introduce complexities in terms of treatment comparability and blinding. Researchers must ensure that the control treatment is appropriate and that the trial design adequately accounts for differences between the investigational product and the active comparator. By addressing these ethical considerations, researchers can ensure that the choice of control groups aligns with the principles of ethical research and participant protection.

24.5.3 Regulatory Requirements for Control Group Studies

Regulatory authorities have established specific requirements for the inclusion of control groups in clinical trials, and the ICH E10 guideline outlines key considerations that researchers must adhere to. These requirements ensure that the design of control group studies meets ethical standards and provides reliable data for regulatory evaluation. Researchers are typically required to provide detailed justifications for the chosen control group, including the rationale for its selection and how it aligns with the trial objectives.

Regulatory submissions should include comprehensive information about the control group, including the methods used for randomization, blinding, and allocation concealment. This information is essential for demonstrating the scientific rigor and integrity of the study. Additionally, regulatory authorities may require that researchers outline plans for monitoring the safety and efficacy of both the investigational product and the control group throughout the trial, ensuring that participant welfare is prioritized.

Moreover, adherence to regulatory requirements extends beyond the design phase of the trial. Researchers must ensure ongoing compliance throughout the study, including timely reporting of any adverse events or safety concerns related to both the investigational product and the control group. By aligning their study designs with regulatory guidelines and requirements, researchers contribute to the credibility and acceptability of their findings in the eyes of regulatory authorities and the scientific community.

24.6 Clinical Investigation of Medicinal Products in Pediatrics (ICH E11)

24.6.1 Special Considerations for Pediatric Trials

The **ICH E11 guideline** addresses the unique challenges and considerations involved in conducting clinical trials in pediatric populations. Children are not merely small adults; they have distinct physiological, developmental, and psychological characteristics that can significantly affect their responses to medications. As a result, the design and conduct of pediatric trials must be tailored to account for these differences, ensuring that the research is both scientifically valid and ethically sound.

One of the critical considerations in pediatric trials is the need for age-appropriate formulations and dosing strategies. Researchers must carefully evaluate the pharmacokinetics and pharmacodynamics of the investigational product in children, taking into account factors such as growth and development that may impact drug metabolism and efficacy. The ICH E11 guideline encourages researchers to engage with pediatric experts to ensure that trial designs are appropriate and that the data generated is relevant to the pediatric population.

Moreover, ethical considerations are paramount in pediatric research. Researchers must prioritize the welfare and rights of child participants, ensuring that informed consent processes are rigorous and that assent is obtained from older children whenever possible. The guidelines advocate for the inclusion of parents or guardians in the decision-making process, fostering a collaborative approach to pediatric research. By addressing these special considerations, researchers can conduct ethically sound and scientifically rigorous studies that contribute to the advancement of pediatric medicine.

24.6.2 Ethical Guidelines for Pediatric Research

The ethical guidelines for pediatric research outlined in the ICH E11 guideline emphasize the need for protecting the rights and well-being of child participants. Given that children may have limited capacity to understand complex medical information, researchers must ensure that the informed consent process is accessible and comprehensible. This involves providing age-appropriate information and engaging parents or guardians in discussions about the study's objectives, risks, and potential benefits.

Additionally, the guidelines stress the importance of conducting risk-benefit assessments specific to pediatric populations. Researchers are required to ensure that the potential benefits of the research outweigh the risks, and that the study addresses a critical health need for children. In cases where the research may pose more than minimal risk, additional safeguards must be implemented to protect the rights and welfare of child participants.

Moreover, researchers must be sensitive to the emotional and psychological needs of pediatric participants. The study environment should be designed to minimize anxiety and discomfort, ensuring that children feel safe and supported throughout the research process. By adhering to ethical guidelines and prioritizing the well-being of child participants, researchers can foster trust and collaboration, ultimately contributing to the advancement of pediatric healthcare.

24.6.3 Regulatory Submission of Pediatric Data

The regulatory submission of pediatric data is a crucial aspect of the drug approval process, and the ICH E11 guideline provides specific recommendations for researchers in this area. When submitting data from pediatric studies to regulatory authorities, researchers must provide comprehensive information about the study design, methods, and results, clearly demonstrating the relevance of the findings to the pediatric population. This includes presenting data on pharmacokinetics, safety, and efficacy outcomes that are specific to children.

Additionally, the ICH E11 guideline emphasizes the importance of transparent communication with regulatory authorities throughout the submission process. Researchers should be prepared to address any questions or concerns raised by regulators regarding the pediatric data, including justifications for the study design and the appropriateness of the chosen endpoints. Timely and thorough responses to regulatory inquiries are essential for facilitating the review process and promoting a positive outcome for pediatric drug approvals.

Moreover, researchers must adhere to any specific requirements set forth by regulatory authorities regarding the reporting of pediatric data. This may include additional analyses or follow-up studies to further evaluate the safety and efficacy of the investigational product in children. By ensuring compliance with regulatory expectations and providing robust pediatric data, researchers contribute to the responsible development of new therapies that meet the needs of young patients.

Review Questions

1. What is the importance of ICH E4 guidelines regarding dose-response information for drug registration?
2. How do the ICH E7 guidelines address clinical studies involving geriatric populations?
3. What considerations are outlined in the ICH E8 guidelines for general clinical trial design and conduct?
4. Why are dose-response studies critical for determining drug efficacy and safety?
5. What are the challenges of conducting clinical studies in special populations, such as pediatrics and geriatrics, as outlined in ICH E7 and E11?
6. How do the ICH E10 guidelines address the selection of control groups in clinical trials?
7. What are the ethical and regulatory considerations when conducting pediatric clinical trials as per ICH E11?
8. How do the ICH guidelines ensure harmonization of clinical trials across different regulatory regions?

CHAPTER TWENTY-FIVE

Post-Market Surveillance and Safety Reporting

25.1 Introduction to Post-Market Surveillance

25.1.1 Purpose of Post-Marketing Studies

Post-market surveillance is a critical aspect of the drug development lifecycle, aimed at monitoring the safety and efficacy of medicinal products after they have received regulatory approval and are available in the market. The primary purpose of post-marketing studies is to identify any potential adverse effects, drug interactions, or long-term consequences that may not have been fully evident during clinical trials. While pre-market studies provide valuable information regarding the safety and efficacy of a drug, they often involve a limited population size and a controlled environment, which may not fully capture the complexities of real-world use.

Post-marketing studies serve several essential functions. They enable ongoing assessment of a drug's benefit-risk profile in diverse patient populations, including those with comorbidities or those taking multiple medications. This real-world data is invaluable for informing healthcare professionals and patients about the long-term safety of the product, ultimately contributing to informed decision-making regarding treatment options. Additionally, these studies help identify rare adverse events that may not have been observed in pre-market trials due to insufficient sample sizes or duration of follow-up. By continuously monitoring the safety of drugs, regulatory authorities can take appropriate actions, such as issuing safety alerts, updating labeling information, or even withdrawing a product from the market if necessary.

25.1.2 Differences Between Pre-Market and Post-Market Safety Monitoring

The distinction between pre-market and post-market safety monitoring is significant in understanding how drug safety is evaluated throughout the product lifecycle. Pre-market safety monitoring is primarily conducted during clinical trials, which are designed to assess the safety and efficacy of a drug in a controlled environment. These trials have strict inclusion and exclusion criteria, and participants are closely monitored for any adverse effects. However, pre-market studies may not capture the full range of potential risks associated with a drug, as they often involve a limited number of participants and controlled conditions that may not reflect real-world usage.

In contrast, post-market safety monitoring occurs once a drug is available to the public. It encompasses a broader and more diverse population, including patients with varying health conditions, demographics, and concurrent medications. This expanded monitoring allows for the identification of adverse events that may arise from the drug's use in real-world settings. Post-market surveillance relies on various data sources, including spontaneous reporting systems, electronic health records, and large-scale observational studies, to capture comprehensive safety data. This ongoing assessment is crucial for detecting long-term safety issues and ensuring that healthcare providers have the most current information regarding a drug's safety profile.

25.1.3 Regulatory Requirements for Post-Market Surveillance

Regulatory authorities, such as the FDA, EMA, and CDSCO, have established specific requirements for post-market surveillance to ensure the ongoing safety of medicinal products. These regulations mandate that pharmaceutical companies implement robust pharmacovigilance systems to monitor and report adverse events associated with their products. Companies are required to submit Periodic Safety Update Reports (PSURs) at regular intervals, summarizing the safety data collected since the drug's approval, including any new information that may impact its benefit-risk profile.

Additionally, regulatory authorities may require specific post-marketing studies to further evaluate the safety and efficacy of a drug in diverse populations. These studies can be a condition of approval and must be conducted according to predefined protocols that align with regulatory guidelines. Companies are also responsible for reporting serious adverse events and providing timely updates on safety signals to the regulatory authorities. By adhering to these regulatory requirements, pharmaceutical companies play a vital role in safeguarding public health and ensuring that the risks associated with medicinal products are continuously assessed and communicated.

25.2 Pharmacovigilance in Post-Market Research

25.2.1 Definition and Role of Pharmacovigilance

Pharmacovigilance is defined as the science and activities related to the detection, assessment, understanding, and prevention of adverse effects or any other drug-related problems. Its primary goal is to improve patient safety and ensure that the benefits of a medicinal product outweigh its risks. Pharmacovigilance plays a crucial role in post-market research by continuously monitoring the safety profile of drugs once they are available to the public. It involves the collection and analysis of data regarding adverse events, drug interactions, and other safety concerns that may arise during the use of a drug in the real-world setting.

The role of pharmacovigilance extends beyond merely identifying adverse events; it also involves evaluating the significance of these events in relation to the overall safety profile of the drug. This includes conducting signal detection analyses to identify potential safety issues, as well as risk assessments to determine the need for regulatory actions, such as changes to labeling, additional warnings, or even withdrawal from the market. By systematically monitoring and analyzing safety data, pharmacovigilance contributes to informed decision-making by healthcare providers, patients, and regulatory authorities, ultimately enhancing the safety and efficacy of medicinal products.

25.2.2 Global Pharmacovigilance Systems (FDA MedWatch, EMA, CDSCO)

Pharmacovigilance operates through various global systems designed to ensure the safe use of medicines across different regions. In the United States, the **FDA MedWatch** program serves as a critical component of the pharmacovigilance system, allowing healthcare professionals and the public to report adverse events, product defects, and safety concerns related to FDA-regulated products. The MedWatch system enables the FDA to collect real-time safety data, facilitating rapid assessments and timely communication of safety information to stakeholders.

Similarly, the **European Medicines Agency (EMA)** has established a robust pharmacovigilance framework that includes the **EudraVigilance** database, which collects and analyzes reports of suspected adverse reactions to medicines in the European Economic Area. The EMA plays a vital role in coordinating the safety monitoring of medicinal products across member states, ensuring that relevant safety information is disseminated to healthcare professionals and patients. In India, the **Central Drugs Standard Control Organization (CDSCO)** oversees pharmacovigilance activities through the **Pharmacovigilance Programme of India (PvPI)**, which aims to enhance patient safety by monitoring the safety of drugs on the market.

These global pharmacovigilance systems work collaboratively to ensure that safety data is shared and analyzed, enabling a comprehensive understanding of the safety profiles of medicines. By fostering international collaboration and information sharing, pharmacovigilance enhances the overall effectiveness of drug safety monitoring efforts and promotes public health on a global scale.

25.2.3 Reporting Requirements for Post-Market Studies

Regulatory authorities impose specific reporting requirements on pharmaceutical companies and healthcare professionals involved in post-market studies to ensure timely and accurate reporting of adverse events and safety data. Companies are obligated to report serious adverse events (SAEs) and unexpected adverse reactions associated with their products to the relevant regulatory authorities within defined timeframes. These reporting requirements are essential for maintaining a comprehensive understanding of the safety profile of a drug and for facilitating timely regulatory actions if necessary.

In addition to individual case reports, companies are required to submit periodic safety update reports (PSURs), which summarize the safety data collected during the reporting period. PSURs must include an analysis of the benefit-risk balance, an assessment of new safety signals, and any changes to the product's labeling or risk management strategies. By adhering to these reporting requirements, companies contribute to the ongoing monitoring of drug safety and support the regulatory authorities' efforts to protect public health.

Furthermore, healthcare professionals are encouraged to report any suspected adverse events related to medications they prescribe or administer. This reporting can provide valuable real-world data on drug safety, allowing regulatory authorities to identify trends and potential safety signals that may not have been evident during clinical trials. By fostering a culture of reporting and transparency, regulatory authorities can enhance their pharmacovigilance efforts and ensure the ongoing safety of medicinal products.

25.3 Periodic Safety Update Reports (PSURs)

25.3.1 Structure and Content of PSURs

Periodic Safety Update Reports (PSURs) are critical documents required by regulatory authorities to monitor the ongoing safety profile of medicinal products in the market. The structure of PSURs typically includes a comprehensive summary of safety data collected during a defined reporting period, along with an assessment of the benefit-risk balance of the product. Key components of a PSUR include information on adverse events, changes in the product's safety profile, risk management activities, and any new safety information that may impact the therapeutic use of the drug.

The content of PSURs is guided by regulatory requirements and best practices, ensuring that they provide meaningful and actionable information to regulatory authorities. PSURs must present a clear narrative of the safety data, emphasizing any significant safety signals identified during the reporting period and the implications for patient management and drug utilization. Additionally, the reports should include relevant analyses, such as statistical evaluations of adverse events and comparisons with prior reporting periods, to facilitate the assessment of trends and patterns in safety data.

By adhering to established guidelines for PSUR content and structure, companies can enhance the effectiveness of their safety monitoring efforts and provide regulatory authorities with the information needed to make informed decisions regarding the safety of medicinal products.

25.3.2 Frequency of PSUR Submissions

Regulatory authorities establish specific requirements for the frequency of PSUR submissions to ensure that safety data is reported in a timely manner. The frequency of PSUR submissions may vary depending on the regulatory jurisdiction and the nature of the product. In general, companies are required to submit PSURs at regular intervals, such as every six months during the first two years post-approval and annually thereafter, or according to a schedule agreed upon with the regulatory authority.

This regular submission of PSURs allows regulatory authorities to conduct ongoing evaluations of a drug's safety profile, identifying any emerging safety signals or trends that may necessitate further action. Companies are encouraged to align their PSUR submission timelines with the requirements of the regulatory authorities in the regions where their products are marketed, ensuring compliance and maintaining open lines of communication regarding safety monitoring.

Moreover, the ICH guidelines encourage companies to continuously update their PSURs with relevant safety information as it becomes available, rather than waiting for the scheduled submission date. By adopting a proactive approach to safety reporting, companies can demonstrate their commitment to patient safety and regulatory compliance, fostering trust and transparency with stakeholders.

25.3.3 Regulatory Requirements for PSURs Across Regions

Regulatory requirements for PSURs can vary significantly across different regions, and it is essential for companies to understand and comply with these requirements to ensure successful market access. In the European Union, for example, PSURs must comply with the guidelines outlined in **Directive 2001/83/EC** and the **EudraLex Volume 9A** guidelines, which detail the structure, content, and submission timelines for PSURs. Companies must ensure that their PSURs are in line with the specific expectations of the European Medicines Agency (EMA) and that they address any regional considerations relevant to the product's safety profile.

In the United States, the **FDA** has established its own set of requirements for PSUR submissions, often referred to as **Post-Marketing Safety Reports**. These reports must include a comprehensive overview of adverse event data and any actions taken in response to safety concerns. Companies are responsible for ensuring that their PSURs meet the regulatory expectations of both the FDA and other relevant authorities, such as the **CDSCO** in India, which has its own guidelines and requirements for post-marketing safety reporting.

Navigating these regulatory requirements can be complex, and companies must remain vigilant in staying updated on any changes to guidelines or expectations from regulatory authorities. By doing so, they can ensure that their PSURs are submitted in compliance with regional regulations, ultimately contributing to the ongoing safety monitoring of their medicinal products.

25.4 Risk Management Plans (RMPs)

25.4.1 Developing RMPs for New Medicinal Products

Risk Management Plans (RMPs) are comprehensive documents that outline a proactive approach to identifying, assessing, and mitigating risks associated with a new medicinal product. The development of RMPs is a regulatory requirement for many new drug applications and is crucial for ensuring the ongoing safety of medications in the market. The ICH E2E pharmacovigilance guidelines emphasize the importance of having a structured plan in place to manage potential risks throughout the lifecycle of the drug.

When developing an RMP, researchers must conduct thorough risk assessments to identify potential safety concerns associated with the drug. This involves analyzing data from preclinical and clinical studies, as well as considering real-world evidence and existing safety data from similar products. Based on this analysis, researchers should outline strategies for minimizing identified risks, including risk communication plans, safety monitoring activities, and educational initiatives for healthcare providers and patients.

Moreover, RMPs should include contingency plans for responding to emerging safety signals or adverse events that may arise post-marketing. This proactive approach to risk management not only enhances patient safety but also fosters regulatory compliance and builds trust with stakeholders, including healthcare providers, regulatory authorities, and patients.

25.4.2 Implementation of RMPs Post-Approval

Once an RMP has been developed and submitted as part of the regulatory approval process, its effective implementation is crucial for ensuring the safety of the medicinal product in the market. The implementation of an RMP involves executing the strategies and activities outlined in the plan, including ongoing safety monitoring, risk communication, and educational initiatives. Companies must establish dedicated teams responsible for overseeing the implementation of the RMP and ensuring that all activities are conducted in accordance with regulatory requirements and best practices.

One of the key components of RMP implementation is the establishment of robust pharmacovigilance systems to monitor the safety of the product continuously. This includes collecting and analyzing data on adverse events, conducting signal detection analyses, and maintaining open lines of communication with regulatory authorities regarding any emerging safety concerns. Companies are encouraged to engage with healthcare professionals and patients to disseminate information about potential risks and safety measures associated with the product.

Additionally, the effectiveness of the RMP should be regularly evaluated, and companies should be prepared to adapt their risk management strategies based on new safety data or changes in the regulatory landscape. This ongoing evaluation and adaptation contribute to the continuous improvement of risk management practices, ensuring that patient safety remains the top priority throughout the lifecycle of the medicinal product.

25.4.3 Regulatory Oversight of RMPs

Regulatory authorities play a vital role in overseeing the implementation of Risk Management Plans (RMPs) and ensuring that companies adhere to the strategies outlined in their plans. This oversight includes reviewing RMPs submitted during the regulatory approval process, evaluating their adequacy, and providing feedback to companies. Once a product is on the market, regulatory authorities continue to monitor the implementation of RMPs through various mechanisms, including periodic safety update reports (PSURs), inspections, and compliance audits.

Regulatory agencies, such as the FDA, EMA, and CDSCO, may require companies to submit regular updates on the status of their RMPs and any changes made in response to new safety data. These updates allow regulatory authorities to assess the effectiveness of risk management strategies and determine whether additional actions are needed to ensure the safety of the product. If regulatory authorities identify deficiencies or non-compliance with RMP requirements, they may take corrective actions, which could include additional regulatory scrutiny, restrictions on the product's use, or even withdrawal from the market.

Moreover, the regulatory oversight of RMPs emphasizes the importance of collaboration between companies and regulatory authorities in ensuring the ongoing safety of medicinal products. By working together, stakeholders can enhance the effectiveness of risk management efforts and contribute to the overall safety and efficacy of drugs in the market. This collaborative approach is essential for maintaining public trust in the pharmaceutical industry and ensuring that patient safety remains a top priority.

25.5 Real-World Evidence in Post-Market Surveillance

25.5.1 Role of Real-World Evidence in Drug Safety

Real-world evidence (RWE) plays an increasingly vital role in the post-market surveillance of medicinal products, providing insights into the safety and efficacy of drugs as they are used in diverse patient populations outside of controlled clinical trial environments. RWE encompasses data derived from various sources, including electronic health records, insurance claims databases, patient registries, and patient-reported outcomes. By analyzing this data, researchers and regulatory authorities can gain a comprehensive understanding of how a drug performs in real-world settings, identifying potential safety concerns and efficacy patterns that may not have been evident during pre-market trials.

The significance of RWE in drug safety monitoring lies in its ability to capture long-term outcomes and rare adverse events that might not be detected in traditional clinical trials due to limited sample sizes and short follow-up durations. For instance, RWE can help identify safety signals related to specific patient populations, such as the elderly or those with comorbid conditions, providing essential information that informs clinical practice and regulatory decision-making. By integrating RWE into post-market safety assessments, regulatory authorities can make more informed evaluations of a drug's benefit-risk profile, ultimately enhancing patient safety.

25.5.2 Data Collection from Real-World Use

The collection of data from real-world use is a fundamental component of leveraging RWE for post-market surveillance. Various methodologies can be employed to gather this data, including observational studies, cohort studies, and patient registries. These approaches allow researchers to monitor drug utilization patterns, treatment adherence, and adverse events in large, diverse populations over extended periods. Additionally, patient-reported outcomes collected through surveys and digital health applications can provide valuable insights into the subjective experiences of patients using a drug, contributing to a more holistic understanding of its safety and effectiveness.

It is essential for organizations conducting real-world data collection to ensure that robust data governance practices are in place. This includes implementing measures to protect patient confidentiality, ensure data accuracy, and maintain compliance with regulatory requirements. By establishing reliable data collection systems, researchers can produce high-quality evidence that enhances the understanding of drug safety and informs regulatory actions as needed.

Moreover, collaboration among stakeholders—such as healthcare providers, researchers, regulatory authorities, and patients—is crucial for effective data collection. Engaging with these stakeholders can facilitate the sharing of information and resources, ultimately leading to a more comprehensive understanding of the drug's performance in real-world settings.

25.5.3 Incorporating Real-World Data into Regulatory Submissions

Integrating real-world data (RWD) into regulatory submissions is a growing trend that enhances the robustness of safety evaluations for medicinal products. Regulatory authorities, such as the FDA and EMA, recognize the value of RWD in providing additional context for clinical trial data, particularly when assessing the long-term safety and effectiveness of a drug. The incorporation of RWD into regulatory submissions can support the identification of safety signals, inform post-marketing commitments, and assist in risk-benefit assessments.

When submitting RWD to regulatory authorities, companies must ensure that the data is collected using scientifically sound methodologies and that it complies with regulatory standards. Clear documentation of the data collection process, analytical methods, and interpretations is essential for regulatory review. Companies should also outline how the RWD complements existing clinical trial data and contributes to the overall understanding of the drug's safety profile.

Furthermore, collaboration with regulatory agencies during the submission process can facilitate the acceptance and integration of RWD. By proactively engaging with regulators and addressing any concerns or questions about the RWD, companies can enhance the credibility of their submissions and promote informed regulatory decision-making. This collaboration ultimately contributes to the ongoing monitoring of drug safety and the continuous improvement of patient care.

25.6 Case Studies in Post-Marketing Safety Surveillance

25.6.1 Successful Post-Marketing Surveillance Programs

Several case studies illustrate the effectiveness of post-marketing surveillance programs in identifying safety issues and enhancing drug safety. For instance, the **FDA's MedWatch program** has successfully facilitated the reporting of adverse events and safety signals related to various medications. By encouraging healthcare professionals and patients to report suspected adverse reactions, the program has contributed to the identification of rare but serious side effects that may not have been captured during clinical trials.

Another notable example is the **European Medicines Agency's EudraVigilance** system, which collects and analyzes reports of suspected adverse drug reactions across the European Economic Area. The system allows for efficient signal detection and provides a platform for regulatory authorities to monitor the safety of marketed products continuously. These successful post-marketing surveillance programs highlight the importance of robust reporting mechanisms and the active involvement of stakeholders in ensuring drug safety in real-world settings.

Additionally, the integration of real-world evidence into post-marketing surveillance has led to significant advancements in understanding drug safety. By leveraging data from electronic health records and patient registries, regulatory authorities can gain insights into the long-term effects of medications and make informed decisions regarding risk management strategies. The success of these programs underscores the value of ongoing safety monitoring and the need for collaborative efforts among regulatory authorities, healthcare providers, and patients.

25.6.2 Regulatory Interventions Based on Post-Market Data

Regulatory authorities have demonstrated their responsiveness to post-market data through various interventions aimed at ensuring patient safety. When safety signals are identified through post-marketing surveillance, regulatory agencies may issue safety alerts, update labeling information, or recommend additional studies to further assess the safety profile of a product. For example, the FDA has been known to require risk evaluation and mitigation strategies (REMS) for certain medications that pose significant safety risks based on post-marketing data.

A notable case involved the pain medication **oxycodone**, which was found to have a higher risk of addiction and overdose than previously understood. In response to emerging data, the FDA implemented risk management strategies, including enhanced labeling and educational initiatives to inform healthcare providers and patients about the associated risks. Such regulatory interventions not only protect patients but also reinforce the importance of continuous safety monitoring in the post-marketing phase.

Furthermore, the implementation of risk communication strategies, such as safety announcements and public health advisories, allows regulatory authorities to inform healthcare professionals and the public about potential safety concerns associated with specific products. By taking proactive measures in response to post-marketing data, regulatory authorities can foster greater awareness and encourage safe prescribing practices.

25.6.3 Lessons Learned from Adverse Drug Reaction (ADR) Reports

Adverse drug reaction (ADR) reports play a crucial role in post-marketing safety surveillance, providing valuable insights into the real-world effects of medications. Analyzing ADR reports can uncover patterns that inform regulatory actions and improve drug safety. One lesson learned from ADR reports is the importance of comprehensive reporting mechanisms that allow for timely identification of safety signals. For instance, the case of the anticoagulant **warfarin** demonstrated that ADR reports were essential in understanding the drug's interaction with various medications, leading to updated prescribing guidelines to mitigate potential risks.

Additionally, the evaluation of ADR reports can highlight gaps in knowledge regarding specific populations, such as the elderly or patients with comorbidities. This understanding can guide future research efforts and inform the development of targeted interventions to enhance patient safety. By analyzing these reports, researchers and regulatory authorities can identify risk factors and improve the overall understanding of how medications impact diverse patient groups.

Moreover, lessons learned from ADR reports emphasize the need for effective communication between regulatory authorities, healthcare providers, and patients. Ensuring that healthcare professionals are informed about potential risks associated with medications allows for better risk management in clinical practice. Encouraging patients to report any adverse effects they experience also fosters a culture of transparency and accountability in drug safety monitoring. By learning from ADR reports and implementing these lessons, stakeholders can work collaboratively to enhance the safety of medicinal products and protect public health.

Review Questions

1. What is the primary purpose of post-market surveillance in drug development?
2. How does post-market surveillance differ from pre-market safety monitoring?
3. Define pharmacovigilance and explain its role in post-market research.
4. What are Periodic Safety Update Reports (PSURs), and how are they structured?
5. How do Risk Management Plans (RMPs) contribute to the long-term safety of approved drugs?
6. What is the role of real-world evidence in post-market surveillance?
7. How do global pharmacovigilance systems, such as FDA MedWatch and EMA, handle adverse event reporting?
8. Discuss case studies where post-marketing surveillance data led to significant regulatory actions.

Glossary Of Key Terms And Definitions

Adverse Drug Reaction (ADR): Any harmful or unintended response to a drug that occurs at doses normally used in humans for prophylaxis, diagnosis, or treatment.

Active Control: A treatment that is used as a comparison in clinical trials, which may be a standard therapy or a drug known to produce a specific effect.

Allocation Concealment: A method used to prevent selection bias by ensuring that the random assignment of participants to treatment groups is unknown to those enrolling participants.

Approval: The official authorization by regulatory authorities allowing a drug to be marketed and sold.

Assent: The agreement of a child or an individual with diminished capacity to participate in a clinical trial, which complements parental or guardian consent.

Audit: A systematic and independent examination of trial-related activities and documents to determine whether the study was conducted according to the protocol, GCP, and regulatory requirements.

Blinding: A technique used in clinical trials to prevent participants or researchers from knowing which treatment participants receive to reduce bias.

Case Control Study: An observational study that compares individuals with a specific condition (cases) to those without (controls) to identify risk factors or causes.

Clinical Investigation: A systematic study designed to assess the safety or effectiveness of a medical product.

Clinical Trial Protocol: A document that outlines the objectives, design, methodology, statistical considerations, and organization of a clinical trial.

Cohort Study: An observational study that follows a group of individuals over time to assess the effects of certain exposures on outcomes.

Confidentiality: The ethical and legal obligation to protect the personal information of research participants.

Control Group: A group of participants in a clinical trial that does not receive the experimental treatment but instead receives a placebo or standard treatment for comparison.

Contract Research Organization (CRO): A company that provides outsourced research services to the pharmaceutical, biotechnology, and medical device industries.

Data Safety Monitoring Board (DSMB): An independent group of experts that monitors patient safety and treatment efficacy during a clinical trial.

Dose-Response Relationship: The relationship between the dose of a drug and the magnitude of its effect.

Drug Interaction: A situation in which a drug affects the activity of another drug when both are administered together.

Ethics Committee: An independent body that reviews and approves research studies to ensure that they are ethical and that participants' rights are protected.

Efficacy: The ability of a drug to produce a desired therapeutic effect under ideal conditions.

Equipoise: A state of uncertainty about the best treatment option, which justifies the ethical conduct of a clinical trial.

Experimental Group: The group of participants in a clinical trial that receives the treatment being tested.

External Validity: The extent to which the results of a study can be generalized to settings, people, times, and measures beyond the study conditions.

Geriatric Population: Older adults, typically aged 65 and above, who may have different physiological responses to medications compared to younger individuals.

Good Clinical Practice (GCP): A set of international ethical and scientific quality standards for designing, conducting, recording, and reporting trials that involve the participation of human subjects.

Informed Consent: A process by which participants voluntarily confirm their willingness to participate in a clinical trial after being informed of all aspects that may affect their decision.

Institutional Review Board (IRB): An independent committee that reviews research studies to ensure that they are ethically sound and that participants' rights are protected.

Investigational New Drug (IND): A request submitted to the FDA to begin human clinical trials of a new drug.

Monitoring: The ongoing oversight of a clinical trial to ensure compliance with the protocol and regulations, as well as the safety of

GLOSSARY OF KEY TERMS AND DEFINITIONS

participants.

Multinational Trial: A clinical trial conducted in multiple countries to evaluate the effects of a drug in diverse populations.

NDA (New Drug Application): A formal proposal submitted to regulatory authorities for approval to market a new drug.

Observational Study: A study in which researchers observe and collect data on participants without manipulating any variables.

Placebo: An inactive substance or treatment designed to resemble the drug being tested, used as a control in clinical trials.

Post-Marketing Surveillance: The monitoring of a drug's safety and effectiveness after it has been approved for use.

Pharmacovigilance: The science and activities related to the detection, assessment, understanding, and prevention of adverse effects or any other drug-related problems.

Protocol Deviation: Any change, divergence, or departure from the study design or procedures outlined in the clinical trial protocol.

Randomization: The process of assigning participants to different treatment groups in a way that eliminates bias, often by using random number generation.

Regulatory Authority: An official governmental body responsible for overseeing the safety, efficacy, and quality of drugs and medical products.

Risk Management Plan (RMP): A document that outlines the risk assessment and management strategies for a drug to ensure its safe use post-marketing.

Serious Adverse Event (SAE): An adverse event that results in death, is life-threatening, requires hospitalization, or results in significant disability or incapacity.

Signal Detection: The process of identifying potential safety signals from adverse event reports that may indicate a new or increased risk associated with a drug.

Study Endpoint: A measurable outcome used to evaluate the effectiveness of a treatment in a clinical trial.

Study Population: The group of individuals eligible to participate in a clinical trial, usually defined by specific inclusion and exclusion criteria.

Surrogate Endpoint: A laboratory measure or a physical sign that is used as a substitute for a clinically meaningful endpoint.

Therapeutic Window: The range of doses of a drug that produces a therapeutic effect without causing significant adverse effects.

Treatment Group: A group of participants in a clinical trial that receives the investigational treatment.

Vulnerable Population: Groups of individuals who may be at increased risk of coercion or undue influence when participating in research, such as children, the elderly, or economically disadvantaged individuals.

Withdrawal: The process of removing a participant from a clinical trial, either voluntarily or involuntarily.

World Health Organization (WHO): A specialized agency of the United Nations responsible for international public health, including guidelines for clinical research.

Zygosity: The genetic similarity or difference between individuals, particularly relevant in studies involving twins.

Absorption: The process by which a drug enters the bloodstream after administration.

Bioavailability: The proportion of a drug that enters the circulation when introduced into the body and is made available for activity.

Clinical Trial Registry: A public database that provides information on clinical trials, including their purpose, methodology, and outcomes.

Data Integrity: The accuracy and consistency of data collected during a clinical trial.

Ethical Approval: Authorization granted by an ethics committee or institutional review board to conduct a study based on its ethical considerations.

Field Study: Research conducted in a natural or uncontrolled environment to observe real-world effects.

Good Manufacturing Practice (GMP): Regulations that require manufacturers to ensure that their products are consistently high in quality.

Investigational Product: A pharmaceutical form of an active ingredient or placebo being tested or used as a reference in a clinical trial.

Labeling: Information provided with a drug product, including indications, dosage, side effects, and other important information.

Medical Device: Any instrument, apparatus, or device intended for use in diagnosing, preventing, or treating medical conditions.

Non-Compliance: Failure to adhere to the clinical trial protocol, GCP guidelines, or regulatory requirements.

Outcome Measures: The primary and secondary endpoints used to assess the efficacy and safety of a treatment in a clinical trial.

GLOSSARY OF KEY TERMS AND DEFINITIONS

Patient Reported Outcomes (PROs): Reports directly from patients about how they feel or function in relation to a health condition and its therapy.

Quality of Life (QoL): A measure of the general well-being of individuals and societies, often used as an endpoint in clinical trials.

Research Ethics: A set of principles that guide the conduct of research involving human participants to ensure their rights and welfare are protected.

Safety Profile: A comprehensive description of the safety and efficacy data associated with a drug or treatment.

Therapeutic Class: A category of drugs that share similar pharmacological properties or therapeutic effects.

Validation: The process of confirming that a method or instrument measures what it is intended to measure.

Withdrawal Syndrome: A group of symptoms that occur upon the abrupt discontinuation of a medication.

Trial Monitoring: The ongoing oversight of a clinical trial to ensure compliance with the protocol and regulatory requirements.

Well-Being: A state of health, happiness, and prosperity that may be evaluated in clinical trials, particularly in patient-reported outcomes.

Accrual: The process of enrolling participants into a clinical trial.

Biologics: Products derived from living organisms that are used to treat diseases, including vaccines and gene therapies.

Chronic Condition: A long-lasting health condition that may not have a cure, often requiring ongoing management.

Endpoint: A primary or secondary outcome used to assess the effectiveness of a treatment in a clinical trial.

Feasibility Study: An initial assessment to determine whether a proposed study is viable in terms of logistics, resources, and participant recruitment.

Good Laboratory Practice (GLP): Principles that ensure the quality and integrity of laboratory studies used to support research or marketing applications.

Human Subject: An individual who participates in research and provides data or biological samples for analysis.

In Vitro: Referring to studies or processes conducted outside a living organism, often in a laboratory setting.

GLOSSARY OF KEY TERMS AND DEFINITIONS

In Vivo: Referring to studies or processes conducted within a living organism.

Manufacturing Authorization: The official approval required to produce and market a pharmaceutical product.

Non-Interventional Study: A study in which the investigator does not assign participants to specific interventions, but instead observes the effects of already prescribed treatments.

Orphan Drug: A medication developed for a rare disease that affects a small percentage of the population.

Phase I Trial: A clinical trial conducted to evaluate the safety, tolerability, pharmacokinetics, and pharmacodynamics of a drug in a small group of participants.

Phase II Trial: A clinical trial designed to assess the efficacy and further evaluate the safety of a drug in a larger group of participants.

Phase III Trial: A large-scale clinical trial that compares the new drug to standard treatments, designed to confirm efficacy and monitor side effects.

Phase IV Trial: Post-marketing studies conducted to gather additional information on the drug's risks, benefits, and optimal use.

Randomized Controlled Trial (RCT): A study in which participants are randomly assigned to receive either the experimental treatment or a control, allowing for comparison of outcomes.

Safety Signal: Information that arises from one or multiple sources that suggests a new potentially causal association between a product and an adverse event.

Translational Research: Research that aims to bridge the gap between basic science and clinical application, facilitating the development of new therapies.

Vaccination: The administration of a vaccine to stimulate an individual's immune system to develop adaptive immunity to a pathogen.

Zoster Vaccine: A vaccine designed to prevent herpes zoster (shingles), a painful rash caused by reactivation of the varicella-zoster virus.

Biostatistics: The application of statistical methods to biological, health, and clinical research.

Clinical Endpoint: A characteristic or variable that reflects how a patient feels, functions, or survives, used to determine the effectiveness of a treatment.

GLOSSARY OF KEY TERMS AND DEFINITIONS

Ethical Dilemma: A situation in which a choice must be made between conflicting ethical principles.

Guideline: A document that provides recommendations for the conduct of research, often developed by regulatory authorities or professional organizations.

Longitudinal Study: A study that follows the same subjects over a period of time to observe changes or developments.

Meta-Analysis: A statistical technique that combines the results of multiple studies to arrive at a comprehensive conclusion.

Quality Control: A system for maintaining standards in manufactured products by testing a sample of the output against the specification.

Safety Monitoring Plan: A plan outlining how the safety of participants will be monitored throughout a clinical trial.

Therapeutic Index: The ratio of the toxic dose to the therapeutic dose of a drug, indicating its safety margin.

Utilization Review: A process that evaluates the necessity, appropriateness, and efficiency of healthcare services.

Bias: Any systematic error in the design, conduct, or analysis of a clinical trial that leads to incorrect conclusions.

Confounding Variable: An extraneous variable that correlates with both the dependent and independent variables, potentially misleading results.

Effect Size: A quantitative measure of the magnitude of a phenomenon, often used in the context of clinical trials to assess the strength of treatment effects.

Heuristic Evaluation: A usability inspection method for computer software that helps identify usability problems in a user interface.

Intervention: A treatment or action taken to improve a health outcome in clinical research.

Longitudinal Cohort Study: A study that follows a group of people over time to determine how certain factors affect health outcomes.

Meta-Data: Data that provides information about other data, such as the method of collection or the context of a study.

Observational Cohort Study: A type of study that follows a group of people with shared characteristics to see how different exposures affect their health.

Peer Review: A process where researchers evaluate the work of their peers to ensure quality and credibility before publication.

Randomized Assignment: The process of randomly assigning participants to different treatment groups to eliminate bias.

Systematic Review: A review that summarizes the results of available studies on a specific topic using a structured methodology.

Treatment Efficacy: The ability of a treatment to provide a beneficial effect when administered under ideal conditions.

Volunteer Subject: An individual who agrees to participate in a clinical trial, often compensated for their involvement.

Crossover Study: A clinical trial design in which participants receive multiple interventions in a sequential manner, allowing them to serve as their own control.

Exposure: Refers to the participants' contact with a treatment, drug, or environmental factor being studied.

Informed Consent Form (ICF): A document that outlines the details of a study, ensuring participants are fully informed about their involvement.

Clinical Research Associate (CRA): A professional responsible for monitoring clinical trials to ensure compliance with regulatory requirements.

Subcutaneous: Referring to a method of drug administration involving injection into the fatty tissue just under the skin.

Investigational Device Exemption (IDE): An FDA regulation that allows an investigational medical device to be used in a clinical study.

Study Arm: A specific group of participants in a clinical trial receiving a particular intervention.

Toxicology: The study of the adverse effects of substances on living organisms.

U.S. Food and Drug Administration (FDA): The federal agency responsible for regulating food, drugs, and medical devices in the United States.

European Medicines Agency (EMA): The agency responsible for the scientific evaluation, supervision, and safety monitoring of medicines in the European Union.

Central Drugs Standard Control Organization (CDSCO): The regulatory authority for pharmaceuticals and medical devices in India.

Ethical Dilemma: A situation in which one must choose between conflicting ethical principles or values.

Health Technology Assessment (HTA): A systematic evaluation of properties, effects, and impacts of health technology, including medical

GLOSSARY OF KEY TERMS AND DEFINITIONS

devices and drugs.

Medication Error: A preventable event that may cause or lead to inappropriate medication use or patient harm.

Patient Safety: The prevention of harm to patients during the provision of health care.

Research Protocol: A document that describes the objectives, design, methodology, statistical considerations, and organization of a clinical trial.

Systematic Review: A literature review that collects and critically analyzes multiple research studies or papers.

Withdrawal Symptoms: Physical or mental symptoms that occur when a person stops taking a medication they are dependent on.

Healthcare Professional: A person who provides health care services, including doctors, nurses, pharmacists, and therapists.

Digital Health: The use of digital technologies to facilitate health management, including telemedicine and mobile health applications.

Clinical Significance: The practical importance of a treatment effect, indicating whether it has a real impact on daily life.

Experimental Design: The plan for conducting an experiment, including the selection of participants, treatments, and measurement of outcomes.

Safety Monitoring Board: A group responsible for overseeing the safety of participants during a clinical trial.

Dose Escalation: A method used in Phase I trials where the dose of a drug is gradually increased to determine the maximum tolerated dose.

Health Literacy: The ability of individuals to access, understand, and use health information to make informed health decisions.

Clinical Epidemiology: The study of the determinants and effects of health and disease in populations.

Open Label Study: A type of clinical trial where both the researchers and participants know which treatment is being administered.

Qualitative Research: Research that seeks to understand human behavior and the reasons that govern such behavior.

Quantitative Research: Research that relies on numerical data and statistical analysis to draw conclusions.

Serum Half-Life: The time it takes for the concentration of a drug in the blood to reduce to half its original value.

Therapeutic Class: A group of medications that work in a similar way or treat the same condition.

GLOSSARY OF KEY TERMS AND DEFINITIONS

Adherence: The extent to which patients follow their prescribed treatment regimens.

Compliance: The degree to which a patient correctly follows medical advice and treatment plans.

Clinical Outcome: A measurable change in health or quality of life resulting from an intervention.

Efficacy Trials: Clinical studies designed to test whether a treatment works under ideal circumstances.

Post-Marketing Studies: Research conducted after a drug has been approved, focusing on its long-term safety and effectiveness.

Bibliography

1. Sneader, W. (2005). Drug discovery: A history. John Wiley & Sons.
2. Friedman, L. M., Furberg, C. D., DeMets, D. L., Reboussin, D. M., & Granger, C. B. (2015). Fundamentals of clinical trials (4th ed.). Springer International Publishing.
3. Daemmrich, A. (2004). Pharmacopolitics: Drug regulation in the United States and Germany. UNC Press Books.
4. Abraham, J., & Lewis, G. (2000). Regulating medicines in Europe: Competition, expertise and public health. Routledge.
5. Emanuel, E. J., Wendler, D., & Grady, C. (2000). What makes clinical research ethical? JAMA, 283(20), 2701-2711. https://doi.org/10.1001/jama.283.20.2701
6. Beecher, H. K. (1966). Ethics and clinical research. New England Journal of Medicine, 274(24), 1354-1360. https://doi.org/10.1056/nejm196606162742405
7. Grimes, D. A., & Schulz, K. F. (2002). Descriptive studies: What they can and cannot do. The Lancet, 359(9301), 145-149. https://doi.org/10.1016/S0140-6736(02)07373-7
8. Ioannidis, J. P. A. (2005). Why most published research findings are false. PLOS Medicine, 2(8), e124. https://doi.org/10.1371/journal.pmed.0020124
9. DiMasi, J. A., Grabowski, H. G., & Hansen, R. W. (2016). Innovation in the pharmaceutical industry: New estimates of R&D costs. Journal of Health Economics, 47, 20-33. https://doi.org/10.1016/j.jhealeco.2016.01.012
10. Kola, I., & Landis, J. (2004). Can the pharmaceutical industry reduce attrition rates? Nature Reviews Drug Discovery, 3(8), 711-715. https://doi.org/10.1038/nrd1470
11. Fogel, D. B. (2018). Factors associated with clinical trials that fail and opportunities for improving the likelihood of success: A review. Contemporary Clinical Trials Communications, 11, 156-164. https://doi.org/10.1016/j.conctc.2018.08.001
12. Arrowsmith, J. (2011). Phase II failures: 2008–2010. Nature Reviews Drug Discovery, 10(5), 328-329. https://doi.org/10.1038/nrd3439
13. Roberts, T. G., Goulart, B. H., Squitieri, L., Stallings, S. C., Halpern, E. F.,

Chabner, B. A., & Clark, J. W. (2004). Trends in the risks and benefits to patients with cancer participating in phase 1 clinical trials. Journal of the American Medical Association, 292(17), 2130-2140. https://doi.org/10.1001/jama.292.17.2130

14. Chiba, K., Tanigawa, T., & Inoue, Y. (2009). Pharmacodynamic studies and dose-ranging studies in phase II trials. Current Clinical Pharmacology, 4(2), 87-94. https://doi.org/10.2174/157488409788486596

15. Mullard, A. (2016). A decade of phase II failures. Nature Reviews Drug Discovery, 15(7), 449-450. https://doi.org/10.1038/nrd.2016.152

16. Packer, M., O'Connor, C. M., Ghali, J. K., Pressler, M. L., Carson, P. E., Belkin, R. N., & Califf, R. M. (2002). Effect of amlodipine on morbidity and mortality in severe chronic heart failure. The New England Journal of Medicine, 346(23), 1846-1853. https://doi.org/10.1056/nejmoa022171

17. Giezen, T. J., Mantel-Teeuwisse, A. K., & Leufkens, H. G. M. (2008). Pharmacovigilance of biopharmaceuticals: Challenges remain. Drug Safety, 31(2), 99-107. https://doi.org/10.2165/00002018-200831020-00002

18. Burt, T., & Yoshida, K. (2014). Pharmacokinetics in early-phase trials: Considerations in study design and conduct. Clinical Pharmacology & Therapeutics, 95(2), 135-141. https://doi.org/10.1038/clpt.2013.212

19. Waller, P. (2010). An introduction to pharmacovigilance. Wiley-Blackwell.

20. Edwards, I. R., & Aronson, J. K. (2000). Adverse drug reactions: Definitions, diagnosis, and management. The Lancet, 356(9237), 1255-1259. https://doi.org/10.1016/S0140-6736(00)02799-9

21. Strom, B. L. (2006). Real-world evidence in regulatory decision making. New England Journal of Medicine, 355(18), 1786-1789. https://doi.org/10.1056/NEJMp068207

22. Beninger, P. (2018). Pharmacovigilance: An overview. Clinical Therapeutics, 40(12), 1991-2004. https://doi.org/10.1016/j.clinthera.2018.11.014

23. Hartmann, K., & Doser, A. (2005). Post-marketing safety and surveillance of pharmaceutical products. Clinical Pharmacokinetics, 44(5), 431-433. https://doi.org/10.2165/00003088-200544050-00001

24. Mann, R. D., & Andrews, E. B. (2007). Pharmacovigilance. John Wiley & Sons.

25. Moore, T. J., Furberg, C. D., & Mattison, D. R. (2017). The risk of polypharmacy and adverse drug reactions in older adults. Journal of the American Medical Association, 318(17), 1700-1702. https://doi.org/10.1001/jama.2017.15040
26. Faris, O., & Shuren, J. (2017). An FDA viewpoint on unique considerations for medical-device clinical trials. The New England Journal of Medicine, 376(14), 1350-1357. https://doi.org/10.1056/NEJMp1701981
27. von Tigerstrom, B. (2017). Regulatory challenges for medical devices in Europe and the United States. European Journal of Risk Regulation, 8(1), 76-87. https://doi.org/10.1017/err.2017.6
28. Katz, J. (1992). The Nuremberg Code and the Nuremberg Trial: A reappraisal. The Journal of the American Medical Association, 276(20), 1662-1666. https://doi.org/10.1001/jama.1992.03420200044025
29. Reverby, S. M. (2009). Examining Tuskegee: The Infamous Syphilis Study and Its Legacy. The University of North Carolina Press.
30. World Medical Association. (2013). Declaration of Helsinki: Ethical principles for medical research involving human subjects. JAMA, 310(20), 2191-2194. https://doi.org/10.1001/jama.2013.281053
31. International Conference on Harmonisation. (1996). Guideline for Good Clinical Practice E6(R1). ICH.
32. Gifford, F. (2011). Randomization and the ethics of randomized clinical trials. Bioethics, 25(7), 379-387. https://doi.org/10.1111/j.1467-8519.2010.01829.x
33. Beecher, H. K. (1955). The powerful placebo. JAMA, 159(17), 1602-1606. https://doi.org/10.1001/jama.1955.02960340022006
34. Benedetti, F., Mayberg, H. S., Wager, T. D., Stohler, C. S., & Zubieta, J. K. (2005). Neurobiological mechanisms of the placebo effect. The Journal of Neuroscience, 25(45), 10390-10402. https://doi.org/10.1523/jneurosci.3458-05.2005
35. Smyth, R. L., & Weindling, A. M. (2002). Research in children: Ethical and scientific aspects. The Lancet, 359(9300), 1250-1255. https://doi.org/10.1016/S0140-6736(02)08270-9
36. Rees, S. (2003). Ethical issues in the inclusion of women in clinical trials. The Lancet, 361(9365), 495-496. https://doi.org/10.1016/S0140-6736(03)12428-0
37. Council for International Organizations of Medical Sciences. (2016). International Ethical Guidelines for Health-Related Research Involving

Humans. CIOMS.
38. Friedman, L. M., Furberg, C. D., DeMets, D. L., Reboussin, D. M., & Granger, C. B. (2015). Fundamentals of clinical trials (4th ed.). Springer International Publishing.

Chapter Wise Contents

Chapter 1: Introduction to Clinical Research and Drug Development
   1.1 History of Clinical Research and Drug Development

- 1.1.1 Early drug discovery methods
- 1.1.2 Milestones in clinical research
- 1.1.3 Evolution of drug development regulations

   1.2 Ethical Considerations in Clinical Research

- 1.2.1 Importance of ethics in clinical research
- 1.2.2 Impact of unethical research (examples: Tuskegee, Thalidomide)
- 1.2.3 Development of international ethical guidelines

   1.3 Different Types of Clinical Studies

- 1.3.1 Observational studies
- 1.3.2 Interventional studies
- 1.3.3 Comparative studies (case-control, cohort, randomized controlled trials)

   1.4 Drug Development Process Overview

- 1.4.1 Pre-clinical trials
- 1.4.2 Clinical trials
- 1.4.3 Drug approval and marketing

   1.5 Challenges in Clinical Drug Development

- 1.5.1 Time and cost factors
- 1.5.2 Regulatory hurdles
- 1.5.3 Patient recruitment and retention

   1.6 Globalization of Clinical Trials

- 1.6.1 Multinational trials

- 1.6.2 Regulatory harmonization
- 1.6.3 Impact of globalization on trial design and outcomes

Chapter 2: Phases of Clinical Trials
2.1 Overview of Clinical Trial Phases

- 2.1.1 Introduction to clinical trial phases
- 2.1.2 Differences between trial phases
- 2.1.3 Importance of sequential progression through phases

2.2 Phase 0 Clinical Trials

- 2.2.1 Role of Phase 0 trials in drug development
- 2.2.2 Micro-dosing studies
- 2.2.3 Exploratory IND (Investigational New Drug) applications

2.3 Phase I Clinical Trials

- 2.3.1 Key objectives: Safety and dosing
- 2.3.2 Single ascending dose (SAD) studies
- 2.3.3 Multiple ascending dose (MAD) studies

2.4 Phase II Clinical Trials

- 2.4.1 Proof of concept studies
- 2.4.2 Dose-ranging studies
- 2.4.3 Safety and efficacy balance

2.5 Phase III Clinical Trials

- 2.5.1 Pivotal trials for regulatory approval
- 2.5.2 Multi-center and multinational trials
- 2.5.3 Registration studies and global trials

2.6 Phase IV Clinical Trials (Post-Marketing)

- 2.6.1 Post-marketing surveillance
- 2.6.2 Pharmacovigilance

- 2.6.3 Real-world evidence and long-term safety data

Chapter 3: Phase 0 Studies
3.1 Definition and Purpose of Phase 0 Studies

- 3.1.1 Role of Phase 0 in early drug development
- 3.1.2 Differences from Phase I trials
- 3.1.3 Regulatory requirements for Phase 0 studies

3.2 Micro-Dosing in Phase 0 Trials

- 3.2.1 Concept of micro-dosing
- 3.2.2 Ethical and safety considerations
- 3.2.3 Applications of micro-dosing in drug discovery

3.3 Exploratory IND Applications

- 3.3.1 Requirements for an exploratory IND
- 3.3.2 Key regulatory approvals needed
- 3.3.3 Advantages of exploratory IND applications

3.4 Study Design in Phase 0 Trials

- 3.4.1 Participant selection
- 3.4.2 Drug administration and dosing strategies
- 3.4.3 Data collection and analysis

3.5 Limitations of Phase 0 Trials

- 3.5.1 Limited sample size and power
- 3.5.2 Restrictions in data applicability
- 3.5.3 Ethical challenges

3.6 Regulatory Aspects of Phase 0 Trials

- 3.6.1 Regulatory agencies and Phase 0 trials
- 3.6.2 Reporting requirements
- 3.6.3 Comparison of Phase 0 regulations in different regions

Chapter 4: Phase I Studies
4.1 Objectives of Phase I Trials

- 4.1.1 Safety assessment
- 4.1.2 Determination of appropriate dosing
- 4.1.3 Pharmacokinetic and pharmacodynamic evaluation

4.2 Types of Phase I Trials

- 4.2.1 Single ascending dose (SAD) studies
- 4.2.2 Multiple ascending dose (MAD) studies
- 4.2.3 Special studies (food effect, drug-drug interaction)

4.3 Dose Escalation and Safety Monitoring

- 4.3.1 Dose escalation methods
- 4.3.2 Maximally tolerated dose (MTD) determination
- 4.3.3 Continuous safety monitoring protocols

4.4 Pharmacokinetics and Pharmacodynamics in Phase I

- 4.4.1 PK/PD endpoints
- 4.4.2 Role of bioavailability and bioequivalence
- 4.4.3 Interpretation of PK/PD data

4.5 Ethical Considerations in Phase I Studies

- 4.5.1 Participant safety and informed consent
- 4.5.2 Ethical approval processes
- 4.5.3 Protecting vulnerable populations

4.6 Regulatory Guidelines for Phase I Studies

- 4.6.1 Key regulations governing Phase I trials
- 4.6.2 Regulatory submission and approval process
- 4.6.3 International regulatory harmonization for Phase I trials

Chapter 5: Phase II Studies

5.1 Proof of Concept and Dose-Ranging Studies

- 5.1.1 Establishing initial efficacy
- 5.1.2 Dose-response relationship studies
- 5.1.3 Balancing safety and efficacy

5.2 Study Design in Phase II Trials

- 5.2.1 Randomized controlled trials (RCTs)
- 5.2.2 Double-blind, placebo-controlled designs
- 5.2.3 Adaptive trial designs

5.3 Patient Recruitment and Selection in Phase II Trials

- 5.3.1 Inclusion and exclusion criteria
- 5.3.2 Recruitment challenges and strategies
- 5.3.3 Ethical considerations in patient selection

5.4 Safety Monitoring in Phase II Studies

- 5.4.1 Monitoring adverse events
- 5.4.2 Safety data collection and reporting
- 5.4.3 Role of Data Safety Monitoring Boards (DSMBs)

5.5 Interim Analyses and Adaptive Trials

- 5.5.1 Importance of interim analyses
- 5.5.2 Adaptive trial methodologies
- 5.5.3 Regulatory considerations for adaptive trials

5.6 Regulatory Pathways for Phase II Trials

- 5.6.1 Key regulatory submissions for Phase II
- 5.6.2 Differences in regulatory pathways by region
- 5.6.3 Fast-track, breakthrough, and orphan drug designations

Chapter 6: Phase III Studies
6.1 Objectives of Phase III Trials

- 6.1.1 Confirming safety and efficacy in large populations
- 6.1.2 Establishing clinical endpoints
- 6.1.3 Registration studies for drug approval

6.2 Study Design in Phase III Trials

- 6.2.1 Multi-center and multinational trials
- 6.2.2 Comparative effectiveness studies
- 6.2.3 Statistical power and sample size determination

6.3 Multi-Ethnicity and Global Clinical Trials

- 6.3.1 Designing trials for diverse populations
- 6.3.2 Regulatory and ethical challenges in multinational trials
- 6.3.3 Harmonization of regulatory requirements

6.4 Safety and Efficacy Monitoring in Phase III

- 6.4.1 Long-term safety monitoring
- 6.4.2 Collection of efficacy data
- 6.4.3 Reporting serious adverse events (SAEs)

6.5 Endpoints and Outcomes in Phase III Trials

- 6.5.1 Primary and secondary endpoints
- 6.5.2 Surrogate endpoints vs. clinical outcomes
- 6.5.3 Statistical analysis of endpoints

6.6 Regulatory Approval Process Following Phase III

- 6.6.1 Submission of data to regulatory agencies
- 6.6.2 Common Technical Document (CTD) format
- 6.6.3 Pathways to approval: NDA, BLA, MAA

Chapter 7: Phase IV and Post-Marketing Studies
7.1 Introduction to Post-Marketing Studies

- 7.1.1 Purpose of Phase IV trials

- 7.1.2 Differences from earlier phases
- 7.1.3 Regulatory requirements for post-approval trials

7.2 Post-Marketing Surveillance

- 7.2.1 Role of pharmacovigilance
- 7.2.2 Reporting adverse drug reactions (ADRs)
- 7.2.3 Spontaneous reporting systems (e.g., FDA MedWatch)

7.3 Pharmacovigilance Systems

- 7.3.1 National and international systems
- 7.3.2 Role of the Qualified Person for Pharmacovigilance (QPPV)
- 7.3.3 Regulatory requirements for pharmacovigilance

7.4 Real-World Evidence and Long-Term Safety Monitoring

- 7.4.1 Real-world data collection
- 7.4.2 Importance of long-term safety data
- 7.4.3 Risk management plans (RMPs)

7.5 Periodic Safety Update Reports (PSURs)

- 7.5.1 Structure and content of PSURs
- 7.5.2 Frequency of reporting
- 7.5.3 Regulatory requirements for PSUR submission

7.6 Case Studies in Post-Marketing Studies

- 7.6.1 Examples of successful Phase IV trials
- 7.6.2 Regulatory responses to post-marketing issues
- 7.6.3 Lessons learned from post-marketing surveillance

Chapter 8: Clinical Investigation and Evaluation of Medical Devices
8.1 Introduction to Medical Device Clinical Investigations

- 8.1.1 Definition of medical devices and IVDs
- 8.1.2 Differences between drug and device clinical trials

- 8.1.3 Importance of clinical investigations for devices

8.2 Regulatory Pathways for Medical Devices

- 8.2.1 Regulatory approval for medical devices
- 8.2.2 Investigational Device Exemption (IDE) process
- 8.2.3 Overview of the FDA, EMA, and CDSCO requirements

8.3 Clinical Evaluation Methods for Medical Devices

- 8.3.1 Pre-clinical and clinical evaluation
- 8.3.2 Safety and performance endpoints
- 8.3.3 Ethical considerations in medical device evaluation

8.4 In-Vitro Diagnostics (IVD) Clinical Studies

- 8.4.1 Specific requirements for IVD clinical trials
- 8.4.2 Study design for IVDs
- 8.4.3 Regulatory requirements for IVDs

8.5 Key Concepts of Medical Device Clinical Evaluation

- 8.5.1 Clinical performance vs. safety evaluation
- 8.5.2 Data collection and interpretation
- 8.5.3 Post-market device surveillance

8.6 Global Harmonization of Medical Device Regulations

- 8.6.1 Overview of the Global Harmonization Task Force (GHTF)
- 8.6.2 ISO 14155 guidelines for medical device trials
- 8.6.3 Harmonization efforts across the EU, USA, and India

Chapter 9: Historical Perspectives on Ethics in Clinical Research
9.1 The Nuremberg Code

- 9.1.1 Background and development of the Nuremberg Code
- 9.1.2 Ethical principles established by the Nuremberg Code
- 9.1.3 Impact on modern clinical research ethics

9.2 The Thalidomide Study and Its Impact

- 9.2.1 Overview of the Thalidomide disaster
- 9.2.2 Changes in regulations following Thalidomide
- 9.2.3 Lessons learned in clinical research ethics

9.3 The Nazi Trials and Their Ethical Legacy

- 9.3.1 Ethical violations during Nazi medical experiments
- 9.3.2 Contributions to global ethics standards
- 9.3.3 The role of the trials in shaping clinical trial regulations

9.4 The Tuskegee Syphilis Study

- 9.4.1 The Tuskegee Syphilis Study: A case of unethical research
- 9.4.2 Long-term effects on minority groups and trust in research
- 9.4.3 Ethical reforms in clinical research post-Tuskegee

9.5 The Belmont Report

- 9.5.1 Core principles: Respect for Persons, Beneficence, Justice
- 9.5.2 Application of Belmont principles to clinical research
- 9.5.3 Belmont's role in informed consent and ethical conduct

9.6 The Declaration of Helsinki

- 9.6.1 Introduction to the Declaration of Helsinki
- 9.6.2 Key ethical guidelines from the Declaration
- 9.6.3 Updates and relevance in modern clinical trials

Chapter 10: The Belmont Report and Declaration of Helsinki
10.1 Historical Context of the Belmont Report

- 10.1.1 Development of the Belmont Report
- 10.1.2 The Belmont Report as a response to unethical research
- 10.1.3 Ongoing relevance of Belmont principles

10.2 Core Ethical Principles of the Belmont Report

- 10.2.1 Respect for Persons: Informed consent and autonomy
- 10.2.2 Beneficence: Risk-benefit assessment in research
- 10.2.3 Justice: Fair selection of research subjects

10.3 Implementation of the Belmont Principles

- 10.3.1 Informed consent processes
- 10.3.2 Ensuring beneficence in clinical research
- 10.3.3 Ensuring justice in subject selection and study design

10.4 The Declaration of Helsinki: Overview

- 10.4.1 Background and history of the Declaration
- 10.4.2 Role of the World Medical Association in its development
- 10.4.3 Updates to the Declaration and their importance

10.5 Key Ethical Guidelines in the Declaration of Helsinki

- 10.5.1 Informed consent in human research
- 10.5.2 Clinical research must prioritize subject safety
- 10.5.3 Obligations of researchers to disclose study results

10.6 Influence of the Belmont Report and Declaration of Helsinki on Modern Regulations

- 10.6.1 Integration of these documents into global regulatory frameworks
- 10.6.2 Comparative analysis: Belmont Report vs. Declaration of Helsinki
- 10.6.3 Relevance in the regulatory frameworks of the FDA, EMA, and CDSCO

Chapter 11: The Origin of ICH-GCP Guidelines
11.1 The International Conference on Harmonization (ICH)

- 11.1.1 Formation and goals of ICH
- 11.1.2 Role in international regulatory harmonization
- 11.1.3 Significance for pharmaceutical companies and regulators

11.2 Good Clinical Practice (GCP) Guidelines Overview

- 11.2.1 Key principles of GCP
- 11.2.2 Regulatory compliance and GCP
- 11.2.3 Ethical considerations in GCP

11.3 Development of the ICH-GCP Guidelines

- 11.3.1 Historical context for GCP development
- 11.3.2 Key milestones in the creation of ICH-GCP
- 11.3.3 Global impact of ICH-GCP guidelines

11.4 Core Principles of ICH-GCP Guidelines

- 11.4.1 Roles and responsibilities of the investigator
- 11.4.2 Responsibilities of the sponsor
- 11.4.3 Protection of human subjects in research

11.5 ICH-GCP Guidelines and Regulatory Compliance

- 11.5.1 Compliance requirements for clinical trials
- 11.5.2 Integration into regional regulations: FDA, EMA, CDSCO
- 11.5.3 Monitoring and audits for GCP compliance

11.6 The Role of ICH-GCP in Multinational Clinical Trials

- 11.6.1 Harmonizing standards for global trials
- 11.6.2 Challenges in implementing ICH-GCP across regions
- 11.6.3 Case studies of multinational trials and GCP compliance

Chapter 12: Ethics of Randomized Clinical Trials
12.1 Importance of Randomization in Clinical Trials

- 12.1.1 Why randomization is critical
- 12.1.2 Randomization methods and techniques
- 12.1.3 Reducing bias through randomization

12.2 Blinding in Randomized Trials

- 12.2.1 Single-blind vs. double-blind studies

- 12.2.2 Ethical implications of blinding
- 12.2.3 Challenges in maintaining blinding

12.3 Ethical Challenges in Randomized Controlled Trials (RCTs)

- 12.3.1 The concept of equipoise
- 12.3.2 Ensuring informed consent in RCTs
- 12.3.3 Ethical considerations in randomizing patients to placebo

12.4 The Role of Placebos in Clinical Trials

- 12.4.1 Ethical justification for placebo use
- 12.4.2 Controversies and limitations of placebo-controlled trials
- 12.4.3 Alternatives to placebos: Active control groups

12.5 Balancing Risk and Benefit in RCTs

- 12.5.1 Risk-benefit assessment in randomized trials
- 12.5.2 Mitigating risks to participants
- 12.5.3 Institutional Review Board (IRB) roles in risk management

12.6 Legal and Regulatory Aspects of Randomized Trials

- 12.6.1 Regulatory requirements for RCTs
- 12.6.2 Informed consent documentation
- 12.6.3 Ethical approvals and ongoing safety monitoring

Chapter 13: The Role of Placebo in Clinical Trials
13.1 Understanding Placebo-Controlled Trials

- 13.1.1 Definition of placebo and placebo effect
- 13.1.2 Types of placebo-controlled studies
- 13.1.3 Importance of placebo in drug evaluation

13.2 Ethical Considerations of Placebo Use

- 13.2.1 Informed consent and placebo deception
- 13.2.2 Placebo use in vulnerable populations

- 13.2.3 Ethical guidelines for placebo use

13.3 Controversies Surrounding Placebo-Controlled Trials

- 13.3.1 Is placebo use ethical when effective treatment exists?
- 13.3.2 Balancing scientific rigor with patient welfare
- 13.3.3 Alternatives to placebo controls

13.4 Placebo Effect and Its Implications

- 13.4.1 Mechanisms of the placebo effect
- 13.4.2 Impact on clinical trial outcomes
- 13.4.3 Minimizing placebo effect in drug efficacy studies

13.5 Designing Placebo-Controlled Trials

- 13.5.1 Placebo selection and administration
- 13.5.2 Blinding in placebo-controlled trials
- 13.5.3 Statistical considerations in placebo-controlled studies

13.6 Placebo-Controlled Trials in Global Regulatory Frameworks

- 13.6.1 FDA and EMA guidelines on placebo use
- 13.6.2 Ethical requirements for placebo trials across regions
- 13.6.3 Case studies on the success and challenges of placebo-controlled trials

Chapter 14: Ethical Considerations for Special Populations
14.1 Special Populations in Clinical Research

- 14.1.1 Definition of special populations (children, elderly, pregnant women)
- 14.1.2 Ethical challenges in recruiting special populations
- 14.1.3 Regulatory guidelines for research on special populations

14.2 Clinical Trials in Children

- 14.2.1 Pediatric-specific ethical concerns

- 14.2.2 Assent and consent in pediatric trials
- 14.2.3 Regulatory requirements for pediatric studies (ICH E11)

14.3 Clinical Trials in Pregnant and Lactating Women

- 14.3.1 Ethical issues in research with pregnant women
- 14.3.2 Risk-benefit analysis for trials involving this group
- 14.3.3 Regulatory guidelines for including pregnant women in trials

14.4 Research in the Elderly

- 14.4.1 Challenges in studying older populations
- 14.4.2 Special ethical considerations for geriatric studies
- 14.4.3 Regulatory requirements for geriatric research (ICH E7)

14.5 Vulnerable Populations and Clinical Research

- 14.5.1 Identifying vulnerable populations in research
- 14.5.2 Safeguards for protecting vulnerable participants
- 14.5.3 Ethical guidelines for conducting research in vulnerable groups

14.6 Case Studies on Ethical Issues in Special Population Research

- 14.6.1 Case study: Pediatric trials in oncology
- 14.6.2 Case study: HIV research in pregnant women
- 14.6.3 Lessons learned and guidelines development

Chapter 15: Institutional Review Boards (IRB) and Independent Ethics Committees (IEC)

15.1 Introduction to IRBs and IECs

- 15.1.1 Role and purpose of IRBs/IECs
- 15.1.2 Historical context: Development of ethics committees
- 15.1.3 Global differences in IRBs/IECs

15.2 Composition and Structure of IRBs/IECs

- 15.2.1 Members and their roles

- 15.2.2 Importance of diversity in IRB/IEC membership
- 15.2.3 Structure of an effective IRB/IEC

15.3 Roles and Responsibilities of IRBs/IECs

- 15.3.1 Reviewing and approving clinical trial protocols
- 15.3.2 Ongoing monitoring of approved trials
- 15.3.3 Ensuring compliance with ethical and legal standards

15.4 The Approval Process: How IRBs/IECs Function

- 15.4.1 Protocol submission and review processes
- 15.4.2 Communication between researchers and IRBs/IECs
- 15.4.3 Decision-making and approval timelines

15.5 Ongoing Safety Monitoring by IRBs/IECs

- 15.5.1 Adverse event reporting and review
- 15.5.2 Periodic safety updates and continuing review
- 15.5.3 Responsibilities of IRBs/IECs in trial suspension or termination

15.6 Regulatory Framework Governing IRBs/IECs

- 15.6.1 FDA, EMA, and CDSCO regulations for IRBs/IECs
- 15.6.2 International guidelines: ICH-GCP
- 15.6.3 Case studies of IRB/IEC failures and their consequences

Chapter 16: Data Safety Monitoring Boards (DSMB)
16.1 Introduction to Data Safety Monitoring Boards

- 16.1.1 Purpose and role of DSMBs in clinical trials
- 16.1.2 Legal and ethical significance of DSMBs
- 16.1.3 Formation and selection of DSMB members

16.2 Structure and Composition of DSMBs

- 16.2.1 Members and their expertise
- 16.2.2 Importance of an independent DSMB

- 16.2.3 Criteria for appointing DSMB members

16.3 Responsibilities of DSMBs

- 16.3.1 Safety monitoring and risk-benefit analysis
- 16.3.2 Review of interim data and decision-making
- 16.3.3 Advising on trial continuation, modification, or termination

16.4 DSMB Processes and Decision-Making

- 16.4.1 Data review and interim analysis
- 16.4.2 How DSMBs make recommendations
- 16.4.3 Frequency and scheduling of DSMB meetings

16.5 Ethical Issues Related to DSMBs

- 16.5.1 Conflict of interest concerns
- 16.5.2 Transparency and confidentiality in DSMB operations
- 16.5.3 DSMBs in placebo-controlled trials

16.6 DSMB Case Studies and Lessons Learned

- 16.6.1 Case studies of DSMBs intervening in trials
- 16.6.2 Impact of DSMB decisions on trial outcomes
- 16.6.3 Lessons learned for future DSMB operations

Chapter 17: Informed Consent Process and Documentation
17.1 Importance of Informed Consent in Clinical Research

- 17.1.1 Definition and ethical foundations of informed consent
- 17.1.2 Historical evolution of informed consent
- 17.1.3 Key principles underlying informed consent

17.2 Components of the Informed Consent Process

- 17.2.1 Disclosure of information to participants
- 17.2.2 Comprehension and voluntary participation
- 17.2.3 Documentation of consent

17.3 Informed Consent in Vulnerable Populations

- 17.3.1 Special considerations for children, elderly, and incapacitated individuals
- 17.3.2 Obtaining informed consent from legally authorized representatives
- 17.3.3 Ethical dilemmas in obtaining consent from vulnerable populations

17.4 Patient Information Sheet and Informed Consent Form

- 17.4.1 Key elements of a Patient Information Sheet (PIS)
- 17.4.2 Designing the Informed Consent Form (ICF)
- 17.4.3 Language and cultural considerations in the consent form

17.5 Regulatory Requirements for Informed Consent

- 17.5.1 FDA, EMA, and CDSCO guidelines
- 17.5.2 GCP requirements for informed consent
- 17.5.3 Legal implications of improper consent documentation

17.6 Case Studies in Informed Consent Violations

- 17.6.1 High-profile cases of informed consent violations
- 17.6.2 Regulatory responses and consequences
- 17.6.3 Lessons learned for enhancing consent practices

Chapter 18: Clinical Research Regulations in India – Schedule Y
18.1 Introduction to Schedule Y

- 18.1.1 Overview of Schedule Y and its scope
- 18.1.2 Key objectives and significance for Indian clinical trials
- 18.1.3 Evolution of Schedule Y

18.2 Regulatory Approval Process in India

- 18.2.1 Steps involved in obtaining trial approval
- 18.2.2 Key regulatory bodies: CDSCO and DCGI

CHAPTER WISE CONTENTS

- 18.2.3 Differences between drug and device trials

18.3 Requirements for Clinical Trial Applications (CTA)

- 18.3.1 Documents required for CTA submissions
- 18.3.2 Role of the Investigator's Brochure (IB)
- 18.3.3 Essential elements of a Clinical Trial Protocol

18.4 Ethical Considerations in Indian Clinical Trials

- 18.4.1 Informed consent requirements under Schedule Y
- 18.4.2 Role of Ethics Committees (ECs)
- 18.4.3 Participant protection in Indian trials

18.5 Safety Monitoring and Reporting Requirements

- 18.5.1 Adverse event reporting in Indian clinical trials
- 18.5.2 Guidelines for serious adverse event (SAE) reporting
- 18.5.3 Post-marketing surveillance under Schedule Y

18.6 Amendments and Updates to Schedule Y

- 18.6.1 Major updates to Schedule Y
- 18.6.2 Future directions for Indian clinical research regulations
- 18.6.3 Comparison with international regulations

Chapter 19: USA Clinical Research Regulations (FDA)
19.1 Overview of the FDA's Role in Clinical Research

- 19.1.1 Introduction to the FDA and its regulatory authority
- 19.1.2 Key objectives of FDA clinical trial oversight
- 19.1.3 FDA organizational structure relevant to clinical research

19.2 New Drug Application (NDA) Processes

- 19.2.1 NDA 505(b)(1): New drug approval process
- 19.2.2 NDA 505(b)(2): Approval based on existing data
- 19.2.3 Abbreviated New Drug Application (ANDA) 505(j): Generic drug

approval

19.3 Investigational New Drug (IND) Applications

- 19.3.1 Requirements for IND submissions
- 19.3.2 Clinical trials under IND status
- 19.3.3 Responsibilities of the sponsor and investigator

19.4 FDA Guidance for Industry

- 19.4.1 Acceptance of foreign clinical studies
- 19.4.2 FDA Good Clinical Practice (GCP) guidelines
- 19.4.3 Key FDA guidance documents for clinical trials

19.5 FDA Safety Reporting Requirements

- 19.5.1 IND safety reporting
- 19.5.2 Serious adverse event (SAE) reporting requirements
- 19.5.3 Post-marketing safety surveillance

19.6 FDA Audits and Inspections

- 19.6.1 FDA audit process
- 19.6.2 Key areas of focus during FDA inspections
- 19.6.3 Common findings and responses to FDA audits

Chapter 20: Clinical Research Regulations in the European Union (EMA)

20.1 Introduction to the European Medicines Agency (EMA)

- 20.1.1 Role and responsibilities of the EMA
- 20.1.2 EMA's regulatory framework for clinical trials
- 20.1.3 Structure and key committees of the EMA

20.2 EU Directives on Clinical Trials

- 20.2.1 Overview of Directive 2001/20/EC
- 20.2.2 Requirements for clinical trial approval in the EU

- 20.2.3 Differences between EU and FDA regulations

20.3 EudraLex and Volume 3 Guidelines

- 20.3.1 Overview of EudraLex
- 20.3.2 Volume 3: Scientific guidelines for human medicinal products
- 20.3.3 Key regulations for clinical trials in Europe

20.4 Annual Safety Report (ASR) and Pharmacovigilance

- 20.4.1 Requirements for Annual Safety Reports
- 20.4.2 Role of the Qualified Person for Pharmacovigilance (QPPV)
- 20.4.3 Pharmacovigilance in the European Union

20.5 ISO 14155 and Medical Device Clinical Trials in the EU

- 20.5.1 Overview of ISO 14155: GCP for medical device trials
- 20.5.2 Requirements for clinical investigation of medical devices
- 20.5.3 Key differences between drug and device trial regulations

20.6 Case Studies in EU Clinical Trials

- 20.6.1 Successful clinical trials conducted under EMA guidelines
- 20.6.2 Challenges faced in multinational EU trials

Chapter 21: Good Clinical Practice (GCP) Guidelines – ICH E6
21.1 Introduction to ICH and the ICH E6 GCP Guidelines

- 21.1.1 History and purpose of the ICH
- 21.1.2 Development of the ICH E6 guidelines
- 21.1.3 Scope and objectives of GCP

21.2 Key Principles of ICH-GCP E6 Guidelines

- 21.2.1 Responsibilities of the sponsor
- 21.2.2 Roles and duties of the investigator
- 21.2.3 Protection of human subjects in clinical research

21.3 Investigator's Responsibilities Under GCP

- 21.3.1 Ensuring informed consent
- 21.3.2 Conduct of the clinical trial according to the protocol
- 21.3.3 Reporting requirements and safety monitoring

21.4 Sponsor's Responsibilities Under GCP

- 21.4.1 Trial management, data handling, and record keeping
- 21.4.2 Monitoring and auditing the clinical trial
- 21.4.3 Reporting safety information to regulatory authorities

21.5 Clinical Trial Protocol Development

- 21.5.1 Key components of a GCP-compliant protocol
- 21.5.2 Protocol amendments and ethical approvals
- 21.5.3 Challenges in protocol design and implementation

21.6 GCP Compliance and Monitoring

- 21.6.1 Monitoring and auditing clinical trials for GCP compliance
- 21.6.2 Addressing non-compliance issues
- 21.6.3 Regulatory actions for GCP violations

Chapter 22: Indian Good Clinical Practice Guidelines
22.1 Overview of Indian GCP Guidelines

- 22.1.1 Development and purpose of Indian GCP
- 22.1.2 Comparison with ICH-GCP guidelines
- 22.1.3 Applicability to clinical trials in India

22.2 Ethical Principles in Indian GCP

- 22.2.1 Informed consent requirements in India
- 22.2.2 Ethical review by Indian ethics committees
- 22.2.3 Protecting vulnerable populations in Indian trials

22.3 Roles and Responsibilities in Indian Clinical Trials

- 22.3.1 Investigator responsibilities under Indian GCP
- 22.3.2 Sponsor responsibilities in Indian clinical trials
- 22.3.3 Role of Contract Research Organizations (CROs)

22.4 Regulatory Compliance in Indian GCP

- 22.4.1 Monitoring and auditing for GCP compliance in India
- 22.4.2 Reporting requirements to CDSCO
- 22.4.3 Addressing non-compliance and regulatory actions

22.5 Safety Reporting and Pharmacovigilance

- 22.5.1 Adverse event reporting requirements in India
- 22.5.2 Pharmacovigilance and post-marketing safety monitoring
- 22.5.3 Role of the Pharmacovigilance Program of India (PvPI)

22.6 Case Studies in Indian GCP Compliance

- 22.6.1 Examples of successful GCP-compliant trials in India
- 22.6.2 Challenges faced in implementing Indian GCP
- 22.6.3 Lessons learned from Indian clinical trials

Chapter 23: ICMR Ethical Guidelines for Biomedical Research
23.1 Overview of ICMR Guidelines

- 23.1.1 History and purpose of ICMR guidelines
- 23.1.2 Key ethical principles in ICMR guidelines
- 23.1.3 Scope of ICMR guidelines in clinical and biomedical research

23.2 Ethical Review of Biomedical Research

- 23.2.1 Role of ethics committees in India
- 23.2.2 ICMR guidelines for ethics committee operations
- 23.2.3 Review and approval processes for biomedical research

23.3 Informed Consent Under ICMR Guidelines

- 23.3.1 Requirements for obtaining informed consent

- 23.3.2 Special considerations for vulnerable populations
- 23.3.3 Language and cultural factors in the consent process

23.4 Protection of Participants in Biomedical Research

- 23.4.1 Ensuring participant safety and well-being
- 23.4.2 ICMR guidelines for adverse event reporting
- 23.4.3 Ethical considerations in high-risk research

23.5 Ethical Guidelines for Research in Special Populations

- 23.5.1 ICMR guidelines for pediatric research
- 23.5.2 Research involving pregnant women and the elderly
- 23.5.3 Research in socially or economically disadvantaged populations

23.6 Case Studies in ICMR-Guided Research

- 23.6.1 Ethical dilemmas in Indian biomedical research
- 23.6.2 Examples of successful application of ICMR guidelines
- 23.6.3 Lessons learned from ethical challenges in research

Chapter 24: Regulatory Guidance on Efficacy and Safety (ICH Guidelines)

24.1 Overview of ICH Guidelines on Efficacy

- 24.1.1 ICH E4: Dose-response information to support drug registration
- 24.1.2 ICH E7: Studies in geriatric populations
- 24.1.3 ICH E8: General considerations for clinical trials

24.2 Dose-Response Studies (ICH E4)

- 24.2.1 Purpose of dose-response studies
- 24.2.2 Study design and data collection for dose-response
- 24.2.3 Regulatory submission of dose-response data

24.3 Studies in Special Populations (ICH E7 and E11)

- 24.3.1 ICH E7: Geriatric population studies

- 24.3.2 ICH E11: Pediatric population studies
- 24.3.3 Regulatory challenges in special population studies

24.4 General Considerations for Clinical Trials (ICH E8)

- 24.4.1 Study design, conduct, and analysis
- 24.4.2 Importance of quality assurance in clinical trials
- 24.4.3 Regulatory guidelines for global clinical trials

24.5 Choice of Control Groups (ICH E10)

- 24.5.1 Types of control groups in clinical trials
- 24.5.2 Ethical considerations in choosing control groups
- 24.5.3 Regulatory requirements for control group studies

24.6 Clinical Investigation of Medicinal Products in Pediatrics (ICH E11)

- 24.6.1 Special considerations for pediatric trials
- 24.6.2 Ethical guidelines for pediatric research
- 24.6.3 Regulatory submission of pediatric data

Chapter 25: Post-Market Surveillance and Safety Reporting
25.1 Introduction to Post-Market Surveillance

- 25.1.1 Purpose of post-marketing studies
- 25.1.2 Differences between pre-market and post-market safety monitoring
- 25.1.3 Regulatory requirements for post-market surveillance

25.2 Pharmacovigilance in Post-Market Research

- 25.2.1 Definition and role of pharmacovigilance
- 25.2.2 Global pharmacovigilance systems (FDA MedWatch, EMA, CDSCO)
- 25.2.3 Reporting requirements for post-market studies

25.3 Periodic Safety Update Reports (PSURs)

- 25.3.1 Structure and content of PSURs
- 25.3.2 Frequency of PSUR submissions
- 25.3.3 Regulatory requirements for PSURs across regions

25.4 Risk Management Plans (RMPs)

- 25.4.1 Developing RMPs for new medicinal products
- 25.4.2 Implementation of RMPs post-approval
- 25.4.3 Regulatory oversight of RMPs

25.5 Real-World Evidence in Post-Market Surveillance

- 25.5.1 Role of real-world evidence in drug safety
- 25.5.2 Data collection from real-world use
- 25.5.3 Incorporating real-world data into regulatory submissions

25.6 Case Studies in Post-Marketing Safety Surveillance

- 25.6.1 Successful post-marketing surveillance programs
- 25.6.2 Regulatory interventions based on post-market data
- 25.6.3 Lessons learned from adverse drug reaction (ADR) reports

Printed in Great Britain
by Amazon